Annie Brassey

Around the World in the Yacht Sunbeam

Our home on the ocean for eleven months

Annie Brassey

Around the World in the Yacht Sunbeam
Our home on the ocean for eleven months

ISBN/EAN: 9783337037949

Printed in Europe, USA, Canada, Australia, Japan

Cover: Foto ©Andreas Hilbeck / pixelio.de

More available books at **www.hansebooks.com**

AROUND THE WORLD IN THE YACHT "SUNBEAM"

OUR HOME ON THE OCEAN FOR ELEVEN MONTHS

BY

MRS. BRASSEY

With Illustrations. Chiefly after Drawings by the Hon. A. Y. Bingham

NEW YORK
HENRY HOLT AND COMPANY
1878

DEDICATION.

To THE FRIENDS in many climes and countries, of the white and colored races, and of every grade in society, who have made our year of travel a year of happiness, these pages are dedicated by the ever grateful Author,

Annie Brassey

PREFACE.

THIS volume needs no elaborate preface. A general sketch of the voyage which it describes was published in the 'Times' immediately after our return to England. That letter is reprinted here as a convenient summary of the 'Sunbeam's' performances. But these prefatory lines would indeed be incomplete if they did not contain a well-deserved tribute to the industry and accuracy of the author. The voyage would not have been undertaken, and assuredly it would never have been completed, without the impulse derived from her perseverance and determination. Still less would any sufficient record of the scenes and experiences of the long voyage have been preserved had it not been for her painstaking desire not only to see everything thoroughly, but to record her impressions faithfully and accurately. The practiced skill of a professional writer cannot reasonably be expected in these simple pages, but their object will have been attained if they are the means of enabling more home-keeping friends to share in the keen enjoyment of the scenes and adventures they describe.

THOMAS BRASSEY.

CONTENTS.

CHAPTER		PAGE
I.	Farewell to Old England.	1
II.	Madeira, Teneriffe, and Cape de Verde Islands	12
III.	Palma to Rio de Janeiro	31
IV.	Rio de Janeiro	42
V.	The River Plate	62
VI.	Life on the Pampas	76
VII.	More about the Argentine Republic	91
VIII.	River Plate to Sandy Point, Straits of Magellan	104
IX.	Sandy Point to Lota Bay	126
X.	Chili	144
XI.	Santiago and Valparaiso	163
XII.	Valparaiso to Tahiti	179
XIII.	The South Sea Islands	194
XIV.	At Tahiti	209
XV.	Tahiti to Sandwich Islands.—Kilauea by Day and by Night	235
XVI.	Hawaiian Sports	256
XVII.	Honolulu—Departure for Japan	271
XVIII.	Honolulu to Yokohama	282

CHAPTER		PAGE
XIX.	YOKOHAMA	293
XX.	KIOTO, LATE MIACO	308
XXI.	THE INLAND SEA	327
XXII.	TO CANTON UP THE PEARL RIVER	348
XXIII.	FROM MACAO TO SINGAPORE	362
XXIV.	SINGAPORE	378
XXV.	CEYLON	395
XXVI.	TO ADEN	412
XXVII.	VIA SUEZ CANAL	424
XXVIII.	'HOME'	440
APPENDIX		455

LIST OF ILLUSTRATIONS.

	PAGE
THE YACHT 'SUNBEAM'	*Frontispiece*
GENERAL CHART SHOWING TRACK OF THE YACHT 'SUNBEAM'	*To face page* 1
FAMILY GROUP	1
NEARLY OVERBOARD	5
A COZY CORNER	20
LULU AND HER PUPPIES	37
THE THREE NAVIGATORS	62
'MONKSHAVEN' ON FIRE	105
SHIPWRECKED CREW COMING ON BOARD	108
BARTERING WITH FUEGIANS	127
CATCHING CAPE-PIGEONS IN THE GULF OF PEÑAS	142
WHAT MAKES HORSES GO IN CHILI	167
JUVENILE SCRUBBERS	180
GOING UP THE MAST IN A CHAIR	192
CHILDREN LOOKING UP	192
MAITEAN BOATMAN	203
A TAHITIAN LADY	227
TATTOO IN THE TROPICS	237
AMATEUR NAVIGATION	286
THE YACHT ON FIRE	334
HOW THE JOURNAL WAS WRITTEN	392
VASCO DE GAMA	449
HOME AT LAST	453

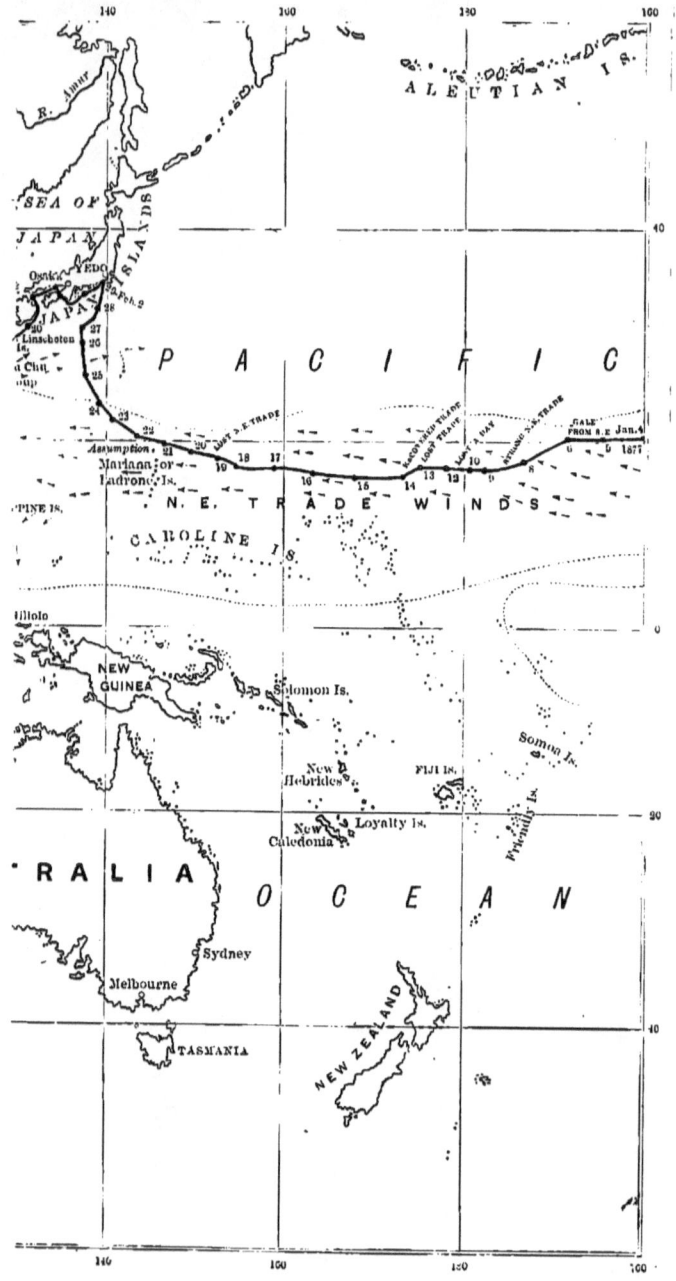

AROUND THE WORLD IN THE YACHT 'SUNBEAM.'

CHAPTER I.

FAREWELL TO OLD ENGLAND.

*Masts, spires, and strand receding on the right,
The glorious main expanding on the bow.*

AT noon on July 1st, 1876, we said good-by to the friends who had come to Chatham to see us off, and began the first stage of our voyage by steaming down to Sheerness, saluting our old friend the 'Duncan,' Admiral Chads's flagship, and passing through a perfect fleet of craft of all kinds. There was a fresh contrary wind, and the Channel was as disagreeable as usual under the circumstances. Next afternoon we were off Hastings, where we had intended to stop and dine and meet some friends; but, unfortunately, the weather was not sufficiently favorable for us to land; so we made a long tack out to sea, and, in the evening, found ourselves once more near the land, off Beachy Head. While becalmed off Brighton, we all—children included—availed ourselves of the opportunity to go overboard and have our first swim, which we thoroughly enjoyed. We had steam up before ten, and again proceeded on our course. It was very hot, and sitting under the awning turned out to be the pleasantest occupation. The contrast between the weather of the two following days was very great, and afforded a forcible illustration of the uncertainties, perhaps the fascinations, of yachting. We steamed quietly on, past the 'Owers' lightship, and the crowds of yachts at Ryde, and dropped anchor off Cowes at six o'clock.

On the morning of the 6th a light breeze sprang up, and enabled us to go through the Needles with sails up and funnel down, a performance of which all on board felt very proud, as many yachtsmen had pronounced it to be an impossibility for our vessel to beat out in so light a breeze.

We were forty-three on board, all told, as will be seen by reference to the list I have given. We had with us, besides, two dogs, three birds, and a charming Persian kitten belonging to the baby. The kitten soon disappeared, and it was feared she must have gone overboard down the hawse pipe. There was a faint hope, however, that she might have been packed away with the new sails, which had been stowed in a great hurry the day before. Unhappily she was never found again, and the children were inconsolable until they discovered, at Torquay, an effective substitute for 'Lily.'

The Channel was tolerably smooth outside the Isle of Wight, and during the afternoon we were able to hold on our course direct for Ushant. After midnight, however, the wind worked gradually round to the W. S. W., and blew directly in our teeth. A terribly heavy sea got up; and, as we were making little or no progress, it was decided to put in to Torquay or Dartmouth, and there await a change. We anchored in Torbay, about half a mile from the pier, at 8.30 a.m., and soon afterwards went ashore to bathe. We found, however, that the high rocks which surround the snug little bathing cove made the water as cold as ice.

Nothing more having been heard of our poor little kitten, we can only conclude that she has gone overboard. Just as we were leaving the railway-station, however, we saw a small white kitten with a blue ribbon round its neck; and all the children at once exclaimed, 'There's our Lily!' We made inquiries, and found that it belonged to the young woman at the refreshment room, who, after some demur, allowed us to take it away with us, in compliance with Muriel's anxious wish, expressed on her face.

About ten o'clock we got under way, but lay-to for breakfast. We then had a regular beat of it down Channel—everybody being ill. We formed a melancholy-looking little row down the lee side of the ship, though I must say that we were quite as cheery as might have been expected under the circumstances. It was bright and sunny overhead, which made things more bearable.

Sunday, July 9th.—A calm at 2 a.m. Orders were given to get up steam; but the new coals from Chatham were slow to light, though good to keep up steam when once fairly kindled. For four long hours, therefore, we lolloped about in the trough of a heavy sea, the sails flapping as the vessel rolled. By the time the steam was up so was the breeze—a contrary one, of course. We accordingly steamed and sailed all day, taking more water on board, though not really in any great quantity, than I had ever seen the good ship do before. She carries a larger supply of coal and other stores than usual, and no doubt the square yards on the foremast make her pitch more heavily. We were all very sorry for ourselves, and 'church,' postponed from eleven until four o'clock, brought together but a small congregation.

On the 8th we were fairly away from Old England, and on the next day off Ushant, which we rounded at about 4.30 p.m., at the distance of a mile and a half; the sea was tremendous, the waves breaking in columns of spray against the sharp needle-like rocks that form the point of the island. The only excitement during the day was afforded by the visit of a pilot-boat (without any fish on board), whose owner was very anxious to take us into Brest, 'safe from the coming storm,' which he predicted. In addition to our other discomforts, it now rained hard; and by half-past six I think nearly all our party had made up their minds that bed would be the most comfortable place.

Two days later we sailed into lovely, bright, warm, sunny weather, with a strong north-easterly breeze, a following sea, and an occasional long roll from the westward. But as the sun rose, the wind increased, and we got rather knocked about by the sea. A good deal of water came on board, and it was impossible to sit anywhere in comfort, unless lashed or firmly wedged in. We were, however, going ten knots through the water, on our course, under our new square head canvas; and this fact made up for a good deal of discomfort.

The thirty extra tons of spare sails, spars, and provisions, the fifteen tons of water, and the eighty-four tons of coal, made a great difference in our buoyancy, and the sea came popping in and out at the most unexpected places; much to the delight of the children, who, with bare feet and legs, and armed with mops and sponges, waged mimic war against the intruder and each other, singing and dancing to their hearts' content. This amusement was occasionally interrupted by a heavier roll than usual, sending them all into the lee scuppers, sousing them from head to foot, and necessitating a thorough change of clothing, despite their urgent protest that seawater never hurt anybody.

After our five o'clock dinner, however, we very nearly met with a most serious accident. We were all sitting or standing about the stern of the vessel, admiring the magnificent dark blue billows following us, with their curling white crests, mountains high. Each wave, as it approached, appeared as if it must overwhelm us, instead of which, it rushed grandly by, rolling and shaking us from stem to stern, and sending fountains of spray on board. Tom was looking at the stern compass, Allnutt being close to him. Mr. Bingham and Mr. Freer were smoking, half-way between the quarter-deck and the after-companion, where Captain Brown, Dr. Potter, Muriel, and I, were standing. Captain Lecky, seated on

Nearly Overboard.

a large coil of rope, placed on the box of the rudder, was spinning Mabelle a yarn. A new hand was steering, and just at the moment when an unusually big wave overtook us, he unfortunately allowed the vessel to broach-to a little. In a second the sea came pouring over the stern, above Allnutt's head. The boy was nearly washed overboard, but he managed to catch hold of the rail, and, with great presence of mind, stuck his knees into the bulwarks. Kindred, our boatswain, seeing his danger, rushed forward to save him, but was knocked down by the return wave, from which he emerged gasping. The coil of rope on which Captain Lecky and Mabelle were seated was completely floated by the sea. Providentially, however, he had taken a double turn round his wrist with a reefing point, and, throwing his other arm round Mabelle, held on like grim death; otherwise nothing could have saved them. She was perfectly self-possessed, and only said quietly, 'Hold on, Captain Lecky, hold on!' to which he replied, 'All right.' I asked her afterwards if she thought she was going overboard, and she answered, 'I did not *think* at all, mamma, but felt sure we were gone.' Captain Lecky, being accustomed to very large ships, had not in the least realized how near we were to the water in our little vessel, and was proportionately taken by surprise. All the rest of the party were drenched, with the exception of Muriel, whom Captain Brown held high above the water in his arms, and who lost no time in remarking in the midst of the general confusion, 'I'm not at all wet, I'm not.' Happily, the children don't know what fear is. The maids, however, were very frightened, as some of the sea had got down into the nursery, and the skylights had to be screwed down. Our studding-sail boom, too, broke with a loud crack when the ship broached-to, and the jaws of the fore-boom gave way.

Soon after this adventure we all went to bed, full of thankfulness that it had ended as well as it did; but, alas! not, so far as I was concerned, to rest in peace. In about two hours I was awakened by a tremendous weight of water suddenly descending upon me and flooding the bed. I immediately sprang out, only to find myself in another pool on the floor. It was pitch dark, and I could not think what had happened; so I rushed on deck, and found that, the weather having moderated a little, some kind sailor, knowing my love of fresh air, had opened the skylight rather too soon; and one of the angry waves had popped on board, deluging the cabin.

I got a light, and proceeded to mop up, as best I could, and then endeavored to find a dry place to sleep in. This, however, was no easy task, for my own bed was drenched, and every other berth occupied. The deck, too, was ankle-deep in water, as I found when I tried to get across to the deck-house sofa. At last I lay down on the floor, wrapped up in my ulster, and wedged between the foot stanchion of our swing bed and the wardrobe athwart-ship; so that as the yacht rolled heavily, my feet were often higher than my head. Consequently, what sleep I snatched turned into nightmare, of which the fixed idea was a broken head from the three hundredweight of lead at the bottom of our bed, swinging wildly from side to side and up and down, as the vessel rolled and pitched, suggesting all manner of accidents. When morning came at last, the weather cleared a good deal, though the breeze continued. All hands were soon busily employed in repairing damages; and very picturesque the deck and rigging of the 'Sunbeam' looked, with the various groups of men, occupied upon the ropes, spars, and sails. Towards evening the wind fell light, and we had to get up steam. The night was the first really warm one we had enjoyed, and the stars shone out brightly. The sea, which had been of a lovely blue color during the day, showed a slight phosphorescence after dark.

Thursday, July 13th.—When I went on deck, at half-past six, I found a gray, steamy, calm morning, promising a very hot day, without wind.

About 10.30 a.m., the cry of 'Sail on the port beam!' caused general excitement, and in a few minutes every telescope and glass in the ship had been brought to bear upon the object which attracted our attention, and which was soon pronounced to be a wreck. Orders were given to starboard the helm, and to steer direct for the vessel; and many were the conjectures hazarded, and the questions asked of the fortunate holders of glasses. 'What is she?' 'Is there any one on board?' 'Where does she come from?' 'Can you read her name?' 'Does she look as if she had been long abandoned?' Soon we were near enough to send a boat's crew on board, whilst we watched their movements anxiously from the bridge. We could now read her name—the 'Carolina'—surmounted by a gorgeous yellow decoration on her stern. She was of between two and three hundred tons burden, and was painted a light blue, with a red streak. Beneath her white bowsprit the gaudy image of a woman served as a figure-head. The two masts had been snapped short off about three feet from the deck, and the bulwarks were gone, only the covering board and stanchions remaining, so that each wave washed over and through her. The roof and supports of the deck-house and the companions were still left standing, but the sides had disappeared, and the ship's deck was burst up in such a manner as to remind one of a quail's back.

We saw the men on board poking about, apparently very pleased with what they had found; and soon our boat returned to the yacht for some breakers,* as the 'Carolina' had been laden with port wine and cork, and the men wished to bring some of the former on board. I changed my dress, and, putting on my sea boots, started for the wreck.

We found the men rather excited over their discovery. The wine must have been *very* new and *very* strong, for the smell from it, as it slopped about all over the deck, was almost enough to intoxicate anybody. One pipe had already been emptied into the breakers and barrels, and great efforts were made to get some of the casks out whole; but this was found to be impossible, without devoting more time to the operation than we chose to spare. The men managed to remove three half-empty casks with their heads stove in, which they threw overboard, but the

---

* Small casks, used for carrying water in boats, frequently spelled *barricos*, evidently from the time of the old Spanish navigators.

full ones would have required special appliances to raise them through the hatches. It proved exceedingly difficult to get at the wine, which was stowed underneath the cork, and there was also a quantity of cabin bulkheads and fittings floating about, under the influence of the long swell of the Atlantic. It was a curious sight, standing on the roof of the deck-house, to look into the hold, full of floating bales of cork, barrels, and pieces of wood, and to watch the sea surging up in every direction, through and over the deck, which was level with the water's edge. I saw an excellent modern iron cooking-stove washing about from side to side; but almost every other movable article, including spars and ropes, had apparently been removed by previous boarders.

It would have delayed us too long to tow the vessel into the nearest port, 375 miles distant, or we might have claimed the salvage money, estimated by the experts at £1,500. She was too low in the water for it to be possible for us, with our limited appliances, to blow her up; so we were obliged to leave her floating about as a derelict, a fertile source of danger to all ships crossing her track. With her buoyant cargo, and with the trade winds slowly wafting her to smoother seas, it may probably be some years before she breaks up. I only hope that no good ship may run full speed on to her, some dark night, for the 'Carolina' would prove almost as formidable an obstacle as a sunken rock.

Tom was now signaling for us to go on board again, and for a few minutes I was rather afraid we should have had a little trouble in getting the men off, as their excitement had not decreased; but after a trifling delay and some rather rough play amongst themselves, they became steady again, and we returned to the yacht with our various prizes.

A 'Mother Carey's chicken' hovered round the wreck while we were on board, and followed us to the 'Sunbeam;' and although a flat calm and a heavy swell pre-ied at the time, we all looked upon our visitor as the harbinger of a breeze. In this instance, at least, the well-known sailor's superstition was justified; for, before the evening, the wind sprang up, and 'fires out and sails up' was the order of the day. We were soon bowling merrily along at the rate of seven knots an hour, while a clear starlight night and a heavy dew gave promise of a fine morrow.

Friday, July 14th.—We still have a light wind, right aft, accompanied by a heavy roll from the westward, which makes it impossible to sit anywhere with comfort, and difficult even to read. By 6 a.m. the sun had become very powerful, though its heat was tempered by the breeze, which gradually increased throughout the day, until, having set all our fore-and-aft canvas, as well as our square sails, we glided steadily along, in delightful contrast to the uneasy motion of the morning, and of the past few days. Under the awning—with the most heavenly blue sky above, and the still darker clear blue sea beneath, stretching away in gentle ripples as far as the eye could reach—it was simply perfect.

Our little party get on extremely well together, though a week ago they were strangers to each other. We are all so busy that we do not see much of one another except at meals, and then we have plenty to talk about. Captain Lecky imparts to us some of his valuable information about scientific navigation and the law of storms, and he and Tom and Captain Brown work hard at these subjects. Mr. Freer follows in the same path; Mr. Bingham draws and reads; Dr. Potter helps me to teach the children, who, I am happy to say, are as well as possible. I read and write a great deal, and learn Spanish, so that the days are all too short for what we have to do. The servants are settling down well into their places, and the commissariat department does great credit to the cooks and stewards. The maids get on satisfactorily, but are a little nervous on rough nights. We hope not to have many more just at present, for we are now approaching calmer latitudes.

In the course of the day, whilst Tom and I were sitting in the stern, the man at the wheel suddenly exclaimed, 'There's land on the port bow.' We knew, from the distance we had run, that this could not be the case, and after looking at it through the glasses, Tom pronounced the supposed land to be a thick wall of fog, advancing towards us *against* the wind. Captain Brown and Captain Lecky came from below, and hastened to get in the studding-sails, in anticipation of the coming squall. In a few minutes we had lost our fair breeze and brilliant sunshine, all our sails were taken flat aback, and we found ourselves enveloped in a dense fog, which made it impossible for us to see the length of the vessel. It was an extraordinary phenomenon. Captain Lecky, who, in the course of his many voyages, has passed within a few miles of this exact spot more than a hundred and fifty times, had never seen anything in the least like it. As night came on the fog increased, and the boats were prepared ready for lowering. Two men went to the wheel, and two to the bows to look out, while an officer was stationed on the bridge with steam-whistle and bell ready for an emergency; so that, in case we ran into anything, or anything ran into us, we should at least have the satisfaction of knowing that, so far as we were concerned, it had all been done strictly according to Act of Parliament.

Saturday, July 15th.—Between midnight and 4 a.m. the fog disappeared, as suddenly as it had come on. We must have passed through a wide belt of it. At 5.30 a.m., when Tom called me to see a steamer go by, it was quite clear. The vessel was the 'Roman,' and she passed so close to us that we made our number, and exchanged salutations with the officers on the bridge.

Towards the afternoon a nice breeze sprang up, and we were able to bank fires and sail.

CHAPTER II.

MADEIRA, TENERIFFE, AND CAPE DE VERDE ISLANDS.

*Full many a green isle needs must be
In this wide sea of misery,
Or the mariner worn and wan
Never thus could voyage on.*

Sunday, July 16*th.*—Porto Santo being visible on the port bow, a quarter of a mile ahead, by 3.55 a.m. this morning, our three navigators congratulated themselves and each other on the good land-fall they had made.

It looks a curious little island, and is situated about thirty-five miles north-east of Madeira, with a high peak in the center, of which we could only see the extreme point appearing above the clouds.

It is interesting to know that it was from his observation of the drift-wood and débris washed on to the eastern shore that Columbus, who had married the daughter of the Governor of Porto Santo, derived his first impressions of the existence of the New World. Here it was that he first realized there might possibly be a large and unknown country to the westward; here it was that he first conceived the project of exploring the hitherto unknown ocean and of discovering what new countries might bound its western shores.

An hour later we saw Fora and its light, at the extreme east of Madeira, and could soon distinguish the mountains in the center of the latter island. As we rapidly approached the land, the beauty of the scenery became more fully apparent. A mass of dark purple volcanic rocks, clothed on the top with the richest vegetation, with patches of all sorts of color on their sides, rises boldly from the sea. There are several small detached rocks, and one curious pointed little island, with an arch right through the middle of it, rather like the Percé Rock on the coast of Nova Scotia. We steamed slowly along the east coast, passing many pretty hamlets, nestled in bays or perched on the side of the hills, and observing how every possible nook and corner seemed to be terraced and cultivated. Sugar-canes, Indian corn, vines, and many varieties of tropical and semi-tropical plants, grow luxuriantly in this lovely climate. Nearly all the cottages in the island are inhabited by a simple people, many of whom have never left their native villages, even to look at the magnificent view from the top of the surrounding mountains, or to gaze on the sea, by which they are encompassed.

We dropped our anchor in the bay of Funchal at about twelve o'clock, and before breakfast was over found ourselves surrounded by a perfect flotilla of boats, though none of them dared approach very near until the health-officer had come alongside and pronounced us free from infection. At this moment all are complaining much of the heat, which since yesterday has been very great, and is caused by the wind called 'Este,' blowing direct from the African deserts. It was $79°$ in the coolest place on board, and $84°$ on shore in the shade, in the middle of the day.

The African mail steamer, 'Ethiopia,' last from Bonny, West Coast of Africa, whence she arrived the day before yesterday, was lying in the bay, and the children went on board with some of our party to see her cargo of monkeys, parrots, and pineapples. The result was an importation of five parrots on board the 'Sunbeam;' but the monkeys were too big for us. Captain Dane, who paid us a return visit, said that the temperature here appeared quite cool to him, as for the last few weeks his thermometer had varied from $82°$ to $96°$ in the shade.

We had service at 4 p.m., and at 5 p.m. went ashore

in a native boat, furnished with bilge pieces, to keep her straight when beached, and to avoid the surf, for it was too rough for our own boats. At the water's edge a curious sort of double sleigh, drawn by two oxen, was waiting. Into this we stepped, setting off with considerable rapidity up the steep shingly beach, under a beautiful row of trees, to the 'Praça,' where the greater portion of the population were walking up and down, or sitting under the shade of the magnolias. These plants here attain the size of forest-trees, and their large white wax-like flowers shed a most delightful fragrance on the evening air. There were graceful pepper vines too, and a great variety of trees only known to us in England in the form of small shrubs. This being a festival day, the streets were crowded with people from town and country, in their holiday attire. The door-posts and balconies of the houses were wreathed with flowers, the designs in many cases being very pretty. One arcade in particular was quite lovely, with arches made of double red geranium, mixed with the feathery-looking pepper leaves, while the uprights were covered with amaryllis and white arum lilies. The streets were strewn with roses and branches of myrtle, which, bruised by the feet of the passers-by and the runners of the bullock sleigh, emitted a delicious aromatic odor.

The trellises in the garden seem overgrown with stephanotis, mauve and purple passion-flowers, and all kinds of rare creepers; the purple and white hibiscus shoots up some fourteen to sixteen feet in height; bananas, full of fruit and flower, strelitzias, heliotrope, geraniums, and pelargoniums, bloom all around in large shrubs, mixed with palms and mimosas of every variety; and the whole formed such an enchanting picture that we were loath to tear ourselves away.

A ride of about twenty minutes in the bullock sleigh, up a steep hill, by the side of a rocky torrent, whose banks were overgrown with caladiums and vines, brought us to our destination, Til, whence we had a splendid view of the town and bay stretching beneath us. During the ascent we passed several cottages, whose inhabitants stood airing themselves on the threshold after the great heat of the day, and through the open doorways we occasionally got a peep into the gardens beyond, full of bright flowers and luxuriant with vines, fig-trees, and bananas. As we sat in the terrace garden at Til we enjoyed the sweet scent of the flowers we could no longer see, and listened to the cool splash of the water in the fountain below; whilst Allnutt, with unceasing energy, searched amongst the bushes for moths, of which he found a large number.

We jogged down the hill a great deal faster than we had come up, stopping only for a short time in the now more than ever crowded 'Praça,' to listen to one or two airs played by the Portuguese band, before we got back to the yacht at about half-past ten.

Next morning we were off to the fish-market by seven o'clock, but it was not a good time for our visit, as there had been no moon on the previous night; and, though there were fish of various kinds, we saw nothing specially worthy of notice. The picturesque costumes of the people were, however, interesting. We afterwards went to the fruit-market, though it was not specially worth seeing, for most of the fruit and vegetables are brought in boats from villages on the sea-shore; and, as it is necessary to wait until the sea-breeze springs up, they do not arrive until midday. After our walk the children and I went down to the beach and bathed, taking care not to go too far out on account of the sharks, of which we had been warned. We undressed and dressed in tents, not unlike clothes-horses, with a bit of matting thrown over them, in which the heat was intense. The beach is very steep; and as one gets out of one's depth immediately, indifferent swimmers put on a couple of bladders—which stick out behind their backs and produce a strange effect—

or else take a bathing-man into the water with them. I preferred the latter course; and we all had a pleasant bathe.

The natives seem almost amphibious in their habits, and the yacht is surrounded all day by boats full of small boys, who will dive to any depth for sixpence, a dozen of them spluttering and fighting for the coin in the water at the same time. They will go down on one side of the yacht too, and bob up on the other, almost before you have time to run across the deck to witness their reappearance.

The Loo Rock, with its old fortress, close to our anchorage, forms a picturesque object; and the scene from the yacht, enlivened by the presence of numerous market-boats, laden with fruit and vegetables, is very pretty. We lie about 150 yards from the shore, just under Mr. Danc-ro's quinta. The cliff just here is overhung with bougainvillæas, geraniums, fuchsias, aloes, prickly pears, and other flowers, which grow luxuriantly quite down to the water's edge, wherever they can contrive to find a roothold.

After five-o'clock tea we rode up the Mount and through the woods on horseback, along a road gay with masses of wild geranium, hydrangea, amaryllis, and fuchsias. We dismounted at a lovely place, which contains a large number of rare trees and plants, brought from all parts of the world. Here were enormous camellias, as well as purple, red, and white azaleas, Guernsey lilies, all growing in the greatest profusion.

Our descent of the Mount, by means of a form of conveyance commonly used on the island, was very amusing. At the summit we found basket-work sleighs, each constructed to hold two people, and attended by a couple of men lashed together. Into these we stepped, and were immediately pushed down the hill at a tremendous pace. The gliding motion is delightful, and was altogether a novelty to us. The men manage the sleighs with great skill, steering them in the most wonderful manner round the sharp angles in the zigzag road, and making use of their bare feet as breaks when necessary. The turns were occasionally so abrupt, that it seemed almost impossible that we could avoid being upset; but we reached the bottom quite safely. The children were especially delighted with the trip, and indeed we all enjoyed it immensely. The only danger is the risk of fire from the friction of the steel runners against the gravel road.

After paying a visit to Mr. and Mrs. Blandy, whose house is beautifully situated, we dined at the hotel, and afterwards sat in the lovely semi-tropical garden until it was time to go on board to bed.

Tuesday, July 18th.—We were called at 4.30 a.m., and went ashore soon after six to meet some friends, with whom we had arranged to ride up to the Gran Corral, and to breakfast there, 5,000 feet above the level of the sea.

It soon became evident that the time we had selected for landing was the fashionable bathing hour. In fact, it required some skill on our part to keep the boat clear of the crowds of people of both sexes and all ages, who were taking their morning dip. It was most absurd to see entire families, from the bald-headed and spectacled grandfather to the baby who could scarcely walk, all disporting themselves in the water together, many of them supported by the very inelegant-looking bladders I have mentioned. There was a little delay in mounting our horses, under the shade of the fig-trees; but when we were once off, a party of eleven, the cavalcade became quite formidable. As we clattered up the paved streets, between vineyard and garden walls, 'curiosity opened her lattice,' on more than one occasion, to ascertain the cause of the unwonted commotion. The views on our way, as we sometimes climbed a steep ascent or descended a deep ravine, were very varied, but always beautiful. About half-way up we stopped to rest under a delightful trellis of vines, by the side of a rushing mountain-stream, bordered with ferns; then, leaving the vineyards and gardens behind us, we passed through forests of shady Spanish chestnut-trees, beneath which stretched the luxurious greensward.

At ten o'clock we quitted this grateful shade, and arrived at the neck of the pass, facing the Gran Corral, where we had to make our choice of ascending a conical hill, on our left, or the Torrinhas Peak, on our right. The latter was chosen, as promising the better view, although it was rather farther off, so we were accordingly seized upon by some of the crowd of peasants who surrounded us, and who at once proceeded to push and pull us up a steep, slippery grass slope, interspersed with large bowlders. The view from the top, looking down a sheer precipice of some 1,500 feet in depth into the valley below, was lovely. Quite at the bottom, amid the numerous ravines and small spurs of rocks by which the valley is intersected, we could distinguish some small patches of cultivated ground. Above our heads towered the jagged crests of the highest peaks, Pico Ruivo and others, which we had already seen from the yacht, when we first sighted the island.

A pleasant walk over some grassy slopes, and two more hard scrambles, took us to the summit of the Torrinhas Peak; but the charming and extensive view towards Camara de Lobos, and the bay and town of Funchal, was an ample reward for all our trouble. It did not take us long to get back to the welcome shade of the chestnut-trees, for we were all ravenously hungry, it being now eleven o'clock. But, alas! breakfast had not arrived: so we had no resource but to mount our horses again and ride down to meet it. Mr. Miles, of the hotel, had not kept his word; he had promised that our provisions should be sent up to us by nine o'clock, and it was midday before we met the men carrying the hampers on their heads. There was now nothing for it but to organize a picnic on the terrace of Mr. Veitch's deserted villa, beneath the shade of camellia, fuchsia, myrtle, magnolia, and pepper-trees, from whence we could also enjoy the fine view of the fertile valley beneath us and the blue sea sparkling beyond.

Wednesday, July 19*th.*—We were so tired after our exertions of yesterday, that it was nine o'clock before we all mustered for our morning swim, which I think we enjoyed the more from the fact of our having previously been prevented by the sharks, or rather by the rumor of sharks.

We were engaged to lunch at Mr. and Mrs. Blandy's, but I was so weary that I did not go ashore until about six o'clock in the evening, and then I went first to the English cemetery, which is very prettily laid out and well kept. The various paths are shaded by pepper-trees, entwined with bougainvillæa, while in many places the railings are completely covered by long trailing masses of stephanotis in full bloom. Some of the inscriptions on the tombs are extremely touching, and it is sad to see, as is almost always the case in places much resorted to by invalids, how large a proportion of those who lie buried here have been cut off in the very flower of their youth. Indeed, the residents of Madeira complain that it is a melancholy drawback to the charms of this beautiful island, that the friendship frequently formed between them and people who come hither in search of health is in so many cases brought to an early and sad termination. Having seen and admired Mrs. Foljambe's charming garden by daylight, we returned on board to receive some friends. Unfortunately they were not very good sailors, and, out of our party of twenty, one lady had to go ashore at once, and another before dinner was over.

They all admired the yacht very much, particularly the various cozy corners in the deck-house. It was a lovely night; and after the departure of our guests, at about ten o'clock, we steamed out of the bay, where we found a nice light breeze, which enabled us to sail.

Thursday, July 20*th.*—All to-day has been taken up in arranging our photographs, journals, &c., &c., and in preparing for our visit to Teneriffe. About twelve o'clock the wind fell light and we tried fishing, but without success, though several bonitos or flying-fish were seen. It was very hot, and it seemed quite a relief when, at eight

A Cozy Corner.

o'clock in the evening we began steaming, thus creating a breeze for ourselves.

Friday, July 21st.—We all rose early, and were full of excitement to catch the first glimpse of the famous Peak of Teneriffe. There was a nice breeze from the northeast, the true trade wind, we hope, which ought to carry us down nearly to the Line. The morning being rather hazy, it was quite ten o'clock before we saw the Peak, towering above the clouds, right ahead, about fifty-nine miles off. As we approached, it appeared less perpendicular than we had expected, or than it is generally represented in pictures. The other mountains too, in the center of the island, from the midst of which it rises, are so very lofty that, in spite of its conical sugar-loaf top, it is difficult at first to realize that the Peak is 12,180 feet high.

We dropped anchor under its shadow in the harbor of Orotava in preference to the capital, Santa Cruz, both on account of its being a healthier place, and also in order to be nearer to the Peak, which we wished to ascend.

The heat having made the rest of our party rather lazy, Captain Lecky and I volunteered to go on shore to see the Vice-Consul, Mr. Goodall, and try to make arrangements for our expedition. It was only 2 p.m., and very hot work, walking through the deserted streets, but luckily we had not far to go, and the house was nice and cool when we got there. Mr. Goodall sent off at once for a carriage, dispatching a messenger also to the mountains for horses and guides, which there was some difficulty in obtaining at such short notice.

Having organized the expedition we re-embarked to dine on board the yacht, and I went to bed at seven, to be called again, however, at half-past ten o'clock. After a light supper, we landed and went to the Vice-Consul's, arriving there exactly at midnight. But no horses were forthcoming, so we lay down on our rugs in the patio, and endeavored to sleep, as we knew we should require all our strength for the expedition before us.

There were sundry false alarms of a start, as the horses arrived by ones and twos from the neighboring villages, accompanied by their respective owners. By two o'clock all our steeds, twelve in number, had assembled, and in another quarter of an hour we were leaving the town by a steep stony path, bordered by low walls. There was no moon, and for the first two hours it was very dark. At the end of that time we could see the first glimmer of dawn, and were shortly afterwards able to distinguish each other and to observe the beautiful view which lay below us as we wended our way up and up between small patches of cultivation. Soon we climbed above the clouds, which presented a most curious appearance as we looked down upon them. The strata through which we had passed was so dense and so white, that it looked exactly like an enormous glacier, covered with fresh-fallen snow extending for miles and miles; while the projecting tops of the other Canary Islands appeared only like great solitary rocks.

The sun had already become very oppressive, and at half-past seven we stopped to breakfast and to water the horses. Half-past eight found us in the saddle again, and we commenced to traverse a dreary plain of yellowish white pumice-stone, interspersed with huge blocks of obsidian, thrown from the mouth of the volcano. At first the monotony of the scene was relieved by large bushes of yellow broom in full flower, and still larger bushes of the beautiful *Retama blanca*, quite covered with lovely white bloom, scenting the air with its delicious fragrance, and resembling huge tufts of feathers, eight or nine feet high. As we proceeded, however, we left all traces of vegetation behind us. It was like the Great Sahara. On every side a vast expanse of yellow pumice-stone sand spread around us, an occasional block of rock sticking up here and there, and looking as if it had indeed been fused in a mighty furnace. By half-past ten we had reached the 'Estancia de los Ingleses,' 9,639 feet above the level of the sea, where the baggage and some of the horses had to be left behind, the saddles being transferred to mules for the very steep climb before us. After a drink of water all round, we started again, and commenced the ascent of the almost perpendicular stream of lava and stone, which forms the only practicable route to the top. Our poor beasts were only able to go a few paces at a time without stopping to regain their breath. The loose ashes and lava fortunately gave them a good foothold, or it would have been quite impossible for them to get along at all. One was only encouraged to proceed by the sight of one's friends above, looking like flies clinging to the face of a wall. The road, if such it can be called, ran in zigzags, each of which was about the length of two horses, so that we were in turns one above another. There were a few slips and slides and tumbles, but no important casualties; and in about an hour and a half we had reached the 'Alta Vista,' a tiny plateau, where the horses were to be left.

The expedition so far had been such a fatiguing one, and the heat was so great, that the children and I decided to remain here, and to let the gentlemen proceed alone to the summit of the Peak. We tried to find some shade, but the sun was so immediately above us that this was almost an impossibility. However, we managed to squeeze ourselves under some slightly overhanging rocks, and I took some photographs while the children slept. The guides soon returned with water-barrels full of ice, procured from a cavern above, where there is a stream of water constantly running; and nothing could have been more grateful and refreshing.

It was more than three hours before Tom and Captain Lecky reappeared, to be soon followed by the rest of the party. Whilst they rested and refreshed themselves with ice, they described the ascent as fatiguing in the extreme, in fact almost an impossibility for a lady. First they had scrambled over huge blocks of rough lava to the tiny plain of the Rambleta, 11,466 feet above the level of the sea, after which they had to climb up the cone itself, 530 feet in height, and sloping at an angle of 44 degrees. It is composed of ashes and calcined chalk, into which their feet sank, while, for every two steps they made forwards and upwards, they slipped one backwards. But those who reached the top were rewarded for their exertions by a glorious view, and by the wonderful appearance of the summit of the Peak. The ground beneath their feet was hot, while sulphurous vapors and smoke issued from various small fissures around them, though there has been no actual eruption from this crater of the volcano since 1704. They brought down with them a beautiful piece of calcined chalk, covered with crystals of sulphur and arsenic, and some other specimens. Parched and dry as the ground looked where I was resting, a few grains of barley, dropped by mules on the occasion of a previous visit, had taken root and had grown up into ear; and there were also a few roots of a sort of dog-violet, showing its delicate lavender-colored flowers, 11,000 feet above the sea, and far beyond the level of any other vegetation

It was impossible to ride down to the spot where we had left the baggage animals, and the descent was consequently very fatiguing, and even painful. At every step our feet sank into a mass of loose scoriæ and ashes; and so we went slipping, sliding, and stumbling along, sometimes running against a rock, and sometimes nearly pitching forward on our faces. All this too beneath a blazing sun, with the thermometer at 78°, and not a vestige of shade. At last Tom and I reached the bottom, where, after partaking of luncheon and draughts of quinine, we lay down under the shadow of a great rock to recruit our weary frames.

Refreshed by our meal, we started at six o'clock on our return journey, and went down a good deal faster than we came up. Before the end of the pumice-stone or Retama plains had been reached, it was nearly dark. Sundry small accidents occurring to stirrup-leathers, bridles, and girths—for the saddlery was not of the best description—delayed us slightly, and as Tom, Dr. Potter, Allnutt, and the guide had got on ahead, we soon lost sight of them. After an interval of uncertainty, the other guides confessed that they did not know the way back in the dark. This was not pleasant, for the roads were terrible, and during the whole of our journey up, from the port to the Peak, we had met only four people in all

—two goatherds with their flocks, and two 'neveros,' bringing down ice to the town. There was therefore not much chance of gaining information from any one on our way down. We wandered about among low bushes, down watercourses, and over rocks for a long time. Horns were blown, and other means of attracting attention were tried; first one and then another of the party meanwhile coming more or less to grief. My good little horse fell down three times, though we did not part company, and once he went up a steep bank by mistake, instead of going down a very nasty watercourse, which I do not wonder at his objecting to. I managed to jump off in time, and so no harm was done; but it was rather anxious work.

About ten o'clock we saw a light in the distance, and with much shouting woke up the inhabitants of the cottage whence it proceeded, promising to reward them liberally if they would only show us our way back. Three of them consented to do this, and provided themselves accordingly with pine-torches, wrapped round with bracken and leaves. One, a very fine man, dressed in white, with his arm extended above his head, bearing the light, led the way; another walked in front of my horse, while the third brought up the rear. They conducted us down the most frightfully steep paths until we had descended beneath the clouds, when the light from our torches threw our shadows in gigantic form upon the mists above, reminding us of the legend of the 'Specter of the Brocken.' At last the torches began to go out, one by one, and just as the last light was expiring, we arrived at a small village, where we of course found that everybody was asleep. After some delay, during which Mabelle and I were so tired that we lay down in the street to rest, more torches were procured and a fresh guide, who led us into the comparatively good path towards Puerto Orotava. Finally, half an hour after midnight, we arrived at the house of the Vice-Consul, who had provided refreshments for us, and whose nephew was still very kindly sitting up awaiting our return. But we were too tired to do anything but go straight on board the yacht, where, after some supper and champagne, we were indeed glad to retire to our berths. This was at 3.30 a.m., exactly twenty-nine hours since we had been called on Friday night.

It is certainly too long an expedition to be performed in one day. Tents should be taken, and arrangements made for camping out for one, if not two, nights; but, in the case of such a large party as ours, this would have been a great business, as everything must be carried to so great a height, up such steep places, and over such bad roads. Still, there are so many objects and places of interest, not only on, but around, the Peak, that it is a pity to see them only when hurried and fatigued.

Sunday, July 23d.—Orders had been given not to call us nor to wash decks, and it was consequently half-past ten before any one awoke, and midday before the first of our party put in an appearance on deck.

Long before this, the 'Sunbeam' had been inundated with visitors from the shore. We had given a general invitation to the friends of the Vice-Consul to come and see the yacht; and they accordingly arrived in due course, accompanied in many cases by a large circle of acquaintances. Those who came first were conducted below and all over the vessel, but the number ultimately became so great, that, in self-defense, we were obliged to limit their wanderings to the deck, opening the skylights wide, however, to enable them to see as much as possible of the saloon and cabins.

From breakfast-time until prayers, at three o'clock, when the yacht was closed for an hour, there was a constant stream of visitors from the shore. It was a great nuisance; but still it seemed unkind to refuse to allow them to see what they had never seen before, and might possibly never have an opportunity of seeing again. All steamers and sailing-ships, as a rule, go to Santa Cruz;

and the fame of our vessel having been spread abroad by our visitors of Friday, many of the poor people had come from villages far away over the mountains. We could not help feeling a certain respect for the determined way in which physical infirmity was mastered by curiosity, for, though many experienced very serious inconvenience from the motion of the vessel, they still persevered in their examination.

About five o'clock we went ashore ourselves, and drove up to Villa Orotava. The wide road is macadamized and marked with kilometer stones, and is planted on either side with pepper-trees, plane-trees, and the *Eucalyptus globulus*, which has grown 35 meters, or 115 feet, in seven years. The hedges are formed of blue plumbago, scarlet geranium, yellow acacia, lavender-colored heliotrope, white jasmine, and pink and white roses.

After driving a few miles, we turned down an old paved road towards the sea, and, by dint of a considerable amount of shaking, arrived at the celebrated Botanical Gardens, mentioned by Humboldt and others. We passed through a small house, with a fine dragon-tree on either side, and entered the gardens, where we found a valuable collection of trees and shrubs of almost every known species. The kind and courteous Curator, Don Hermann Wildgaret, accompanied us, and explained the peculiarities of the many interesting plants, from Europe, Asia, Africa, America, Australia, New Zealand, and the various islands of the North and South Pacific and Indian Oceans. The climate of Teneriffe is so equable that the island forms a true garden of acclimatization for the vegetable productions of the various countries of the world; by the judicious expenditure of a little more money, this establishment might be made an important means of introducing to Europe many new and valuable plants. At present the annual income is 5,000 francs, the salary of the Curator being 1,000 francs.

A rough drive over paved roads, commanding extensive views of sea and rocks, and of some palm-trees on a promontory in the distance, brought us, at about seven o'clock, to the boat, which was waiting our return. We arrived in due course on board the 'Sunbeam,' laden with bouquets of the choicest flowers, and soon after dinner we all retired to bed, not having yet recovered from the fatigues of yesterday.

Monday, July 24th.—What one gains in the beauty and abundance of vegetable life here, one loses in its rapid and premature decay. Fruit gathered in the morning is scarcely fit to eat at night, and the flowers brought on board yesterday evening were dead to-day at 4.30 a.m.; whilst some of the roses we brought from Cowes lasted until we reached Madeira, though it must be owned so many fell to pieces that my cabin used to be daily swept with rose-leaves instead of tea-leaves.

We went ashore soon after six, and drove straight to the garden of the Marquis de Sonzal, where there is a beautiful palm-tree, 101 feet high, the remains of an enormous dragon-tree, old even in the fifteenth century, besides hedges of myrtle, jasmine, and clematis, and flowers of every description in full bloom. The dragon-tree is a species of dracæna, and looks rather like a gigantic candelabrum, composed of a number of yuccas, perched on the top of a gnarled and somewhat deformed stem, half palm, half cactus. Another beautiful garden was next visited, belonging to the Marquis de la Candia, who received us and showed us his coffee and plantains in full growth, as well as a magnificent Spanish chestnut-tree, coëval with the dragon-tree. Out of one of its almost decayed branches a so-called young tree was growing, but it would have been thought very respectable and middle-aged in any other locality.

Every one here, as in Madeira, has been more or less ruined by the failure of the vines. Most of the large landed proprietors have left their estates to take care of themselves; and the peasants, for the last few years, have been emigrating by hundreds to Caraccas, in Venezuela. Things are, however, beginning to look up a little now. The cultivation of cochineal appears to succeed, though the price is low; coffee answers well; and permission has been obtained from the Spanish Government to grow tobacco, accompanied by a promise to purchase, at a certain fixed rate, all that can be produced. Still, people talk of the Island of Teneriffe as something very different now from what it was twenty-five or thirty years ago, both as regards the number of its inhabitants and the activity of its commerce, and mourn over 'the good old times;'—a custom I have remarked in many other places!

The Marquis de la Candia and Don Hermann Wildgaret returned on board with us to breakfast. The anchor had been weighed, and the 'Sunbeam' was slowly steaming up and down, waiting for us. The stream of visitors had been as great and as constant as ever during our absence, in spite of the heavy roll of the sea, and the deck seemed quite covered with baskets of flowers and fruit, kindly sent on board by the people who had been over the yacht the day before. Amongst the latest arrivals were some very handsome Spanish ladies, beautifully dressed in black, with mantillas, each of whom was accompanied by a young man carrying a basin. It must, I fear, be confessed that this was rather a trial to the gravity of all on board. It certainly was an instance of the pursuit of knowledge, or the gratification of curiosity, under considerable difficulties.

Immediately after breakfast, our friends bade us adieu, and went ashore in the shore-boat, while we steamed along the north side of the island, past the splendid cliffs of Buenavista, rising 2,000 feet sheer from the sea, to Cape Teno, the extreme western point of Teneriffe. In the distance we could see the Great Canary, Palma, and Hierro, and soon passed close to the rocky island of Gomera. Here, too, the dark cliffs, of volcanic form and origin, are magnificent, and as we were almost becalmed by the high land whilst we sailed along the north shore of the island, we had ample opportunities of admiring its rugged beauty. During the night we approached Palma, another large island of the Canary group, containing one of the most remarkable calderas, or large basins, formed by volcanic action in the world.

CHAPTER III.

PALMA TO RIO DE JANEIRO.

A wet sheet and a flowing sea,
A wind that follows fast
And fills the white and rustling sail,
And bends the gallant mast.

Tuesday, July 25th.—There was not much wind during the night, and Palma was consequently still visible when I came on deck at daybreak. We had a light fair wind in the morning, accompanied by a heavy swell, which caused us to roll so much that I found it very difficult to do anything. Several shoals of flying-fish skimmed past us along the surface of the water, occasionally rising to a considerable height above it. Their beautiful wings, glittering in the bright sunlight, looked like delicate silver filigree-work. In the night one flew on board, only to be preserved in spirits by Dr. Potter.

Saturday, July 29th.—For the last three days we have been going on quietly with fair, warm weather, but a nice fresh breeze sprang up to-day. At midday the sun was so exactly vertical over our heads, that it was literally possible to stand under the shadow of one's own hatbrim, and be sheltered all round. Our navigators experienced considerable difficulty in taking their noontide observations, as the sun appeared to dodge about in every direction.

About two o'clock we made the high land of St. Antonio, one of the Cape de Verde Islands, and, soon afterwards, the lower land of St. Vincent. Some doubt existing as to the prevalence of fever at the latter place,

Tom decided not to stop there, for fear of having to undergo quarantine at Rio de Janeiro. We therefore shortened sail, and passed slowly between the islands to the anchorage beyond the Bird Rock. This is a very small island, of perfectly conical form, covered with thousands of sea-fowl, who live here undisturbed by any other inhabitants. The town of Porto Grande, with its rows of white houses on the sea-shore, at the base of the rocky crags, looked clean and comfortable in the evening light. During the day, however, it must be a hot and glaring place, for there are no trees to afford shade, nor, indeed, any kind of vegetation. The water, too, is bad, and all supplies for passing steamers are brought from the other islands, at very uncertain intervals. It is still a great coaling station, though not so much used as it was formerly, before the opening of the Suez Canal. The ships come out with coal, and go away in ballast (there is nothing else to be had here), procured from a point near the town, to Rio or elsewhere, where they pick up the homeward cargo of fruit, &c.

The absence of twilight in these latitudes, both at dawn and sunset, is certainly very remarkable. This morning, at four o'clock, the stars were shining brightly; ten minutes later the day had commenced to break; and at half-past four the sun had risen above the horizon, and was gilding the surrounding mountain tops.

Sunday, July 30th.—About 10 a.m. we were off Tarafal Bay—a most hopeless-looking place for supplies. High rocky mountains, sandy slopes, and black volcanic beach composed a scene of arid desolation, in the midst of which was situated one small white house, with four windows and a thatched roof, surrounded by a little green patch of sugar-canes and cocoa-nut palms.

But the result proved the sageness of the advice contained in the old proverb, not to trust to appearances only; for, whilst we were at breakfast, Mr. Martinez, the son of the owner of the one whitewashed cottage to be seen, came on board. To our surprise, he spoke English extremely well, and promised us all sorts of supplies, if we could wait until three o'clock in the afternoon. Having agreed to do this, we shortly afterwards went ashore in his boat, with a crew of more than half-naked negroes, and a hot row of about three miles brought us to the shore, where, after some little difficulty, we succeeded in effecting a landing. Our feet immediately sank into the hot black sand, composed entirely of volcanic deposits and small pieces, or rather grains, of amber, through which we had a fatiguing walk until we reached some palm-trees, shading a little pool of water. Here we left some of the men, with instructions to fill the breakers they had brought with them, while we walked on along the beach, past the remains of an English schooner that caught fire not far from this island, and was run ashore by her captain, thirty years ago. Her iron, anchor, chain, and wheel still remained, together with two queer little iron cannon, which I should have much liked to carry off as a memorial of our visit. We then turned up a narrow shadeless path, bordered by stone walls, leading away from the sea, past a sugar-mill and a ruin. A few almond, castor-oil, and fig trees were growing amongst the sugar-canes, and as we mounted the hill we could see some thirty round straw huts, like beehives, on the sandy slopes beside the little stream. An abrupt turn in the mountains, amid which, at a distance of three leagues, this tiny river takes its rise, hides it from the sea, so that the narrow valley which it fertilizes looks like a small oasis in the desert of rocks and sand.

Mr. Martinez's house, where we sat for some time, and beneath the windows of which the one stream of the island runs, was comparatively cool. Outside, the negro washerwomen were busy washing clothes in large turtle-shell tubs, assisted, or hindered, by the 'washerwoman-bird,' a kind of white crane, who appeared quite tame, playing about just like a kitten, pecking at the clothes or the women's feet, and then running away and hiding behind a tree. The stream was full of water-cresses, while the burned-up little garden contained an abundance of beautiful flowers. There were scarlet and yellow mimosas, of many kinds, combining every shade of exquisite green velvety foliage, alpinias, with pink, waxy flowers and crimson and gold centers, oleanders, begonias, hibiscus, allamandas, and arum and other lilies.

Mr. Bingham sketched, I took some photographs, Dr. Potter and the children caught butterflies, and the rest of our party wandered about. Every five minutes a negro arrived with a portion of our supplies. One brought a sheep, another a milch-goat for baby, while the rest contributed, severally, a couple of cocoa-nuts, a papaya, three mangoes, a few water-cresses, a sack of sweet potatoes, a bottle of milk, three or four quinces, a bunch of bananas, a little honey, half a dozen cabbages, some veal and pork, and so on; until it appeared as if every little garden on either side of the three leagues of stream must have yielded up its entire produce, and we had accumulated sacks full of cocoa-nuts and potatoes, hundreds of eggs, and dozens of chickens and ducks. It was very amusing to see the things arrive. They were brought in by people varying in color from dark yellow to the blackest ebony, and ranging in size from fine stalwart men, over six feet in height, to tiny little blackies of about three feet six, with curly hair, snowy teeth, and mischievous, beady eyes. The arrival of the provision boat and the transfer of its miscellaneous cargo to the 'Sunbeam' was quite an amusing sight. The pretty black goat and the sheep bleated, the fowls cackled, and the ducks quacked, while the negroes chatted and laughed as they handed and hauled on board fish of all shapes and sizes, bunches of bananas, piles of cocoa-nuts, sacks of potatoes, and many other things, finishing up with a tiny black boy, about three years old, whom I think they would rather have liked to leave behind with us, if we would only have taken him. The fish proved excellent, though some of them really seemed almost too pretty to eat. A brilliant gold-fish, weighing about three pounds, and something like a gray mullet in flavor, was perhaps the best. The prices were very curious. Chickens a shilling each, ducks five shillings, goats thirty shillings, and sheep ten shillings. Vegetables, fruit, and flowers were extremely cheap; but the charge for water, fetched from the spring in our own breakers by our own crew, with but little assistance from four or five negroes, was £3 18s. However, as ours is the only yacht, with one exception, that has ever visited this island, there was nothing for it except to pay the bill without demur.

I never in my life felt so warm as I did to-day on shore, though the inhabitants say it will not be *really* hot for two months yet; I never before saw cocoa-nut palms growing; and I never tasted a mango until this morning; so I have experienced three new sensations in one day.

The night was fearfully close, muggy, and thundery, the temperature in the cabins being 89°, in spite of open skylights and port-holes. Generally speaking, it has not hitherto been as hot as we expected, especially on board the yacht itself. On deck there is almost always a nice breeze, but below it is certainly warm.

Tuesday, August 1st.—Yesterday we were still under sail, but to-day it has been necessary to steam, for the wind has fallen too light. There was a heavy roll from the south, and the weather continued hot and oppressive. In the cabins the thermometer stood at 89° during the whole of the night, in spite of all our efforts to improve the temperature. We therefore put three of the children in the deck-house to sleep, opening the doors and windows; and some of the rest of our party slept on deck in hammocks. In anticipation of the heavy equatorial rains, which Captain Lecky had predicted might commence to-day, we had the awnings put up; a fortunate piece of foresight, for, before midnight, the rain came down in torrents.

Wednesday, August 2d.—At daybreak the sky was covered with heavy black clouds, and the atmosphere was as hot and muggy as ever. We had a great deal of rain during the day, and took advantage of the opportunity to fill every available tub, bucket, and basin, to say nothing of the awnings. It came down in such sheets that mackintoshes were comparatively useless, and we had soon filled our seventeen breakers, the cistern, and the boats, from which we had removed the covers, with very good, though somewhat dirty, washing water.

Friday, August 4th.—We were only 289 miles off Sierra Leone in the morning, and at noon therefore Tom decided to put about. Having done so, we found that we went along much more easily and quite as fast on the other tack. We maintained a good rate of speed on our new course, which was now nearly due west, passing a large bark with every stitch of canvas set, hand over hand.

We are still in the Guinea current, and the temperature of the water is 82°, even in the early morning; but the heat of the sun does not seem to have much effect upon it, as it does not vary to any great extent during the day.

In the evening we saw the Southern Cross for the first time, and were much disappointed in its appearance. The fourth star is of smaller magnitude than the others; and the whole group is only for a very short time in a really upright position, inclining almost always either to one side or the other, as it rises and sets.

Tuesday, August 8th.—We crossed the line at daylight. This event caused much fun and excitement, both in cabin and forecastle. The conventional hair was put across the field of the telescope for the unsophisticated 'really to see the line,' and many firmly believed they did see it, and discussed its appearance at some length. Jim Allen, one of our tallest sailors, and coxswain of the gig, dressed in blue, with long oakum wig and beard, gilt paper crown and trident, and fish impaled in one hand, was seated on a gun-carriage, and made a capital Father Neptune. Our somewhat portly engineer, Mr. Rowbotham, with fur-trimmed dressing-gown and cap, and bent form, leaning on a stick, his face partially concealed by a long gray beard, and a large bandbox of pills on one arm, made an equally good doctor to his Marine Majesty, while the part of Mrs. Trident was ably filled by one of the youngest sailors, dressed in some of the maids' clothes.

Soon afterwards we saw an enormous shoal of grampuses, large black fish, about 25 feet in length, something between a dolphin and a whale, with the very ugliest jaws, or rather snouts, imaginable. They are of a predatory and ferocious disposition, attacking not only sharks, dolphins, and porpoises, but even whales, more than twice their own size. We also passed through enormous quantities of flying fish, no doubt driven to the surface by dolphins and bonitos. They were much larger and stronger in the wing than any we have hitherto seen.

Lulu and her Puppies.

Lulu's puppies, born yesterday, have been respectively named Butterfly (who survived her birth only an hour), Poseidon, Aphrodite, Amphitrite, and Thetis—names suggested by their birthplace on the ocean close to his Marine Majesty's supposed equatorial palace.

At noon we were 250 miles off St. Paul's Rocks.

Thursday, August 10*th.*—A very hot, showery day. Saw two large ships in the distance. In the morning we were almost becalmed for a time, but the breeze returned during the afternoon, and we were able to proceed on our course. I think this has been the most lovely of the many exquisite days we have enjoyed since we left England. It commenced with a magnificent sunrise, and ended with an equally gorgeous sunset, only to be succeeded by a beautiful moonlight night, so clear and bright that we could see to read ordinary print on deck.

Saturday, August 12*th.*—At noon we were 300 miles off Bahia, a place we have made up our minds not to visit, as it would lengthen our voyage considerably, and there is not much to see there. We have therefore decided to proceed direct to Rio, where we are looking forward to arrive on Wednesday or Thursday next.

The night was showery, with a good deal of wind and sea.

Sunday, August 13*th.*—Sailing in the tropics is really very delightful! When going to the westward, there is almost always, at this season of the year, a favorable breeze, and the weather is generally either quite fair or moderately so.

> Whispered to it, westward, westward,
> And with speed it darted forward.

We had service at 11.15 a.m., and again at 5.30 p.m. The choir has considerably improved; one of our new men plays the violin very well, and frequently accompanies the children and the nurse in their songs. On a clear calm night, beneath a tropical sky, when the members of this little group assemble on deck, and, by the light of a lantern, sing some of their simple songs, the effect produced is both melodious and picturesque.

The wind dropped at about 10 p.m., and we had an unpleasant amount of roll during the night, sails flapping, spars creaking, and booms swinging as if they would pull the masts out of the vessel.

Monday, August 14*th.*—This morning we saw a small schooner ahead, and thinking from her manœuvres that she wished to speak us, we made our number and ran towards her. We soon found out, however, that she was a whaler, in chase of two large grampuses. She had two men on the lookout in the cross-trees, in a sort of iron cage; and though she was of much smaller tonnage than the 'Sunbeam,' she carried five big boats, one of which, full of men, was ready to be lowered into the water the instant they had approached sufficiently near to the whale or grampus. The seas used formerly to abound with whalers, but they are now much less numerous, the seasons having been bad of late.

To-night the stars were especially brilliant, and we spent some hours in trying to make out their names. Vega, our polar star for some time to come, shone conspicuously bright, and the Southern Cross could be seen to great advantage.

Wednesday, August 16*th.*—We had a fine fair breeze all day, and at 5 p.m. there was a cry from the mast-head of 'Land ahead!' Great excitement immediately prevailed on board, and Tom and Captain Brown rushed, for about the twelfth time, to the foretop to see if the report was true. They were soon able to announce that Cape Frio was visible on the port bow, about thirty-five miles distant. After even a fortnight at sea, an indescribable sensation is produced by this cry, and by the subsequent sight of the land itself. When we came up on deck this evening, after dinner, we all gazed on the light-house on the still distant shore as if we had never beheld such a thing in our lives before. The color and temperature of the water had perceptibly changed, the former from a beautiful, clear, dark ultramarine to a muddy green; innumerable small birds, moths, locusts, and grasshoppers came on board; and, having given special orders that we were to be called early the next morning, we went to bed in the fond hope that we should be able to enter Rio harbor at daybreak.

Thursday, August 17th.—'L'homme propose; Dieu dispose.' Steam was up at midnight, but by that time it was blowing half a gale of wind from the south-west, with such a steep, short sea that the screw was scarcely ever properly immersed, but went racing round and round in the air with tremendous velocity, as we pitched and rolled about. Our progress was therefore at the rate of something rather under a mile an hour, and at daybreak, instead of entering the harbor of Rio, as we had hoped to do, we found ourselves close to Cape Frio.

About 8 a.m. matters mended, the wind moderating and changing its direction slightly; so that, under steam and sail, we were soon going along the coast at the rate of four or five miles an hour. The surf was breaking with a loud roar upon the white sandy beach, while the spray was carried by the force of the wind far inland, over the strip of flat fertile-looking country, lying between the sea and a chain of low sugar-loaf-shaped mountains, parallel with the shore, and only a short distance off.

Our course lay between the mainland and the islands of Maya and Payo, where the groves of bananas and other trees looked very miserable in the wind. The tall isolated palm-trees, whose elastic stems bowed readily before the fury of the blast, looked, as they were twisted and whirled hither and thither, like umbrellas turned inside out. Passing the false Sugar-loaf mountain, as it is called, we next opened out the true one, the Gavia, and the chain of mountains beyond, the outlines of which bear an extraordinary resemblance to the figure of a man lying on his back, the profile of the face being very like that of the late Duke of Wellington. As the sun sank in gorgeous splendor behind these hills, I think I never saw a grander or more beautiful sight; though the sky was so red and stormy-looking that our hopes of a fine day to-morrow were but faint.

Before entering the harbor, a bar had to be crossed, which is a dangerous operation all the world over. The skylights and hatches were fastened down, and those of our party who did not like being shut up below took their places on the bridge, where, for the first time since we left England, it felt really quite cold. As we advanced, the beautiful harbor, with its long rows of glittering gaslights, extending for miles on either side of the bay, and illuminating the city and suburbs, gradually became visible. On our left lay the two islands, Rodonda and Raza, on the latter of which is situated a lighthouse. The wind was blowing off the land when we reached the bar, so that, after all our preparations, there was hardly any sea to encounter, and the moment we were over, the water on the other side was perfectly smooth. A gun and a blue light from Fort Santa Cruz, answered immediately by a similar signal from Fort Santa Lucia, announced our arrival, and we shortly afterwards dropped our anchor in the quarantine ground of Rio close to Botafogo Bay, in the noble harbor of Nictherohy.

After dinner it rained heavily, and continued to do so during the whole night.

CHAPTER IV.

RIO DE JANEIRO.

The sun is warm, the sky is clear,
The waves are dancing fast and bright,
Blue isles and snowy mountains wear
The purple noon's transparent light.

Friday, August 18*th*.—The clouds still hung heavy on the hills, or rather mountains, which surround the bay, occasionally descending in the form of torrents of rain, and hiding everything from our view.

Early in the morning we weighed anchor and steamed up the bay to the man-of-war anchorage, a much pleasanter situation than the quarantine harbor, where we had brought up last night. About 9.30 a.m. the health officers came on board, and half an hour later we had a visit from the custom-house official, who required Tom to sign and seal a declaration upon oath that he had no cargo on board, and not more coal than we absolutely required for our own consumption.

About eleven o'clock we put on our mackintoshes and thick boots, and, accompanied by an interpreter, who (together with several washerwomen) had suddenly made his appearance on board, rowed ashore, pushing our way through crowds of boats laden with fruit and vegetables. The landing-place was close to the market, at some broken-down steps, and was crowded with chattering negroes, of every shade of color. The quays seemed covered with piles of fruit and vegetables, discharged from the boats, the principal produce being sugar-cane, bananas, and oranges. Each side street that we came to was a little river, which had to be crossed, or rather forded, after paddling through the mud in the main thoroughfare.

Our first visit was to the post-office—'no letters'—then to the British Consulate—'no letters'—and finally to the Legation, but there was nobody at home there; so we set off for the Hôtel des Etrangers, to breakfast. Our way lay through the straggling suburbs of the city for about two miles, and as we drove along we could see and admire, despite the heavy rain, the magnificent groves of palm-trees, and the brilliancy and beauty of the tropical vegetation in the various private and public gardens that we passed.

After breakfast we returned to the Legation, where we were most kindly received, but, much to our regret, no letters were forthcoming. We next paid a visit to some of the shops in the Rua do Ouvidor, for the sale of imitations of flowers, made from the undyed feathers of birds, and a large number of the more expensive varieties of ordinary artificial flowers, each petal consisting of the entire throat or breast of a humming-bird, and the leaves are made from the wings of beetles. They are very rare and beautiful, their manufacture being quite a *spécialité* of this city. The prices asked astonished us greatly; the cost of five sprays, which I had been commissioned to buy, was £29, and the price of all the others was proportionately high. But then they wear forever. I have had some for nine years, and they are as good now as when they were bought.

Saturday, August 19*th.*—Though far from brilliant, the weather improved, and we were able to enjoy occasional glimpses of the beautiful scenery around us.

Mr. Gough and Mr. O'Conor breakfasted with us on board, and we afterwards proceeded in a 'bond' to the Botanical Gardens, about seven miles out of the city. These 'bonds,' which are a great institution here, are large carriages, either open or closed, drawn sometimes by one, sometimes by two, sometimes by three mules. They go at a great pace, and run very smoothly. Ordinary carriages are dear; and as tramways have been laid down in almost every street and road, driving is a rather difficult affair. On our road we passed several delightful-looking private gardens. The railings were completely covered, some with white stephanotis and scarlet lapageria, others with a beautiful orange-colored creeper and lilac bougainvillæa, or passion-flowers of many colors and variety. Inside we could see large trees with green and yellow stripes, croton-oil plants, spotted and veined caladiums, and dracænas, the whole being shaded by orange-trees.

Along the edge of Botafogo Bay there is a delightful drive, beneath a splendid avenue of imperial palms, extending to the gates of the Botanical Gardens. Each specimen rises straight up like the column of an Egyptian temple, and is crowned with a feathery tuft of large shiny dark-green leaves, some thirty feet in length. The clumps of bamboos, too, were very fine, and nearly all the trees seemed to be full of curious orchids and parasites of every sort and kind.

We had an agreeable drive back in the cool evening to dinner at the Hôtel de l'Europe. The food was excellent, and included some delicious, tiny, queer-shaped oysters, which are found on the mangrove-trees, overhanging the water, higher up the bay. We afterwards went to a pleasant little reception, where we enjoyed the splendid singing of some young Brazilian ladies, and the subsequent row off to the yacht, in the moonlight, was not the least delightful part of the programme.

Sunday, August 20th.—At last a really fine day. We could now, for the first time, thoroughly appreciate the beauties of the noble bay of Nictherohy, though the distant Organ mountains were still hidden from our view. In the morning we went to church on board H.M.S. 'Volage,' afterwards rowing across the bay to Icaraky, where we took the tramway to Santa Rosa. On our way we again passed many charming villas and gardens, similar to those we had admired yesterday, while the glorious and ever-attractive tropical vegetation abounded everywhere. In spite of the great heat, the children seemed untiring in the pursuit of butterflies, of which they succeeded in catching many beautiful specimens.

Monday, August 21*st.* — After an early breakfast, we started off to have a look at the market. The greatest bustle and animation prevailed, and there were people and things to see and observe in endless variety. The fish-market was full of finny monsters of the deep, all new and strange to us, whose odd Brazilian names would convey to a stranger but little idea of the fish themselves. There was an enormous rockfish, weighing about 300 pounds, with hideous face and shiny back and fins; there were large ray, and skate, and cuttle-fish—the *pieuvre* of Victor Hugo's 'Travailleurs de la Mer'—besides baskets full of the large prawns for which the coast is famous, eight or ten inches long, and with antennæ of twelve or fourteen inches in length. They make up in size for want of quality, for they are insipid and tasteless, though, being tender, they make excellent curry. The oysters, on the other hand, are particularly small, but of the most delicious flavor. They are brought from a park, higher up the bay, where, as I have said, they grow on posts and the branches of the mangrove-tree, which hang down into the water. We also saw a large quantity of fine mackerel, a good many turtle and porpoises, and a few hammer-headed sharks. The latter are very curious creatures, not unlike an ordinary shark, but with a remarkable hammer-shaped projection on either side of their noses for which it is difficult to imagine a use.

In the fruit-market were many familiar bright-colored fruits; for it is now the depth of winter at Rio, and the various kinds that we saw were all such as would bear transport to England. Fat, jet-black negresses, wearing turbans on their heads, strings of colored beads on their necks and arms, and single long white garments, which appeared to be continually slipping off their shoulders, here presided over brilliant-looking heaps of oranges, bananas, pineapples, passion-fruit, tomatoes, apples, pears, capsicums and peppers, sugar-cane, cabbage-palms, cherimoyers, and bread-fruit.

In another part of the market all sorts of live birds were for sale, with a few live beasts, such as deer, monkeys, pigs, guinea-pigs in profusion, rats, cats, dogs, marmosets, and a dear little lion-monkey, very small and rather red, with a beautiful head and mane, who roared exactly like a real lion in miniature. We saw also cages full of small flamingoes, snipe of various kinds, and a great many birds of smaller size, with feathers of all shades of blue, red, and green, and metallic hues of brilliant luster, besides parrots, macaws, cockatoos innumerable, and torchas, on stands. The torcha is a bright-colored black-and-yellow bird, about as big as a starling, which puts its little head on one side and takes flies from one's fingers in the prettiest and most enticing manner. Unfortunately, it is impossible to introduce it into England, as it cannot stand the change of climate. The other birds included guinea-fowls, ducks, cocks and hens, pigeons, doves, quails, &c., and many other varieties less familiar or quite unknown to us. Altogether the visit was an extremely interesting one, and well repaid us for our early rising.

At eleven o'clock we started for the Petropolis steamer, which took us alongside a wooden pier, from the end of which the train started, and we were soon wending our way through sugar and coffee plantations, formed in the midst of the forest of palms and other tropical trees. An Englishman has made a large clearing here, and has established a fine farm, which he hopes to work successfully by means of immigrant labor.

After a journey of twenty minutes in the train, we reached the station, at the foot of a hill, where we found several four-mule carriages awaiting our arrival. The drive up from the station to the town, over a pass in the Organ mountains, was superb. At each turn of the road we had an ever-varying view of the city of Rio and its magnificent bay. And then the banks of this tropical high-road! From out a mass of rich verdure grew lovely scarlet begonias, and spotted caladiums, shaded by graceful tree-ferns and overhung by trees full of exquisite parasites and orchids. Among these the most conspicuous, after the palms, are the tall thin-stemmed sloth-trees, so called from their being a favorite resort of the sloth, who with great difficulty crawls up into one of them, remains there until he has demolished every leaf, and then passes on to the next tree.

The pace of the mules, up the steep incline, under a broiling sun, was really wonderful. Half-way up we stopped to change, at a buvette, where we procured some excellent Brazilian coffee, of fine but exceedingly bitter flavor. Our next halt, midway between the buvette and the top of the hill, was at a spring of clear sparkling water, where we had an opportunity of collecting some ferns and flowers; and on reaching the summit we stopped once more, to enjoy the fine view over the Pass and the bay of Nictherohy. The descent towards Petropolis then commenced: it lies in the hollow of the hills, with a river flowing through the center of its broad streets, on either side of which are villas and avenues of noble trees. Altogether it reminded me of Bagnères-de-Luchon, in the Pyrenees, though the general effect is unfortunately marred by the gay and rather too fantastic painting of some of the houses.

Tuesday, August 22d.—We were called at half-past five, and, after a hasty breakfast, started on horseback by seven o'clock for the Virgin Forest, about six miles from Petropolis. After leaving the town and its suburbs, we pursued our way by rough winding paths, across which huge moths and butterflies flitted, and humming-birds buzzed in the almond-trees. After a ride of an hour and a half, we entered the silence and gloom of a vast forest. On every side extended a tangled mass of wild, luxuriant vegetation: giant-palms, and tree-ferns, and parasites are to be seen in all directions, growing wherever they can find root-hold. Sometimes they kill the tree which they favor with their attentions—one creeper, in particular, being called 'Mata-pao' or 'Kill-tree;' but, as a rule, they seem to get on very well together, and to depend mutually upon one another for nourishment and support. The most striking of these creepers is, perhaps, the liane, whose tendrils grow straight downwards to the ground, twisting themselves together in knots and bundles. Occasionally one sees, suspended from a tree, at a height of some fifty feet, a large lump of moss, from which scarlet orchids are growing, looking like an enormous hanging flower-basket. All colors in Brazil, whether of birds, insects, or flowers, are brilliant in the extreme. Blue, violet, orange, scarlet, and yellow are found in the richest profusion, and no pale or faint tints are to be seen. Even white seems purer, clearer, and deeper than the white of other countries.

We had a long, wet walk in the forest; the mosses and ferns being kept moist and green by the innumerable little streams of water which abound everywhere. Owing to the thickness of the surrounding jungle, it was impossible to stray from our very narrow path, notwithstanding the attractions of humming-birds, butterflies, and flowers. At last we came to an opening in the wood, whence we had a splendid view seawards, and where it was decided to turn round and retrace our steps through the forest. After walking some distance we found our horses waiting, and after a hot but pleasant ride reached Petropolis by twelve o'clock, in time for breakfast. Letter-writing and butterfly-catching occupied the afternoon until four o'clock, when I was taken out for a drive in a comfortable little phaeton, with a pretty pair of horses, while the rest of the party walked out to see a little more of Petropolis and its environs. We drove past the Emperor's palace—an Italian villa, standing in the middle of a large garden—the new church, and the houses of the principal inhabitants, most of which are shut up just now, as everybody is out of town, but it all looked very green and pleasant. It was interesting to see a curious breed of dogs, descended from the bloodhounds formerly used in hunting the poor Indians.

Wednesday, August 23d.—At six o'clock we all assembled on the balcony of the hotel to wait for the coach, which arrived shortly afterwards. There was some little delay and squabbling before we all found ourselves safely established on the coach, but starting was quite another matter, for the four white mules resolutely refused to move, without a vast amount of screaming and shouting and plunging. We had to pull up once or twice before we got clear of the town to allow more passengers to be somehow or other squeezed in, and at each fresh start similar objections on the part of the mules had to be overcome.

The air felt fresh when we started, but before we had proceeded far we came into a thick, cold, wet fog, which, after the heat of the last few weeks, seemed to pierce us to the very marrow. Eight miles farther on the four frisky white mules were exchanged for five steady dun-colored ones, which were in their turn replaced after a seven-mile stage by four nice bays, who took us along at a tremendous pace. The sun began by this time to penetrate the mist, and the surrounding country became visible. We found that we were following the course of the river, passing through an avenue of coral-trees, loaded with the most brilliant flowers and fruit imaginable, and full of paroquets and fluttering birds of many hues.

We stopped at several small villages, and at about 11 a.m. reached Entre Rios, having changed mules seven times, and done the 59½ miles in four hours and fifty minutes, including stoppages—pretty good work, especially as the heat during the latter portion of the journey had been as great as the cold was at the commencement. The term 'cold' must here be taken only in a relative sense, for the thermometer was never lower than 48°, though, having been accustomed for a long while to 85°, we felt the change severely.

After a capital breakfast at the inn near the station, we got into the train and began a very hot dusty journey over the Serra to Palmeiras, which place was reached at 4 p.m. We were met on our arrival by Dr. Gunning, who kindly made room for Tom and me at his house, the rest of our party proceeding to the hotel. The view from the windows of the house, which is situated on the very edge of a hill, over the mountains of the Serra, glowing with the light of the setting sun, was perfectly enchanting; and after a refreshing cold bath one was able to appreciate it as it deserved. A short stroll into the forest adjoining the house proved rich in treasures, for in a few minutes I had gathered twenty-six varieties of ferns, including gold and silver ferns, two creeping ferns, and many other kinds. The moon rose, and the fireflies flashed about among the palm-trees, as we sat in the veranda before dinner, while in several places on the distant hills we could see circles of bright flames, where the forest had been set on fire in order to make clearings.

We were up next morning in time to see the sun rise from behind the mountains, and as it gradually became warmer the humming-birds and butterflies came out and buzzed and flitted among the flowers in front of our windows. We had planned to devote the day to a visit to Barra, and it was therefore necessary to hurry to the station by eight o'clock to meet the train, where we stopped twenty minutes to breakfast at what appeared to be a capital hotel, built above the station. The rooms were large and lofty, everything was scrupulously clean, and the dishes most appetizing-looking. Our carriage was then shunted and hooked on to the other train, and we proceeded to the station of Santa Anna, where Mr. Faro met us with eight mules and horses, and a large old-fashioned carriage, which held some of us, the rest of the party galloping on in front. We galloped also, and upset one unfortunate horse, luckily without doing him any harm. After a couple of miles of a rough road we arrived at the gates of the Baron's grounds, where the old negro slave-coachman amused us very much by *ordering* his young master to conduct the equestrians round to the house by another way. Beneath the avenue of palm-trees, leading from the gates to the house, grew orange, lemon, and citron trees, trained as espaliers, while behind them again tall rose-bushes and pomegranates showed their bright faces. Driving through an archway we arrived at the house, and, with much politeness and many bows, were conducted in-doors, in order that we might rest ourselves and get rid of some of the dust of our journey.

Santa Anna is one of the largest coffee fazendas in this part of Brazil. The house occupies three sides of a square, in the middle of which heaps of coffee were spread out to dry in the sun. The center building is the dwelling-house, with a narrow strip of garden, full of sweet-smelling flowers, in front of it; the right wing is occupied by the slaves' shops and warehouses, and by the chapel; while the left wing contains the stables, domestic offices, and other slave-rooms.

By law, masters are bound to give their slaves one day's rest in every seven, and any work the slaves may choose to do on that day is paid for at the same rate as free labor. But the day selected for this purpose is not necessarily Sunday; and on adjoining fazendas different days are invariably chosen, in order to prevent the slaves from meeting and getting into mischief. Thursday (to-day) was Sunday on this estate, and we soon saw all the slaves mustering in holiday attire in the shade of one of the verandas. They were first inspected, and then ranged in order, the children being placed in front, the young women next, then the old women, the old men, and finally the young men. In this order they marched into the corridor facing the chapel, to hear mass. The priest and his acolyte, in gorgeous robes, performed the usual service, and the slaves chanted the responses in alternate companies, so that sopranos, contraltos, tenors, and basses contrasted in a striking and effective manner. The singing, indeed, was excellent; far better than in many churches at home. After the conclusion of the mass the master shook hands with everybody, exchanged good wishes with his slaves, and dismissed them. While they were dawdling about, gossiping in the veranda, I had a closer look at the babies, which had all been brought to church. They seemed of every shade of color, the complexions of some being quite fair, but the youngest, a dear little woolly-headed thing, was black as jet, and only three weeks old. The children all seemed to be on very good terms with their master and his overseers, and not a bit afraid of them. They are fed most liberally, and looked fat and healthy. For breakfast they have coffee and bread; for dinner, fresh pork alternately with dried beef, and black beans (the staple food of the poor of this country); and for supper they have coffee, bread, and mandioca, or tapioca.

Returning to the house, we sat down, a party of thirty, to an elaborate breakfast, the table being covered with all sorts of Brazilian delicacies, after which several complimentary speeches were made, and we all started off to walk round the fazenda. Our first visit was to the little school-children, thirty-four in number, who sang very nicely. Then to the hospital, a clean, airy building, in which there were happily but few patients, and next we inspected the new machinery, worked by water-power, for cleaning the coffee and preparing it for market. The harvest lasts from May to August. The best quality of coffee is picked before it is quite ripe, crushed to free it from the husk, and then dried in the sun, sometimes in heaps, and sometimes raked out flat, in order to gain the full benefit of the heat. It is afterwards gathered up into baskets and carefully picked over, and this, being very light work, is generally performed by young married women with babies. There were nineteen tiny pickaninnies, in baskets, beside their mothers, in one room we entered, and in another there were twenty just able to run about.

Cassava is an important article of food here, and it was interesting to watch the various processes by which it is turned into flour, tapioca, or starch. As it is largely exported, there seems no reason why it should not be introduced into India, for the ease with which it is cultivated and propagated, the extremes of temperature it will bear, and the abundance of its crop, all tend to recommend it. We went on to look at the maize being shelled, crushed, and ground into coarse or fine flour, for cakes and bread, and the process of crushing the sugar-cane, turning its juice into sugar and rum, and its refuse into potash. All the food manufactured here is used on the estate; coffee alone is exported. I felt thoroughly exhausted by the time we returned to the house, only to exchange adieus and step into the carriage on our way to Barra by rail *en route* to Rio de Janeiro. After passing through several long tunnels at the top of the Serra, the line drops down to Palmeira, after which the descent became very picturesque, as we passed, by steep inclines, through virgin forests full of creepers, ferns, flowers, and orchids. The sunset was magnificent, and the subsequent coolness of the atmosphere most grateful. Leaving the Emperor's palace of São Christovão behind, Rio was entered from a fresh side. It seemed a long drive through the streets to the Hôtel de l'Europe, where, after an excellent though hurried dinner, we contrived to be in time for a private representation at the Alcazar. As a rule, ladies do not go to this theater, but there were a good many there on the present occasion. Neither the play nor the actors, however, were very interesting, and all our party were excessively tired; so we left early, and had a delightful row off to the yacht, in the bright moonlight.

Monday, August 28*th.*—We have all been so much interested in the advertisements we read in the daily papers of slaves to be sold or hired, that arrangements were made with a Brazilian gentleman for some of our party to have an opportunity of seeing the way in which these transactions are carried on. No Englishman is allowed to hold slaves here, and it is part of the business of the Legation to see that this law is strictly enforced. The secrets of their trade are accordingly jealously guarded by the natives, especially from the English. The gentlemen had therefore to disguise themselves as much as possible, one pretending to be a rich Yankee, who had purchased large estates between Santos and San Paulo, which he had determined to work with slave instead of coolie labor. He was supposed to have come to Rio to select some slaves, but would be obliged to see and consult his partner before deciding on purchase. They were taken to a small shop in the city, and, after some delay, were conducted to a room upstairs, where they waited a quarter of an hour. Twenty-two men and eleven women and children were then brought in for inspection. They declared themselves suitable for a variety of occupations, in-door and out, and all appeared to look anxiously at their possible purchaser, with a view to ascertain what they had to hope for in the future. One couple in particular, a brother and sister, about fourteen and fifteen years old respectively, were most anxious not to be separated, but to be sold together; and the tiny children seemed quite frightened at being spoken to or touched by the white men. Eight men and five women having been specially selected as fit subjects for further consideration, the visit terminated.

The daily Brazilian papers are full of advertisements of slaves for sale, and descriptions of men, pigs, children, cows, pianos, women, houses, &c., to be disposed of, are inserted in the most indiscriminate manner. In one short half-column of the 'Jornal do Commercio,' published within the last day or two, the following announcements, amongst many similar ones, appear side by side :—

VENDE-SE uma escrava, de 22 annos, boa figura, lava, engomma e cose bem ; informa-se na rua de S. Pedro n. 97.

FOR SALE.—A female slave, 22 years of age, a good figure, washes, irons, and sews well ; for particulars apply at No. 97 rua de S. Pedro.

VENDE-SE ou aluga-se um rico piano forte do autor Erard, de 3 cordas, por 280$, garantido ; na rua da Quitanda n. 42, 2 andar.

FOR SALE, OR TO BE LET ON Hire.—A splendid trichord pianoforte by Erard, for $280, guaranteed; apply at rua da Quitanda No. 42, 2d floor.

VENDE-SE, por 1,500$, um escravo de 20 annos, para serviço de padaria ; na rua da Princeza dos Cajueiros n. 97.

TO BE SOLD FOR $1,500.—A male slave 20 years of age, fit for a baker's establishment ; apply at rua da Princeza dos Cajueiros No. 97.

VENDE-SE uma machima Singer, para qualquer costura, trabalha perfeitamente, por preço muito commodo ; trata-se na rua do Sabão n. 95.

FOR SALE.—On very reasonable terms, a Singer's sewing-machine, adapted for any description of work ; works splendidly ; apply at No. 95 rua do Sabão.

VENDE-SE uma preta moça, boa figura e de muito boa indole, com tres filhos, sendo uma negrinha de 6 annos, um moleque de 5 e uma ingenua de 3, cabenda cozinhar bem, lavar e engommar ; na mesma casa vende-se só uma negrinha de 12 annos, de conducta afiançada e muito propria para serviço de casa de familia, por ja ter bons principios, tendo vindo de Santa Catharina ; na rua da Uruguayana n. 90 sobrado.

FOR SALE.—A good black woman, good figure, good disposition, with three children, who are a little black girl 6 years of age, a black boy of 5, and a child 3 years of age ; she is a good cook, washes and irons well. At the same house there is likewise for sale a little black girl 12 years of age : her character will be guaranteed ; she is well adapted for the service of a family, as she has had a good beginning, having come from Santa Catharina ; apply at No. 90 rua da Uruguayana, first floor.

VENDE-SE o Diccionario portuguez de Lacerda, em dous grandes volumes, novo, vindo pelo ultimo paquete, por 30$, custão aqui 40$; na rua do Hospicio n. 15, 2º andar.

FOR SALE.—Lacerda's Portuguese Dictionary, in two large volumes, quite new, arrived by the last mail, price $30, costs here $40; No. 15 rua do Hospicio, 2d floor.

VENDE-SE uma preta de meia idade, que cozinha, lava, e engomma com perfeição ; para tratar na rua do Viscande de Itaúna n. 12.

FOR SALE.—A middle-aged black woman, who is a first-rate cook, washes and irons splendidly ; for particulars apply at No. 12 rua do Viscande de Itaúna No. 12.

VENDEM-SE arreios para carrocinhas de pão ; na rua do General Camara n. 86, placa.

FOR SALE.—Harnesses for small carts for delivery of bread ; apply at No. 86 rua do General Camara.

VENDEM-SE 20 moleques, de 14 a 20 annos, vindos do Maranhão no ultimo vapor ; na rua da Prainha n. 72.

FOR SALE.—20 young blacks from 14 to 20 years of age just arrived from Maranham by the last steamer ; No. 72 rua da Prainha.

We had many visitors to breakfast to-day, and it was nearly two o'clock before we could set off for the shore *en route* to Tijuca. We drove nearly as far as the Botanical Gardens, where it had been arranged that horses should meet us ; but our party was such a large one, including children and servants, that some little difficulty occurred

at this point in making a fair start. It was therefore late
before we started, the clouds were beginning to creep
down the sides of the hills, and it had grown very dusk
by the time we reached the Chinisi river. Soon afterwards the rain began to come down in such tropical torrents, that our thin summer clothing was soaked through
and through long before we reached the Tijuca. At last,
to our great joy, we saw ahead of us large plantations of
bananas, and then some gaslights, which exist even in
this remote locality. We followed them for some little
distance, but my horse appeared to have such a very decided opinion as to the proper direction for us to take,
that we finally decided to let him have his own way, for
it was by this time pitch dark, and none of us had ever
been this road before. As we hoped, the horse knew his
own stables, and we soon arrived at the door of White's
hotel, miserable, drenched objects, looking forward to a
complete change of clothing. Unfortunately the cart
with our luggage had not arrived, so it was in clothes
borrowed from kind friends that we at last sat down, a
party of about forty, to a sort of table-d'hôte dinner, and
it continued to pour with rain during the whole evening,
only clearing up just at bed-time.

Tuesday, August 29th. —After all the fine weather we
have had lately, it was provoking to find, on getting up
this morning, that the rain still came steadily down.
Daylight enabled us to see what a quaint-looking place
this hotel is. It consists of a series of low, wooden detached buildings, mostly one story high, with verandas
on both sides, built round a long courtyard, in the center
of which are a garden and some large trees. It is more
like a boarding-house, however, than an hotel, as there is
a fixed daily charge for visitors, who have to be provided
with a letter of introduction! The situation and gardens
are good; it contains among other luxuries a drawing-
room, with a delightful swimming-bath for ladies, and
another for gentlemen. A mountain stream is turned into

two large square reservoirs, where you can disport yourself under the shade of bananas and palm-trees, while orange-trees, daturas, poinsettias, and other plants, in full bloom, drop their fragrant flowers into the crystal water. There is also a nice little bathing-house, with a douche outside; and the general arrangements seem really perfect. The views from the walks around the hotel and in the forest above are beautiful, as, indeed, they are from every eminence in the neighborhood of Rio.

During the morning the weather cleared sufficiently for us to go down to 'The Bowlders,' huge masses of rock, either of the glacial period, or else thrown out from some mighty volcano into the valley beneath. Here they form great caverns and caves, overhung with creepers, and so blocked up at the entrance, that it is difficult to find the way into them. The effect of the alternate darkness and light, amid twisted creepers, some like gigantic snakes, others neatly coiled in true man-of-war fashion, is very striking and fantastic. Every crevice is full of ferns and orchids and curious plants, while moths and butterflies flit about in every direction. Imagine, if you can, scarlet butterflies gayly spotted, yellow butterflies with orange edgings, butterflies with dark-blue, velvety-looking upper wings, the under surface studded with bright, owl-like peacock eyes, gray Atlas moths, and, crowning beauty of all, metallic blue butterflies, which are positively dazzling, even when seen in a shop, dead. Imagine what they must be like, as they dart hither and thither, reflecting the bright sunshine from their wings, or enveloped in the somber shade of a forest. Most of them measure from two to ten inches in length from wing to wing, and many others flit about, equally remarkable for their beauty, though not so large. Swallow-tails, of various colors, with tails almost as long, in proportion to their bodies, as those of their feathered namesakes; god-parents and 'eighty-eights,' with the figures 88 plainly marked on the reverse side of their rich blue or crimson wings. In fact, if Nature could by any possibility be gaudy, one might almost say that she is so in this part of the world.

From 'The Bowlders' we went down a kind of natural staircase in the rock to the small cascade, which, owing to the recent rains, appeared to the best advantage, the black rocks and thick vegetation forming a fine background to the sheet of flowing white water and foam. Our way lay first through some castor-oil plantations, and then along the side of a stream, fringed with rare ferns, scarlet begonias, and gray ageratum. We returned to the hotel, too late for the general luncheon, and, after a short rest, went out for a gallop in the direction of the peak of Tijuca, past the large waterfall, the 'Ladies' Mile,' and 'Grey's View.' The forest is Government property; the roads are therefore excellent, and are in many places planted with flowers and shrubs, rare even here. It seems a waste of money, however; for there is hardly any one to make use of the wide roads, and the forest would appear quite as beautiful in its pristine luxuriance. To our eyes the addition of flowers from other countries is no improvement, though the feeling is otherwise here. More than once I have had a bouquet of common stocks given to me as a grand present, while orchids, gardenias, stephanotis, large purple, pink, and white azaleas, orange-blossom, and roses, were growing around in unheeded profusion.

Wednesday, August 30th.—Once more a wet morning; but as it cleared towards noon, we ordered horses and some luncheon, and went up to Pedro Bonito. The ride was pleasant enough at first, but as we mounted higher and higher, we got into the clouds and lost the view. Finally there seemed nothing for it but to halt near the top, under a grove of orange-trees, lunch in the pouring rain, and return without having reached the summit.

Friday, September 1st.—At three o'clock this morning, when I awoke, I saw at last a bright, clear sky, and at five, finding that there was every prospect of a beautiful sunrise, we sent for horses, ate our early breakfast, and set off for the peak of Tijuca. Step by step we climbed, first through the grounds of the hotel, then through the forest, till we reached 'The Bamboos,' a favorite halting-place, by the side of a stream, near which grow, in waving tufts, the graceful trees which lend their name to the spot. It was very beautiful in the hill-side forest, with a new prospect opening out at every step, and set in an ever-varying natural framework of foliage and flowers. There was not sufficient time to linger, however, as we would fain have done, in the cool and shady paths, occasionally illumed by the bright rays of the sun, shining through the foliage of noble palms, the fronds of tree-ferns, and the spiral stems of many-colored creepers.

Before reaching the top of the peak, there are twenty-nine wooden and ninety-six stone steps to be ascended, at the foot of which we tied our horses. An iron chain is hung by the side to assist you, without which it would be rather giddy work, for the steps are steep, and there is a sheer precipice on one side of them. Arrived at the top, the scene was glorious; on every side mountains beyond mountains stretch far away into the distance, and one can see as far north as Cape Frio, and southwards as far as Rio Grande do Sul, while beneath lies the bay of Rio with its innumerable islands, islets, and indentations. All too soon we had to scramble down again, and mount our horses for a hurried return to the hotel, there being barely time for lunch and a scramble to the yacht.

Monday, September 4th.— We were all up very early this morning, superintending the preparations for our eldest boy's departure for England. The yacht had been gayly dressed with flags, in honor of the anniversary of the Emperor's wedding-day; but it must be confessed that our own feelings were hardly in accordance with these external symbols of joy. Breakfast was a melancholy meal, and I fear that the visitors from the 'Volage' were not very well entertained. After breakfast, we went ashore to the market, to get a couple of lion-monkeys, which had been kept for us, and which Tab was to take home with him to present to the Zoological Gardens. At one o'clock the steam launch from the 'Volage' came alongside and embarked the luggage and servants. Half an hour later it returned for us; then came many tearful farewells to the crew, and we set off. We knew the parting had to be made, but this did not lessen our grief; for although it is at all times hard to say good-by for a long period to those nearest and dearest to you, it is especially so in a foreign land, with the prospect of a long voyage on both sides. Moreover, it is extremely uncertain when we shall hear of our boy's safe arrival; not, I fear, until we get to Valparaiso, and then only by telegram—a long time to look forward to. Over the next half-hour I had better draw a vail.

At two o'clock precisely, just after we had left the steamer, the starting bell rang, and the 'Cotopaxi' steamed away. As she passed the yacht, all our flags were dipped and the guns fired. Then we could see her rolling on the bar, for, calm as the water was in the bay, there was a heavy swell outside; and then, all too soon, we lost sight of her, as she sank,

'. . . with all we love, below the verge.'

We heard to-day that, the Saturday before our first arrival at Rio, the bar was quite impassable, even for a man-of-war, and that, although she succeeded the next day, the sea was extremely rough.

On our return to the 'Sunbeam,' I went to bed to rest, and the remainder of the party went ashore. A great many visitors came on board in the course of the afternoon; some remained to dine with us. At half-past nine we all went on shore again to a ball at the Casino, the grand public room in Rio, to which we had been invited some days ago. It seemed a splendid place, beautifully decorated in white and gold and crimson, with frescos and pictures let into the walls, and surrounded by galleries. It is capable of containing fifteen hundred persons, and I believe that there were even more than that number present on the occasion of the ball given to the Duke of Edinburgh some years ago. The arrangement of the large cloak-rooms, refreshment-rooms, and passages downstairs, and the balconies and supper-rooms upstairs, is very convenient. The ball this evening being comparatively a small affair, the lower rooms only were used, and proved amply sufficient. There were not a great many ladies present, but amongst those we saw some were extremely pretty, and all were exquisitely dressed in the latest fashions from Paris. The toilets of the younger ones looked fresh and simple, while those of the married ladies displayed considerable richness and taste; for although Brazilian ladies do not go out much, and, as a rule, remain *en peignoir* until late in the afternoon, they never fail to exhibit great judgment in the selection of their costumes.

The floor was excellent, but the band made rather too much noise, and the dancing was different, both in style and arrangement, from what we are accustomed to at home.

The time had now come when we had to say farewell to the many kind friends whom we have met here, and who have made life so pleasant to us during the last three weeks, in order that we might return to the yacht, to complete our preparation for an early start. The last leave-takings were soon over, and, with mutually expressed hopes that we might ere long meet some of our friends in England, Tom and I drove off, in the bright moonlight, to the quay, where our boat was waiting for us. The other members of our party found the attractions of the ball so irresistible that they were unable to tear themselves away until a much later hour.

The Three Navigators.

CHAPTER V.

THE RIVER PLATE.

*Blue, glossy green, and velvet black,
They coiled and swam ; and every track
Was a flash of golden fire.*

Tuesday, September 5th.—We got under way at 6 a.m., and soon bade adieu to Rio, where we have spent so many happy days, and to our friends on board H.M.S. 'Volage' and 'Ready,' with whom we interchanged salutes in passing. It was a dull, wet morning, and we could not see much of the beauties we were leaving behind us. The peak of Tijuca and the summit of the Corcovado were scarcely visible, and the Sugarloaf and Gavia looked cold and gray in the early mist. It was not long before we were rolling on the bar, and then tumbling about in very uncomfortable fashion in the rough sea outside. One by one we all disappeared below, where most of us remained during the greater part of the day. As for me, I went to bed for good at six o'clock in the evening, but was called up again at ten, to see some large bonitos playing about the bows of the yacht. It was really worth the trouble of getting up and climbing quite into the bows of the vessel to watch them, as they gamboled and frisked about, brightly illumined by the phosphorescence of the water, now swimming together steadily in pairs or fours, now starting in sudden pursuit of one of their number, who would make an independent rush forward in advance of his companions.

Saturday, September 9th.—The last three days have been showery, with squalls which have freshened to a gale, and we are now scudding along, under all storm canvas, followed by crowds of cape-pigeons and cape-hens, and a few albatrosses. Towards this evening, however, the wind fell light, and we got up steam, in order to be prepared for any emergency, as a calm is frequently succeeded on this coast by a *pampero*, and we are now approaching a lee shore.

Sunday, September 10th.—Tom has been on deck nearly all night. The shore is very low and difficult to distinguish, and the lights are badly kept. If the lighthouse-keeper happens to have plenty of oil, and is not out shooting or fishing, he lights his lamp; otherwise, he omits to perform this rather important part of his duties. The lighthouses can therefore hardly be said to be of much use. About 5 a.m., Kindred rushed down into our cabin, and woke Tom, calling out, 'Land to leeward, sir!' and then rushed up on deck again. The first glimmer of dawn had enabled him to see that we were running straight on to the low sandy shore, about three miles off, a very strong current having set us ten miles out of our course. The yacht's head was accordingly at once put round, and steaming seaward we soon left all danger behind. The sun rose brilliantly, and the weather during the day was very fine. Morning service was impossible, owing to the necessity for a constant observation of the land; but, after making the lighthouse on Santa Maria, we had prayers at 4.30 p.m., with the hymn, 'For those at Sea.' In the night we made the light on Flores, burning brightly, and before morning those in the harbor of Monte Video.

Monday, September 11*th.*—After making the Flores light we proceeded slowly, and dropped our anchor in the outer roads of Monte Video at 4 a.m. At seven o'clock we got it up again, and by eight were anchored close to the shore. We found that our arrival was expected, and the health-officers' boat was soon alongside. Next came an officer from the United States' man-of-war 'Frolic,' with polite messages and offers of service; and then a steam-launch belonging to the Pacific Company, and another from the Consul, Major Monro, with piles of letters and newspapers for us.

Monte Video, as seen from the water, is not an imposing-looking place. On the opposite side of the entrance to the harbor rises a hill, called the Cerro, 450 feet high, from which the town derives its name, and further inland, on the town side, is another eminence, 200 feet high, called the Cerrito. With these exceptions the surrounding country looks perfectly flat, without even a tree to break the monotony.

Soon after breakfast we went ashore—in more senses of the word than one; for they have commenced to build a mole for the protection of small vessels, which, in its unfinished state, is not yet visible above the water. The consequence was that, at a distance of about half a mile from the landing-steps, we rowed straight on to the submerged stonework, but fortunately got off again very quickly, without having sustained any damage. On landing, we found ourselves opposite the Custom House, a fine building, with which we afterwards made a closer acquaintance.

There is a large and very good hotel here, l'Hôtel Oriental. It is a handsome building outside, and the interior is full of marble courts, stone corridors, and lofty rooms, deliciously cool in the hottest weather. Having procured a carriage, Tom and I and the children drove through the streets, which are wide and handsome, though badly paved, and so full of holes that it is a wonder how the springs of a carriage can last a week. The houses seem built chiefly in the Italian style of architecture, with fine stucco fronts, and in many cases marble floors and facings, while the courtyards, seen through the grilles, blazed with flowers. All the lower windows were strongly barred, a precaution by no means unnecessary against the effects of the revolutions, which are of such frequent occurrence in this country. To enable the inhabitants the better to enjoy the sea-breeze, the tops of the houses are all flat, which gives the town, from a distance, somewhat of an Eastern appearance. There are a great many Italian immigrants here, and most of the building and plastering work is done by them.

The Paseo del Molino is the best part of the town, where all the rich merchants reside in quintas, surrounded by pretty gardens. They are very fantastic in their ideas of architectural style, and appear to bestow their patronage impartially, not to say indiscriminately, upon Gothic cathedrals, Alhambra palaces, Swiss cottages, Italian villas, and Turkish mosques. Except for this variety, the suburb has somewhat the appearance of the outskirts of many of the towns on the Riviera, with the same sub-tropical surroundings. These are, however, hard times on the River Plate, and more than half the quintas are deserted and falling into ruins. On our way back, by the Union Road, we met a great many of the native bullock-carts going home from market. These huge conveyances are covered with hides, and are drawn by teams of from two to twelve bullocks, yoked in pairs, and driven by a man on horseback, who carries a sharp-pointed goad, with which he prods the animals all round, at intervals. Dressed in a full white linen shirt and trousers, with his bright poncho and curious saddle-gear, he forms no unimportant figure in the picturesque scene. In the large market-place there are hundreds of these carts, with their owners encamped around them.

When we at last arrived on board the yacht again, at three o'clock, we found that the miseries of coaling were not yet over, and that there had been numerous visitors from the shore. Everything on deck looked black, while below all was pitch dark and airless, every opening and crevice having been closed and covered with tarpaulin, to keep out the coal dust. It took seven hours to complete the work, instead of two, as was hoped and promised, so our chance of starting to-day is over. This seemed the more disappointing, because, had we foreseen the delay, we might have made other arrangements for seeing more on shore.

Tuesday, September 12*th.*—The anchor was up, and we were already beginning to steam away, when I came on deck this morning, just in time to see the first faint streaks of dawn appearing in the gray sky. The River Plate here is over a hundred miles wide, and its banks are very flat; so there was nothing to be seen, except the two little hills of Cerro and Cerrito, and the town of Monte Viedo, fast vanishing in the distance. The channels are badly buoyed, and there are shoals and wrecks on all sides. The lightships are simply old hulks, with no special marks by which to distinguish them; and as they themselves look exactly like wrecks, they are not of much assistance in the navigation, which is very confusing, and sometimes perilous. Once we very nearly ran aground, but discovered just in time that the vessel we were steering for with confidence was only a wreck, on a dangerous shoal, and that the light-ship itself was further ahead. The yacht was immediately put about, and we just skirted the bank in turning.

The weather improved during the day, and a fine sunset was followed by a clear starlight night. At 10.30 p.m.

we dropped our anchor outside all the other vessels in the roads at Buenos Ayres, eight miles from the shore. The light-ship only carried an ordinary riding light, like any other vessel, so that it was almost impossible, unless you knew the port very well, to go in closer to the land at night.

Wednesday, September 13*th.*—Daylight did not enable us to distinguish the town, for the river here is wide and the banks are low, and we were lying a long way from the shore, outside a great many fine-looking ships at anchor in the roads. About nine o'clock a German captain, in a large whale-boat, came alongside and told us we were nearly eight miles from Buenos Ayres. Tom arranged with him to take us ashore; and accordingly we soon started. The water was smooth and there was a nice breeze, and we sailed gallantly along for about two hours, until we reached the town. After anchoring, we transhipped ourselves into a small boat, in which we were rowed to some steps, at the end of the long rickety mole, where we landed. Some of the planks of the pier were missing, leaving great holes, big enough to fall through, and others were so loose that when you stepped upon one end of them the other flew up almost into your face.

Our first business was to secure the services of a pilot, to take us up to Rosario. The best man on the river was sent for; but when he came he did not recommend our undertaking the voyage, as the water is very low at present, and we might get stuck on a sandbank, and be detained for some days, although no further harm would be likely to occur to us. We decided, therefore, as our time is precious, to give up the idea of making the expedition in the yacht, and to go in the ordinary river-boat instead.

Under the guidance of some gentlemen, we then went to the Central Railway Station to send off some telegrams, and thence to the River Plate Bank. The treasury contains £600,000 in British sovereigns, locked up in three strong safes, besides paper-money and securities to the amount of £2,000,000. It was the Rosario branch of this bank which was recently robbed of £15,000 by an armed government force; an unprecedented proceeding in the history of nations, and one that might have led to the interference of foreign powers.

There was time afterwards to go round and see something of the city, which, like many other South American towns, is built in square blocks, all the streets running exactly at right angles one to another. There is a fine plaza, or grand square, in which are situated the cathedral, theater, &c., the center being occupied by a garden, containing statues and fountains. The various banks, with their marble facings, Corinthian columns, and splendid halls, are magnificent buildings, and look more like palaces than places of business. Some of the private houses, too, seem very handsome. Outside they are all faced with marble, to a certain height from the ground, the interior, consisting of courtyard within courtyard, being rather like that of a Pompeian house.

We next went to the agricultural show, which, though not an imposing affair to our eyes, appeared really very creditable to those who had organized it. The horses and cattle looked small, but there were some good specimens of sheep—specially the *rombouellis* and *negrettis*, whose long fine wool was, however, only to be discovered by first turning aside a thick plaster of mud, beneath which it was concealed. We saw also some curious animals, natives of the country, such as vicuñas, llamas, bizcachas, and various kinds of deer, a very mixed lot of poultry and dogs, and two magnificent Persian cats. Another department of the show was allotted to the commercial products of the country, animal, vegetable, and mineral; the whole forming a very interesting collection.

In re-embarking, the disagreeable process of this morning had to be repeated—rickety pier, rotten steps, and small boat included—before we reached the whale-boat, after which we had an eight miles' sail out to the yacht. It was a cold, dull night, and getting on board proved rather difficult work, owing to the rough sea.

Thursday, September 14th.—The pilot came on board at seven o'clock to take us in nearer the shore, but, after all, we found ourselves obliged to anchor again five miles off. No ship drawing more than ten feet can get inside the sandbanks, which makes it a wretched place to lie in, especially as the weather at this time of year is very uncertain. You may go ashore from your ship on a fine clear morning, and before you return a gale may have sprung up, accompanied by a frightful sea. Open boats are therefore quite unsafe, a state of things which has given rise to the existence of a class of fine boats, specially built for the service, which attend all the ships lying in the roads. They are half-decked, will sail in any weather, and can be easily managed by two men.

About ten o'clock we went ashore again in the whale-boat, which Tom had engaged to wait on us during our stay, and made the best of our way to a warehouse to look at some ponchos, which are the specialty of this part of South America. Everybody wears one, from the beggar to the highest official. The best kind of ponchos are very expensive, being made from a particular part of the finest hair of the vicuña, hand-woven by women, in the province of Catamarca. The genuine article is difficult to get, even here. In the shops the price usually varies from £30 to £80; but we were shown some at a rather lower price—from £20 to £60 each. They are soft as silk, perfectly waterproof, and will wear, it is said, forever. We met a fine-looking man in one of beautiful quality yesterday. He told us that it originally cost £30 in Catamarca, twenty years ago, and that he gave £20 for it, second-hand, ten years ago; and, with the exception of a few slight tears, it is now as good as ever. Before we came here, we were strongly advised, in case we should happen to go on a rough expedition up country, not to be tempted to take with us any *good* ponchos, as the Guachos, or half-bred Indians of the Pampas, who are great connoisseurs of these articles, and can distinguish their quality at a glance, would not hesitate to cut our throats in order to obtain possession of them.

The material of which they are made is of the closest texture, and as the hair has never been dressed or dyed, it retains all its natural oil and original color, the latter varying from a very pretty yellow fawn to a pale cream-color. The majority of the ponchos worn here are, however, made at Manchester, of a cheap and inferior material. They look exactly like the real thing at first sight, but are neither so light nor so warm, nor do they wear at all well. Occasionally they are made of silk, but more often of bright-colored wool. In shape a poncho is simply a square shawl with a hole in the middle for the head of the wearer. On horseback the appearance is particularly picturesque, and it forms also a convenient cloak, which comes well over the saddle, before and behind, and leaves the arms, though covered, perfectly free.

The natives, as a rule, wear a second poncho, generally of a different color, tucked into the waistband of their long full linen drawers (*calzonillas*), so as to make a pair of short baggy over-trousers. A poor man is content with a shirt, drawers, and two ponchos. A rich man has many rows of fringe and frills of lace at the bottom of his *calzonillas*, and wears a short coat, with silver buttons, and a gorgeous silver belt, covered with dollars. His horse-fittings and massive stirrups (to say nothing of his enormous spurs) will be of solid silver, and his arms inlaid with the same metal. He will sometimes give as much as from £10 to £20 for a pair of stirrups alone, and the rest of his dress and equipment is proportionately expensive. The cost of the silver articles is little more than the value of the metal itself, which is of very pure quality, and is only roughly worked by the

Indians or Guachos. But as Manchester provides the ponchos, so does Birmingham the saddlery and fittings, especially those in use in the neighborhood of towns.

After inspecting the ponchos, we breakfasted with some friends, and about noon started in the train for Campana. The line passes at first through the streets of Buenos Ayres, and thence into the open country, beautifully green, and undulating like the waves of the sea. Near the town and the suburb of Belgrano are a great many peach-tree plantations, the fruit of which is used for fattening pigs, while the wood serves for roasting them. There is also some scrubby brushwood, and a few large native trees; but these are soon left behind, and are succeeded by far-spreading rich pasture land, and occasional lagunes.

We saw for the first time the holes of the bizcachas, or prairie-dogs, outside which the little prairie-owls keep guard. There appeared to be always one, and generally two, of these birds, standing, like sentinels, at the entrance to each hole, with their wise-looking heads on one side, pictures of prudence and watchfulness. The bird and the beast are great friends, and are seldom to be found apart. We also passed several enormous flocks of sheep and herds of cattle, most of them quite unattended, though some were being driven by men on horseback. There were quantities of plovers, and a great many partridges, of two kinds, large and small, and the numerous lagunes were covered with and surrounded by water-fowl of all kinds—wild swans and ducks, snipe, white storks, gray herons, black cormorants, and scarlet flamingoes, the last-named standing at the edge of the water, catching fish, and occasionally diving below the surface. On the very top of some of the telegraph-posts were the nests of the oven-bird, looking like carved round blocks of wood, placed there for ornament. These nests are made of mud, and are perfectly spherical in form, the interior being divided into two quite distinct chambers.

Campana was reached by four o'clock, the train running straight on to the pier, alongside of which the two vessels were lying with steam up. Passengers, baggage, and freight were immediately transferred from the train to the boats; and we soon found ourselves steaming along in the 'Uruguay,' between the willow-hung banks of the broad Parana. The country, though otherwise flat and uninteresting, looks very pretty just now, in its new spring coat of bright green.

We passed several small towns, amongst others San Pedro and San Nicolas, which are quite important-looking places, with a good deal of shipping, and occasionally stopped to pick up passengers, who had come in boats and steam-launches from far-distant villages, situated on lagunes, which our steamer could not enter.

Just before arriving at each stopping-place, we had a race with the 'Proveedor,' and whenever she became visible at a bend in the river, half a ton more coal was immediately heaped on to our fires by the captain's order—a piece of reckless extravagance, for, do what they would, they could not make us gain five minutes. The competition is, however, very fierce, and I suppose the two companies will not be satisfied until they have ruined one another; whereas, if each would run a steamer on alternate days, they and the public would be equally benefited. The fares are exceedingly reasonable, being less than £3 for the whole journey from Buenos Ayres to Rosario, including all charges.

Friday, September 15*th.*—A violent storm of thunder and lightning, apparently just above our heads, woke us at six o'clock this morning. Torrents of rain followed, and continued to fall until we dropped our anchor at Rosario, at 8.45 a.m., just as we were in the middle of breakfast, in our cozy little stern cabin. Half an hour later we landed, though the rain still came down in sheets; but the steamer was now alongside the pier, and close carriages had been provided. A few minutes' drive through ill-paved streets brought us to the Hôtel Universel, a handsome, spacious building, with marble courtyards, full of trees, plants, and flowers, into which all the sitting-rooms open. Above are galleries, round which the various bedrooms are in like manner ranged. It all looked nice and cool, and suitable for hot weather, but it was certainly rather draughty and cheerless on such a cold, pouring wet day, and all our efforts to make our large room, in which there were four immense windows, at all comfortable, were in vain.

Rosaria, like Buenos Ayres, is built in squares. The streets are generally well paved with black and white marble, but the roadways are composed of little round stones, and are full of holes and inequalities, so that, in crossing the road after heavy rain, one steps from the *trottoir* into a very slough of despond. The universal tramway runs down the center of every street.

After luncheon we made a fresh start for Carcaraña by a special train, to which were attached two goods-vans, full of horses, and a carriage truck, containing a most comfortable American carriage, in shape not unlike a Victoria, only much lighter and with very high wheels. After a short journey through a rich, flat, grass country, we arrived at Roldan, the first colony of the Central Argentine Land Company. Here we all alighted, the horses were taken out of the vans, saddled, bridled, and harnessed, and the gentlemen rode and I drove round the colony, along what are generally roads, but to-day were sheets of water. We saw many colonists, of every grade, from those still occupying the one-roomed wooden cottages, originally supplied by the Land Company, standing in the midst of ill-cultivated fields, to those who had built for themselves good houses in the town, or nice cottages, with pretty gardens, surrounded by well-tilled lands.

The drive ended at the mill belonging to a retired officer of the British army, who has settled here with his wife and two dear little children. Here we had tea and a pleasant chat, and then returned to the train and proceeded to Carcaraña, the next station on the line. Now, however, instead of the rich pasture lands and flourishing crops which we had hitherto seen on all sides, our road lay through a desolate-looking district, bearing too evident signs of the destructive power of the locust. People traveling with us tell us that less than a week ago, the pasture here was as fresh and green as could be desired and the various crops were a foot high; but that, in the short space of a few hours, the care and industry of the last ten months were rendered utterly vain and useless, and the poor colonists found their verdant fields converted into a barren waste by these rapacious insects.

Carcaraña may be called the Richmond—one might almost say the Brighton—of Rosario. It stands on a river, the Carcarañal, to the banks of which an omnibus runs twice a day from the railway station, during the season, to take people to bathe. Near the station is also an excellent little hotel, containing a large dining-room and a few bed-rooms, kept by two Frenchwomen; and here the Rosarions come out by train to dine and enjoy the fresh air. It was quite dark by the time we arrived, so that we could not see much of the flourishing little colony which has been formed here. We therefore paddled across the wet road to the inn, where, despite the somewhat rough surroundings, we enjoyed a capital dinner, cooked in the true French style. They are specially celebrated here for their asparagus, but the locusts had devoured all but a very few stalks, besides which they were held responsible, on the present occasion, for the absence of other vegetables and salad. Yesterday there was a grand wedding party near here, the complete success of which was, we were told, somewhat marred by the fact that for six hours, in the very middle of the day, it became absolutely necessary to light candles, owing to the dense clouds of locusts, about a league in extent, by which the air was darkened. Trains are even stopped by these insects occasionally;

for they appear to like a hard road, and when they get on the line their bodies make the rails so greasy that the wheels of the engines will not bite. Moreover, they completely obscure the lights and signals, so that the men are afraid to proceed. The only remedy, therefore, is to go very slowly, preceded by a truck-load of sand, which is scattered freely over the rails in front of the engine. Horses will not always face a cloud of locusts, even to get to their stables, but turn round and stand doggedly still, until it has passed.

After dinner we once more stepped into our special train, in which we arrived at Rosario at about half-past nine o'clock, thoroughly tired out.

CHAPTER VI.

LIFE ON THE PAMPAS.

*There's tempest in yon horned moon,
And lightning in yon cloud;
But hark the music, mariners!
The wind is piping loud.*

Saturday, September 16*th.*—Waking at half-past five, we busied ourselves until nine o'clock, when we again started in a special train for Carcarañ. After a short stop at Roldan, it was reached two hours later, and breakfast was followed by a long ride through the Land Company's colony, and from thence to Candelaria, a purely Spanish settlement.

I freely confess that I had hardly believed all the stories they told me last night about the terrible doings of the locusts, and thought they must have been slightly exaggerated. It all seemed too dreadful to be true—as if one of the plagues of Egypt had been revived by the wand of an evil magician. In this somewhat incredulous mood I rashly said that, although I was very sorry to hear of the visit of these destructive creatures, as they *were* unfortunately here, I should like to see them. My wish was shortly to be gratified; for, in the course of our ride, we saw in the distant sky what looked very much like a heavy purple thunder-cloud, but which the experienced pronounced to be a swarm of locusts. It seemed impossible; but as we proceeded they met us, first singly, and then in gradually increasing numbers, until each step became positively painful, owing to the smart blows we received from them on our heads, faces, and hands. We stopped for a time at Mr. Holt's large estancia, where, notwithstanding the general appearance of prosperity, the traces of the ravages of the locusts were only too visible. On remounting, to proceed on our journey, we found that the cloud had approached much nearer, the effect produced by its varying position being most extraordinary. As the locusts passed between us and the sun they completely obscured the light; a little later, with the sun's rays shining directly on their wings, they looked like a golden cloud, such as one sometimes sees in the transformation scene of a pantomime; and, at a greater distance, when viewed from the top of a slight eminence, they looked like a snow-storm, or a field of snow-white marguerites, which had suddenly taken to themselves wings. When on the ground, with their wings closed, they formed a close mass of little brown specks, completely hiding the ground and crops, both grass and grain. In riding over them, though not a quarter of their number could rise, for want of space in which to spread their wings, they formed such a dense cloud that we could see nothing else, and the horses strongly objected to face them. They got into one's hair and clothes, and gave one the creeps all over. I am sure I shall often dream of them for some time to come, and I have quite made my mind that I never wish to see another locust as long as I live. I have, however, secured some fine specimens for any one who is curious about them.

The land we passed through appeared to be well farmed. We spoke to several of the colonists, especially to one Italian family, living in a little mud rancho with a tile roof. They were all gathered together to witness the dying agonies of one of their best cows, perishing from the effects of the drought. The rest of the animals in the corral looked, I am sorry to say, thin and miserable, and as if they intended soon to follow their companion's example. The poor people, nevertheless, seemed very cheery and contented, and hospitably gave us each a drink of some remarkably muddy water.

After a thirty-mile ride under a hot sun, fortunately on the easiest of horses, we were none of us sorry to stop for a short time at Carcaraña, and obtain some refreshment, before proceeding—horses, carriage, and all—by train to Rosario, another colony on the line. Arrived at the latter place, I thought I had had enough riding for the first day, and therefore visited the various farms and houses in the carriage, the rest of the party going, as before, on horseback. After a round of about fifteen miles, we returned to the station, where we were kindly received by the sister of the station-master. An excellent dinner was provided for us in the refreshment-room, before we entered our special train, and Rosario was reached at about ten o'clock.

Sunday, September 17*th*.—A kind friend sent his carriage to take us to the English church, a brick building, built to replace the small iron church that existed here previously, and only opened last month. The service was well performed, and the singing of the choir excellent. We paid a visit to the Sunday-schools after luncheon, and then drove to the quinta of Baron Alvear. The road lies through the town, past the race-course, crowded with Guachos, getting up scratch races amongst themselves, and on, over undulating plains and water-courses, into the open country. Sometimes there was a track, sometimes none. In some places the pastures were luxuriantly green; in others the ground was carpeted with white, lilac, and scarlet verbena, just coming into bloom—for it is still early spring here. Here and there came a bare patch, completely cleared by the locusts, who had also stripped many of the fine timber trees in the garden of the quinta. On the gate-posts, at the entrance, were the nests of two oven-birds, like those we had already seen on the telegraph-posts, so exactly spherical as to look like ornaments. In one of the shrubberies a fine jaguar was shut up in a cage, who looked very like a tiger. Though he had evidently just had his dinner, he was watching with greedy interest the proceedings of some natives in charge of a horse—an animal which he esteems a great delicacy, when procurable.

On our way across the camp we saw a great quantity of the seeds of the *Martynia proboscidea*, mouse-burrs as they call them—devil's claws or toe-nails: they are curious-looking things.

Frank Buckland has a theory—and very likely a correct one—that they are created in this peculiar form for the express purpose of attaching themselves to the long tails of the wild horses that roam about the country in troops of hundreds. They carry them thousands of miles, and disseminate the seed wherever they go at large in search of food and water.

When we returned to Rosario we noticed a great crowd still on the race-course, and were just in time to see the finish of one race, ridden barebacked, and for a very short distance. All the races are short; and as the natives are always engaging in these little contests of speed, the horses get into the habit of extending themselves directly you put them out of a walk. But the least touch is sufficient to stop them immediately, and I never saw horses better broken than they are here. The most fearful bits are used for the purpose; but when once this is accomplished, the mere inclination of the body, or the slightest pressure of the finger upon the bridle, is sufficient to guide them. They will maintain, for almost any length of time, a quick canter—what they call here 'a little gallop'—at the rate of three leagues (ten miles) an hour, without showing the slightest sign of fatigue. They don't like being mounted, and always fidget a little then, but are quite quiet directly you are in the saddle. I rode several horses which had never carried a lady before; but after the first few minutes they did not seem to mind the riding-habit in the least. They evidently dislike standing still, unless you dismount and throw the rein on the ground, when they will remain stationary for hours.

Monday, September 18*th.*—The early part of this morning was spent in much the same way as on Saturday, Tom going as before to the Land Company's Office, whilst I remained at home to write.

At nine o'clock we proceeded to the station, and started in our comfortable railway carriage for Tortugas. We formed quite a large party altogether, and the journey over the now familiar line, past Roldan, Carcarana, and Cañada de Gomez, was a very pleasant one. At Tortugas we left the train, and paid a visit to one of the overseers of the colony and his cheery little French wife, who, we found, had been expecting us all day on Saturday. A few weeks ago this lady's sister was carried off by Indians, with some other women and children. After riding many leagues, she seized her opportunity, pushed the Indian who was carrying her off his horse, turned the animal's head round, and galloped back across the plain, hotly pursued, until within a mile or two of the colony, by the rest of the band. It was a plucky thing for a little bit of a woman to attempt with a great powerful savage, and she is deservedly looked upon in the village as quite a heroine.

The journey between Rosario and Cordova occupies twelve hours by the ordinary train; and as Frayle Muerto is exactly half-way between the two places, the trains going in either direction commence their journey at the same hours (6 a.m. and 6 p.m.), by which means the passengers meet each other here in time to breakfast and dine together. There is a fine bridge over the river near Frayle Muerto, but the place is principally celebrated as having been the site of the Henleyite colony, which caused disappointment to so many young men of family, who were induced to come out here from England and to go up country, with no other result than the loss of all their money. The scheme was supposed to be perfect in all its details, but proved upon a closer acquaintance to be utterly worthless. The iron church at Rosario is still standing, which the members of the expedition took up there, and we have also met some of the young men themselves at various times.

The train did not reach Cordova until 7.30 p.m., and it was therefore too late for us to see much of the approach to the city, but to-morrow we intend to do a good deal in that way. In the middle of the night we were aroused by a violent thunderstorm. The lightning was most vivid, and illuminated our room with many, colors. The rain fell heavily, flooding everything, and making the streets look like rivers, and the courtyard of the hotel like a lake. It is one of the oldest, and, at the same time, one of the most unhealthy, of the cities of South America, for it is built in the hollow of the surrounding hills, where no refreshing breezes can penetrate.

Traveling in Brazil is like passing through a vast hothouse, filled with gorgeous tropical vegetation and forms of insect life. In the neighborhood of Monte Video you might imagine yourself in a perpetual greenhouse. Here it is like being in a vast garden, in which the greenest of turf, the brightest of bedding-out plants, and the most fragrant flowering shrubs abound. Each country, therefore, possesses its own particular beauty, equally attractive in its way.

Shortly after leaving Cordova we passed through an Indian village; but, except at this point, we did not meet many natives during our ride. One poor woman, however, whom we did unfortunately encounter, had a fall from her horse, owing to the animal being frightened at the umbrella I carried, yet my own horse had, after a very brief objection, quietly submitted to the introduction of this novelty into the equipment of his rider.

We found that the hotel on the Caldera for which we were bound was shut up; but one of the party had the keys, and an excellent lunch quickly made its appearance. The view from the veranda, over the river, to the Sierras beyond, was very fine. It had become quite hot by this time, and I was much interested in seeing all our horses taken down to the water to bathe. They appeared to be perfectly familiar with the process; and, the river being shallow, they picked out all the nice holes between the bowlders, where they could lie down and be completely covered by the water. Just as we were starting to return, black clouds gathered from all around; the lightning flashed, the thunder muttered, and big drops began to fall. But the storm was not of long duration, and we escaped the worst part of it, though we had ample evidence of its severity during our homeward ride, in the slippery ground, the washed-away paths, and the swollen ditches. We stopped half-way to see the drowning out of some poor little bizcachas from their holes. The water had been turned into their dwellings by means of trenches, and as the occupants endeavored to make their escape at the other end they were pounced upon by men and dogs; the prairie-owls meanwhile hovering disconsolately overhead. Two of the gentlemen of our party each managed to purchase a living bizcacha, which was then wrapped up in a handkerchief and conveyed home. When young they are pretty little creatures, and are easily tamed.

It was late when we reached Cordova; but I was anxious to visit the Observatory before our departure, as it is one of the best, though not by any means the largest, in the world. Professor Gould, the astronomer, is away just at present, but we were kindly received by Mrs. Gould, who conducted us over the building. They have a fine collection of various instruments and some wonderful photographs of the principal stars—Saturn, with his ring and eight moons, Jupiter, with his four moons, Venus, Mercury, etc. If we could have staid longer we might have seen much more; but it was now quite dark, and we had only just time for a short visit to the observing-room itself. Our ride down to the city in the dark would have been exceedingly risky if our horses had been less sure-footed, for the roads had been washed away in many places, but we reached the bottom of the Observatory hill in safety, and shortly afterwards arrived at the hotel just in time for dinner.

After dinner we drove to the station, where we found all our own party assembled, and many more people, who had come to see us off. I was given the Chilian bit used for the horse I rode to-day, as a remembrance of my visit. It is a most formidable-looking instrument of torture, and one which I am sure my dear little steed did not in the least require; but I suppose the fact of having once felt it, when being broken in, is sufficient for a lifetime, for the horses here have certainly the very lightest mouths I ever met with. A gift of a young puma, or small lion, was also waiting for me. It is about four months old, and very tame; but, considering the children, I think it will be more prudent to pass it on to the Zoo, in London.

The train started at 8.30 p.m. and took an hour to reach Rio Segundo, where we found tea and coffee prepared. After that we proceeded to make our arrangements for the night; some of the gentlemen sleeping in the saloon-carriages, and some on beds made up in the luggage-van. Tom and I turned into our two cozy little berths, and knew nothing more until we were called at 4.30 a.m., at Cañada de Gomez. The lamp had gone out, and we found it rather difficult work dressing and packing in the cold and dark; but it was soon done, and a cup of hot coffee in the refreshment-room afterwards made us feel quite comfortable.

Then we all separated: Captain Dunlop to join his ship; Tom to complete his report on the colonies of the Central Argentine Land Company, which he is preparing in compliance with the request of the Directors in London; while the rest of the party awaited the arrival of the wagonette which was to take us to the estancia of Las Rosas.

Wednesday, September 20th.—At 6.30 p. m. the wagonette arrived, a light but strong, unpainted vehicle, drawn by a pair of active little well-bred horses, both of whom had been raced in their day. There were but a few leagues of cultivated ground to be passed before we reached the broad, undulating, solitary Pampas, where for some time the only visible signs of life were to be found in the Teru-tero birds (a sort of plover), who shrieked discordantly as we disturbed their repose; the partridges, large and small, put up by the retriever who accompanied us; some prairie fowls; a great many hawks, of all sizes; and the pretty little wydah-birds, with their two immense tail feathers, four times the length of their bodies. The first glimpse of the far-spreading prairie was most striking in all its variations of color. The true shade of the Pampas grass, when long, is a light dusty green; when short it is a bright fresh green. But it frequently happens that, owing to the numerous prairie-fires, either accidental or intentional, nothing is to be seen but a vast expanse of black charred ground, here and there relieved by a few patches of vivid green, where the grass is once more springing up under the influence of the rain.

The road, or rather track, was in a bad condition, owing to the recent wet weather, and on each side of the five *cañadas*, or small rivers, which we had to ford, there were deep morasses, through which we had to struggle as best we could, with the mud up to our axletrees. Just before arriving at the point where the stream had to be crossed, the horses were well flogged and urged on at a gallop, which they gallantly maintained until the other side was reached. Then we stopped to breathe the horses and to repair damages, generally finding that a trace had given way, or that some other part of the harness had shown signs of weakness. On one occasion we were delayed for a considerable time by the breaking of the splinter-bar, to repair which was a troublesome matter; indeed, I don't know how we should have managed it if we had not met a native lad, who sold us his long lasso to bind the pieces together again. It was a lucky *rencontre* for us, as he was the only human being we saw during the whole of our drive of thirty miles, except the peon who brought us a change of horses, half-way.

In the course of the journey we passed a large estancia, the road to which was marked by the dead bodies and skeletons of the poor beasts who had perished in the late droughts. Hundreds of them were lying about in every stage of decay, those more recently dead being surrounded by vultures and other carrion-birds. The next *cañada* that we crossed was choked up with the carcasses of the unfortunate creatures who had struggled thus far for a last drink, and had then not had sufficient strength left to extricate themselves from the water. Herds of miserable-looking, half-starved cattle were also to be seen, the cows very little larger than their calves, and all apparently covered with the same rough shaggy coats. The pasture is not fine enough in this part of the country to carry sheep, but deer are frequently met with.

A little later we again began to approach cultivated land, and a mile or two further brought us to a broad road, with high palings on either side, down which we drove, and through the yard, to the door of the estancia. The house is a one-story building, one room wide, with a veranda in front and at the back, one side of which faces the yard, the other a well-kept garden, full of violets and other spring flowers, and roses just coming into bloom. There are several smaller detached buildings, in which the sleeping apartments are situated, and which are also provided with verandas and barred windows. Having visited the various rooms, in company with our hosts, we sat down to a rough but substantial breakfast, to which full justice was done. Traveling all night, and a ride of thirty miles in the fresh morning air, have a tendency to produce a keen appetite; and the present occasion proved no exception to that rule.

After breakfast I rested and wrote some letters, while the gentlemen inspected the farm and stud. The proprietor of this estancia has the best horses in this part of the country, and has taken great pains to improve their breed, as well as that of the cattle and sheep, by importing thorough-breds from England. Unlike the Arabs, neither natives nor settlers here think of riding mares, and it is considered quite a disgrace to do so. They are therefore either allowed to run wild in troops, or are used to trample out corn or to make mud for bricks. They are also frequently killed and boiled down, for the sake of their hides and tallow, the value of which does not amount to more than about 10*s.* per head. Large herds of them are met with at this time of the year on the Pampas, attended by a few horses, and accompanied by their foals.

The natives of these parts pass their lives in the saddle. Horses are used for almost every conceivable employment, from hunting and fishing to brick-making and butter-churning. Even the very beggars ride about on horseback. I have seen a photograph of one, with a police certificate of mendicancy hanging round his neck, taken from life for Sir Woodbine Parish. Every domestic servant has his or her own horse, as a matter of course; and the maids are all provided with habits, in which they ride about on Sundays, from one estancia to another, to pay visits. In fishing, the horse is ridden into the water as far as he can go, and the net or rod is then made use of by his rider. At Buenos Ayres I have seen the poor animals all but swimming to the shore, with heavy carts and loads, from the ships anchored in the inner roads; for the water is so shallow that only very small boats can go alongside the vessels, and the cargo is therefore transferred directly to the carts to save the trouble and expense of transhipment. In out-of-the-way places, on the Pampas, where no churns exist, butter is made by putting milk into a goat-skin bag, attached by a long lasso to the saddle of a peon, who is then set to gallop a certain number of miles, with the bag bumping and jumping along the ground after him.

About four o'clock the horses—much larger and better-bred animals than those we have been riding lately—were brought round from the corral. Mine was a beauty, easy, gentle, and fast. We first took a canter round the cultivated ground, about 300 acres in extent, and in capital condition. Lucern grows here splendidly, and can be cut seven times a year. As we left the yard, Mr. Nield's man asked if he would take the dogs. He replied in the negative; but I suppose he must have referred to the greyhounds only, for we were certainly accompanied on the present occasion by *eleven* dogs of various sorts and sizes, those left behind being shut up and kept without food, in anticipation of the stag-hunt to-morrow. We rode over the race-course, where the horses are trained, and on to the partridge ground. The larger kind of these birds are exceedingly stupid, and are easily ridden down by a horseman, or caught in a noose. They rise three times, and after the third flight they are so exhausted and terrified that it is easy to dismount and catch them with the hand, as they lie panting on the long grass. Partridge-hunting is considered good sport. It is necessary to keep your eye constantly fixed upon the bird, and to watch where he settles, and then to gallop to the spot as hard as possible, leaving your horse to look after himself amid the long grass; and this manœuvre has to be repeated until at last the unfortunate bird is overtaken and caught.

As we were riding along, the dogs found and killed a bizcacha, in a bank. Just as Mr. Elliott had pulled it out, and had laid it, dead, in the field, its little companion owl arrived, and appeared to be in the most dreadful state of mind. It shrieked and cried, as it hovered over us, and finally selected a small white fox terrier, who, I think, really had been principally concerned in the death, as the object of its vengeance, pouncing down upon his head, and giving him two or three good pecks, at the same time flapping its wings violently. The other dogs drove it off; but more than half an hour afterwards, while we were looking at some horses, nearly a mile from the spot, the plucky little owl returned to the charge, and again swooped down upon the same dog, with a dismal cry, and administered a vigorous peck to him. Altogether it was a striking and interesting proof of the attachment existing between these curious birds and beasts; the object of the owl in the present instance clearly being to revenge if possible the death of its friend.

On our return to the farm, we went all around the place, and found that everything was being made secure for the night; after which we watched all the servants come in one by one for their daily ration of grog, and then retired to dress for dinner, shortly after which, being thoroughly tired out, I retired to my bed-room, attended by a very kind old Irishwoman, who had been deputed to look after me. My mind was at first somewhat disturbed by the discovery of one or two enormous toads and long-armed spiders in my apartment; but they fortunately did not interfere with my repose, for I slept like a top. All the rooms being on the ground-floor, it is almost impossible entirely to exclude intruders of this description. I admired very much what I took to be two fine ponchos, of a delicate fawn-color, used as tablecloths, but upon a closer examination I found that they were made of the finest silk, and learned afterwards that they were imported from England. I don't know why the same material should not be employed for a similar purpose at home; but I believe that those manufactured hitherto have been designed expressly for the South American market, to which they are exported in considerable quantities.

Thursday, September 21*st.*—At five o'clock, when I awoke, it was so misty that I could only see about half-way across the yard. By six, the hour at which we were to have started on our hunting expedition, matters had improved a little; but it was still considered unsafe to venture out, for fear of being lost on the vast plains which surrounded us. An hour later, however, it was reported that the fog was clearing off, and a little before eight o'clock we started. Horses, riders, and dogs, all appeared to be in the highest spirits, the former jumping and frisking about, hardly deigning to touch the ground, the latter tearing after one another and barking at every stray bird they met. The pack numbered seventeen, and could hardly be called a level lot of hounds, comprising, as it did, two deerhounds, five well-bred greyhounds, two retrievers, one setter, one spaniel, one French poodle, two fox terriers, one black-and-tan terrier, and two animals of an utterly indescribable breed; but they all did their work well, as the event proved. Even the shaggy, fat old French poodle arrived in each case before the deer was cut up.

Two deer were soon descried in the distance, and we cantered steadily towards them at the rate of about ten miles an hour until the dogs winded and sighted them. Then, directly the first short yelp was heard, every horse extended himself in an instant, galloping away as hard as he could go, almost literally *ventre à terre*. They were nearly all thorough-breds, and had been raced, so that the speed was something delightful. But it only lasted ten minutes, at the end of which time the dogs ran into one of the deer, and thus put a temporary stop to our enjoyment. He proved to be a fine buck, and was soon killed. His legs were cut off for trophies, but, his horns being like velvet, the head was not worth having. Some of the dogs pursued the doe, but failed to pull her down, and returned half an hour later fatigued and panting.

It had become hot by this time, so we rode to the nearest water, to enable the animals to drink and bathe, and then started afresh at a sharp canter. There were plenty of bizcacha holes and boggy places to be avoided; but we allowed the horses to take care of themselves and us in this respect, and occupied ourselves almost exclusively in looking for fresh deer. For some time we found nothing; then two sprang out of the long grass close to the *cañada*, which they crossed, and, on reaching the other side, started off in different directions. The pack pursued and divided, some going after each animal. I, and two others of the party, followed the doe, and after another short burst of ten minutes, at a tremendous pace, we ran into and killed her. As soon as she had been dispatched, we wanted to follow the buck, in pursuit of which the rest of the riders had gone, but there was now nothing to be seen of him or them. Flat as the country looked, the slight undulations of the ground quite hid them from our view. After riding about for two hours in various directions, looking and listening most patiently, we abandoned the search in despair, and returned to the house, where we found that our friends had already arrived. They had enjoyed the best run they had had for many months—seven miles, from point to point—but the dogs had lain down, dead beat, at the end of the first six miles. The horsemen had galloped on, their animals tailing off one by one, until only two remained in it at all. Having mutually agreed to let the stag live till another day, to afford perhaps as good a run and as much pleasure to some one else, they thereupon also abandoned the chase, and turned their horses' heads homewards.

After a change of dress we proceeded to pack up, preparatory to our departure, and then had breakfast, after which we bade adieu to our kind hosts, and started in the wagonette to retrace our steps to the station. It was very bright and hot, and the sun and wind had already begun to have a visible effect upon the vegetation of the Pampas. The streams were much more passable, and we reached Cañada de Gomez at about half-past five, in a shorter time than it had taken us to perform the outward journey yesterday. On reaching Rosario at about ten o'clock, we found several friends waiting to receive us, with invitations to tea; but we felt too tired in body and too disreputable in appearance to accept them, and preferred going straight to our hotel and to bed.

CHAPTER VII.

MORE ABOUT THE ARGENTINE REPUBLIC.

The twilight is sad and cloudy,
The wind blows wild and free,
And like the wings of sea-birds
Flash the white caps of the sea.

Friday, September 22d.—Mr. Fisher called for me at 8 a.m., to drive me in his little carriage to the railway yard and workshops, and then to pay some farewell visits. We also went to see the market, and to get some photographs of Rosario; after which, breakfast, packing-up, and paying the bill occupied our time until one o'clock, when we started for the steamer, to return to Buenos Ayres. On our arrival alongside the 'Proveedor,' I found that nearly all our Rosario friends had come down to the landing-place to see us off, and had brought all manner of remembrances for me and the children. Flowers in profusion; a tame cardinal bird for Muriel; a pair of dear little long-tailed green paroquets; the skin of a seal, shot at the Alexandria colony; a beautiful poncho; an Argentine bit, whip, and stirrups; a carpincha skin; two pretty little muletas—a sort of armadillo, very tame, and often kept in the houses here as a pet; and several other presents, all of which, when I look at them at home, will serve to remind me of the kind donors, and of the happy days spent in the Argentine Republic.

It was not long before we were off, and steaming slowly astern of the 'Uruguay.' This boat is not so large nor so fast as the 'Uruguay,' though the difference in speed does not probably amount to more than fifteen minutes in the twenty-four hours. Her saloon and deck are not so good, but her sleeping cabins are much larger and more comfortable. The Italian captains are equally agreeable on both steamers, the civility is the same, and the fares and food are precisely similar, so that there is not much left to influence one in the choice of vessels. We had a pleasant party at an excellent dinner in the evening, the captain only regretting that we had not been on board two days ago, when Mlle. P. and the opera company went down from Rosario to Buenos Ayres. They had a very cheery evening, and some good music, which Tom told us afterwards he thoroughly enjoyed. There were no musicians on board to-night, and not any temptation to sit up late, which was perhaps as well; one of the reasons for our going back this way being that we wished to have an opportunity of seeing the River Tigré, which we should reach in the early morning. On the upward journey we had, to save time, embarked at Campaña, which is situated above that river.

Saturday, September 23d.—At 4.30 a.m. the captain called me, being anxious that I should not miss any of the beauties of the Tigré. On my arrival on deck he kindly had a chair placed for me right in the bows, provided me with rugs and wraps, and sent for some hot coffee, which was particularly acceptable, as the morning air was fresh and chilly. The sky was flushed with rosy clouds, the forerunners of one of the most beautiful sunrises imaginable. The river itself is narrow and monotonous, the branches of the willow-trees on either bank almost sweeping the sides of the steamer. The center channel is fairly deep; but we managed to run aground once, though we only drew nine feet, and in turning a sharp corner it was necessary to send a boat ashore with a rope, to pull the vessel's head round.

At half-past six we reached the port of Tigré, where we found many fine ships waiting for the tide, to go up the river. Some delay occurred while the passengers' luggage was being examined; but in about half an hour we were able to land and walk to the railway-station, through an avenue of shady trees, round the trunks of which the wisteria, now in full bloom, was climbing, and past several houses, whose pretty gardens were ablaze with all sorts of flowers. At the station I found a letter from Tom, telling me we were expected to breakfast at a quinta, not far from Buenos Ayres.

For about an hour and a half the line ran through a rich and fertile country, quite the garden of Buenos Ayres, until we arrived at the station where we were to alight. Here Mr. Coghlan met us and drove us to his house, which is charmingly situated in the midst of a grove of olive-trees, formerly surrounding the palace of the viceroys. After breakfast the gardener cut us a fine bouquet of roses and violets, and we walked to the tramway, and were conveyed by one of the cars, smoothly and quickly, to the city. The contrast between this mode of traveling and riding in an ordinary carriage through the ill-paved streets is very striking. It is really less fatiguing to walk than to adopt the latter mode of conveyance, and I believe that, but for the look of the thing, most people would prefer to do so. How the vehicles themselves stand the jolting I cannot imagine, for they are all large and handsome, and must suffer tremendous strains.

At noon we went with Mr. Coghlan to see the market and the museum, and to do some shopping. The market is a large open building, well supplied with everything at moderate prices; meat, game, fruit, vegetables, and flowers being especially cheap and good. House-rent and fine clothes—what Muriel would call 'dandy things'—are very dear in Buenos Ayres, but all the necessaries of life are certainly cheap. People of the middle and lower classes live much better here than they do at home, and the development of bone and muscle in large families of small children, owing to the constant use of so much meat and strong soup, is very remarkable. When once they have .

attained the age at which they can run about, children get on very well; but the climate, and the difficulty of obtaining a proper supply of milk in hot weather, often prove fatal to infants. It is very difficult to get good servants here, as they can easily obtain much higher pay in other capacities, and are very soon enabled to set up in business for themselves. Returning to the hotel, we collected our parcels and had some luncheon, and then proceeded to the pier, where we found the children waiting for us to embark in the gig, and we soon arrived safely on board the 'Sunbeam.'

At about half-past six, Tom and Mabelle returned from their expedition to the largest and most comfortable estancia in the country, where they were received most hospitably, and enjoyed themselves very much.

After dinner, some of our party left in the whale-boat, being anxious to be present at Madame Almazilia's benefit performance at the opera, for which I fear they arrived too late, after all. Whilst we were waiting at the railway-station to-day, some of the bouquets, which were to be presented at the theater to-night, arrived by train. The flowers were arranged in all manner of strange shapes and devices—full-sized tables and chairs, music-stands, and musical instruments, and many other quaint conceits, composed entirely of gray Neapolitan violets, marked out with camellias and other colored flowers.

Sunday, September 24th.—Most of us went ashore in the whale-boat at ten o'clock, to attend the English church, re-opened to-day for the first time for some months. After our own service we met many friends, and walked to the Roman Catholic cathedral. The streets were full of well-appointed carriages, and in the interior of the building we found a great many well-dressed ladies, and a few men. Mass had not commenced, and a constant stream of worshipers was still entering; but we remained only for a short time, and then returned to the Mole. By this time the wind had freshened considerably, and several of our friends tried to persuade us to remain on shore; but as we knew Tom was expecting us, and we wanted to get the things we required for our next journey, we thought it better to go off.

It took us two hours and a half, beating against the wind, to reach the yacht, sea-sick, and drenched to the skin. Directly we got outside the bar the sea was very bad, and each wave broke more or less over the little half-deck, under which the children had been packed away for shelter. Seeing how rough it was out at the anchorage— far worse than near the shore—Tom had quite given us up, for it was now half-past three, and was preparing to come ashore, bringing our things with him. On board the yacht we found an unfortunate French maid, and another servant, who had come off early in the morning to spend the day and have dinner with our people, but who were now lying prostrate and ill in the cabin.

Champagne and luncheon revived us a little, and Tom hurried us off to get ashore again by daylight, before the weather became worse. It was a very pleasant twenty minutes' sail to the shore, racing along before the wind, with two reefs in the mainsail—quite a different thing from beating out. The tide was high, and the captain therefore steered for the pier, where he hoped to land us. Unfortunately, however, he missed it; and as it was impossible to make another tack out, all that could be done was to let go the anchor to save running ashore, and wait until they sent out a small boat to fetch us. This took some little time, during which we pitched and tossed about in a very disagreeable fashion. When the boat did at last arrive she turned out to be a wretched little skiff, rowed by two men, with very indifferent oars, and only capable of taking three passengers at a time. Tom went first, taking with him the two children, and the two poor sea-sick maids, and the boat at once put off for the land, Tom steering. It was terrible to watch them from the whale-boat, and when one tremendous sea came, and the skiff broached-to, I thought for a moment that all was over, as did every one who was watching our proceedings from the pier. I could not look any more, till I heard shouts that they were safe ashore. Then came our turn. The boat returned for us, this time provided with better oars, and we were soon landed in safety, if not in comfort; and a third and last trip brought ashore the rest of the party and the luggage, Tom remaining at the tiller.

Mr. Coghlan had come down to meet us, but, seeing the peril of the first boat, had gone away until he heard we were all landed, and now returned to congratulate us on our narrow escape and present safety. After we had rested for a short time in the waiting-room, to recover from our fright and shake our dripping garments, we went to the Hôtel de la Paix, where we dined, and at ten o'clock we walked down to the railway-station, where a large number of people had already assembled, some of whom were to accompany us to Azul, while others had only come to see us off.

Everything had been most comfortably arranged for us in the special train. The interior fittings of two second-class American carriages had been completely taken out, and a canvas lining, divided into compartments, each containing a cozy little bed, had been substituted. Wash-stands, looking-glasses, &c., had been provided, and a profusion of beautiful flowers filled in every available spot. In a third car two tables, occupying its entire length, with seats on one side of each table, had been placed; and here it was intended that we should breakfast, lunch, and dine.

Monday, September 25th.—We slept soundly—speaking for the children and myself—until we were aroused at six o'clock this morning by the agreeable intelligence that we had reached our destination. Azul is about 300 miles south of Buenos Ayres, on the Southern Railway. It is a small and primitive place in itself, but is situated in the midst of splendid pastures, both for rearing sheep and cattle, of which there are large·flocks and herds.

Whilst we were waiting for breakfast, we walked a little distance to see a troop of mares treading mud for bricks. It was a curious, but rather sad sight. Inside a circular inclosure, some fifty yards in diameter, about fifty half-starved animals, up to their houghs in very sloppy mud, were being driven round about, and up and down, as fast as they could go, by a mounted peon, assisted by five or six men on foot, outside the inclosure, armed with long heavy whips, which they used constantly. Some of the poor creatures had foals, which were tied up a little distance off, and which kept up a piteous whinnying, as an accompaniment to the lashings and crackings of the whips. On our way back to the station we saw a horse, attached to a light gig, bolt across the Pampas at full gallop, vainly pursued by a man on horseback. First one wheel came off and then the other; then the body of the gig was left behind, and then the shafts and most of the harness followed suit; until at last—as we afterwards heard—the runaway reached his home, about five miles off, with only his bridle remaining.

At nine o'clock the breakfast-bell rang, and we found an excellent repast spread out for us on two long tables. An hour later we started in seven large carriages and proceeded first to make the tour of the town, afterwards visiting the bank, and a fine new house in the course of construction by a native, built entirely of white marble from Italy. Then we paid a visit to some Indians—an old chief and his four wives, who have settled quietly down in a toldo near the town. They were not bad-looking, and appeared fairly comfortable as they squatted in the open air round the fire, above which was suspended a large iron pot, containing, to judge by the look and smell, a most savory preparation. We next went to a store, where we picked up a few curiosities, and then drove to the mill of Azul, a new establishment, of which the inhabitants of the town, are evidently very proud. There is a pretty walk by the mill-stream, overhung with willows, and close by is another toldo, inhabited by more Indians.

Leaving the town, we now proceeded about two leagues across the Pampas to Mr. Frer's estancia. He is a farmer on a very extensive scale, and possesses about 24,000 sheep and 500 horses, besides goodly herds of cattle. The locusts have not visited this part of the country, and the pastures are consequently in fine condition after the late rains, while the sheep look proportionately well. We passed a large *grasseria*, or place where sheep are killed at the rate of seven in a minute, and are skinned, cut up, and boiled down for tallow in an incredibly short space of time, the residue of the meat being used in the furnace as fuel. Running about loose, outside, were four or five curly-horned rams, between two of which a grand combat took place, apparently conducted in strict accordance with the rules of fighting etiquette. The two animals began by walking round and round, eying each other carefully, and then retiring backwards a certain distance, which might have been measured out for them, they stopped so exactly simultaneously. Then, gazing steadfastly at one another for a few moments, as if to take aim, they rushed forward with tremendous force, dashing their foreheads together with a crash that might have been heard a mile away. It seemed marvelous that they did not fracture their skulls, for they repeated the operation three or four times before Mr. Frer could get a man to help to stop the fight, when the two combatants were led off, in a very sulky state, to be locked up apart.

Arrangements had been made for us to see as much of station-life as possible during our short visit. The peons' dinner had been put back, in order that we might witness their peculiar method of roasting, or rather baking, their food, and eating it; but we were rather later than was expected, and the men were so hungry that we were only able to see the end of the performance. Mr. Frer had also sent a long way across the Pampas for some wild horses, belonging to him, in order that we might see them lassoed; and Colonel Donovan had brought with him one of his best domidors, or horse-breakers, that we might have an opportunity of seeing an unbroken colt caught and backed for the first time.

About a hundred horses were driven into a large corral, and several Guachos and peons, some on horseback and some on foot, exhibited their skill with the lasso, by catching certain of the animals, either by the fore leg, the hind leg, or the neck, as they galloped round and round at full speed. The captured animal got a tremendous fall in each case, and if the mounted horse was not very clever and active, he and his rider were very likely to be thrown down also. There was the risk too of the man receiving an injury from the lasso itself, if it should happen to get round his body, in which case he would probably be almost cut in half by the sudden jerk.

The next proceeding was to cast a lasso at a *potro*, or unbroken colt, who was galloping about in the very center of the troop, at full speed. His fore legs were caught dexterously in the noose, which brought him up, or rather down, instantly, head over heels. Another lasso was then thrown over his head, and drawn quite tight round his neck, and a bridle, composed of two or three thongs of raw hide, was forced into his mouth by means of a slip-knot rein. A sheepskin saddle was placed on his back, the man who was to ride him standing over him, with one foot already in the stirrup. All this time the poor horse was lying on the ground with his legs tied close together, frightened almost out of his life, trembling in every limb, and perspiring from every pore. When the man was ready, the horse's legs were loosened sufficiently to allow him to rise, and he was then led outside the corral. The lassoes were suddenly withdrawn, and he dashed forwards, springing and plunging upwards, sideways, downwards, in every direction, in the vain effort to rid himself of his unaccustomed load. The man remained planted, like a rock, in the saddle, pulling hard at the bridle, while a second domidor, mounted on a tame horse, pursued the terrified animal, striking him with a cruel whip to make him go in the required direction. After about ten minutes of this severe exercise, the captive returned to the corral, exhausted, and perfectly cowed, and showing no desire to rejoin his late companions. In order to complete the process of breaking him in, we were told that it would be necessary to keep him tied up for two or three days, rather short of food, and to repeat daily the operation of saddling, bridling, and mounting, the difficulty being less on each occasion, until at last he would become as quiet as a lamb.

We now saw our train approaching, orders having been given for it to come as far as it could from the station to meet us. We wished good-by to Mr. Frer and his party, and, with many thanks to all, got into our carriages and drove across the plains to the railway. On our way we passed some large lagunes, full of wild fowl, and surrounded by scarlet flamingoes and pelicans. The ground we had to traverse was very boggy; so much so that two of the carriages got stuck, and their occupants had to turn out and walk. At last we reached the train, and climbed into the cars, where we found an excellent luncheon prepared, which we ate whilst the train dashed along at the rate of forty miles an hour. About seven o'clock we stopped for tea and coffee, and the children were put to bed. By nine we had reached the junction for Buenos Ayres, where an engine met us, and took most of our party into the city, in one of the cars, while we went on to Punta Lara, the station for Ensenada.

On arriving we were met by several of our men, who had been allowed to go ashore at Buenos Ayres on Sunday morning, and had not been able to rejoin the yacht since. On Sunday night, when they were to have returned, it was impossible for them to get off. Even the whale-boat was nearly dashed to pieces, at anchor, near the pier. They spent the early part of Monday morning in hunting everywhere with the pilot for the lost steward, and at last left the shore just in time to see the yacht steaming down the river, with only half her crew on board, and without a pilot. It seems they had been waited for from eight o'clock until eleven; it then became necessary to get under way, for fear of losing the tide. As it was, the yacht had not been able to get near the pier at Ensenada, and was now lying in the river, two miles out. The station-master, having been informed of the state of affairs, very kindly had steam got up in the railway tug to take us off. The children, with their nurses, remained in bed in the car, which was shunted into a siding until the morning, the doctor staying on shore in charge. The rest of us then set out for the yacht, which we reached at 1 a.m., only to be greeted with the pleasing intelligence that no fresh provisions had arrived on board for the party of friends we were expecting. The captain of the tug was good enough to promise to do what he could for us on shore; but everything is brought here from Buenos Ayres, and it is too late to telegraph for a supply. We cannot help fearing that something must have happened to our steward, for he has always been most steady and respectable hitherto, and I fancy Buenos Ayres is rather a wild place. Every inquiry is to be made, and I can only trust the morning may bring us some news.

Tuesday, September 26th.—The morning was fine, with a nice breeze, but the tide was so low that we should have been unable to get alongside the pier until ten o'clock, when Tom thought we should just miss our guests. .It was therefore decided that it would be better to send the steam-tug to meet the special train, especially as, if we took the yacht in, it would be impossible to get out again in the middle of the night, when we had arranged to sail.

The steam-tug came off early, bringing two sheep, half

a bullock, and some wild ducks, much to the relief of the cook's mind; but there were no vegetables to be had on shore, and of course it was too late to send to Buenos Ayres for any. We had to do the best we could without them, therefore, and I really do not think any one knew of the dilemma we had been in, until they were told, at the end of the day. The servants all turned to and worked with a will; but it was rather a different matter from having a large luncheon party on board in the Thames, with our London servants and supplies to fall back upon.

For our own part, I think we all felt that the comparative scarcity of meat this morning was an agreeable change, after our recent experiences. Animal food is so cheap and so good in this country that at every meal four or five dishes of beef or mutton, dressed in various ways, are provided. In the camp—as all the country round Buenos Ayres is called—people eat nothing but meat, either fresh or dried, and hardly any flour with it. Especially in the more distant estancias, beef and mutton, poultry and eggs, form the staple food of the inhabitants. Very little bread is eaten, and no vegetables, and an attempt is rarely made to cultivate a garden of any sort. This year, too, the ravages of the locusts have made vegetable food scarcer than ever, and it must now be looked upon quite as a luxury by very many people; for there can be little doubt that to live entirely on meat, even of the best quality, though probably strengthening, must be exceedingly monotonous.

About one o'clock we saw the tug coming off again, this time with her decks crowded. We found she had brought us fifteen ladies and thirty gentlemen—more than we had expected, on account of the shortness of the notice we had been able to give. The luncheon was managed by dividing our guests into three parties, the coffee and dessert being served on deck; but I am afraid the last division got very hungry before their time arrived. It could not, however, be helped, and it is to be hoped that the examination of the various parts of the yacht and her contents served to while away the time. Every one seemed to be pleased with the appearance of the vessel, never having seen one like her before. Indeed, the only yacht that has ever been here previously is the 'Eothen,' which formerly belonged to us.

Mr. St. John's servant brought me a most magnificent bouquet, composed entirely of violets, arranged in the shape of a basket, three feet in width, full of camellias, and marked with my initials in alyssum. Altogether it was quite a work of art, but almost overpoweringly sweet.

It was late before our friends began the task of saying good-by—no light matter where, as in the present case, it is doubtful whether, or at any rate when, we shall meet again. At last they left us, steaming round the yacht in the tug, and giving us some hearty cheers as they passed. The Minister's flag was run up, salutes were exchanged, and the little steamer rapidly started off in the direction of the shore, followed by a dense cloud of her own smoke. Through a telescope we watched our friends disembark at the pier, and saw the train steam away; and then we turned our thoughts to the arrangements for our own departure.

Wednesday, September 27th.—A fine breeze was blowing this morning, in a favorable direction for our start, but as ten and eleven o'clock arrived, and there were still no signs of the expected stores, Tom was in despair, and wanted to sail without them. I therefore volunteered to go ashore in the gig and see what had happened to them, and telegraph, if necessary, to Mr. Crabtree. Fortunately, we met the tug on our way, and returned in tow of her to the yacht. Then, after settling a few bills, and obtaining our bill of health, we got the anchor up, and proceeded down the river under sail. Between one and two o'clock we commenced steaming, and in the course of the evening were clear of the River Plate and fairly on our way to the Straits of Magellan.

CHAPTER VIII.

RIVER PLATE TO SANDY POINT, STRAITS OF MAGELLAN.

I have seen tempests, when the scolding winds
Have riv'd the knotty oaks ; and I have seen
The ambitious ocean swell and rage and foam,
To be exalted with the threat'ning clouds :
But never till to-night, never till now
Did I go through a tempest dropping fire.

Thursday, September 28*th.*—A fine bright morning, with a strong, fair wind. The order to stop firing was given at noon, and we ceased steaming shortly after. There had evidently been a gale from the southward during the last few days, for the swell was tremendous, and not only made us all feel very uncomfortable after our long stay in harbor, but considerably diminished our speed. Still, we managed to go twenty-seven knots in two hours and a half.

I was lying down, below, after breakfast, feeling very stupid, when Mabelle rushed into the cabin, saying, 'Papa says you are to come up on deck at once, to see the ship on fire.' I rushed up quickly, hardly knowing whether she referred to our own or some other vessel, and on reaching the deck I found everybody looking at a large bark, under full sail, flying the red union-jack upside down, and with signals in her rigging, which our signal-man read as 'Ship on fire.' These were lowered shortly afterwards, and the signals, 'Come on board at once,' hoisted in their place. Still we could see no appearance of smoke or flames, but we nevertheless hauled to the wind, tacked, hove-to, and sent off a boat's crew, well armed, thinking it not impossible that a mutiny had taken place on board, and that the captain or officers, mistaking the yacht for a gunboat, had appealed to us for assistance. We were now near enough to the bark to make out her name through a glass—the 'Monkshaven,' of Whitby—and we observed a puff of smoke issue from her deck simultaneously with the arrival of our boat alongside. In the course of a few minutes, the boat returned, bringing the mate of the 'Monkshaven,' a fine-looking Norwegian, who spoke English perfectly, and who reported his ship to be sixty-eight days out from Swansea, bound for Val-

'Monkshaven' on Fire.

paraiso, with a cargo of smelting coal. The fire had first been discovered on the previous Sunday, and by 6 a.m. on Monday the crew had got up their clothes and provisions on deck, thrown overboard all articles of a combustible character, such as tar, oil, paint, spare spars and sails, planks, and ropes, and battened down the hatches. Ever since then they had all been living on deck, with no protection from the wind and sea but a canvas screen. Tom and Captain Brown proceeded on board at once. They found the deck more than a foot deep in water, and all a-wash; when the hatches were opened for a moment dense clouds of hot suffocating yellow smoke immediately poured forth, driving back all who stood near. From the captain's cabin came volumes of poisonous gas, which had found its way in through the crevices, and one man, who tried to enter, was rendered insensible.

It was perfectly evident that it would be impossible to save the ship, and the captain therefore determined, after consultation with Tom and Captain Brown, to abandon her. Some of the crew were accordingly at once brought on board the 'Sunbeam,' in our boat, which was then sent back to assist in removing the remainder, a portion of whom came in their own boat. The poor fellows were almost wild with joy at getting alongside another ship, after all the hardships they had gone through, and in their excitement they threw overboard many things which they might as well have kept, as they had taken the trouble to bring them. Our boat made three trips altogether, and by half-past six we had them all safe on board, with most of their effects, and the ship's chronometers, charts, and papers.

The poor little dinghy, belonging to the 'Monkshaven,' had been cast away as soon as the men had disembarked from her, and there was something melancholy in seeing her slowly drift away to leeward, followed by her oars and various small articles, as if to rejoin the noble ship she had so lately quitted. The latter was now hove-to, under full sail, an occasional puff of smoke alone betraying the presence of the demon of destruction within. The sky was dark and lowering, the sunset red and lurid in its grandeur, the clouds numerous and threatening, the sea high and dark, with occasional streaks of white foam. Not a breath of wind was stirring. Everything portended a gale. As we lay slowly rolling from side to side, both ship and boat were sometimes plainly visible, and then again both would disappear, for what seemed an age, in the deep trough of the South Atlantic rollers.

For two hours we could see the smoke pouring from

various portions of the ill-fated bark. Our men, who had brought off the last of her crew, reported that, as they left her, flames were just beginning to burst from the fore-hatchway; and it was therefore certain that the rescue had not taken place an hour too soon. Whilst we were at dinner, Powell called us up on deck to look at her again, when we found that she was blazing like a tar-barrel. The captain was anxious to stay by and see the last of her, but Tom was unwilling to incur the delay which this would have involved. We accordingly got up steam, and at 9 p.m. steamed round the 'Monkshaven,' as close as it was deemed prudent to go. No flames were visible then: only dense volumes of smoke and sparks; issuing from the hatches. The heat, however, was intense, and could be plainly felt, even in the cold night air, as we passed some distance to leeward. All hands were clustered in our rigging, on the deck-house or on the bridge, to see the last of the poor 'Monkshaven,' as she was slowly being burned down to the water's edge.

She was a large and nearly new (three years old) composite ship, built and found by her owners, Messrs. Smales, of Whitby, of 657 tons burden, and classed A .1 for ten years at Lloyd's. Her cargo, which consisted of coal for smelting purposes, was a very dangerous one; so much so that Messrs. Nicholas, of Sunderland, from whose mines the coal is procured, have great difficulty in chartering vessels to carry it, and are therefore in the habit of building and using their own ships for the purpose. At Buenos Ayres we were told that, of every three ships carrying this cargo round to Valparaiso or Callao, one catches fire, though the danger is frequently discovered in time to prevent much damage to the vessel or loss of life.

The crew of the 'Monkshaven,'—Danes, Norwegians, Swedes, Scotch, and Welsh—appear to be quiet, respectable men. This is fortunate, as an incursion of fifteen rough, lawless spirits on board our little vessel would have been rather a serious matter. In their hurry and fright, however, they left all their provisions behind them, and it is no joke to have to provide food for fifteen extra hungry mouths for a week or ten days, with no shops at hand from which to replenish our stores. The sufficiency of the water supply, too, is a matter for serious consideration. We have all been put on half-allowance, and sea-water only is to be used for washing purposes.

Shipwrecked Crew coming on Board.

Some account of the disaster, as gathered from the lips of various members of the crew at different times, may perhaps be interesting. It seems that, early on Monday morning, the day following that on which the fire was discovered, another bark, the 'Robert Hinds,' of Liverpool, was spoken. The captain of that vessel offered to stand by them or do anything in his power to help them; but at that time they had a fair wind for Monte Video, only 120 miles distant, and they therefore determined to run for that port, and do their best to save the ship, and possibly some of the cargo. In the course of the night, however, a terrible gale sprang up, the same, no doubt, as the one of which we had felt the effects on first leaving the River Plate. They were driven hither and thither, the sea constantly breaking over them and sweeping the decks, though fortunately without washing any of them overboard. After forty-eight hours of this rough usage the men were all exhausted, while the fire was gradually increasing in strength beneath their feet, and they knew not at what moment it might burst through the decks and envelop the whole ship in flames. They were beginning to abandon all hope of a rescue, when a sail was suddenly discovered; and as soon as the necessary flags could be found, the same signal which attracted us was displayed. The vessel, now quite close to them, proved to be a large American steamer, but she merely hoisted her own ensign and code-pennant, and then coolly steamed away to the southward. 'I think that captain deserved tarring and feathering, anyway,' one of the men said to me. Another observed, 'I wonder what will become of that man; for we had put all our lives in his hand by signaling as we did, and every seaman knows that right well.' Another said, 'When we saw that ship go away, we all gave in and lay down in despair to die. But our captain, who is very good to his crew, and a religious man too, said, "There is One above who looks after us all." That was true enough, for, about ten minutes afterwards, as I was talking to the cook, and telling him it was all over with us, I saw a sail to leeward, and informed the captain. We bore down a little, but did not like to go out of our course too much, fearing you might be a "Portuguese," and play us the same trick as the American.' (They could not understand our white ensign; for, our funnel being stowed, we looked like a sailing vessel, while all gunboats of our size are steamers.) 'When we saw it was an English vessel, and that you answered our signals and sent a boat off, we were indeed thankful; though that was nothing to what we feel now at once more having a really dry ship under our feet. Not that we have really suffered anything very terrible, for we had a bit of shelter, and plenty to eat, and the worst part was seeing our things washed overboard, and thinking perhaps we might go next. We have not had a dry deck since we left Swansea, and the pumps have been kept going most of the time. Why, with this sea, ma'am, our decks would be under water.' (This surprised me; as, though low in the water, the 'Monkshaven' did not appear to be overladen, and the Plimsoll mark was plainly visible.) 'Our boats were all ready for launching, but we had no sails, and only one rudder for the three; so we should have had hard work to fetch anywhere if we had taken to them. We lashed the two boys—apprentices, fourteen and sixteen years old—in one of the boats, for fear they should be washed overboard. The youngest of them is the only son of his mother, a widow; and you could see how she loved him by the way she had made his clothes, and fitted him out all through. He was altogether too well found for a ship like ours, but now most of his things are lost. His chest could not be got up from below, and though I borrowed an old bread-bag from the steward, it was not half big enough, and his sea-boots and things his mother had given him to keep him dry and cover his bed—not oilskins, like ours.'—' Mackintoshes,' I suggested.—' Yes, that's the name—they were all lost. It did seem a pity. The boy never thought there was much danger till this morning, when I told him all hope was gone, as the American ship had sailed away from us. He said, "Will the ship go to the bottom?" and I replied, "I fear so; but we have good boats, so keep up your heart, little man." He made no further remark, but laid down gently again, and cried a little.'

This poor child was dreadfully frightened in the small boat coming alongside, and his look of joy and relief, when once he got safely on board, was a treat to me. Every one on board, including the captain, seems to have been very kind to him. One of the men had his foot broken by the sea, and the captain himself had his leg severely injured; so the doctor has some cases at last.

It was almost impossible to sleep during the night, owing to the heavy rolling, by far the most violent that we have yet experienced.

Friday, September 29th.— Again a fine morning. A fair breeze sprang up, and, the dreaded storm having apparently passed over, we ceased steaming at 6 a.m.

All on board are now settling down into something like order. The stewards are arranging matters below, and measuring out the stores, to allowance the men for twelve days. The men belonging respectively to the port and starboard watches of the 'Monkshaven' have been placed in the corresponding watches on board the 'Sunbeam.' The cook and steward are assisting ours below, and the two boys are very happy, helping in the kitchen, and making themselves generally useful. The deck does not look quite as neat as usual. Such of the men's sea-chests as have been saved are lashed round the steam-chest, so that they can be got at easily, while their bags and other odd things have been stowed on deck, wherever they can be kept dry; for every inch of available space below is occupied. Captain Runciman is writing, with tears in his eyes, the account of the loss of his fine ship. He tells me that he tried in vain to save sixty pounds' worth of his own private charts from his cabin, but it was impossible, on account of the stifling atmosphere, which nearly overpowered him. Fortunately, all his things are insured. He drowned his favorite dog, a splendid Newfoundland, just before leaving the ship; for although a capital watch-dog, and very faithful, he was rather large and fierce; and when it was known that the 'Sunbeam' was a yacht, with ladies and children on board, he feared to introduce him. Poor fellow! I wish I had known about it in time to save his life.

The great danger of smelting coal, as a ship's cargo, besides its special liability to spontaneous combustion, appears to be that the fire may smolder in the very center of the mass for so long that, when the smoke is at last discovered, it is impossible to know how far the mischief has advanced. It may go on smoldering quietly for days, or at any moment the gas that has been generated may burst up the vessel's decks from end to end, without the slightest warning. Or it may burn downwards, and penetrate some portion of the side of the ship below water; so that, before any suspicion has been aroused, the water rushes in, and the unfortunate ship and her crew go to the bottom. On board the 'Monkshaven' the men dug down into the cargo in many places on Sunday night, only to find that the heat became more intense the deeper they went; and several of them had their hands or fingers burned in the operation.

This has been about the best day for sailing that we have had since we left the tropics. The sea has been smooth, and a fair breeze has taken us steadily along at the rate of nine knots an hour. The sun shone brightly beneath a blue sky, and the temperature is delightful. The sunset was grand, though the sky looked threatening; but the moon rose brilliantly, and until we went to bed, at ten o'clock, the evening was as perfect as the day had been. At midnight, however, Tom and I were awakened by a knock at our cabin door, and the gruff voice of Powell, saying: 'The barometer's going down very fast, please, sir, and it's lightning awful in the sou'-west. There's a heavy storm coming up.' We were soon on deck, where we found all hands busily engaged in preparing for the tempest. Around us a splendid sight presented itself. On one side a heavy bank of black clouds could be seen rapidly approaching, while the rest of the heavens were brilliantly illuminated by forked and sheet lightning, the thunder meanwhile rolling and rattling without intermission. An ominous calm followed, during which the men had barely time to lower all the sails on deck, without waiting to stow them, the foresail and jib only being left standing, when the squall struck us, not very severely, but with a blast as hot as that from a furnace. We thought worse was coming, and continued our preparations; but the storm passed rapidly away to windward, and was succeeded by torrents of rain, so that it was evident we could only have had quite the tail of it.

Saturday, September 30*th.*—The morning broke bright and clear, and was followed by a calm, bright, sunny day, of which I availed myself to take some photographs of the captain and crew of the 'Monkshaven.' The wind failed us entirely in the afternoon, and it became necessary to get up steam. In the ordinary course of things, we should probably have had sufficient patience to wait for the return of the breeze; but the recent large addition to our party made it desirable for us to lose as little time as possible in reaching Sandy Point. Another grand but wild-looking sunset seemed like the precursor of a storm; but we experienced nothing worse than a sharp squall of hot wind, accompanied by thunder and lightning.

Sunday, October 1*st.*—A fine morning, with a fair wind. At eleven we had a short service, at four a longer one, with an excellent sermon from Tom, specially adapted to the rescue of the crew of the burning ship. As usual, the sunset, which was magnificent, was succeeded by a slight storm, which passed over without doing us any harm.

I have said that it was found impossible to save any provisions from the 'Monkshaven.' As far as the men are concerned, I think this is hardly to be regretted, for I am told that the salt beef with which they were supplied had lain in pickle for so many years that the saltpeter had eaten all the nourishment out of it, and had made it so hard that the men, instead of eating it, used to amuse themselves by carving it into snuff-boxes, little models of ships, &c. I should not, however, omit to mention that Captain Runciman managed to bring away with him four excellent York hams, which he presented to us, and one of which we had to-day at dinner.

Wednesday, October 4th.—At 6 a.m., on going on deck, I found we were hove-to under steam and closely-reefed sails, a heavy gale blowing from the south-west right ahead. The screw was racing round in the air every time we encountered an unusually big wave; the spray was dashing over the vessel, and the water was rushing along the deck—altogether an uncomfortable morning. As the sun rose, the gale abated, and in the course of the day the reefs were shaken out of the sails, one by one, until, by sunset, we were once more under whole canvas, beating to windward. There were several cries of 'land ahead' during the day, but in each case a close examination, through a glass, proved that the fancied coast-line or mountain-top existed only in cloud-land.

Thursday, October 5th.—We made the land early, and most uninteresting it looked, consisting, as it did, of a low sandy shore, with a background of light clay-colored cliffs. Not a vestige of vegetation was anywhere to be seen, and I am quite at a loss to imagine what the guanacos and ostriches, with which the chart tells us the country hereabouts abounds, find to live upon. About twelve o'clock we made Cape Virgin, looking very like Berry Head to the north of Torbay, and a long spit of low sandy land, stretching out to the southward, appropriately called Dungeness.

Some of the charts brought on board by Captain Runciman were published by Messrs. Imray, of London, and in one of them it is represented that a fine fixed light has been established on Cape Virgin.* This we knew to be an impossibility, not only on account of the general character of the country, but because no indication is given of the light in our newest Admiralty charts. Captain Runciman, however, had more confidence in the correctness of his own chart, and could hardly believe his eyes when

---

* I have since received a letter from Messrs. Imray requesting me to state that the light was inserted on erroneous information from the hydrographic office at Washington, and has since been erased from their charts.

he saw that the light really had no existence on the bare bleak headland. His faith was terribly shaken, and I hope he will not omit to call Messrs. Imray's attention to the matter on his return home; for the mistake is most serious, and one which might lead to the destruction of many a good ship.

About two o'clock we saw in the far distance what looked at first like an island, and then like smoke, but gradually shaped itself into the masts, funnel, and hull of a large steamer. From her rig we at once guessed her to be the Pacific Company's mail boat, homeward bound. When near enough, we accordingly hoisted our number, and signaled 'We wish to communicate,' whereupon she bore down upon us and ceased steaming. We then rounded up under her lee and lowered a boat, and Tom, Mabelle, and I, with Captain Runciman and four or five of the shipwrecked crew, went on board. Our advent caused great excitement, and seamen and passengers all crowded into the bows to watch us. As we approached the ladder the passengers ran aft, and directly we reached the deck the captain took possession of Tom, the first and second officers of Mabelle and myself, while Captain Runciman and each of his crew were surrounded by a little audience eager to know what had happened, and all about it. At first it was thought that we all wanted a passage, but when we explained matters Captain Thomas, the commander of the 'Illimani,' very kindly undertook to receive all our refugees and convey them to England. We therefore sent the gig back for the rest of the men and the chests of the whole party, and then availed ourselves of the opportunity afforded by the delay to walk round the ship. It was most amusing to see the interest with which we were regarded by all on board. Passengers who had never been seen out of their berths since leaving Valparaiso, and others who were indulging, at the time of our visit, in the luxury of a 'day sleep,' between the twelve-o'clock luncheon and four-o'clock dinner, suddenly made their appearance, in dressing-gowns and wraps, with disheveled hair and wide-opened eyes, gazing in mute astonishment at us, quite unable to account for our mysterious arrival on board in this out-of-the-way spot. A mail steamer does not stop for a light cause, and it was therefore evident to them that the present was no ordinary occurrence. The captain told us that the last time he passed through the Straits he picked up two boats' crews, who had escaped from a burning ship, and who had suffered indescribable hardships before they were rescued.

Captain Runciman is convinced, after comparing notes with the chief officer of the 'Illimani,' that the vessel which refused to notice his signal of distress was the 'Wilmington,' sent down from New York, with a party of forty wreckers, to try and get the steamer 'Georgia' off the rocks near Port Famine, in the Straits of Magellan. If this be so, it is the more surprising that no attempt was made to render assistance to the 'Monkshaven,' provided her signals were understood, as the 'Wilmington' had plenty of spare hands, and could not have been in a particular hurry. Moreover, one would think that, with her powerful engines, she might have made an attempt to tow the distressed vessel into Monte Video, and so secure three or four thousand pounds of salvage money.*

The captain of the 'Illimani' kindly gave us half a bullock, killed this morning, a dozen live ducks and chickens, and the latest newspapers. Thus supplied with food for body and mind, we said farewell, and returned to the 'Sunbeam;' our ensigns were duly dipped, we steamed away on our respective courses, and in less than an hour we were out of sight of each other. It is a sudden change for the 'Monkshaven' men, who were all very reluctant to leave the yacht. Many of them broke down at the last moment, particularly when it came to saying

---

* See p. 125.

good-by to Tom and me, at the gangway of the steamer. They had seemed thoroughly to appreciate any kindnesses they received while with us, and were anxious to show their gratitude in every possible way. The two boys, especially, were in great grief at their departure, and were very loath to part with their boatswain, who remains with us to make up our complement.*

About 8 p.m we anchored for the night in Possession Bay. It was thick at sunset, but afterwards clear and cold, with a splendid moon.

Friday, October 6th.—We got under way at 5.30 a.m., and steamed past the low sandy coast of Patagonia and the rugged mountains of Terra del Fuego, and through the First and Second Narrows, to Cape Negro, where the

---

* After our return to England the following letter reached us from Messrs. Smales :—

            Whitby, June 30th, 1877.
'Thomas Brassey, Esq.

 'Dear Sir,—Observing by the newspapers that you have returned home after your cruise, we take this opportunity of thanking you most heartily for the valuable assistance you rendered to the crew of our late bark "Monkshaven," in lat. 43 28 S., lon. 62 21 W., after she proved to be on fire and beyond saving. Your kind favor of October 1 last duly reached us, and it was very satisfactory to know from an authority like your own, that all was done under the trying circumstances that was possible to save the ship and cargo. The inconvenience of having so many extra hands for the time on board your vessel must have tried your resources ; but you will be probably aware that the Board of Trade willingly compensate for loss sustained in rescuing a crew, when a claim is made. You will be glad to learn that the master and crew arrived all well, in due course, at Liverpool, by the " Illimani," and were very grateful for your kindness to them. Our ill-fated vessel must have sunk very soon after you took off the crew, as nothing more has been heard of her, and it was a most fortunate circumstance that you were so near at hand ; more especially as the captain reported to us that a vessel carrying the American colors took no notice of his signal of distress. As shipowners, we generally find that our own countrymen are more heroic, and always ready to lend a helping hand to brother mariners in distress, so that, as you say, we do not doubt you experienced some satisfaction in rendering this service.—Trusting that you have enjoyed your trip, we beg to remain yours, truly obliged,

               'Smales Brothers.'

character of the scenery began to improve a little, the vegetation gradually changing from low scrubby brushwood to respectable-sized trees. When passing between Elizabeth Island, so named by Sir Francis Drake, and the island of Santa Madalena, we looked in vain for the myriads of seals, otters, and sea-lions with which this portion of the Straits is said to abound ; but we saw only seven or eight little black spots on the shore, in the distance, which disappeared into the sea as we approached.

At 3 p.m. we reached Sandy Point, the only civilized place in the Straits. It is a Chilian settlement, and a large convict establishment has been formed here by the Government. Almost before we had dropped our anchor, the harbor-master came on board, closely followed by the officers of the two Chilian men-of-war lying in the harbor. The rain, which had been threatening all day, now descended in torrents, and we landed in a perfect downpour. We thought the pier at Buenos Ayres unsafe and rickety, but here matters were still worse, for the head of the structure had been completely washed away by a gale, and no little care was necessary in order to step across the broken timbers in safety. The town, which contains between 1,200 and 1,300 inhabitants, is composed entirely of one-storied log huts, with slate or tile roofs, and with or without verandas. They are all arranged in squares, separated from each other by wide roads; and the whole settlement is surrounded by stockades. At the farther end of the town stands the convict prison, distinguished by its tower, and the Governor's house, which, though built of wood, is the most pretentious-looking edifice in the place. There is a nice little church close by, and some tidy-looking barracks.

We went straight to the house of the British Vice-Consul, who received us very kindly, and promised to do what he could to assist us in obtaining supplies; but the resources of the place are limited, and eggs, ship's beef and biscuits, and water, will, I expect, be the sum total of what we shall be able to procure. In fact, it is rather doubtful whether we shall even be able to renew our stock of coal. In the meantime we started off to potter about the town, finding, however, very little to amuse us. There were some new-laid ostrich eggs to be bought, and some queer-looking worked Patagonian saddle-bags.

I fear we shall not see any of the Patagonians themselves, for they come to the colony only three or four times a year, to purchase supplies, and to sell skins and ostrich eggs. They are a mounted tribe of Indians, living on the northern plains, and are now on their way down here, to pay one of their periodical visits; but, being encumbered with their families, they move very slowly, and are not expected to arrive for another ten days. They will no doubt bring a splendid supply of skins, just too late for us, which is rather disappointing, particularly as we are not likely to have another opportunity of meeting with them at any of the places we touch at. They live so far in the interior of the country that they very seldom visit the coast.

We went to see three Fuegian females, who are living in a house belonging to the medical officer of the colony. They were picked up a short time since by a passing steamer from a canoe, in which they had evidently sought refuge from some kind of cruelty or oppression. The biggest of them, a stout, fine-looking woman, had a terrible gash in her leg, quite recently inflicted, and the youngest was not more than eight years old. They appeared cheerful and happy, but we were told that they are not likely to live long. After the free life and the exposure to which they have been accustomed, civilization—in the shape of clothing and hot houses—almost always kills them. Their lungs become diseased, and they die miserably. Their skin is slightly copper-colored, their complexions high-colored, their hair thick and black; and, though certainly not handsome, they are by no means so repulsive as

I had expected from the descriptions of Cook, Dampier, Darwin, and other more recent travelers.

Saturday, October 7th.—My birthday. Tom gave me a beautiful guanaco-skin robe, and the children presented me with two ostrich rugs. The guanaco is a kind of large deer, and it is said that the robes made from its skin are the warmest in the world. People here assure me that with the hair turned inside, these robes have afforded them sufficient protection to enable them to sleep in comfort in the open air, exposed to snow, frost, and rain. They are made from the skin of the young fawns, killed before they are thirteen days old, or, better still, from the skins of those which have never had an independent existence. In color, the animals are a yellowish brown on the back, and white underneath, and they are so small that when each skin is split up it produces only two triangular patches, about the size of one's hand. A number of these are then, with infinite trouble, sewed neatly together by the Indian women, who use the fine leg-sinews of the ostrich as thread. Those worn by the caciques, or chiefs, have generally a pattern in the center, a brown edging, and spots of red and blue paint on the part which is worn outwards. Such robes are particularly difficult to obtain, on account of the labor and time necessary to produce them. Each cacique keeps several wives constantly employed in making them, of the best as well as of the ordinary description. The ostrich rugs, which are made here, are more ornamental, though not so warm and light as the guanaco robes. They are made of the entire skin of the ostrich, from which the long wing-feathers have been pulled out. Mabelle has been given a beautiful little rug composed of the skins of thirty little ostriches, all from one nest, killed when they were a fortnight old, each skin resembling a prettily marked ball of fluff.

At eleven o'clock we went ashore. The Governor had kindly provided horses for all the party, and while they were being saddled I took some photographs. There are plenty of horses here, but the only saddles and bridles to be had are those used by the natives. The saddles are very cumbrous and clumsy to look at, though rather picturesque. They are formed of two bits of wood, covered with about a dozen sheepskins and ponchos; not at all uncomfortable to ride in, and very suitable for a night's bivouac in the open. 'Plenty of nice soft rugs to lie upon and cover yourself with, instead of a hard English saddle for your bed and stirrups for blankets,' as a native once said, when asked which he preferred. About one o'clock we started, accompanied by the officers commanding the garrison and two attendant cavaliers, equipped in Chilian style, with enormous carved modern stirrups, heavy bits and spurs much bigger than those whose size struck us so much in the Argentine Republic. We had a pleasant ride, first across a sandy plain and through one or two small rivers, to a saw-mill, situated on the edge of an extensive forest, through which we proceeded for some miles. The road was a difficult one, and our progress was but slow, being often impeded by a morass or by the trunk of a tree which had fallen right across the path, and was now rapidly rotting into touchwood under the influence of the damp atmosphere and incessant rain. Lichens of every color and shape abounded, and clothed the trunks gracefully, contrasting with the tender spring tints of the leaves, while the long hairy tillandsia, like an old man's beard, three or four feet long, hung down from the topmost branches. The ground was carpeted with moss, interspersed with a few early spring flowers, and the whole scene, though utterly unlike that presented by any English forest, had a strange weird beauty of its own. Not a sound could be heard; not a bird, beast, or insect was to be seen. The larger trees were principally a peculiar sort of beech and red cedar, but all kinds of evergreens, known to us at home as shrubs, such as laurestina and various firs, here attain the proportions of forest-trees. There is also a tree called Winter's Bark (*Drimys Winteri*), the leaves and bark of which are hot and bitter, and form an excellent substitute for quinine. But the most striking objects were the evergreen berberis and mahonia, and the Darwinii, the larger sort of which was covered with brilliant orange, almost scarlet, flowers, which hung down in bunches of the shape and size of small outdoor grapes.

On our way back we took a sharp turn leading to the sea-shore, to which the forest extends in places, and rode along the beach towards the town. It was low water, or this would not have been possible, and as it was, we often had considerable difficulty in making our way between wood and water. The day was bright and clear, with a bitterly cold wind and occasional heavy showers of rain; a fair average day for Sandy Point. It is farther west, they say, that the weather is so hopeless. Lieutenant Byron, in his terribly interesting account of the wreck of the 'Wager,' says that one fine day in three months is the most that can be expected. I wonder, not without misgivings, if we really shall encounter all the bad weather we not only read of but hear of from every one we meet. Though very anxious to see the celebrated Straits, I shall not be sorry when we are safely through, and I trust that the passage may not occupy the whole of the three weeks which Tom has been advised to allow for it.

We saw a few sea-birds, especially some 'steamer-ducks,' so called from their peculiar mode of progression through the water. They neither swim nor fly, but use their wings like the paddles of a steamer, with a great noise and splutter, and go along very fast. On reaching the plains we had an opportunity of testing the speed of our horses, which warmed us up a little after our slow progress by the water's edge in the bitter wind. We rode all round the stockades, outside the town, before dismounting, but I saw nothing of special interest. Before the party broke up, arrangements were made for us to go to-morrow to one of the government corrals, to see the cattle lassoed and branded—an operation which is always performed twice a year.

We reached the yacht again at half-past five. Dr. Fenton came on board to dinner, and from him we heard a great deal about the colony, the Patagonians or Horse Indians, and the Fuegians or Canoe Indians. The former inhabit, or rather roam over, a vast tract of country. They are almost constantly on horseback, and their only shelter consists of toldos, or tents, made of the skins of the old guanacos, stretched across a few poles. They are tall and strong, averaging six feet in height, and are bulky in proportion; but their size is nothing like so great as old travelers have represented. Both men and women wear a long flowing mantle of skins, reaching from the waist to the ankle, with a large loose piece hanging down on one side, ready to be thrown over their heads when necessary, which is fastened by a large flat pin hammered out either from the rough silver or from a dollar. This, their sole garment, has the effect of adding greatly in appearance to their height. They never wash, but daub their bodies with paint and grease, especially the women. Their only weapons are knives and bolas, the latter of which they throw with unerring precision. During their visits to the Sandy Point settlement their arms are always taken from them, for they are extremely quarrelsome, particularly when drunk. Nobody has been able to ascertain that they possess any form of sacred belief, or that they perform any religious ceremonies. Their food consists principally of the flesh of mares, troops of which animals always accompany them on their excursions. They also eat ostrich-flesh, which is considered a great delicacy, as well as the fish the women catch, and the birds' eggs they find. Vegetable food is almost unknown to them, and bread is never used, though they do sometimes purchase a little flour, rice, and a few biscuits, on the occasion of their visits to the colony.

The Fuegians, or Canoe Indians, as they are generally

called, from their living so much on the water, and having no settled habitations on shore, are a much smaller race of savages, inhabiting Terra del Fuego—literally Land of Fire—so called from the custom the inhabitants have of lighting fires on prominent points as signals of assembly. The English residents here invariably call it Fireland—a name I had never heard before, and which rather puzzled me at first. Whenever it is observed that a ship is in distress, or that shipwrecked mariners have been cast ashore, the signal-fires appear as if by magic, and the natives flock together like vultures round a carcass. On the other hand, if all goes well, vessels often pass through the Straits without seeing a single human being, the savages and their canoes lying concealed beneath the overhanging branches of trees on the shore. They are cannibals, and are placed by Darwin in the lowest scale of humanity. An old author describes them as 'magpies in chatter, baboons in countenance, and imps in treachery.' Those frequenting the eastern end of the Straits wear—if they wear anything at all—a deerskin mantle, descending to the waist: those at the western end wear cloaks made from the skin of the sea-otter. But most of them are quite naked. Their food is of the most meager description, and consists mainly of shell-fish, sea-eggs, for which the women dive with much dexterity, and fish, which they train their dogs to assist them in catching. These dogs are sent into the water at the entrance to a narrow creek or small bay, and they then bark and flounder about and drive the fish before them into shallow water, where they are caught.

Bishop Selwyn, of the Falkland Islands, has been cruising about these parts in a small schooner, and visiting the natives for the last twelve years, and the Governor here tells us that he has done much good in promoting their civilization; while the hardships he has endured, and the difficulties and dangers he has surmounted, have required almost superhuman energy and fortitude on his part.

The Fuegians, as far as is known, have no religion of their own.

The 'Wilmington' came in this morning. Her captain declares that as the 'Monkshaven' was not hove-to, he never thought that there could be anything seriously amiss with her. His glass was not good enough to enable him to make out the union-jack reversed, or the signal of distress, which he therefore supposed to be merely the ship's number. It was satisfactory to hear this explanation; and as not only the interests of humanity, but his own, were involved, there is every reason to believe that his account of the transaction is perfectly true.

CHAPTER IX.

SANDY POINT TO LOTA BAY.

And far abroad the canvas wings extend,
Along the glassy plain the vessel glides,
While azure radiance trembles on her sides ;
The lunar rays in long reflection gleam,
With silver deluging the fluid stream.

Sunday, October 8th.—At 6 a.m. we weighed anchor, and proceeded on our voyage. At first there was not much to admire in the way of scenery, the shores being low and sandy, with occasional patches of scrubby brushwood, and a background of granite rocks and mountains.

Soon after passing Port Famine we saw the bold outline of Cape Froward, the southernmost point of South America, stretching into the Straits. It is a fine headland, and Tom ordered the engines to be stopped in order to enable Mr. Bingham to sketch, and me to photograph, both it and the splendid view back through the channel we had just traversed to the snowy range of mountains in the distance, crowned by Mount Sarmiento, not unlike the Matterhorn in appearance.

At this point the weather generally changes, and I suppose we must look forward to living in mackintoshes for some little time to come.

In the afternoon, when in English Reach, where many vessels have been lost, great excitement was caused on board by the appearance of a canoe on our port bow. She was stealing out from the Barbara Channel, and as she appeared to be making direct for us, Tom ordered the engines to be slowed. Her occupants thereupon redoubled their efforts, and came paddling towards us, shouting and making the most frantic gesticulations, one man waving a skin round his head with an amount of energy that threatened to upset the canoe. This frail craft, upon a nearer inspection, proved to be made only of rough planks, rudely tied together with the sinews of animals; in fact, one of

Bartering with Fuegians.

the party had to bale constantly, in order to keep her afloat. We flung them a rope, and they came alongside, shouting 'Tobáco, galléta' (biscuit), a supply of which we threw down to them, in exchange for the skins they had been waving; whereupon the two men stripped themselves of the skin mantles they were wearing, made of eight or ten sea-otter skins sewed together with finer sinews than those used for the boat, and handed them up, clamoring for more tobacco, which we gave them, together with some beads and knives.* Finally, the woman, influenced by this

---

* These skins proved to be the very finest quality ever plucked, and each separate skin was valued in England at from £4 to £5.

example, parted with her sole garment, in return for a little more tobacco, some beads, and some looking-glasses I had thrown into the canoe.

The party consisted of a man, a woman, and a lad; and I think I never saw delight more strongly depicted than it was on the faces of the two latter, when they handled, for the first time in their lives probably, some strings of blue, red, and green glass beads. They had two rough pots, made of bark, in the boat, which they also sold, after which they reluctantly departed, quite naked but very happy, shouting and jabbering away in the most inarticulate language imaginable. It was with great difficulty we could make them let go the rope, when we went ahead, and I was quite afraid they would be upset. They were all fat and healthy-looking, and, though not handsome, their appearance was by no means repulsive; the countenance of the woman, especially, wore quite a pleasing expression, when lighted up with smiles at the sight of the beads and looking-glasses. The bottom of their canoe was covered with branches, amongst which the ashes of a recent fire were distinguishable. Their paddles were of the very roughest description, consisting simply of split branches of trees, with wider pieces tied on at one end with the sinews of birds or beasts.

Steaming ahead, past Port Gallant, we had a glorious view over Carlos III. Island and Thornton Peaks, until, at about seven o'clock, we anchored in the little harbor of Borja Bay. This place is encircled by luxuriant vegetation, overhanging the water, and is set like a gem amid the granite rocks close at hand, and the far-distant snowy mountains.

Our carpenter had prepared a board, on which the name of the yacht and the date had been painted, to be fixed on shore, as a record of our visit; and as soon as the anchor was down we all landed, the gentlemen with their guns, and the crew fully armed with pistols and rifles, in case of accident. The water was quite deep close to the shore, and we had no difficulty in landing, near a small waterfall. To penetrate far inland, however, was not so easy, owing to the denseness of the vegetation. Large trees had fallen, and, rotting where they lay, under the influence of the humid atmosphere, had become the birthplace of thousands of other trees, shrubs, plants, ferns, mosses, and lichens. In fact, in some places we might almost be said to be walking on the tops of the trees, and first one and then another of the party found his feet suddenly slipping through into unknown depths below. Under these circumstances we were contented with a very short ramble, and having filled our baskets with a varied collection of mosses and ferns, we returned to the shore, where we found many curious shells and some excellent mussels. While we had been thus engaged, the carpenter and some of the crew were employed in nailing up our board on a tree we had selected for the purpose. It was in company with the names of many good ships, a portion of which only were still legible, many of the boards having fallen to the ground and become quite rotten.

Near the beach we found the remains of a recent fire, and in the course of the night the watch on deck, which was doubled and well armed, heard shouts and hoots proceeding from the neighborhood of the shore. Towards morning, too, the fire was relighted, from which it was evident that the natives were not far off, though they did not actually put in an appearance. I suppose they think there is a probability of making something out of us by fair means, and that, unlike a sealing schooner, with only four or five hands on board, and no motive power but her sails, we are rather too formidable to attack.

Monday, October 9th.—We are indeed most fortunate in having another fine day. At 6 a.m. the anchor was weighed, and we resumed our journey. It was very cold, but that was not to be wondered at, surrounded as we are on every side by magnificent snow-clad mountains and superb glaciers. First we passed Snowy Sound, in Terra del Fuego, at the head of which is an immense blue glacier. Then came Cape Notch, so called from its looking as if it had had a piece chopped out of it. Within a few yards of the surrounding glaciers, and close to the sea, the vegetation is abundant, and in many places semi-tropical, a fact which is due to the comparatively mild winters, the temperate summers, the moist climate, and the rich soil of these parts. Passing up English Reach, we now caught our first glimpse of the Pacific Ocean, between Cape Pillar on one side, and Westminster Hall, Shell Bay and Lecky Point, on the other. Steering to the north, and leaving these on the left hand, we issued from the Straits of Magellan, and entered Smyth's Channel, first passing Glacier Bay and Ice Sound, names which speak for themselves. Mount Joy, Mount Burney, with its round snow-covered summit, rising six thousand feet from the water, and several unnamed peaks, were gradually left behind; until, at last, after threading a labyrinth of small islands, we anchored for the night in Otter Bay, a snug little cove, at the entrance to the intricacies of the Mayne Channel.

It was almost dark when we arrived, but the children, Captain Brown, and I, went on shore for a short time, and gathered a few ferns and mosses. We also found the embers of a fire, which showed that the natives were not far off, and we therefore thought it prudent to hurry on board again before nightfall. No names of ships were to be seen; but, in our search for ferns, we may possibly have overlooked them. We have not come across any Fuegians to-day, though in two of the places we have passed—Shell Bay and Deep Harbor, where a few wigwams are left standing as a sort of head-quarters—they are generally to be met with. During the night the watch again heard the natives shouting; but no attempt was made to re-light the fire we had noticed, until we were steaming out of the bay the next morning.

Tuesday, October 10*th.*—In the early morning, when

we resumed our voyage, the weather was still fine; but a few light clouds were here and there visible, and an icy wind, sweeping down from the mountains, made it appear very cold, though the thermometer—which averages, I think, 40° to 50° all the year round—was not really low. The line of perpetual snow commences here at an elevation of from 2,500 to 3,500 feet only, which adds greatly to the beauty of the scene; and as it is now early spring the snow is still unmelted 500 feet, and even less, from the shore. The stupendous glaciers run right down into the sea, and immense masses of ice, sometimes larger than a ship, are continually breaking off, with a noise like thunder, and falling into the water, sending huge waves across to the opposite shore, and sometimes completely blocking up the channels. Some of these glaciers, composed entirely of blue and green ice and the purest snow, are fifteen and twenty miles in length. They are by far the finest we have, any of us, ever seen; and even those of Norway and Switzerland sink into comparative insignificance beside them. The mountains here are not so high as those of Europe, but they really appear more lofty, as their entire surface, from the water's edge to the extreme summit, is clearly visible. At this end of the Straits they terminate in peaks, resembling Gothic spires, carved in the purest snow; truly 'virgin peaks,' on which the eye of man has but seldom rested, and which his foot has never touched. They are generally veiled in clouds of snow, mist, and driving rain, and it is quite the exception to see them as distinctly as we now do.

After leaving Mayne's Channel, and passing through Union and Collingwood Sounds, we found ourselves beneath the shadow of the splendid Cordilleras of Sarmiento —quite distinct from Mount Sarmiento, already referred to—along the foot of which extended the largest glacier we have yet seen.* With Tarleton Pass on our right

---

* I should explain that the names of places in these Straits frequently occur in duplicate, and even triplicate, which is rather confusing.

hand, and Childer's Pass on the left, we came in sight of Owen's Island, one extremity of which is called Mayne Head, and the other Cape Brassey, these places having all been so named by Captain Mayne, during his survey in the 'Nassau,' in 1869. Near the island of Esperanza, the clouds having by that time completely cleared away, and the sun shining brightly, we had a splendid view of another range of snowy mountains, with Stoke's Monument towering high in their midst. The numerous floating icebergs added greatly to the exquisite beauty of the scene. Some loomed high as mountains, while others had melted into the most fanciful and fairy-like shapes— huge swans, full-rigged ships, schooners under full sail, and a hundred other fantastic forms and devices. The children were in ecstasies at the sight of them.

As we gradually opened out our anchorage—Puerto Bueno—we found a steamer already lying there, which proved to be the 'Dacia,' telegraph ship, just in from the Pacific coast. Having dropped our anchor at about 5 p.m., we all went on shore, armed as before, some of the gentlemen hoping to find a stray duck or two, at a freshwater lake, a little way inland. We met several of the officers of the 'Dacia,' who, being the first comers, did the honors of the place, and told us all they knew about it. The vegetation was as luxuriant and beautiful as usual— in fact, rather more so; for we are now advancing northwards at the rate of about a hundred miles a day. There were no ducks in the lake, but we enjoyed the scramble alongside it, to the point where it falls over some rocks into the sea. The gig was drawn under this waterfall, and having been loaded to her thwarts with about three tons and a half of excellent water, she was then towed off to the yacht, where the water was emptied into our tanks, which were thus filled to the brim. A small iceberg, also towed alongside, afforded us a supply of ice; and we were thus cheaply provided with a portion of the requisite supplies for our voyage. The 'Dacia' had an iceberg half as big as herself lying alongside her, and all hands were at work until late at night, aided by the light of lanterns and torches, chopping the ice up and stowing it away.

Our boat being thus engaged, we were obliged to wait on shore until long past dark; but as we were a large and strong party, it did not much matter. Our men amused themselves by collecting a number of large and excellent mussels, some of which, distinguishable by the peculiar appearance of their shells, arising from a diseased condition of the fish, contained from ten to thirty very small seed pearls. The captain of the 'Dacia' came to dinner, and the officers in the evening; and they gave us much valuable information about the anchorages farther up the Straits, and many other things. The captain kindly gave Tom all his Chilian charts of the Darien Channel, which has not yet been fully surveyed by the English Government, though the 'Nassau' passed through in 1869.

Wednesday, October 11th.—I never in my life saw anything so beautiful as the view when I came on deck this morning, at a quarter to five. The moon was shining, large and golden, high in the heavens; the rosy streaks of dawn were just tingeing the virgin snow on the highest peaks with faint but ever-deepening color; whilst all around, the foliage, rocks, and icebergs were still wrapped in the deepest shade. As the sun rose, the pink summits of the mountains changed to gold and yellow, and then to dazzling white, as the light crept down into the valleys, illuminating all the dark places, and bringing out the shades of olive-greens, grays, and purples, in the most wonderful contrasts and combinations of color. The grandeur of the scene increased with every revolution of the screw, and when fairly in the Guia narrows we were able to stop and admire it a little more at our leisure, Mr. Bingham making some sketches, while I took some photographs. To describe the prospect in detail is quite impossible. Imagine the grandest Alpine scene you ever saw, with tall snowy peaks and pinnacles rising from huge domed tops, and vast fields of unbroken snow; glaciers, running down *into* the sea, at the heads of the various bays; each bank and promontory richly clothed with vegetation of every shade of green; bold rocks and noble cliffs, covered with many-hued lichens; the floating icebergs; the narrow channel itself, blue as the sky above, dotted with small islands, each a mass of verdure, and reflecting on its glassy surface every object with such distinctness that it was difficult to say where the reality ended and the image began. I have seen a photograph of the Mirror Lake, in California, which, as far as I know, is the only thing that could possibly give one an idea of the marvelous effect of these reflections. Unfit Bay, on Chatham Island, looking towards the mountains near Pill Channel, and Ladder Hill, which looks as if a flight of steps had been cut upon its face, were perhaps two of the most striking points amid all this loveliness.

All too soon came the inevitable order to steam ahead; and once more resuming our course, we passed through Innocents and Conception Channels, and entered Wide Channel, which is frequently blocked up with ice at this time of year, though to-day we only met with a few icebergs on their way down from Eyre Sound.

I have already referred to the extraordinary shapes assumed by some of the mountain peaks. That appropriately called Singular Peak — on Chatham Island — and Two-peak Mountain and Cathedral Mountain—both on Wellington Island—specially attracted our attention to-day. The first-named presents a wonderful appearance, from whichever side you view it; the second reminds one of the beautiful double spires at Tours; while the last resembles the tapering spire of a cathedral, rising from a long roof, covered with delicate towers, fret-work, and angles. In Wide Channel we felt really compelled to stop again to admire some of the unnamed mountains. One we christened Spire Mountain, to distinguish it from the rest: it consisted of a single needle-like point, piercing deep into the blue vaults of heaven, and surrounded by a cluster of less lofty but equally sharp pinnacles. This group rose from a vast chain of exquisitely tinted snow-peaks, that looked almost as if they rested on the vast glacier beneath, seamed with dark blue and green crevasses and fissures.

All this time the weather continued perfect. Not a cloud was to be seen, the sun was hot and bright, and the sky was blue enough to rival that of classic Italy. If we could but be sure that this delightful state of things would continue, how pleasant it would be to stop and explore some of these places! We have, however, been so frequently warned of the possibility of detention of days and even weeks at anchor, owing to bad weather, that we are hurrying on as fast as we can, expecting that every day will bring the much-dreaded deluge, gale, or fog. In thick weather it is simply impossible to proceed; and if it comes on suddenly, as it generally does, and finds you far from an anchorage, there is nothing to be done but to heave-to and wait till it clears, sending a party ashore if possible to light a fire, to serve as a landmark, and to enable you to maintain your position. How thankful I am that we have been hitherto able to make the passage under such favorable circumstances! It has been a vision of beauty and variety, the recollection of which can never be effaced.

Europe Inlet, on our right, going up Wide Channel, was full of ice. Husband's Inlet looked as if it was frozen over at the farther end, and Penguin Inlet seemed quite choked up with huge hummocks and blocks of ice. Tom therefore decided not to attempt the passage of Icy Reach, for fear of being stopped, but to go round Saumarez Island to Port Grappler by way of Chasm Reach, rather a longer route. It was a happy decision; for nothing could exceed the weird, impressive splendor of this portion of the Straits. We were passing through a deep, gloomy mountain gorge, with high perpendicular cliffs on either side. Below, all was wrapped in the deepest shade. Far above, the sun gilded the snowy peaks and many-tinted foliage with his departing light, that slowly turned to rose-color ere the shades of evening crept over all, and the stars began to peep out, one by one. We could trace from the summit to the base of a lofty mountain the course of a stupendous avalanche, which had recently rushed down into the sea, crushing and destroying everything in its way, and leaving a broad track of desolation behind it. It must for a time have completely filled up the narrow channel; and woe to any unfortunate vessel that might happen to be there at such a moment!

Port Grappler is rather a difficult place to make in the dark; but Tom managed it with much dexterity, and by eight o'clock we were safely anchored for the night. We all wanted Tom to stay here to-morrow to get some rest, which we much need, but he was determined to start at five o'clock in the morning as usual, for fear of being caught by bad weather. Even I, who have of course had no anxiety as to the navigation, felt so fatigued from having been on the bridge the whole day since very early this morning, that I went straight to bed before dinner, in order to be ready for to-morrow.

Thursday, October 12*th.*—A day as perfect as yesterday succeeded a clear cold night. We weighed anchor at 5.15 a.m., and, retracing our course for a few miles, passed round the end of Saumarez Island, and entered the narrow channel leading to Indian Reach. The greatest care is here necessary to avoid several sunken rocks, which have already proved fatal to many ships, a large German steamer having been wrecked as recently as last year. The smooth but treacherous surface of the channel reflected sharply the cliffs and foliage, and its mirror-like stillness was only broken at rare intervals, by the sudden appearance of a seal in search of a fresh supply of air, or by the efforts, delayed until the very last moment, of a few steamer-ducks, gannets, or cormorants, to get out of our way.

Having accomplished the passage of Indian Reach in safety, we were just passing Eden Harbor, when the cry of 'Canoe ahead!' was raised. A boat was seen paddling out towards us from behind Moreton Island, containing about half-a-dozen people, apparently armed with bows and arrows and spears, and provided with fishing-rods, which projected on either side. One man was standing up and waving, in a very excited manner, something which turned out ultimately to be a piece of cotton-waste. Our engines having been stopped, the canoe came alongside, and we beheld six wild-looking half-naked creatures —two men, three women, and a very small boy, who was crouching over a fire at the bottom of the boat. There were also four sharp, cheery-looking little dogs, rather like Esquimaux dogs, only smaller, with prick ears and curly tails, who were looking over the side and barking vigorously in response to the salutations of our pugs. One man had on a square robe of sea-otter skins, thrown over his shoulders, and laced together in front, two of the women wore sheepskins, and the rest of the party were absolutely naked. Their black hair was long and shaggy, and they all clamored loudly in harsh guttural tones, accompanied by violent gesticulations, for 'tabáco' and 'galléta.' We got some ready for them, and also some beads, knives, and looking-glasses, but through some mistake they did not manage to get hold of our rope in time, and as our way carried us ahead they were left behind. The passage was narrow, and the current strong, and Tom was anxious to save the tide in the dangerous English Narrows. We could not, therefore, give them another chance of communicating with us, and accordingly we went on our way, followed by what were, I have no doubt, the curses—not only deep, but loud—of the whole party, who indulged at the same time in the most furious and threatening gestures. I was quite sorry for their disappointment at losing their hoped-for luxuries, to say nothing of our own at missing the opportunity of bargaining for some more furs and curiosities.

Shortly afterwards there were seen from the masthead crowds of natives among the trees armed with long spears, bows, and arrows, busily engaged pushing off their canoes from their hiding-places in creeks and hollows; so perhaps it was just as well we did not stop, or we might have been surrounded. Not far from here are the English Narrows, a passage which is a ticklish but interesting piece of navigation. A strong current prevails, and, to avoid a shoal, it is necessary at one point to steer so close to the western shore that the bowsprit almost projects over the land, the branches of the trees almost sweep the rigging, and the rocks almost scrape the side of the vessel. Two men were placed at the wheel, as a matter of precaution, and we appeared to be steering straight for the shore, at full speed, till Tom suddenly gave the order 'Hard a port!' and the 'Sunbeam' instantly flew round and rushed swiftly past the dangerous spot into wider waters. It is just here that Captain Trivett was knocked off the bridge of his vessel by the boughs—a mishap he warned Tom against before we left England.

Whilst in the Narrows we looked back, to see everything bright and cheerful, but ahead all was black and dismal: the sky and sun were obscured, the tops of the mountains hidden, and the valleys filled up with thick fog and clouds—all which seemed to indicate the approach of a storm of rain, although the glass was still very high. We went up South Reach and North Reach, in the Messier Channel, till, just as we were off Liberta Bay, in lat. 48° 50' S., long. 74° 25'. W., the blackest of the black clouds came suddenly down upon us, and descended upon the deck in a tremendous shower—not of rain, but of *dust* and *ashes*. Windows, hatches, and doors were shut as soon as we discovered the nature of this strange visitation, and in about half an hour we were through the worst of it: whereupon dust-pans, brooms, and dusters came into great requisition. It took us completely by surprise, for we had no reason to expect anything of the sort. Assuming the dust to be of volcanic origin, it must have traveled an immense distance; the nearest volcano, as far as we know, being that of Corcovado, in the island of Chiloe, nearly 300 miles off. We had heard from Sir Woodbine Parish, and others at Buenos Ayres, of the terrible blinding dust-storms which occur *there*, causing utter darkness for a space of ten or fifteen minutes; but Buenos Ayres is on the edge of a river, with hundreds and thousands of leagues of sandy plains behind it, the soil of which is only kept together by the roots of the wiry pampas grass. For this dust to reach the Messier Channel, where we now are, it would have to surmount two chains of snowy mountains, six or seven thousand feet in height, and in many places hundreds of miles in width, and traverse a vast extent of country besides.

The weather was still so fine, and the barometer so high—30.52 inches—that Tom determined to go to sea to-day, instead of stopping at Hale Cove for the night, as we had originally intended. Directly we got through the English Narrows, therefore, all hands were busily engaged in once more sending up the square-yards, top-masts, &c., and in making ready for sea. Just before sunset, as we were quitting the narrow channels, the sun pierced through the clouds and lightened up the lonely landscape as well as the broad waters of the Pacific Ocean. Its surface was scarcely rippled by the gentle breeze that wafted us on our course; the light of the setting sun rested, in soft and varied tints, on the fast-fading mountains and peaks; and thus, under the most favorable and encouraging circumstances, we have fairly entered upon a new and important section of our long voyage.

Although perhaps I ought not to say so, I cannot help

admiring the manner in which Tom has piloted his yacht through the Straits, for it would do credit, not only to any amateur, but to a professional seaman. He has never hesitated or been at a loss for a moment, however intricate the part or complicated the directions; but having thoroughly studied and mastered the subject beforehand, he has been able to go steadily on at full speed the whole way. It has, however, been very fatiguing work for him, as he hardly ever left the bridge whilst we were under way.

We steamed the whole distance from Cape Virgin to the Gulf of Peñas, 659 knots, in 76 hours, anchoring six times. This gives seven days' steaming of an average length of eleven hours each; and as we stopped two or three hours, at different times, for Fuegians, photographs, and sketches, our average speed was nine and a half knots, though sometimes, when going with strong currents, it was twelve or fourteen, and, when going against them, barely six knots.

Just at dark we passed between Wager Island and Cheape Channel, where H.M.S. 'Wager,' commanded by Captain Cheape, was wrecked, and we spent the night in the Gulf of Peñas, almost becalmed.

Friday, October 13*th*.—We ceased steaming at 7.30 a.m., and made every effort throughout the rest of the day, by endless changes of sail, to catch each fleeting breath of wind. We did not, however, make much progress, owing to the extreme lightness of the breeze.

Sorry as we are to lose the scenery of the Straits, it is pleasant to find the weather getting gradually warmer, day by day, and to be able to regard the morning bath once more as a luxury instead of a terror. The change is also thoroughly appreciated by the various animals we have on board, especially the monkeys and parrots, who may now be seen sunning themselves in every warm corner of the deck. In the Straits, though the sun was hot, there was always an icy feeling in the wind, owing to the presence of enormous masses of snow and ice on every side.

Saturday, October 14*th.*—Light winds and calms prevailed the whole day. About 2 p.m. we were off the island of Socorro. In the afternoon a large shoal of whales came round the yacht. I was below when they first made their appearance, and when I came on deck they were spouting up great jets of water in all directions, suggestive of the fountains at the Crystal Palace. We were lying so still that they did not seem to be in the least afraid of us, and came quite close, swimming alongside, round us, across our bows, and even diving down under our keel. There was a shoal of small fish about, and the whales, most of which were about fifty or sixty feet in length, constantly opened their huge pink whalebone-fringed mouths so wide that we could see right down their capacious throats. The children were especially delighted with this performance, and baby has learned quite a new trick. When asked, 'What do the whales do?' she opens her mouth as wide as she can, stretches out her arms to their fullest extent, then blows, and finishes up with a look round for applause.

Soon after 8 p.m. the wind completely died away, and, fearing further detention, we once more got up steam.

Sunday, October 15*th.*—Still calm. We had the litany and hymns at 11 a.m.; prayers and hymns and a sermon at 5 p.m. In the course of the afternoon we were again surrounded by a shoal of whales. We passed the island of Chiloe to-day, where it always rains, and where the vegetation is proportionately dense and luxuriant. It is inhabited by a tribe of peculiarly gentle Indians, who till the ground, and who are said to be kind to strangers thrown amongst them. Darwin and Byron speak well of the island and its inhabitants, who are probably more civilized since their time, for a steamer now runs regularly once a week from Valparaiso to San Carlos and back for garden produce. The potato is indigenous to the island.

Tuesday, October 17*th*.—At 6 a.m., there being still no wind, Tom, in despair of ever reaching our destination under sail alone, again ordered steam to be raised. Two hours later a nice sailing breeze sprang up; but we had been so often disappointed that we determined to continue steaming. Just before sunset we saw the island of Mocha

Catching Cape-Pigeons in the Gulf of Peñas.

in the distance. It is said to have been inhabited at one time by herds of wild horses and hogs, but I think they have now become extinct.

One of our principal amusements during the calm weather has been to fish for cape-pigeons, cape-hens, gulls, and albatrosses, with a hook and line. We have caught a good many in this way, and several entangled themselves in the threads left floating for the purpose over the stern. The cape-pigeons were so tame that they came almost on board, and numbers of them were caught in butterfly-nets. Their plumage is not unlike grebe, and I mean to have some muffs and trimmings for the children made out of it. Allen, the coxswain of the gig, skins them very well, having had some lessons from Ward before we left England. I want very much to catch an albatross, in order to have it skinned, and to make tobacco-pouches of its feet and pipe-stems of the wing-bones, for presents.

CHAPTER X.

CHILI.

Sunbeam of summer, oh, what is like thee?
Hope of the wilderness, joy of the sea.

Wednesday, October 18th.—At 3.30 a.m. we were close to the land lying south of the Bay of Lota; at 4 a.m. the engines were stopped on account of the mist; and at 6 a.m. we began to go slowly ahead again, though it was still not very easy to make out the distance and bearing of the coast. The passage into the bay, between the island of Santa Maria and Lavapié Point, is narrow and difficult, and abounds with sunken rocks and other hidden dangers, not yet fully surveyed. Tom said it was the most arduous piece of navigation he ever undertook on a misty morning; but happily he accomplished it successfully. Just as he entered the sun broke through the mist, displaying a beautiful bay, surrounded on three sides by well-wooded hills, and sheltered from all winds except the north. One corner is completely occupied by the huge establishment belonging to Madame Cousiño, consisting of coal-mines, enormous smelting-works, and extensive potteries. The hill just at the back is completely bare of vegetation, which has all been poisoned by the sulphurous vapors from the furnaces. This spot, from its contiguity to the works, has been selected as the site of a village for the accommodation of the numerous laborers and their families. It is therefore to be hoped that sulphur fumes are not as injurious to animal as they evidently are to vegetable life. As we drew nearer to the shore we could distinguish Madame Cousiño's house, in the midst of a park on the summit of a hill, and surrounded on all sides by beautiful gardens. Every prominent point had a little summer-house perched upon it, and some of the trees had circular seats built round their trunks half-way up, approached by spiral staircases, and thatched like wigwams. The general aspect of the coast, which is a combination of rich red earth, granite cliffs, and trees to the water's edge, is very like that of Cornwall and Devonshire.

We had scarcely dropped our anchor before the captain of the port came on board, and told us we were too far from the shore to coal, which was our special object in coming here; so up went the anchor again, and we steamed a few hundred yards farther in, and then let go close to the shore, in deep water. Captain Möller waited to go ashore with us, introduced our steward to the butcher and postmaster of the place, and then accompanied us to Madame Cousiño's gardens.

It was a steep climb up the hill, but we were well rewarded for our labor. Tended by over a hundred men, whose efforts are directed by highly paid and thoroughly experienced Scotch gardeners, these grounds contain a collection of plants from all the four quarters of the globe, and from New Zealand, Polynesia, and Australia. Amid them were scattered all kinds of fantastic grottoes, fountains, statues, and ferneries; flights of steps, leading downwards to the beach, and upwards to sylvan nooks; arcades, arched over with bamboos, and containing trelliswork from Derbyshire, and Minton tiles from Staffordshire; seats of all sorts and shapes, *under* trees, *in* trees, and *over* trees; besides summer-houses and pagodas, at every corner where there was a pretty view over land or sea.

One of the heads of the establishment, a great friend of Madame Cousiño's, was unfortunately very ill, and as she was nursing him, she could not come out to see us; but she kindly gave orders to her gardener to send some cut flowers and some ferns on board the yacht, to decorate the saloon; and as she was unable to invite us to luncheon at the big house, she sent some champagne and refreshments down to the Casa de la Administracion, where we were most hospitably entertained. She has had the latter place comfortably fitted up for the use of the principal employés on the works, and has provided it with a billiard-table, a very fair library, and several spare bedrooms for the accommodation of visitors.

After luncheon we went to see the copper-smelting works, which were very interesting. The manager walked through with us, and explained the processes very clearly. He could tell at once, on taking up a piece of rough ore, fresh from the mine, what percentage of copper or iron it contained, the amount varying from ten to seventy-five per cent. of the gross weight. The furnaces are kept burning night and day, and are worked by three gangs of men; and the quantity of copper produced annually is enormous. In fact, three parts of the copper used in Europe comes from here. The ore is brought from various parts of Chili and Peru, generally in Madame Cousiño's ships; and coal is found in such abundance, and so near the surface, that the operation of smelting is a profitable one. Our afternoon, spent amid smoke, and heat, and dirt, and half-naked workmen, manipulating with dexterous skill the glowing streams of molten ore, was a great contrast to our morning ramble.

Having seen the works, and received a curious and interesting collection of copper ore, as a remembrance of our visit, we started in a little car, lined with crimson cloth, and drawn by a locomotive, to visit the various coal-mines. First we went through the park, and then along a valley near the sea, full of wild flowers and ferns, and trees festooned with 'copigue,' the Chilian name for a creeper which is a specialty of this country, and which imparts a character of its own to the landscape during the month of May, when its wreaths of scarlet, cherry, or pink flowers are in full bloom. We went to the mouths of three coal-pits, and looked down into their grimy depths, but did not descend, as it would have occupied too much time. They are mostly about 1,000 yards in depth, and extend for some distance under the sea.

We next visited a point of land whence we could see an island which closely resembles St. Michael's Mount. It is quite uninhabited, except by a few wild goats and rabbits. The sea-shore is lined with trees to the water's edge, and there are many bold rocks and fine white sandy caves in different parts of it. Some boats were drawn up high and dry on the beach, along which several picturesque-looking groups of shell-fish collectors were scattered. The mussels that are found here are enormous—from five to eight inches in length—and they, together with cockles and limpets, form a staple article of food.

A steam-launch had been sent to meet us, but it could not get near enough to the shore for us to embark. A rickety, leaky small boat, half full of water, was therefore, after some delay, procured, and in this we were sculled out, two by two, till the whole party were safely on board. Outside there was quite a swell, and a north wind and rain are prophesied for to-morrow. Mr. Mackay returned with us to the yacht, and staid to dinner. Before he left, the prognostications of bad weather were to some extent justified; for the wind changed, and rain, the first we have felt for some time, began to fall.

Thursday, October 19*th*.—We have been persuaded by our friends here to try and see a little more of the interior of Chili than we should do if we were to carry out our original intention of going on to Valparaiso in the yacht, and then merely making an excursion to Santiago from that place. We have therefore arranged to proceed at once overland to Santiago, by a route which will enable us to see something of the Cordillera of the Andes, to have a peep at the Araucanian Indians on the frontier, and to visit the baths of Cauquenes. Tom, however, does not like to leave the yacht, and has decided to take her up to Valparaiso, and then come on to Santiago, and meet us in about five or six days' time. The anchor was accordingly hove short, and the mizzen hoisted, when we landed this morning, in a drenching rain.

A coach runs daily from Lota to Concepcion, the first stage of our journey, but a special vehicle was engaged for our accommodation, and a curious affair it was to look at. It seemed to be simply a huge wooden box, suspended, by means of thick leather straps, from C springs, without windows or doors, but provided with two long, narrow openings, through which you squeezed yourself in or out, and which could be closed at pleasure by roll-up leather blinds. Inside, it was roomy, well-padded, and comfortable.

The rain had made the road terribly greasy, and several times the carriage slued half-way round and slid four or five feet sideways down the hill, causing us to hold on, in expectation of a spill. At last we reached the bottom in safety, and crossing a small river, emerged upon the seashore at Playa Negra, or Black Beach, along which we drove for some distance through the deep, loose sand, the horses being up to their fetlocks in water most of the time. Then we forded another little river, and leaving the beach, proceeded up a steep road, not more than three yards wide, with a ditch on one side and a steep precipice on the other, to the little village of Coronel, overlooking the bay of the same name. While the horses were being changed, we walked down to the little wooden pier, on the sea-shore, and saw the 'Sunbeam' just coming out of Lota Bay.

Drawn up by the side of the pier was a picturesque-looking market-boat, full of many sorts of vegetables, and little piles of sea-eggs, with their spines removed, and neatly tied up with rushes in parcels of three. The people seemed to enjoy them raw, in which state they are considered to be most nutritious; and when roasted in their shells, or made into omelets, they are a favorite article of food with all classes. Coronel is a great coaling station, and the bay, which is surrounded by tall chimneys, shafts, and piers, connected with the mines, was full of steamers and colliers.

Our road now ran for some time through undulating pasture-land, in which were many large trees, the scene resembling a vast park. Masses of scarlet verbena, yellow calceolaria, and white heath grew on all sides, while the numerous myrtle, mimosa, and other bushes were entwined with orange-colored nasturtiums, and a little scarlet tropæolum, with a blue edge, whose name I forget. Beneath the trees the ground was thickly carpeted with adiantum fern. The road over which we traveled was of the worst description, and our luncheon was eaten with no small difficulty, but with a considerable amount of merriment. Once, when we jolted into an unusually big hole, the whole of our provisions, basket and all, made a sudden plunge towards one side of the coach, and very nearly escaped us altogether.

Half-way between Coronel and Concepcion, we met the return stage-coach, crowded with passengers, and looking as if it had just come out of the South Kensington Museum or Madame Tussaud's, or like the pictures of a coach of Queen Elizabeth's time. It was a long, low vehicle, with unglazed windows all round it, painted bright scarlet, decorated with brilliant devices on every panel, and suspended, like our own, by means of innumerable leather straps, from huge C springs. The seats on either side held three passengers, and there was a stool in the middle, like the one in the Lord Mayor's coach, on which four people sat, back to back.

Soon after we drew up to rest the horses at a little posada, kept by two Germans, called 'Half-way House,' and seven miles more brought us to a rich and well-cultivated farm belonging to Mr. Hermann, where we stopped to change horses.

It was six o'clock in the evening when we reached the Bio-Bio, a wide shallow river, at the entrance of the town of Concepcion; it had to be crossed in a ferry-boat, carriage and all, and as it was after hours, we had some difficulty in finding any one to take us over. At last, in consideration of a little extra pay, six men consented to undertake the job, and having set a square-sail, to keep us from being carried down the river by the current, they punted us over with long poles. Sometimes there was nine feet of water beneath us, but oftener not more than four or five. The boat could not get close to the opposite shore, and it was a great business to get the carriage out and the horses harnessed, in some eighteen inches of water. First the carriage stuck in the sand, and then the horses refused to move, but after a great deal of splashing, and an immense display of energy in the way of pulling, jerking, shrieking, shouting—and, I am afraid, swearing—we reached the bank, emerged from the water, struggled through some boggy ground, and were taken at full gallop through the streets of the town, until we reached the Hotel Comercio, where we found comfortable rooms and a nice little dinner awaiting us.

This was all very well, as far as it went, but when we came to inquire about our onward route we were disappointed to learn that the line to Angol was closed, owing to the breaking down of a bridge, and would remain so until next month, and that, with the exception of a contractor's train, which runs only once a week, there was nothing by which we could travel. 'To-morrow is Friday,' added Monsieur Letellier, 'and that is so near Monday, what can Madame do better than wait here till then?' By way of consolation, he informed us that there were no Indians now at Angol, as the Araucanian*

---

* I have lately received a letter from a friend in Paris, who says: 'Strange to tell, it is only a few days ago that poor Orélie Antoine I., ex-King of Araucania, died at Bordeaux, in a hospital. He reigned for some years, and then made war upon Chili, which gave him a

Indians had recently all been driven farther back from the frontier by the Chileños, but that, if we were still bent on trying to get there, we could go by boat as far as Nacimiento, where we might, with some difficulty, procure a carriage. The river just now, however, is so low that the boat frequently gets aground, and remains for two or three days; therefore, taking everything into consideration, we have decided to abandon this part of our programme, for otherwise we shall not reach Santiago in time. In any case, the journey will be a much longer one than we expected.

Friday, October 20th.—We went out for a short stroll round the Plaza before breakfast, which meal was scarcely over when Mr. Mackay arrived in a carriage, and took us off to see what there was to see in the town. The Plaza was full of bright-looking flower-beds, in which were superb roses, and many English flowers, shaded by oranges, pomegranates, and deutzias. Each plot belongs to one of the principal families in the town, and great emulation is displayed as to whose little garden shall be in the best order and contain the finest collection of plants and flowers.

Concepcion has suffered, and still suffers, much from earthquakes. The existing town is only thirty-five years old. The houses are all one story high only, and the streets, or rather roads, between them are wide, in order to afford the inhabitants a chance of escape, should their dwellings be thrown down by a sudden shock. In summer everybody rushes out into the street, no matter what hour of the day or night it may be, as soon as the first symptoms of an earthquake are felt; but during the win-

---

warm reception; even captured his Majesty and sent him back to his native land. I met him here a few years ago, surrounded by a small court, which treated him with great deference. I found him a dignified, intelligent sovereign. He attempted to return to his kingdom, but was captured on the high seas by a Brazilian cruiser, and sent back to France to die a miserable death.'

ter, when the shocks are never so severe, the alarm caused is not so great. The old town was about two miles distant from the present site, near a place now called Pinco, but after being demolished in the ordinary way, an immense wave rolled up and completely destroyed all traces of its existence.

We drove out to Puchacai, Mr. Mackay's hacienda, a pretty little thatched cottage, surrounded by a veranda, in the midst of a garden, where laburnums and lilacs bloom side by side with orange-trees and pomegranates. Round the garden are groves of shady English oaks (the first we have seen since leaving home) and Norfolk Island pines, the effect of the whole scene being strangely suggestive of the idea that a charming little bit of English rural scenery has in some mysterious manner been transported to this out-of-the-way spot in Chili. The interior of the house, which is simply but tastefully furnished, and at the time of our visit was full of fresh flowers, arranged with an artistic eye to color, bears the same indescribable *homelike* air. We were kindly received and regaled with luncheon, including, amongst other good things, fried *pesca-reye* (king of fish), deservedly so called.

In the afternoon we strolled about the garden, and looked at the farm and stable, and were shown the probable winner of one of the prizes at the forthcoming race-meeting. In the cottages on the estate some specimens of Miniaca lace were offered to us—a lace made by most of the peasants in this part of the country. It varies considerably in quality, from the coarse kind, used for covering furniture, to the finest description, used for personal adornment. It is very cheap, wears forever, and strongly resembles the *torchon* lace, now so fashionable in Paris and London for trimming petticoats and children's frocks. The women also spin, dye, and weave the wool from the fleece of their own sheep into the bright-colored ponchos universally worn, winter and summer, by the men in this country. These ponchos are not made of nearly such good material as those used in the Argentine Republic, but they are considerably gayer and more picturesque in appearance.

After dinner, there was nothing to do except to stroll about the town and buy photographs. They are extremely good in Chili—both views and portraits—but proportionately dear, the price being double what would be charged in London or Paris for the same thing.

Saturday, October 21st.—Having wished good-by to Mr. Mackay, and taken our seats in the train for Linares, we were now fairly launched on our own resources in a strange country, I being the only one of the party who could speak even a little Spanish. At San Romde we stopped half an hour to allow the train from Chillan to pass. Most of the passengers took the opportunity of breakfasting, but as we were not hungry we occupied the time in having a chat with the engine-driver, a very intelligent Canadian. He told us that, as it happened, we might have gone to Angol to-day after all, as a special car and engine were going there to take a doctor to see a patient, returning early to-morrow morning.

The railroad runs alongside the Bio-Bio all the way to San Romde. On either bank are low wooded hills, on whose sides vines are cultivated in considerable quantities. The wild flowers grow luxuriantly everywhere: calceolarias, especially, in huge bushes of golden bloom, two or three feet high. At San Romde we left the river, and traveled through a pretty and well-cultivated country to Chillan, which derives its name from an Indian word, signifying 'saddle of the sun,' and is so called from the fact that the sun shines upon it through a saddle-shaped pass in the chain of the Andes.

Like Concepcion, the existing town has been recently built at a distance of about a mile from the remains of the old place of the same name, which was overthrown by an earthquake about thirty years ago. The destruction was, however, not so complete as in the case of Concepcion, and some few of the better-conditioned houses are still inhabited by very poor people, though the walls have great cracks in them from top to bottom, and they are otherwise in a deplorable state. A large cattle and horse market is held at Chillan every Saturday, and it is said that, on these occasions, 100,000 dollars frequently change hands in the course of the morning, in the open market-place. All the business of the day was over by the time we got there, and there was nothing to be seen but a few stray beasts and quaint bullock-carts, and some peasants selling refreshments, Miniaca lace, and other trifles. In several of the old-fashioned shops on the Plaza there were curious-looking stirrups, bits, spurs, and other horse-gear, all made of solid silver, roughly worked by the Indians themselves.

Having had our baths, we returned to the hotel, where we found dinner laid out in my bed-room, which happened to be the largest, for our host did not approve of our dining at the table-d'hôte, as we should have preferred to do. He gave us an excellent dinner, with good wine, and attended to us most assiduously himself.

While the gentlemen were smoking, I went to see a poor engine-driver who had met with a bad accident, and who was lying at this hotel. He is a fine healthy-looking Englishman, and he told me that, until this misfortune, he had never known a day's illness in his life. It seems that, at four o'clock in the afternoon of this day week, he was sent off with a special engine to convey an important message. Something going wrong during the journey, he slackened speed, and, in stepping off the engine to see what was the matter, his foot slipped, and the wheel of the tender went over it. He had no one with him who could manage the engine alone, so he was obliged to get up again, and endeavored to struggle on to Talca; but after going a few miles farther, the engine suddenly ran off the track, at a part of the unfinished line that had not yet been sufficiently ballasted. They could not get it on again unaided, and one of the men had to start off and walk many miles before he could procure assistance. Altogether, poor Clarke underwent forty-two hours of intense agony from the time of the accident until he received any medical attention. In spite of this he is now doing well; and though the foot, which is in a bath of carbolic acid and water, looks very bad, he is in great spirits, because the three local doctors, in consultation, have decided that amputation will not be necessary. He spoke in the highest terms of the kindness of our French host and his Spanish wife, the latter of whom, he says, has nursed him like a mother. He certainly has the one large room in the house, and when I saw him his bed was comfortably made and arranged, flowers and fruit were on a table by his side, and everything looked as neat and snug as possible. It was a treat to him to see some one fresh from the old country, and to hear all the news, and our voyage appeared to interest him greatly. While I was with him one of his friends came in, who remembered me quite well, and who knew one or two people with whom we are acquainted, including the manager of Messrs. Bowdler and Chaffers' yard, where the 'Sunbeam' was built.

Sunday, October 22*d.*—Though it was Sunday, we had no choice but to travel on, or we should not have been able to start until Tuesday. We were therefore up at five o'clock, and at the station before seven. From San Carlos, where we arrived at 8.15 a.m., we started for Linares, which was reached a couple of hours later. It is a much smaller town than Chillan, but is built exactly on the same plan—Plaza, cathedral, and all. To-day the streets were crowded with men on horseback, who had brought their wives in, seated pillion-fashion on the crupper behind them, to attend mass.

Our road lay through a rich country, intersected by small rivers, with the distant snowy chain of the Andes as a background, and through thickly planted groves of poplars, growing in long shady avenues, fragrant with perfume from the magnificent roses which blossomed beneath their shade. In the course of our four hours' drive, we crossed a great many streams, in some of which the water was deep enough to come in at the bottom of the carriage, and cause us to tuck ourselves up on the seats; there was always a little pleasing excitement and doubt, as we approached one of these rivulets, as to whether we were to be inundated or not. We met a good many people riding and walking about in their holiday clothes, and at all the cabarets groups of talkers, drinkers, and players were assembled.

The cottages we have seen by the roadside have been picturesque but wretched-looking edifices, generally composed of the branches of trees stuck in the ground, plastered with mud and thatched with reeds. Two outhouses, or arbors, consisting of a few posts and sticks, fastened together and overgrown with roses and other flowers, serve respectively as a cool sitting-room and a kitchen, the oven being invariably built on the ground outside the latter, for the sake of coolness. The women, when young, are singularly good-looking, with dark complexions, bright eyes, and luxuriant tresses, which they wear in two plaits, hanging down their backs far below the waist. The men are also, as a rule, fine-looking. In fact, the land is good, and everybody and everything looks prosperous. The beasts are up to their knees in rich pasture, are fat and sleek, and lie down to chew the cud of contentment, instead of searching anxiously for a scanty sustenance. The horses are well fed, and their coats are fine and glossy, and the sheep, pigs, and other animals are in equally good condition. It is therefore a cheery country to travel through, and at this spring-time of the year one sees it in its highest perfection.

Before reaching Talca we had to cross the Maule, a wide, deep river, with a swift current. The carriage was first put on board a large flat-bottomed boat, into which the horses then jumped, one by one, the last to embark tumbling down and rolling among the legs of the others. With a large oar the boat was steered across the stream, down which it drifted about 200 yards into shallow water, where the boatmen jumped out and towed us to a convenient landing-place. Here we found several people waiting to be ferried over. A troop of mules having been driven into the water, which they seemed rather to enjoy, swam across safely, though they were carried some distance down the river.

About five o'clock we arrived at Talca, and went straight to the Hotel Colon, kept by Gassaroni. Every Italian who starts a hotel in this part of the world calls it, as a matter of course, 'The Columbus Hotel;' for they are very anxious to claim the great navigator as a countryman, though the Spaniards dispute their right to do so, on the ground that Genoa, where he was really born, was at that time an independent state. While we were waiting for dinner we walked about the town, which so exactly resembles Concepcion and Chillan in the arrangement of its streets, buildings, and trees, that I doubt whether any one familiar with the three places could tell immediately which town he was in, if transported suddenly to the middle of the Plaza, though I believe Talca is rather the largest. It still retains its old Indian name, meaning, 'thunder,' doubtless on account of the frequency and violence of the thunder-storms by which it is visited.

Monday, October 23d.—Soon after midnight I was aroused by a great noise. At first I thought I was dreaming, but a very brief reflection convinced me of the existence of an energetically played big-drum, somewhere in the immediate neighborhood of my bed-room. I at once got up, and peeping through the window in the door, saw a military band of twenty-five performers, standing on the other side of the courtyard, blowing and hitting their hardest. It must be confessed that they played well, and that their selection of music was good, but it was, nevertheless, rather annoying, after a long and fatiguing day, and with the prospect of an early start, to be kept awake until half-past three in the morning, while they serenaded and toasted the *prima donna*, and each of the other members of the theatrical company who are staying here. The noise was, of course, increased by the reverberation from the walls of the courtyard, and finding it impossible to sleep, I abandoned the attempt, and took to writing instead. At last the welcome notes of the Chilian national air gave me hope that the entertainment was over for the night—or rather morning—and soon afterwards all was once more quiet.

We left Talca by the 7.30 train, Mr. Budge, who had business at Curico, accompanying us. All the engines and rolling stock this side of Santiago are of American make and pattern. Mr. Budge had secured one of the long cars, with a passage down the center, and a saloon at each end, for us, so we were very comfortable, and he told us a great deal about the country as we went along. Like all Chileños, he is very patriotic, and is especially proud of the financial stability of his country. He often said, ' If English people would only invest their money here, instead of in Peru or the Argentine Republic, they would get eight per cent. on good security.' We heard the same thing from many other sources; and it certainly does seem that this country is the most settled, and the least liable to be disturbed by revolutions, of any in South America. At Curico* we breakfasted at a little restaurant on Chilian dishes and the wine of the country. The latter is excellent and of various kinds, but it is so cheap that none of the innkeepers can be persuaded to supply it to travelers, whose only chance of tasting it, therefore, is at some small inn.

Mr. Budge left us at Pelequen, the next station to San Fernando, having put us in charge of the conductor, who

---

* An Indian name, signifying ' black waters,' having reference to the mineral springs in the neighboring mountains.

promised to see after us at Cauquenes, but who wofully betrayed his trust. There was no regular station at the latter place, but as the train stopped, and we saw 'Bains de Cauquenes' on a hotel close by, we jumped out just in time to see it go on again. Luckily the other passengers were kind enough to interest themselves on our behalf, and shrieked and hallooed to such good purpose that the engine was once more brought to a standstill, and our luggage was put out. Half a dozen little boys carried it to the inn, where I had to explain to the *patron*, in my best Spanish, that we wanted a carriage to go to the baths, seven leagues off. In a wonderfully short space of time four good horses were harnessed to a queer sort of vehicle, which held four inside and one out, besides the driver, and which had to be entered by means of a ladder. Having all packed in, and paid our fare beforehand, we were rattled off at a merry pace towards the Andes. The road went up and down and round about, and crossed many rivers, but was fairly good throughout. We changed once at a large hacienda, where a man went into a large yard, containing about sixty horses, and dexterously lassoed the particular four required for our use. Several horsemen were waiting about, and I looked at their saddles, which were made of a dozen or more sheepskins, laid one on the top of the other, forming a soft seat to ride in by day and a comfortable bed to sleep on at night.

Early in the afternoon we saw some buildings in the distance, which we rightly guessed to be the baths, and soon afterwards we passed in at the entrance gate of the establishment, by the side of which was a rock with the word 'Welcome' painted upon its face. The whole distance from the station was twenty-three miles, which we had accomplished in a little over two hours. Driving between hedgerows of roses in full bloom, we were not long in reaching the door of the hotel, where we were received by the proprietor. He told us he was very full, but he managed to find us some small rooms, and then conducted us to the luxuriously fitted bathing establishment. After this came the table-d'hôte, to which about seventy sat down, though many of the visitors were dining in their own rooms. In the evening we walked about the garden and chatted with several people, who all seemed to have heard of us and our voyage, and to be anxious to know what we thought of the Straits. We saw some English papers too, which was a great treat, though there did not seem to be much news in them.

Tuesday, October 24th.—This is a wonderful place, built entirely of wood. The center part is a square, seventy yards in extent, surrounded by a single row of one-storied rooms, with doors opening into the courtyard, and windows looking over the river or up into the mountains. In the middle of the square are a pavilion containing two billiard-tables, a boot-blacking arbor, covered with white and yellow jessamine and scarlet and cream-colored honeysuckle, plenty of flower-beds, full of roses and orange-trees, and a monkey on a pole, who must, poor creature, have a sorry life of it, as it is his business to afford amusement to all the visitors to the baths. He is very good-tempered, does several tricks, and is tormented 'from early dawn to dewy eve.' I remonstrated with our host on his behalf; but he merely shrugged his shoulders and said, ' Mais il faut que le monde se divertisse, Madame.' From the center square, marble steps lead to a large hall, with marble baths on either side, for ladies and gentlemen respectively. A few steps farther bring one to a delightful swimming-bath, about forty feet square, filled with tepid water. The water, as it springs from the rock, is boiling hot, and contains, I believe, a good deal of magnesia and other salts, beneficial in cases of rheumatism and gout; but the high temperature of the water makes the air very muggy, and we all found the place relaxing, though perhaps it was because we indulged too freely in the baths, which are a great temptation.

In the afternoon we went for a ride, to see a celebrated view of the Andes. Unfortunately it was rather misty, but we could see enough to enable us to imagine the rest. Some condors were soaring round the rocky peaks, and the landscape, though well clothed with vegetation, had a weird, dreary character of its own, partly due to the quantity of large cacti that grew in every nook and corner, singly, or in groups of ten or twelve, to the height of twenty or thirty feet. Though they say it hardly ever rains in Chili, a heavy shower fell this afternoon, and our landlord thoughtfully sent a boy on horseback after us with umbrellas.

Wednesday, October 25th.—The bath was so delightful this morning, that we felt quite sorry it was to be our last. One could very well spend a week or two here, and find plenty to do in the way of excursions into the valleys of the Andes, which look most inviting in the distance.

At half-past ten we set out on our return journey to the railway, changing horses at the same place where we had stopped at coming up, and which we reached half an hour before the train was due; when it arrived we were allowed to get in with our belongings in rather a less hurried fashion than we had alighted. Luncheon was procured at Rancagua, and we finally reached Santiago at about 4.50 p.m. No sooner had we got fairly into the station than the car was invaded by a crowd of porters touting for employment. They are all dressed in white, and wear red caps, on which is a brass number, by means of which they are easily recognized. The landlord from the Hotel Ingles, M. Tellier, met us, and we at once drove off, leaving our luggage to follow, in charge of one of the red-capped gentlemen. The drive from the station was along the Alameda, on either side of which were many fine houses; but the road was ill-paved and shaky as usual.

The Grand Hotel, which used to be considered the best in South America, is now shut up, the company who owned it having recently failed; so all the smaller hotels, none of which are very good, are crowded to overflowing. The Hotel Ingles is considered the best, though I cannot say much in its favor. The rooms are good, but the situation is noisy, being at the corner of two streets; the servants are attentive, but the cuisine and arrangements are bad. Independently of all this, we have great reason to complain of the conduct of the landlord, for my first question, as soon as he had introduced himself, was, of course, 'Have Mr. and Miss Brassey arrived?' 'Yes, Madame, and went away this morning.' 'What! and left no letter?' 'No; but Monsieur returns to-morrow.' Imagine my surprise and disappointment! But there was nothing to be done but to go to the hotel and wait patiently. We afterwards found that *Tom had left a long letter, and that he had never said a word about returning.* The wretched man would not give me the letter, because he thought he could detain us, and he never sent the telegram I handed to him to forward to Tom at once, asking for an answer.

Our luggage arrived just in time to enable us to dress for the second table-d'hôte at six o'clock, after which we went for a walk through some arcades, paved with marble, and full of fine shops, past the Grand Hotel, which was situated at the end of the Alameda, and is built over an arcade of shops. It is a handsome building, and must command a fine view. The cathedral and the archbishop's palace, large but rather dull-looking brick buildings, are close by. The surrounding gardens looked pretty by gaslight, and the scent of roses pervaded the evening air.

CHAPTER XI.

SANTIAGO AND VALPARAISO.

Gems of the changing autumn, how beautiful you are,
Shining from your glassy stems, like many a golden star!

Thursday, October 26th.—Our kind hostess at Lota had given us a letter of introduction to her manager at Santiago, who called this morning to inquire what arrangements he could make which would be most agreeable to us during our stay. She had also given orders that her carriages and horses should be placed at our disposal, and at about ten o'clock we all started in an open break, drawn by a pair of good-looking half-bred brown horses, bigger than any we had seen before in this country.

We went first to the Compañia, a large open square, planted with flowers, the site of the old Jesuit Church, which was burned down on December 8th, 1863. Well known as the story is, I may here recall the tragic details, standing on the very spot where they took place. It was the Feast of the Virgin, and the church was densely crowded with a congregation composed almost entirely of women, principally young, many of whom were servant-girls. Some of the draperies used in the decoration of the building caught fire, the flames spread rapidly, destroying in their course the cords by which the numerous paraffin and oil lamps were suspended across the nave and aisles, and precipitating their burning contents upon the people beneath. The great doors opened inwards; the crowd, trying to press out, closed them, and kept them hermetically sealed. The priests, anxious to save the church properties and sacred relics, shut the large iron gates across the chancel and kept them fastened, notwithstanding the agonizing shrieks of the unhappy victims, many of whom might otherwise have escaped. Their conduct on this terrible occasion created at the time a feeling of bitter and universal indignation, and caused a shock to the popularity and authority of the priesthood in this country, from which it will take them a long time to recover.

Mr. Long told us that, between seven and eight o'clock on the evening of the catastrophe, he was walking with some friends on the Alameda, when he saw smoke rising in dense volumes from the quarter of the city where the house in which he resided was situated. He and his friends ran quickly in the direction of the fire, giving the alarm as they went, and on reaching the church they found the doors closely shut, while fearful screams were issuing from the interior, and smoke and flames pouring from the windows. They got a party of men together accustomed to the use of the lasso—no difficult task here—and with them climbed from the neighboring houses to the top of the church. Making a hole in the roof, they then dropped their lassos over some of the women beneath, and so dragged them out of the building; but the number thus saved was necessarily very small, and it happened too often that many of the poor creatures below, in their eagerness to escape, hung on to the legs or body of the one they saw lassoed, and by their weight literally dragged her to pieces. Sometimes even a lasso broke, and those clinging to it, when almost within reach of safety, were again precipitated into the burning mass below. Any one who has seen a rawhide lasso, capable of withstanding the sudden rush of the fiercest bull ever captured, will be able to realize the immense strain which would be required to cause one to give way. The next morning at daybreak, the interior of the church presented a terrible spectacle. Mr. Long described it as being full of women, standing up, tightly wedged together, their hands stretched out as if in an attitude of supplication, their faces and the upper part of their bodies charred beyond recognition, the lower part, from the waist downwards, completely untouched.

Their remains were buried in one large grave, in the cemetery of the Recoleta, and the spot is now marked by a square piece of ground, full of bright flowers; inclosed by iron railings, almost hidden by the creepers that entwine them, and shaded by willows, orange-trees, cypresses, and pomegranates. In the center is a large cross, and on either side of the iron railings there is a marble tablet with the simple but touching inscription, in Spanish—

'Incendio de la Iglesia
de la Compañia,
8 de Diciembre, 1863.
Restos de las Victimas ;
2000, mas o menos.'
(Burning of the Church of the Compañia, December 8th, 1863.
Remains of the victims. 2,000, more or less.)

Almost every household in Santiago had lost one of its members. One lovely girl of seventeen was pulled out through the roof and taken to Madame Cousiño's residence, where she lay for nearly a fortnight. She suffered the greatest agonies, but was sensible to the last, and gave a graphic account of the whole harrowing scene. The site of the church, hallowed by such sad memories, has never been built upon, but is preserved as an open space, surrounded by a strip of garden, and having in its center a finely carved monument.

The Houses of Congress were the next thing we went to see, after which we drove through a great part of the city and over a handsome bridge, with statues and small niches on either side. Beneath it, however, there is little more than a dry torrent bed; and it is said that an American, when visiting this spot with a Santiago friend, who was showing him round, remarked, 'I guess you ought either to buy a river or sell this here bridge.' We also went to the Church of La Recoleta. From the church we went to the cemetery of the same name, which is prettily laid out, and well stocked with flowers and trees.

It being now past eleven o'clock, we began to think about breakfast, and accordingly returned to the hotel, where I was disappointed to find no news from Tom and no answer to the telegram I sent last night.

At one o'clock we started again, and had a pleasant but rather dusty drive of eight miles to Macul, the stud-farm established by the late Don Luis Cousiño.

We had some luncheon at Mr. Canning's house, in a room that had recently been split from top to bottom by an earthquake, and afterwards sat in the veranda to see the horses and some of the cattle, which were brought round for our inspection. Among them were Fanfaron, Fandango, and other beautiful thorough-breds, three fine Cleveland coach-horses, Suffolk cart-horses and percherons, and some of the young stock. We saw only a few of the beasts, as at this time they are away feeding on the hills, but I believe they are as good as the horses. Mr. Long had arranged for us all to ride round the farm, and I was mounted on a lovely chestnut mare, sixteen hands high, daughter of Fanfaron, and niece to Kettledrum. I should have liked to have bought her and sent her home, but she was not for sale, though her value was £400. English horses here are as dear, in proportion, as native horses are cheap. The latter may be bought for from twenty to sixty dollars apiece; and some of them make capital little hacks.

We rode all over the farm, attended by half a dozen peons, who drove the young thorough-bred stock together, in the enormous fields, for us to see, and afterwards did the same thing with some of the cattle. We also went through the farm buildings, in one part of which we saw the operation of making lassos. The best are composed of neatly plaited strips of cured hide, about a quarter of an inch wide, the commoner sort being made from an undressed cow's hide, with the hair on, cut from the center in an ever-increasing circle, so that they are in one piece, many yards in length. In another part of the farm there were a few acres more of flower-gardens, orange-trees, and kitchen-gardens.

What makes Horses go in Chili.

Beautiful as the whole place is, it loses much in interest from its vastness. You never seem to know where you are, or when you have come to an end. I hear that Madame Cousiño talks of extending the park still farther, right up into the mountains, which seems almost a pity, as it is already too big to be kept in really perfect order, even with a hundred and twenty men employed upon it. Everything is completely surrounded and overgrown with flowers. Even the fields are separated by hedges of sweet-smelling double pink roses, and these hedges are larger than many a 'bullfinch' in the old country.

After a delightful gallop of about two hours, we returned to the farmhouse, where we found a fresh pair of horses waiting for us in the break, and drove back to Santiago by moonlight.

It was eight o'clock when we reached the hotel, and as the table-d'hôte dinner only lasts from five till half-past seven, I asked for a private dinner in our own room or in the general dining-room, for our own party and two guests in addition. But the landlord said he was not at all sure about giving us dinner; he must see what there was in the kitchen first. We then declared we would go and dine at a café, and in less than half an hour managed to get an excellent little dinner at the Café Santiago, though even Mr. Long, who ordered it for us, could not induce them to give us native wine. I am bound to confess, however, that we punished ourselves at least as much as the landlord, for as we paid so much a day for board and lodging, he was of course bound to provide us with dinner, and we had thus to pay for our food twice over.

Friday, October 27th.—Still no news from Tom. Mr. Long called at half-past eight, to take me to the market, and my first step was to send another telegram, this time taking care to see that it really was dispatched.

We then walked through the streets to the market-hall, a handsome iron building, commodiously arranged, which was sent out from England in pieces, and put together here. All round it are stalls, where you can get a capital breakfast, generally consisting of coffee, tender beef-steak, buttered toast, and boiled beans, for a small sum. One of our party, who had been at the market since half-past five, tried one, and fully confirmed the report we had heard as to their excellence and cleanliness. At the time of our visit all these refreshment stalls were crowded, and I felt rather tempted to join one of the hungry merry-looking groups myself. The market was well supplied with meat, fish, vegetables, fruit, and flowers of all kinds, green peas, French beans, and strawberries being specially abundant. There were quantities of queer-looking baskets to be seen, and some curious pottery, made by the nuns from a kind of cement. Outside the building there were men and women hanging about with ponchos, of their own manufacture, which they had brought in from the country, for sale. We bought some bright specimens as presents for the children, but it took some time to collect them, as each individual had only one to offer. They are the work of the women, in the intervals of household labor, and as soon as one is completed it is sold, in order that materials for a fresh one may be purchased. We also bought some of the carved wooden stirrups, made in the country, and used by all the natives. They are rather like a small coal-scuttle in shape, and must be heavy and cumbersome.

From the market we went to hear high mass at the cathedral. This is a fine building, though the interior seemed very dark. The high altar was illuminated by hundreds of candles, whose light shone on a crowd of kneeling women, all dressed in black, and with black veils over their heads, the contrast between their somber appearance and the gilding and paintings on the walls—handsome at a distance, but tawdry on a closer examination—being very striking. The organ is of splendid tone and quality, and reverberated grandly through the aisles, and the whole scene was not without a certain impressiveness. I had not thought of paying a visit to the cathedral when I went out this morning, and it was not until I saw every one staring at me that I remembered I had committed the terrible mistake of going to church in a hat, and without any veil; but we remained in a dark corner most of the time, and emerged into open daylight again before any of the authorities of the place had time to observe or remonstrate with me. My wearing a hat was, however, quite as much against all church rules as a similar proceeding on the part of a man would have been. The women of this city are almost always good-looking when young, and they glide gracefully about the streets in their long black clinging gowns and *mantos*, by which they are completely enveloped from head to foot.

In the afternoon we went for a drive in the park, and to see Santa Lucia, of which, as the only hill in Santiago, the inhabitants of the city are very proud, and from thence drove to the Cousiño Park, an extensive piece of ground near the Alameda, laid out and arranged under the direction of the late Don Luis Cousiño, and presented by him to the city of Santiago.

After a stroll round the park, Mr. Long took us to an emporium for Panama hats, which are made in Lima, Guayaquil, and other states of Chili, as well as in Panama, from a special kind of grass, split very fine, and worn by almost everybody on this coast. The best made cost 340 dollars, or about sixty guineas, and fifty pounds is not at all an uncommon price to pay, though the inferior kind may be had for two pounds. Those ordinarily worn by the gentlemen here cost from twenty to thirty pounds each, but they are so light, pliable, and elastic that they will wear forever, wash like a pocket-handkerchief, do not get burned by the sun, and can be rolled up and sat upon—in fact, ill-treated in any way you like—without fear of their breaking, tearing, or getting out of shape. For the yacht, however, where so many hats are lost overboard, they would, I fear, prove a rather unprofitable investment.

We now drove back to the hotel, past the Mint, a handsome building, guarded by soldiers, and with windows protected by iron gratings. On our return I found that one of the valuable ponchos, given to me in the Argentine Republic, had been taken from our room. The landlord declined to trouble himself about its recovery, as he said it was 'most unlikely that any one would take a thing of no value to him here;' the real truth being that the guanaco ponchos are worth nearly double as much in Chili as they are on the other side of the Andes.

After dinner we walked to the theater, where we saw *La Sonnambula*, well put on the stage, and well sung and acted by an Italian opera company. The *prima donna*, contralto, baritone, and bass were all good, but the scenery was occasionally somewhat deficient. The house, which is highly decorated—perhaps too much so for the ladies' dresses—looked well by night, though if it had been full the effect would have been still better. The box-tiers are not divided into pigeon-holes, as they are with us, and everybody can therefore see equally well. The Presidential box seemed commodious and handsome, and had the Chilian coat of arms in front of it, making it look very much like a Royal box.

The walk back by moonlight was delightful. Some of our party afterwards went to the Union Club, where they met several English gentlemen, who were most kind and pressing in their invitations to them to stay a few days longer, and go up the mountains to see the views and to have some guanaco shooting. About twenty-four hours from here they say you can have your first shot, and a little farther on you meet them in herds which may be counted by thousands. There are also wild horses and wild donkeys. Quaggas and hemuels used to be found, but are now extinct. The last named is a rare animal, exactly resembling a horse in every particular, except that its hoofs are cloven. It used only to be found in the mountains of Chili, and it is one of the supporters of the national coat of arms.

Saturday, October 28*th.*—At 5 a.m. we were called, and soon afterwards parting gifts of flowers began to arrive, and even I was obliged to confess that four large clothes-baskets full of rosebuds were more than I quite knew what to do with. At seven o'clock Mr. Long came to know if he could help us in any way, and a little later Madame Cousiño's coachman appeared with the carriage, to take us to the station.

We had a pleasant drive down the Alameda, the sun shining brilliantly in a bright blue sky, and the distant mountains for the first time being clearly visible. The station was crowded with venders of pottery, curious things in buffalo horn, sweetmeats, &c. The rolling stock on this line is of English manufacture, and we were therefore put into the too familiar, close, stuffy, first-class carriage, and duly locked up for the journey down to Valparaiso. The line, running as it does through mountain gorges for a great portion of the way, must have been a difficult one to make.

Just now the whole country wears a golden tint from the bloom of the espinosa, which seems to grow everywhere, and which is now in perfection. The branches of this shrub are so completely covered with little yellow balls of flowers, which come before the leaves, and which have no separate stalk, but grow along the shiny, horny branches, that they look as if they were made of gold. It is called the 'burning bush' here, and its wood is said to be the hardest in the country. The flowers are often plucked off and dried, in which state they are most fragrant, and are used for scenting linen and for keeping away moths. The thorns, however, are a terrible nuisance to the shepherds and owners of cattle, catching their clothes and tearing them as they gallop swiftly across over the plains. If I bore you by saying too much about the flowers, forgive me. I want to make you all realize, if possible, what a lovely flowery land Chili is. The whole air is quite perfumed with roses, principally large double pink roses, something like the old-fashioned cabbage rose, though there are a good many of the monthly kind and a few white and deep scarlet ones. They formed hedgerows on either side of the road, and in many places climbed thirty or forty feet up the trees, and then threw down long brambles laden with bloom, almost producing the effect of a wall of pink. There were also plenty of wild flowers of other sorts, such as scarlet and white lilies, larkspurs, eschscholtzias, evening primroses, and many others whose names I do not know.

At Llaillai we stopped for breakfast, procured at a small restaurant at the station. While waiting for the train for Santiago to come in, we had plenty of time to observe the half-Indian girls selling fruit, flowers, cakes, &c., and jabbering away in a sort of *patois* Spanish, in recommendation of their wares. Some of them were really pretty, and all were picturesquely dressed in bright-colored stuffs, their hair neatly done up and decorated with flowers, their faces clean and smiling. At 11.15 a.m. we reached Quillota, where the train was literally besieged by men, women, and children, offering bouquets for sale —two or three of which were thrust in at every carriage window—and baskets of strawberries, cherimoyers, mespilas, melons, oranges, sugar-cane, plantain, bananas, asparagus, green peas, French beans, eggs, chickens, and even fish—nice little pesca-reyes, fresh from the stream close by. It must evidently be the custom of the Chileños to visit by rail these fertile districts, for the purpose of doing their marketing; for the occupants of the train soon absorbed the entire stock of the venders, who were left with empty baskets.

I never saw such a country as this is for eggs and chickens. A hen seems never to have a smaller brood than ten, and I have often counted from seventeen to twenty-one chickens with the mother, and, more than once, as many as twenty-four. However well you may have breakfasted or dined, the waiters always come at the end of the meal to ask, not *whether* you will have any eggs, but *how* you will have them — fried, boiled, poached, or in some sort of omelet. If you refuse altogether, the chances are that two very lightly boiled eggs will be placed by your side, with the suggestion that you should beat them up and drink them. The inhabitants of the country always seem to finish their meals with eggs in some form or another.

The celebrated 'Bell of Quillota,' a mountain which derives its name from its peculiar shape, and which serves as a good landmark in entering the harbor of Valparaiso, is well seen from the railway, a little below Quillota Station. We stopped again at Limache, a little village situated in the midst of a fertile country, about twenty-five miles from Valparaiso, where fruit, flowers, &c., were as freely offered for sale as before, and again at Viña del Mar, the next station to Valparaiso. There is a good hotel here, in the midst of a pretty garden, where you can get an excellent breakfast or dinner.

From this spot the line runs close along the edge of the sea, and we strained our eyes in vain, trying to discover the yacht. At the station we were assailed by porters and touts of every description, but, seeing no one to meet us, and not knowing where to go, we contented ourselves with collecting our baggage in a little heap, while a fight went on close by between a policeman and a coachman, who had been too persistent in his endeavors to obtain a fare. They knocked one another about a good deal, and broke one or two windows, after which they appeared quite satisfied, shook hands, and were good friends again. Tom, Mabelle, and Muriel arrived before it was over, and we were very glad to meet again after our short absence.

A long dusty drive brought us to the mole, and while the luggage was being packed in the boat, Tom and I went to call on the British Consul, where we found some letters. We were on board in time for two-o'clock luncheon, after which, amid many interruptions from visitors, we devoured our news from home and other parts—for amongst our letters were some from Natal, India, Japan, Canada, Teneriffe, South American ports, St. Petersburg, Constantinople, and several other places, besides those from dear old England.

About four o'clock Tom and I went ashore. We had intended going alone in the 'Flash' (our lightest boat), but a strong southerly wind had sprung up, which at once made the sea so rough that we went in the 'Gleam' (the gig) instead, with six oars. It took the men all their time to get us ashore, though we had not far to go, for wind, tide, and waves were all against us.

Valparaiso consists mainly of two interminable streets, running along the edge of the sea, at the foot of the hills, which rise immediately behind them, and on which are built all the residences and villas of the gentlemen of the place. Very few live in the town itself, which is composed almost entirely of large warehouses and fine shops, where you can get almost anything you want by paying between three and four times as much for it as you would do in England. For instance, the charge for hair-cutting is a dollar and a half (4*s*.), a three-and-sixpenny Letts's Diary costs two dollars and a half (10*s*.), a tall hat costs fifty-eight shillings, you must pay sixpence each for parchment luggage-labels, threepence apiece for quill pens, four shillings for a quire of common note-paper, and so on in proportion.

We had, as I have said, seen the yacht leave Lota Bay, with a strong head-wind blowing, on Thursday, the 19th instant. In a few hours the wind fell to a calm, which then changed to a light favorable breeze, and the 'Sunbeam' reached Valparaiso on the following Saturday afternoon, anchoring out in the bay, not far from H.M.S. 'Opal.' Here they rolled and tumbled about even more than if they had been at sea, the swinging capacities of the saloon tables and lamps being tried to the utmost. On Sunday half the men went ashore for a few hours' leave, but neither they nor the boat returned until the next morning, as they had not been allowed to leave the shore after nine o'clock. In the meantime Tom had been told that the small-pox was raging in the town, and he was much annoyed at their having to pass the night on shore, owing to proper inquiries as to the regulations of the port not having been made by them on landing. The next day the doctor went to see some medical *confrères* at the hospital, and found that the reports were much exaggerated, the reality being that small-pox is always more or less prevalent both here and at Santiago. Three months ago it was very bad, but at the present time it is not worse than usual. Tom and Mabelle started for Santiago on Monday, but unfortunately left their letters of introduction behind; and as they did not like the hotel, they found it rather dull. We could not telegraph to them from Cauquenes, or anywhere *en route*, for there were no wires; so on Wednesday morning, not hearing or seeing anything of us, they returned to Valparaiso. Tom left a long letter for me, with inclosures (which I never received), in the innkeeper's hands, asking for a telegraphic reply as to our plans and intentions, and, as I have already mentioned, never said a word about coming back. Thursday was spent in seeing what little there is to see in Valparaiso, and in visiting the 'Opal.' On Friday Tom went for a sail, moved the yacht close in shore, had a dinner party on board, and went to a pleasant ball afterwards, given by the Philharmonic Society, an association of the same sort as the one at Rio. It was not, however, called a regular ball, but a *tertullia*, so the ladies were in *demi-toilette*. Tom described the room as good, the floor first-rate, the music excellent, the ladies good-looking, and the men agreeable. To-day he met us at the station with the children; and now, therefore, one account will describe the movements of the whole reunited party.

Sunday, October 29*th.*—We all went ashore to church, having been told it was only five minutes' walk from the landing-place, instead of which it took us at least a quarter of an hour, in an intensely hot sun, to climb up a steep hill. The building itself was large, airy, and cool, and there is a good organ and choir, but most of the choristers had gone away to-day to a picnic in the country. During the Litany our attention was suddenly drawn to the fact that earthquakes are matters of frequent occurrence in this country, by a special prayer being offered up for preservation from them and their destructive effects.

At four o'clock we went ashore for a ride, and having climbed the hills at the back of the town, which command extensive views over land and sea, we galloped across the downs and through some villages on to the old high road from Valparaiso to Santiago, along which we rode only for a few yards, turning off into a romantic valley, where the path was so narrow that we could barely squeeze through between the thickly growing shrubs and trees. At last we went up a steep hill on to another high road, and re-entered the town quite at the opposite end to that at which we had left it, after which a ride of two miles along the stony, ill-paved streets brought us to the landing-place.

Monday, October 30*th.*—We were to be off directly the sea-breeze sprang up, at about eleven o'clock, and as I had many letters to write, I was called at 4 a.m., and

finished them all before breakfast at eight. But first one
visitor and then another arrived, and it was nearly eleven
o'clock when we landed to make the final preparations
for starting on our long voyage of eleven thousand miles
across the Pacific.

Our route, as at present arranged, will be viâ the
Society, Friendly, and Sandwich Islands. Juan Fernandez (Robinson Crusoe's Island), which we at first thought
of visiting, we have been obliged, I am sorry to say, to
give up, not on account of its distance from Valparaiso,
as it is only 270 miles off, but because it lies too far to
the southward, and is consequently quite out of the
track of the trade wind, which we ought to pick up, according to the charts and sailing directions, about 500
miles to the northward and westward of this place. I
have been trying to persuade Tom to steam out five or six
hundred miles, so that we may make a quick passage and
economize our time as much as possible, but he is anxious
to do *the whole* voyage under sail, and we are therefore taking very little coal on board, in order to be in the
best trim. If we do not pick up a wind, however, there
is no knowing how long we may lollop about. I suppose till
we are short of water and fresh provisions, when the fires
will be lighted and we shall steam away to the nearest
island—uninhabited, we will hope, or at any rate peopled
by friendly natives, which is rather the exception than
the rule in the south-east corner of the Low Archipelago.
There we shall fill up with fresh water, bananas, bread-
fruit, and perhaps a wild hog or two, and resume our voyage to Tahiti. But this is the least favorable view of the
matter, and we must hope to fall in with the trades soon,
and that they will blow strong and true.

The island of Juan Fernandez now belongs to the
Chilian Government, but is let on a long lease to a man
who, they say here, is somewhat of a robber. He was
very desirous that we should give him a passage in the
yacht, and another man wanted to come too, with some

pointers, to show us the best spots for game, goats, turtle, crayfish, sea-fish, with all of which the place abounds. Some cattle have also been introduced, and the island is much frequented by whalers, who go there for fresh provisions and water. There is nothing particular to be seen, however, and the scenery of the island is not remarkable; at least, so people who have been there tell us, and the photographs I have bought quite confirm their report. Admiral Simpson, who staid there once for a fortnight, told us a good deal about the place, and strongly recommended us not to go there unless we had plenty of time to spare, as we should not be repaid for our trouble, which would probably only result in the dissipation of all our childish illusions.

Our first step on landing this morning was to go to the Consul's to post our letters. By-the-bye, I hope people in England will appreciate them, for they cost between nine and ten pounds to send home. For our outward letters, although prepaid in England, we had to pay over eight pounds before we were allowed to have them from the office. Twenty-nine cases of stores, provisions, wine, &c., which had also been sent out, all arrived safely, and cost comparatively little. There are very good French hair-dressers here, a tempting hat-shop, and a well-stocked book-shop; but everything, as I have said, is frightfully dear.

It was half-past three when the harbor-tug arrived to tow us out of the harbor and so save our getting up steam. There was not a breath of air stirring, but Tom hoped we should find more outside when the tug cast us off. As we dropped slowly out, we had a good view of the harbor and town; and we soon found ourselves once more fairly embarked on the bosom of the wide ocean.

CHAPTER XII.

VALPARAISO TO TAHITI.

The western sea was all aflame,
The day was well-nigh done!
Almost upon the western wave
Rested the broad bright sun.

Tuesday, October 31st.—Throughout the night a flat calm prevailed. The morning was wet and foggy, or we might still have seen Valparaiso, and perhaps have had a peep at Aconcagua. There was a light contrary wind from the N. W. throughout the day. In the afternoon we saw two whales blowing in the distance.

Wednesday, November 1st.—An almost calm day, with a few light showers, and fitful but unfavorable breezes. Some thirty or forty little birds, which the sailors called Mother Carey's chickens, but which were smaller and more graceful than any I have seen of that name, followed closely in our wake. I was never tired of watching the dainty way in which they just touched the tips of the waves with their feet, and then started off afresh, like a little maiden skipping and hopping along, from sheer exuberance of spirit.

Thursday, November 2d.—A bright sunny morning, with a heavy swell and light contrary wind, but the sea became more tranquil towards the evening. The sunset was superb, and the afterglow, as is often the case in these latitudes, lighted up sky and sea with an indescribable beauty, which attained its greatest magnificence about five minutes after the sun had disappeared, reminding one of the glorious sunsets of the African deserts, so often described by travelers.

Friday, November 3d.—Still a blue sky, bright sunshine, smooth sea, and light head-wind. The crew have all turned tailors, and are making themselves new suits from some dungaree we bought at Valparaiso, the clothes we expected for them not having met us there.

Saturday, November 4th.—As fine as ever. This is certainly sailing luxuriously, if not swifty. We have now settled down into our regular sea-ways, and have plenty to

Juvenile Scrubbers.

do on board; so the delay does not much signify. Still, our time is limited, and we all hope to fall in with the trades shortly to carry us to Tahiti or some of the South Sea islands. We caught half-a-dozen of the little petrels, for stuffing, by floating lines of black cotton astern, in which they became entangled.

To-night's sunset was more superb than ever. Each moment produced a new and ever increasingly grand effect. I mean to try and take an instantaneous photograph of one. It would not, of course, reproduce all the marvelous shades of coloring, but it would perhaps give some idea of the forms of the masses of cloud, which are finer than any I ever saw before. This ocean seems to give one, in a strange way, a sense of solemn vastness, which was not produced to the same extent by the Atlantic. Whether this results from our knowledge of its size, or whether it is only fancy, I cannot say, but it is an impression which we all share.

Sunday, November 5th.—Fine, and considerably hotter, though not unpleasantly so. We had the Litany at eleven, and evening prayers and a sermon at four o'clock. Not a single ship has passed within sight since we left Valparaiso, and the only living creatures we have seen are some albatrosses, a few white boobies, a cape-hen, the little petrels already mentioned, a shoal of porpoises, and two whales.

Monday, November 6th.—Passed, at 3 a.m. to-day, a large bark, steering south, and at 8 a.m. a full-rigged ship, steering the same course. We held—as we do with every ship we pass—a short conversation with her through the means of the mercantile code of signals. (This habit of exchanging signals afterwards proved to have been a most useful practice, for when the report that the 'Sunbeam' had gone down with all hands was widely circulated through England, I might almost say the world,—for we found the report had preceded us by telegram to almost all the later ports we touched at,—the anxiety of our friends was relieved many days sooner than it would otherwise have been by the fact of our having spoken the German steamer 'Sakhara,' in the Magellan Straits, Oct. 13, four days after we were supposed to have gone to the bottom.) The weather continues fine, and we have the same light baffling winds. We hoped, when we started, to average at least 200 miles a day, but now we have been a week at sea, and have only made good a little more than 700 miles altogether, though we have sailed over 800 miles through the water. It is, however, wonderful, in the opinion of the navigators, that we have made even as much progress as this, considering the very adverse circumstances under which the voyage has so far been performed, and we must endeavor to console ourselves with the reflection that the sailing qualities of the yacht have undergone another severe test in a satisfactory manner. How the provisions and water will last out, and what time we shall leave ourselves to see anything of Japan, are questions which, nevertheless, occasionally present themselves to our minds. Independently of such considerations, nothing could be more luxurious and delightful than our present mode of existence. With perfect weather, plenty of books to read, and writing to do, no possibility of interruptions, one can map out one's day and dispose of one's time exactly as one pleases, until the half-past six o'clock dressing-bell—which always seems to come long before it is wanted—recalls one to the duties and necessities of life.

Wednesday, November 8th.—A gray, cloudy morning and a flat calm. At twelve o'clock, to the great joy of everybody on board, Tom decided to get up steam, as we have now been becalmed quite twenty-four hours, and have made but little progress in the right direction for some days. The alacrity with which the order to stow sails and raise the funnel was obeyed—every one lending a hand—and the delight expressed on every countenance must have assured him of at least the popularity of his decision.

Whilst we were waiting for steam to be got up, Tom took Muriel and me for a row in the 'Flash,' his own particular little boat, with about four inches of freeboard. The possibility of doing this will give you a better idea of the tranquillity of this vast ocean than any description I can write. At the same time, when we wanted to get into the boat, we found there was a considerable roll on, and that it was no easy matter without the aid of a gangway or ladder. We rowed a little way from the yacht, and, considering how quiet it had seemed to us when on board, it was wonderful to observe how she rolled in the trough of the sea, without sails to steady her or motive power to guide her. The Lota coals, though black and dirty beyond description, burn up very quickly, and in about an hour we were steaming merrily along, the Arabian horseshoe on our bowsprit's end being now pointed direct for the island of Tahiti, instead of for wherever the wind chose to blow us.

Thursday, November 9th.—A flat calm at 6 a.m.; a very light fair wind at 9 a.m. In spite of my remonstrances, Tom determined, at half-past nine, to cease steaming and try sailing again. About twelve o'clock a puff came that sent us along at the rate of 10½ knots for a short time; but it soon dropped, and during the rest of the afternoon and evening, our average speed was only three or four knots an hour. This is very poor work for the trades, but I don't believe we are really in them yet, in spite of the wind charts. It is possible that they may vary in different years; besides which it is now the height of summer, with the sun south of the line, which would naturally make them lighter.

Saturday, November 11th.—At last we seem to be feeling the influence of the trades, as the wind continues to blow from the same direction, though it varies much in force. Sometimes we are going along at the rate of 11¾ knots, sometimes barely five. In the afternoon we had the usual Saturday singing practice.

Sunday, November 12th.—Another lovely day. We had the Litany and hymns at eleven, evening service and sermon at four.

Just before morning church some one turned on the water in the nursery bath, and forgot to turn it off again, so that when we came aft from the saloon we had the pleasure of finding everything in the children's cabins afloat, and that a good deal of water had got down into the hold. It was rather annoying at the time, but, I dare say, like many other present troubles, it was a good thing in the end. It obliged us, at any rate, to have all the stores brought up on deck, and led to our taking an inventory of our resources sooner than we should otherwise have done. I am sorry to say we found that, owing to the departure of our head steward and the illness of his successor, they have not been husbanded as carefully as they should have been, especially those provided for use forward. Sailors are more like children than grown-up men, and require as much looking after. While there is water in the tanks, for instance, they will use it in the most extravagant manner, without thought for the morrow; and they are quite as reckless with their other stores.

I find, however, that one of the drawbacks to taking a very close personal interest in the housekeeping arrangements on board is the too intimate acquaintance one makes with the various individuals composing the live stock, the result being that the private particular history of every chicken, duck, turkey, and joint of mutton is apt to be remembered with a damaging effect to appetite.

In the afternoon two boobies, the first birds we have seen for some days, paid us a visit. I suppose we are too far out to see anything more of our pretty little friends, the petrels.

Monday, November 13*th.*—We had a regular turn out and re-arrangement of our stores to-day, and discovered that the waste and mismanagement have been greater even than we at first supposed. Fortunately, we found some spare tins of provisions stowed away under the nursery floor and forgotten, and which will now come in very opportunely. But I fear that, even as it is, we may be seriously inconvenienced before getting to the end of our voyage. Of the six sheep, sixty chickens, thirty ducks, and four dozen pigeons, brought on board alive at Valparaiso, we have comparatively few left, and not a great deal to give those few to eat; so we must depend mainly on our potted meats and vegetables, which happen to be excellent. We often wonder how the earlier navigators got on, when there were no such things as tinned provisions, and when the facilities for carrying water were of the poorest description, while they were often months and months at sea, without an opportunity of replenishing their stores, and with no steam-power to fall back upon in case they were becalmed. Still more wonderful, in my opinion, is the successful manner in which the Spaniards managed to convey their horses in tiny vessels, together with a sufficient quantity of forage for them, to the New World, where, according to all accounts, they generally arrived in good condition, fit to go to work or to war immediately.

The wind increased in the evening and blew dead aft. In the middle of the night the mizzen-halyards broke, and blocks and all came down with a tremendous crash, which caused both Tom and me to rush up on deck. About an hour and a half's work put everything straight again, however, though it looked a sad mess at first. We had been remarking at dinner how lucky we had been, with all this rolling about in calms and running before the wind, not to have had anything carried away or any of the ropes chafed. Personally, I think the accident is not to be regretted, for now all the fore and aft canvas is stowed, and we are running under square canvas alone, which is much steadier work, though we still roll considerably.

Tuesday, November 14th.—Fine, with a strong fair wind.

I have been laid up for a few days with a touch of my old enemy, Syrian fever, but am gradually recovering, and enjoy very much lying on deck and reading.

Our victualing arrangements have now been satisfactorily settled, and everybody has been put on an allowance of water, our supply of which will last the whole ship's company of forty persons for five weeks, leaving one tank still in reserve in case of accidents. As we expect to reach our destination in about three weeks from the present time, we have therefore, I hope, an ample supply for all our requirements.

Wednesday, November 15th.—Pleasant as we have found life at sea in the South Pacific hitherto, it is, I fear, monotonous to read about, and I dare say you will find it difficult to realize how quickly the days fly past, and how sorry we are when each one comes to an end. I am afraid they are among those things which do not repeat themselves. At any rate, they afford a golden opportunity for reading, such as we are not likely to have again often, if ever, in our busy lives; and Tom and I are endeavoring to make the best use of it by getting through as many of the seven hundred volumes we brought with us as possible. The weather favors us in our endeavors to be industrious; for, while it is sufficiently warm to indispose one for a very severe course of study, it has never been so hot as to compel us to lie down and do nothing but gasp for breath —which is what we were warned to expect. There is indeed one slight drawback to the perfect enjoyment of our present state of existence, and that is the incessant motion of the vessel. When she rolls as quickly as she has done to-day, it is difficult to settle down steadily to any occupation, and at last one cannot help feeling aggravated at the persistent manner in which everything, including one's self, refuses to be still for a single instant.

Thursday, November 16th.—To-day it is really warm— not to say hot—with a bright cloudless sky, which renders an awning acceptable. We saw some 'bo's'n' birds for the first time, and more shoals of flying-fish. I wish a few of the latter would come on board; they would be an agreeable addition to our breakfast-table.

The rolling still continues, the wind being dead aft, and nothing but our square canvas being set. The effect is rather wearisome, and one longs to be able to say,

'Catch hold of her head and keep her still, if only for five minutes' peace and quietness!' Cooking is difficult, and even eating is a hazardous occupation; and at our evening game of cards we have to pocket our counters and markers and hold on as best we can.

Friday, November 17th.—At 8 a.m. the course was altered, our fore-and-aft canvas was set again, and we were once more gliding along swiftly and smoothly through the water, to the great relief of every one on board. The day was lovely, and though it was warm, a pleasant breeze throughout the ship prevented our feeling uncomfortably hot.

Saturday, November 18th.—The days are so much alike that it is difficult to find anything special to say about them. They fly so quickly that I was surprised to be reminded by the usual singing-practice this afternoon that another week had gone by.

The two green paroquets, 'Coco' and 'Meta,' given to me by Mr. Fisher at Rosario, have turned out dear little pets, with the most amusing ways. They are terrible thieves, especially of sugar, pencils, pens, and paper, and being nearly always at liberty, they follow me about just like dogs, and coax and caress me with great affection. They do not care much for any one else, though they are civil to all and good-tempered even to the children, who, I am afraid, rather bore them with their attempts at petting. The other foreign birds, of which I have a large collection, are doing well, and I begin to hope I shall get them home safely after all. We had at one time about twenty parrots, belonging to the men on board, all running about on deck forward, with their wings clipped, but about half of them have been lost overboard. The dogs keep their health and spirits wonderfully. Félise is quite young again, and she and Lulu have great games, tearing up and down and around the decks as hard as they can go.

Sunday, November 19th.—I am convalescent at last,

and appeared at breakfast this morning for the first time for ten days.

The wind was very variable throughout the day. Between 6 and 7 a.m. we were going twelve knots; between 7 and 8 only three; but as we never stop, we manage to make up a fair average on the whole.

At eleven o'clock we had the Communion Service and two hymns. At midday the week's work was made up, with the following result. Our position was in lat. 15° 38′ S., long. 117° 52′ W.; we were 3,057 miles from Valparaiso,—1,335 of which had been accomplished since last Sunday,—and 1,818 miles from Tahiti.

To-day we were not far from Easter Island, the southernmost island of Polynesia. Here as in the Ladrones, far away in the north-west quarter of the Pacific, most curious inscriptions are sometimes found carved in stone.

The sails had been flapping, more or less, all day, and at the change of the dog-watches, at six o'clock, Tom ordered the men aft to stow the mizzen. This they had scarcely begun to do when a light breeze sprang up, and in a few minutes increased to a strong one, before which we bowled along at the rate of nine knots. These sudden changes are of constant occurrence, and coming as they do without the slightest warning, are quite inexplicable. If only we had our old square sails, and our bigger yards and topmast, we should have saved a good deal of time already; for one or two knots an hour extra amount to from 25 to 50 miles a day, and in a month's run the difference would not be far short of 1,500 miles. But we heard so much from people in England, who had visited these parts, of squalls and hurricanes, that Tom did not like to run the risk of being oversparred, especially with a wife and children as passengers.

Monday, November 20th.—The fore-and-aft sails were taken in, as they were doing no good and the square canvas was drawing. This allowed the mizzen-awning to be spread, making a pleasant place to sit in and a capital playground for the children, who scamper about all day long, and do not appear to feel the heat a bit.

Tuesday, November 21st.—Certainly a *very* hot day. We made steady progress under the same canvas as yesterday.

Wednesday, November 22d.—Between 2 and 3 a.m. a nice breeze sprang up, and between 3 and 4.30 a.m. all the fore-and-aft sails were again set. It was deliciously cool on deck at that time; but the sun rose fierce and hot, and more or less killed the breeze as the day wore on.

Thursday, November 23d. — Twenty-four days out. We had hoped to reach Tahiti to-day, and Tom begins to regret that he did not steam some distance out from Valparaiso, so as to pick up the trades sooner. Still it is satisfactory to know how well the 'Sunbeam' can and does sail against light contrary winds, and to have an opportunity of developing some of her good points, of which we were previously hardly aware. How she manages to slip along as she does, four or five knots an hour, with not sufficient wind to blow a candle out, is a marvel to every one on board. More than once, when the hand-log has shown that we were going five knots, I have carried a naked light from one end of the deck to the other without its being extinguished.

The sunrise was magnificent, and a splendid albatross, the largest we have yet seen, was at the same time visible in mid-air, floating against the rose-colored clouds. He looked so grand, and calm, and majestic, that one could almost fancy him the bird of Jove himself, descending direct from the sun. Where do these birds rest? How far and how fast do they really fly? are questions for the naturalist. We have seen them many times at a distance of at least two thousand miles from the nearest land.

About nine o'clock there was a slight breeze, but it fell as the sun rose, and the day was intensely hot.

Friday, November 24th.—A fine breeze in the early morning, which, however, gradually died away. Having now quitted the regular track of the trade winds and got into the variables, we lighted fires at two o'clock. Then another light breeze sprang up for a few minutes, only to fall away again immediately, and at six o'clock we commenced to steam.

Saturday, November 25th.—A very wet morning, the sky clearing at about ten, but the weather remaining dull, heavy, hot, and oppressive, throughout the day. But we were making good progress under steam, which rendered the state of things more endurable than it would otherwise have been.

Whilst I was standing on deck at night, a flying-fish flew against my throat and hung there, caught in the lace of my dress. He is a pretty specimen, but only his wings are to be preserved, for Muriel will have his body for breakfast to-morrow.

Sunday, November 26th.—Our fourth consecutive Sunday at sea, and out of sight of land. At 4 a.m. the sails were spread to a good breeze. At 7 we stopped steaming, but at 10 the wind again fell light. The Litany was read on deck this morning on account of the heat. The observations at noon showed that we were in lat. 15° 47′ S., long. 135° 20′ W., the distance accomplished during the last twenty-four hours being 181 miles. We have now made good 4,067 miles from Valparaiso, and are 815 miles distant from Tahiti. At 5 p.m. we had prayers and a sermon, also on deck. It was then almost calm, and at eight o'clock we again began steaming, in order to insure our making the island of Tatakotoroa, 200 miles off, before dark to-morrow.

Monday, November 27th.—I was on deck at 3.30 a.m. Everybody on board was more or less excited at the prospect of making land, after twenty-eight days at sea.

It was a delicious morning, with a favorable breeze, and under steam and sail we progressed at the rate of from 10 to 11½ knots an hour. Several birds flew on board, amongst whom were two boobies, who hovered round us and appeared to examine everything with great curiosity, especially the little wind-vanes at the extremity of the masts. At last they settled on the foretopmast, whereupon one of the sailors went up to try and catch them. They observed his movements closely, and appeared to be specially interested in his cap; but as he approached, first one and then the other flew away, for a few yards, and then returned to his former position. At last the man, watching his opportunity, managed to seize one of them by his legs and bring him down in triumph, despite flapping wings and pecks from a sharp beak. He was shut up in the fowl-pen—now, alas! empty of its proper denizens—where we had an opportunity of examining him before he was killed. He was a fine, handsome, gray bird, with large blue eyes, and a wild hawk-like look.

At one o'clock we were almost sailing over the spot marked by Findlay as the situation of Tatakotopoto, or Anonymous Island; but there was nothing whatever visible in the shape of land, even from the masthead, where a man was stationed, and from which it was possible to see a distance of ten or fifteen miles. Tom went up himself several times and scanned the horizon carefully, but in vain. It is therefore evident either that the position of the island is incorrectly stated, or that it has become submerged. I believe that in these seas there are many islands marked that have no existence, and that several that do exist are not marked, which renders it necessary to keep a constant good lookout. What a charming task it would be to thoroughly survey these parts, and to correct the present charts where necessary, and how much I should like to be one of the officers appointed for the service!

At 1.30 p.m. land was sighted from the masthead,

and at two o'clock I saw from the deck what looked like plumes of dark ostrich feathers rising from the sea. This was the island of Tatakotoroa—also known as Narcissus, or Clarke Island—to the eastward of the Pamotu or Low Archipelago of the South Seas. The sailing directions describe the inhabitants as 'hostile,' and Sir Edward Belcher mentions that some of them tried to cut off the boats sent from a man-of-war for water. We were therefore afraid to attempt a landing, but sailed as near as we could to the shore, which, surrounded by a rampart of snow-white coral, and clothed almost to the water's edge with feathery palms, cocoanut-trees, and luxuriant vegetation of various kinds, looked very tempting. A few canoes were drawn up on the beach near a large hut, out of which three or four natives came, and, having looked at us for some time, ran off into the woods. Blue smoke could be seen curling up from several points of the forest, no doubt indicating the presence of more natives, whose dwellings were concealed by the trees.

After lunch, Tom had me hoisted up to the foretop-masthead in a 'boatswain's chair,' which is simply a small plank, suspended by ropes at the four corners, and used by the men to sit on when they scrape the masts. I was very carefully secured with a rope tied round my petticoats, and, knocking against the various ropes on my way, was then gently hoisted up to what seemed at first a giddy height; but when I once got accustomed to the smallness of the seat, the airiness of my perch, and the increased roll of the vessel, I found my position by no means an unpleasant one. Tom climbed up the rigging and joined me shortly afterwards. From our elevated post we could see plainly the formation of the island, and the lagune in the center, encircled by a band of coral, in some places white, bare, and narrow, in others wide and covered with palm-trees and rich vegetation; it was moreover possible to understand better the theory of the formation of these coral islands. I was so happy up aloft that I did not care to descend; and it was almost as interesting to observe what a strange and disproportioned appearance everything and everybody on board the yacht presented from my novel position, as it was to examine the island we were passing. The two younger children and the dogs took the greatest interest in my aërial expedition, and never ceased calling to me and barking, until I was once more let down safely into their midst. As soon as we had seen all we could of the island, fires were banked, and we proceeded under sail alone throughout the evening and night.

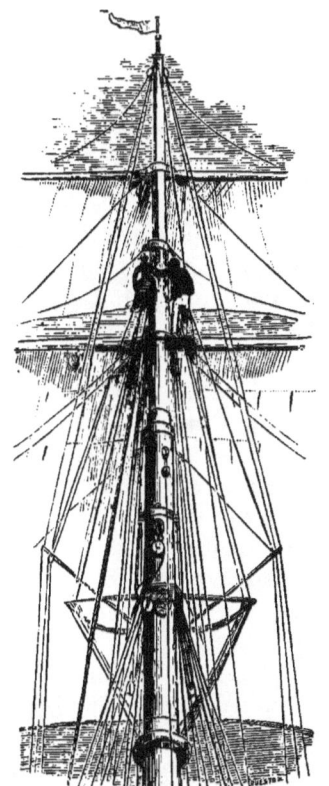

Going up the Mast in a Chair.

Children looking up.

CHAPTER XIII.

THE SOUTH SEA ISLANDS.

And all throughout the air there reigned the sense
Of waking dream with luscious thoughts o'erladen,
Of joy too conscious made and too intense
By the swift advent of excessive Aiden,
Bewilderment of beauty's affluence.

Tuesday, November 28th.—We passed Anaa, or Chain Island, in the morning watch, before daybreak. I came on deck to try and get a glimpse of it, and was rewarded by a glorious sunrise. We had a nice eight-knot breeze and a strong current in our favor, and just before breakfast Tom descried from the masthead Amanu, or Möller Island, which we had hardly expected to make before ten or eleven o'clock. Some one remarked that it seemed almost as if it had come out to meet us. The reef encircling this island varies much in height and vegetation. In some places it supports a noble grove of trees, in others the sea breaks over the half-submerged coral-bed, the first obstacle it has met for 4,000 miles, with a roar like thunder.

Before we had lost sight of Amanu, the island of Hao Harpe, or Bow Island, was visible on our port bow. I wished very much to land, and at last persuaded Tom, who was rather anxious on the score of the natives, to allow some of us to make the attempt, cautioning us to turn away from the shore directly, in case the islanders looked at all doubtful in their attitude and intentions. After lunch, therefore, we hove-to, and the gig's crew were ordered to arm themselves with revolvers and rifles,

which they were not to show unless required to do so.
All the gentlemen had revolvers, and Mabelle and I were
also provided with two small ones, Phillips and Muriel
being the only unarmed members of the party. I took
a bag full of beads, knives, looking-glasses, and pictures,
for barter and presents, and with these preparations we
set off to make our first personal acquaintance with the
islanders of the South Pacific. Tom gave us a tow to
windward, and we then rowed direct to a point on one
side of the entrance to the lagune, where we saw some
natives waving something white. As we approached we
could distinguish several figures standing on the point,
under the shade of some cocoanut-trees, and on the opposite side of the entrance some canoes were drawn up
on the beach, by the side of a hut, close to a large clump
of low trees. We were by this time surrounded by breakers, and it required no little skill to steer the boat safely
through the broken water, between the race of the tide
on one side, and the overfall from the coral reef on the
other. It was successfully done, however, and, having
rounded the point, we found ourselves at once in the
waters of the tranquil lagune. We should have preferred
to land at the point, had it been possible, as it was doubtful whether it would be safe to go round the corner, and
so lose sight of the yacht; but the intentions of the natives seemed peaceable, several of them running into the
water up to their waists to meet us, while others could be
seen hurrying along the beach, the women carrying what
looked like bunches of fruit.

It is really impossible to describe the beauty of the
scene before us. Submarine coral forests, of every color,
studded with sea-flowers, anemones, and echinidæ, of a
brilliancy only to be seen in dreamland, shoals of the
brighest and swiftest fish darting and flashing in and out;
shells, every one of which was fit to hold the place of
honor in a conchologist's collection, moving slowly along
with their living inmates: this is what we saw when we

looked down, from the side of the boat, into the depths below. The surface of the water glittered with every imaginable tint, from the palest aquamarine to the brightest emerald, from the pure light blue of the turquois to the deep dark blue of the sapphire, and was dotted here and there with patches of red, brown, and green coral, rising from the mass below. Before us, on the shore, there spread the rich growth of tropical vegetation, shaded by palms and cocoanuts, and enlivened by the presence of native women in red, blue, and green garments, and men in motley costumes, bringing fish, fowls, and bunches of cocoanuts, borne, like the grapes brought back from the land of Canaan by the spies, on poles.

As soon as we touched the shore the men rushed forward to meet us, and to shake hands, and, having left the muskets and revolvers judiciously out of sight in the boat, we were conducted to a cluster of huts, made of branches, or rather leaves, of the palm-tree, tied by their foot-stalks across two poles, and hanging down to the ground. Here we were met by the women and children, who, likewise, all went through the ceremony of shaking hands with us, after which the head-woman, who was very good-looking, and was dressed in a cherry-colored calico gown, with two long plaits of black hair hanging down her back, spread a mat for me to sit upon just outside the hut. By this time there was quite a little crowd of people assembled round, amongst whom I noticed one woman with a baby, who had her hair sticking straight out all round her head, and another who held a portion of her dress constantly before her face. After the gentlemen had walked away she removed the cloth, and I then saw that her nose had been cut off. Most of the women were good-looking, with dark complexions and quantities of well-greased, neatly-plaited black hair, but we did not see a single young girl, though there were plenty of children and babies, and lots of boys, the latter of whom, like some of the older women, had only a piece of palm matting round their loins. We therefore came to the conclusion that the girls must have been sent away intentionally when the approach of the yacht was observed.

As soon as I was seated, the head-woman told one of the men to knock down some cocoanuts from the trees close by, and after cutting off the ends she offered us a drink of the fresh cool milk, which was all the sweeter and better for the fact that the nuts were not nearly ripe. While this was going on, the natives brought piles of cocoanuts, fish, and fowls, and laid them at our feet as a present. Some of the fish were of a dark-brown color, like bream, others were long and thin, with a pipe-like nose and four fins, somewhat resembling the wings of a flying-fish.

Seeing smoke in the distance, rising from under some high palm-trees, we thought we should like to go and see whence it proceeded, and accordingly set off to walk through a sort of bush, over sharp coral that cut one's boots terribly, the sun blazing down upon us fiercely all the time, until we reached a little settlement, consisting of several huts, the inhabitants of which were absent. Fine plaited mats for beds, cocoanut shells for cups, mother-of-pearl shells for plates, and coral, of various kinds and shapes, for dishes and cooking utensils, formed their only furniture. We saw three women, one very old, with nothing but a palm-leaf mat as a covering, the others dressed in the apparently universal costume, consisting of a long bright-colored gown, put into a yoke at the shoulders, and flowing thence loosely to the ground, which completely conceals the wearer's form, even to the tips of her toes. I think these dresses must come from England or America, for they are evidently machine-made, and the cotton-stuff of which they are composed has the most extraordinary patterns printed on it I ever saw. Cherry and white, dark blue and yellow or white stripes, red with yellow spots, and blue with yellow crosses, appear to be the favorite designs. The women seemed gentle and kind, and were delighted with some beads, looking-glasses, and knives I gave them, in return for which they brought us quantities of beautiful shells.

We saw the large iron knee of a vessel in one spot during our walk, and wondered how it came there. In another place we saw a canoe in process of construction, ingeniously made of boards, sewed together with plaited palm-leaves. The canoes in use here are very high, long, and narrow, and are only kept from upsetting by means of a tremendous outrigger, consisting of a log fastened to the extremity of two bent pieces of wood, projecting sideways from each end of the boat. The only animals we met with in our ramble were four pigs and a few chickens, and no other live stock of any kind was visible. No attempt seemed to be made at the cultivation of the ground; and I think if there had been, we must have observed it, for our party separated and walked a good distance in various directions.

The natives made us understand that on the other side of the entrance to the lagune, in the better sort of house we had noticed, there resided a white man. He did not, however, make his appearance during our visit, and I imagine he must have been one of those individuals called 'beach-combers,' referred to in so many of the books that treat of the South Sea Islands—a sort of ne'er-do-well Englishman or American, rather afraid of meeting any of his own countrymen, but very clever at making a bargain between a ship's crew and the natives, with considerable profit to himself.

Among the bushes we found numbers of large hermit crabs, crawling, or rather running, about in whelk shells, half a dozen of them occasionally having a grand fight amongst themselves. We picked up at least twenty different sorts of gracefully shaped pieces of coral, and quantities of shells of an infinite variety of form and color; cowries, helmet-shells, the shells from which cameos are sometimes cut, mother-of-pearl, shells, and a large spiral univalve, nearly a foot long, with dark brown spots and stripes on a delicate cream-colored ground, like the skin of a tiger or leopard. On our way back to the huts we peeped into several of the canoes drawn up on the beach, in which were some fish-spears and a fish-hook, nearly three inches long, made of solid mother-of-pearl, the natural curve of the shell from which it was cut being preserved. A piece of bone was securely fastened to it by means of some pig's hair, but there was no bait, and it seems that the glitter of the mother-of-pearl alone serves as a sufficient allurement to the fish.

In nearly all accounts of voyages in the South Seas much space is devoted to the description of the purchase, or rather barter, of hogs. We thought we could not do better than follow as far as possible the example of our predecessors, and accordingly bought two little pigs for two shillings each. They were evidently quite pets, lying on the mats outside the huts, and coming when called, just like dogs. The one I first bought appeared to be quite happy and content to be carried under my arm. The natives seemed quite to understand the value of money, and did not hesitate to ask for it in return for the cocoanuts full of shells which they brought us. I fancy some of the Tahiti schooners trade here for pearl, shells, and bêche-de-mer.

The cocoanuts, fowls, fish, and coral, &c., having been put into our boat, we shook hands with the friendly islanders and embarked, and having rounded the point we soon found ourselves again in the broken water outside the lagune, where the race of the tide and the overfall were now much more violent than they had been when we landed. If we had once been drawn into the current, we should have stood a good chance of being knocked to pieces on the coral reefs, strong as our boat was; but the danger was happily avoided, and we reached the yacht safely, much to Tom's relief.

The natives did not exhibit the slightest curiosity

about us during our visit to the island, and though they received us with courtesy, and assisted us as far as they could on our arrival and departure, they did not follow us about while on shore, nor, with the exception of one or two of them, did they take the trouble to walk across the point to see us get into the open sea and join the yacht. In this respect they might have given a lesson to many civilized people, so gentle, genial, and graceful, yet dignified, were their manners.

The screw having been feathered and the sails set, our voyage was at once resumed. A few miles from where we had landed, we saw, high and dry on the coral reef skirting the island, a large square-built schooner, of about 500 tons, her masts gone, her hull bleached white by the sun, and a great hole in her side. She was on the inside of the reef, and must therefore either have drifted there from the lagune, or else have been lifted bodily across by one of the big Pacific rollers, in some terrible storm. No doubt the iron knee we had seen on the island originally formed part of this vessel.

Wednesday, November 29th.—We seem to have got into the real south-east trades, just as the chart tells us we ought to expect to lose them; for there was a strong fair breeze all day, which made it very pleasant on deck in the shade of the sails. But it was exceedingly hot in the saloon, where some of the woodwork has been pulled down, in order to secure better ventilation for the galley and the berths of some of the men, who, I hope, appreciate the alteration, for it is a source of considerable discomfort to us.

We had the bigger of our two little pigs for dinner to-day, and a welcome change it was from the salt and potted meats. He was most excellent, and fully corroborated Captain Cook's statement as to the superiority of South Sea Island pork to any other—a fact which is doubtless due to the pigs being fed entirely on cocoanuts and breadfruit. Still it seemed a pity to eat such a tame creature, and I mean to try and preserve the other one's life, unless we are much longer than we expect in reaching Tahiti. He is only about ten inches long, but looks at least a hundred years old, and is altogether the most quaint, old-fashioned little object you ever saw. He has taken a great fancy to the dogs, and trots about after me with them everywhere, on the tips of his little toes, even up and down the steep cabin stairs. I call him Agag, because he walks so delicately, whilst others accost him as Beau, not only on account of his elegant manners, but as being the name of his former home.

The moon was more brilliant this evening than we have yet seen her during our voyage, and we could enjoy sitting on deck reading, and even doing some coarse needlework, without any other light. One splendid meteor flashed across the sky. It was of a light orange color, with a fiery tail about two degrees in extent, and described in its course an arc of about sixty degrees, from S.S.E. to N.N.W., before it disappeared into space, far above the horizon. If the night had been darker, the spectacle would have been finer; but even as it was, the moon seemed quite paled for a few minutes afterwards. We have seen many meteors, falling-stars, and shooting-stars since we left Valparaiso, but none so fine as the one this evening.

Friday, December 1st.—The sun rose grandly, but the heavy black and red clouds, looking like flames and smoke from a furnace, gave promise of more rain. The heat was greater to-day than any we have yet felt; and it is now nearly mid-winter at home.

At 5 a.m. we made the island of Maitea, and expected to reach it in about an hour and a half; but the wind fell light, and it was a quarter to ten before we got into the gig and set out for the shore. There are not many instructions about landing, either in Captain Cook or Findlay, but the latter mentions that houses are to be found on the south side of the island. We thought, however, we could distinguish from the yacht a little cove, close to some huts, at another part of the shore, where the surf did not break so heavily. We accordingly rowed straight for it, and as we approached we could see the natives coming down from all parts to meet us, the women dressed in the same sort of long, bright, flowing garments we had seen at Hao Harpe, with the addition of garlands round their necks and heads, the men wearing gay-colored loin-cloths, shirts of Manchester cotton stuff, flying loose in the wind, and sailors' hats with garlands round them, or colored silk handkerchiefs—red and orange evidently having the preference—tied over their heads and jauntily knotted on one side. Several of the men waded out into the surf to meet us, sometimes standing on a rock two feet above the water, sometimes buried up to their necks by a sudden wave. But the rocks were sharp, the only available passage was narrow, and the rollers long and high; and altogether it looked, upon a closer inspection, too unpromising a place to attempt a landing. Much to the disappointment of the natives, therefore, we decided to go round and try the other side of the island. Seeing us prepare to depart, the people on shore immediately launched a tiny canoe, with an enormous outrigger, and a man dressed in a pale green shirt, dark blue and yellow under-garment, and with a silk handkerchief and garland on his head, came alongside and made signs that he would take us ashore one by one in his frail-looking craft. But the heavy Pacific rollers and the sharp rocks daunted us, and we declined his offer with thanks, and rowed off to the southward. Anything more enticing than the cove we were quitting can hardly be imagined. A fringe of cocoanuts and bread-fruit trees, overhanging an undergrowth of bright glossy foliage and flowers, a few half-hidden palm-leaf covered huts, from one of which—I suppose the chief's—a tattered Tahitian flag floated in the breeze, a small schooner drawn up among the trees and carefully covered with mats, the steep sugar-loaf point, at the entrance to the cove, clothed to its summit with grass and vegetation: these were the objects which attracted our attention in our hurried survey of the scene.

We had to give the island a wide berth in rowing round it, on account of the heavy rollers, which seemed to come from every side, breaking in surf against the dark brown cliffs, and throwing columns of white spray, from which

Our Boatman.

the brilliant sunsnine was reflected in rainbow hues, high into the air. As we proceeded matters looked worse and worse, and the motion of the boat became so disagreeable that both Muriel and I were very ill. At last we came to a spot where we could see some people sitting on the shore, and several others, who had probably come over from the other side to meet us, running swiftly down the sides of the cliffs to the beach. The island was of a different character from the one we had already visited, and was evidently of volcanic origin. No coral was anywhere to be seen, but there were big rocks jutting out at intervals into the sea all round it, one of which seemed large enough to afford us a sort of shelter in landing. The natives waved and pointed towards the channel beyond this rock, and one or two swam out to meet us; but we soon found that the channel would not be wide enough to admit our big boat, though it was no doubt sufficient for a light canoe, drawing some two inches of water. We therefore reluctantly turned away and resumed our uneasy coasting voyage, in the course of which we passed some nearly leafless trees, full of white patches, too large for flowers, which afterwards turned out to be booby-birds, who here find a resting-place. They are so numerous that it is hardly possible to walk beneath the trees without treading on their eggs.

Having completed the circuit of the island, we found ourselves once more opposite the spot where we had first thought of landing, and the tide being by this time a little higher, we decided to make another attempt. Some of the natives seeing us approach, plunged into the water as before, and seized the gunwale of the boat, while others, on shore, brought down rollers to put beneath our keel. We went in on the top of a big wave, and thus at last found ourselves—boat and all—high and dry on the beach of Maitea.

The people came down to meet us, and conducted us to the house of the chief, who, with his pretty wife, received us kindly, but with much gravity and dignity. Mats were placed for me to sit upon, wreaths were offered me for my head and neck, and cocoanut milk to drink. We wished for some bananas, and they immediately cut down a tree in order to obtain a bunch. Cocoanuts were at the same time thrown down from the trees, and a collection of fruit, poultry, and meat—the latter consisting of the immemorial hog—was laid at our feet, as a present from the chief. The rest of the natives brought us pearls, shells, mother-of-pearl, small canoes, fish-hooks, young boobies, and all sorts of things for barter; but the chief himself refused any return for his gift. Perhaps the greatest curiosity they offered us was about six fathoms of fine twine, made from human hair. Before these islands were visited by Europeans this was the material from which fishing-lines were made; but it is now rarely used, and is consequently very difficult to procure. The young boobies they brought us looked just like a white powder-puff, and were covered with down far thicker and softer than any swan's down I ever saw.

The natives seemed quite *au fait* in the matter of monetary transactions and exchanges. For an English sovereign they would give you change at the rate of five dollars. Chilian or United States dollars they accepted readily, but Brazilian currency they would not look at. They were pleased with knives, beads, looking-glasses, and picture papers I had brought on shore, and we did a brisk trade. We experienced great difficulty in explaining to them that we wanted some fresh eggs, Muriel's especial fancy, and a luxury which we have been without for some time. At last, by pointing to the fowls and picking up some small egg-shaped stones, we managed to procure a few, though, from the time it took to collect them, I should think the island must have been scoured in the search for them.

Most of the natives seemed puzzled to comprehend why we had visited the island at all. 'No sell brandy?' —'No.' 'No stealy men?'—'No.' 'No do what then?' Their knowledge of English was too limited to enable us to make them understand that we were only making a voyage of circumnavigation in a yacht.

It was now time to bid farewell to our amiable hosts and their beautiful island. As we reached the landing-place, a small schooner, which we had previously noticed in the distance, came close to the shore, and a canoe put off from the island to meet it. We found that the vessel was bringing back from Tahiti and other places some of the inhabitants of the island, who had been away on a visit or in search of work. The meeting of the reunited friends and relatives was in some cases quite touching.

Two women, in particular, sat and embraced each other for nearly a quarter of an hour, without moving, but with tears running down their faces.

All our gifts and purchases having been placed in the boat, and one or two of us having embarked, she was shoved out over the wooden rollers into the narrow channel, where she lay-to while the rest of the party were brought alongside, one by one, in a frail canoe—an operation which occupied some time, during which we had leisure once more to admire the little bay I have already attempted to describe. We asked the captain of the schooner, who spoke French, to give us a tow off to the yacht, which he willingly consented to do, chatting cheerfully all the time, but evidently fearful of approaching too close to the yacht, and positively refusing our invitation to him to come on board. There can be little doubt that he mistrusted our intentions, and feared we might attempt to kidnap him and his crew; for the whites have, in too many cases, behaved in a most villainous manner to the inhabitants of these islands, who are, as a rule—to which there are of course exceptions—a kind and gentle people. I think if the many instances of the murder of ships' and boats' crews could be thoroughly sifted to the bottom, it would be found that most of them were acts of reprisal and revenge for brutal atrocities committed on the defenseless natives, who have been kidnapped, plundered, and murdered by unscrupulous traders and adventurers. Unfortunately, the good suffer for the bad, and such lives as those of Captain Goodenough and Bishop Patteson are sacrificed through the unpardonable misconduct of others —perhaps their own countrymen. It is still quite a chance how you may be received in some of the islands; for if the visit of the last ship was the occasion of the murder, plunder, and ill-treatment of the inhabitants, it is not to be wondered at that the next comers should be received with distrust, if not with treachery and violence.

We reached the yacht at four o'clock, rather exhausted by so many hours' exposure to the broiling sun, having had nothing to eat since breakfast, at 7 a.m., except cocoanuts and bananas. The ship was put about, the sails filled, and, continuing steadily on our course throughout the evening, we made the smaller of the two peninsulas that form the island of Tahiti at 10.30 p.m.

Saturday, December 2d. — We were dodging on and off all night, and at daybreak the weather was thick and rainy. At 4.30 a.m. we made the land again, and crept slowly along it, past Point Venus and the lighthouse in Matavai Bay (Captain Cook's first anchorage), until we were off the harbor of Papiete. The rain was now descending in torrents, and we lay-to outside the reef for a short time, until a French pilot came on board and took us in through the narrow entrance. It was curious, while we were tumbling about in the rough sea outside, to see the natives placidly fishing in the tiniest of canoes on the lagune inside the reef, the waves beating all the time furiously on the outer surface of the coral breakwater, as if anxious to seize and ingulf them.

At nine o'clock we were safely anchored in the chief port of the island of Tahiti.

Perhaps I cannot better bring this account of our long voyage from Valparaiso to a conclusion than by a quotation from a charming book, given to me at Rio, which I have lately been reading—Baron de Hubner's 'Promenade autour du Monde' :—' Les jours se suivent et se ressemblent. Sauf le court épisode du mauvais temps, ces trois semaines me font l'effet d'un charmant rêve, d'un conte de fée, d'une promenade imaginaire à travers une salle immense, tout or et lapis-lazuli. Pas un moment d'ennui ou d'impatience. Si vous voulez abréger les longueurs d'une grande traversée, distribuez bien votre temps, et observez le règlement que vous vous êtes imposé. C'est un moyen sûr de se faire promptement à la vie claustrale et même d'en jouir.'

We have been five weeks at sea, and have enjoyed them quite as much as the Baron did his three. We saw but two ships between Valparaiso and Tatakotoroa: he saw only one between San Francisco and Yokohama. It is indeed a vast and lonely ocean that we have traversed.

CHAPTER XIV.

AT TAHITI.

The cava feast, the yam, the cocoa's root,
Which bears at once the cup, and milk, and fruit,
The bread-tree which, without the plowshare, yields
The unreap'd harvest of unfurrowed fields.

. . . . . .

These, with the luxuries of seas and woods,
The airy joys of social solitudes,
Tamed each rude wanderer.

Saturday, December 2d.—The anchor was dropped in the harbor of Papiete at nine o'clock, and a couple of hours later, by which time the weather had cleared, we went ashore, and at once found ourselves in the midst of a fairy-like scene, to describe which is almost impossible, so bewildering is it in the brightness and variety of its coloring. The magnolias and yellow and scarlet hibiscus, overshadowing the water, the velvety turf, on to which one steps from the boat, the white road running between rows of wooden houses, whose little gardens are a mass of flowers, the men and women clad in the gayest robes and decked with flowers, the piles of unfamiliar fruit lying on the grass, waiting to be transported to the coasting vessels in the harbor, the wide-spreading background of hills clad in verdure to their summits—these are but a few of the objects which greet the new-comer in his first contact with the shore.

We strolled about, and left our letters of introduction; but the people to whom they were addressed were at breakfast, and we were deliberating how best to dispose of our time, when a gentleman accosted us, and, seeing how new it all was to us strangers, offered to show us round the town.

The streets of Papiete, running back at right angles with the beach, seem to have wonderfully grand names, such as the Rue de Rivoli, Rue de Paris, &c. Every street is shaded by an avenue of high trees, whose branches meet and interlace overhead, forming a sort of leafy tunnel, through which the sea-breeze passes refreshingly. There is also what is called the Chinamen's quarter, through which we walked, and which consists of a collection of regular Chinese-built bamboo houses, whose occupants all wore their national costume, pigtail included. The French commandant lives in a charming residence, surrounded by gardens, just opposite the palace of Queen Pomare, who is at present at the island of Bola-Bola, taking care of her little grandchild, aged five, the queen of the island. She went down in a French man-of-war, the 'Limier,' ten days ago, and has been obliged to remain, owing to some disturbances amongst the natives. I am rather disappointed that she is absent, as I should like to see a person of whom I have heard so much.

Having completed our tour, we next went to call on the British Consul, who received us kindly, and entertained us with an interesting account of the island and its inhabitants, its pearl-fisheries and trade, the French policy, the missionaries, &c., on all of which subjects he is well informed. He has just completed an exhaustive consular report on the condition of the island, which will, no doubt, appear in due course in the form of a blue book.

On our return to Messrs. Brander's office, where we had left one of our letters of introduction, we found the manager, with whom we had a long chat before returning on board.

At 5 p.m. we went for a row in the 'Glance' and the 'Flash' to the coral reef, now illumined by the rays of the setting sun. Who can describe these wonderful gardens of the deep, on which we now gazed through ten and twenty fathoms of crystal water? Who can enumerate or describe the strange creatures moving about and darting hither and thither, amid the masses of coral forming their submarine home? There were shells of rare shape, brighter than if they had been polished by the hand of the most skillful artist; crabs of all sizes, scuttling and sidling along; sea-anemones, spreading their delicate feelers in search of prey; and many other kinds of zoophytes, crawling slowly over the reef; and scarlet, blue, yellow, gold, violet, spotted, striped, and winged fish, short, long, pointed, and blunt, of the most varied shapes, were darting about like birds among the coral trees.

At last, after frequent stoppages, to allow time for admiration, we reached the outer reef, hauled the boat up and made her fast, and, in bathing shoes, started on a paddling expedition. Such a paddle it was too, over the coral, the surf breaking far above our heads, and the underflow, though only a few inches deep, nearly carrying me and the children off our legs! There were one or two native fishermen walking along the reef, whipping the water; but they appeared to have caught only a few small rock-fish, pretty enough to look at, but not apparently good to eat.

The shades of night compelled us to return to the yacht, laden with corals of many different species. After dinner the bay was illuminated by the torches of the native fishermen, in canoes, on the reef. Tom and I went to look at them, but did not see them catch anything. Each canoe contained at least three people, one of whom propelled the boat, another stood up waving about a torch dipped in some resinous substance, which threw a strong light on the water, while the third stood in the bows, armed with a spear, made of a bundle of wires, tied to a long pole, not at all unlike a gigantic egg-whip, with all its loops cut into points. This is aimed with great dexterity at the fish, who are either transfixed or jammed between the prongs. The fine figures of the natives, lighted up by the flickering torches, and standing out in bold relief against the dark blue starlit sky, would have served as models for the sculptors of ancient Greece.

Sunday, December 3d.—At a quarter to five this morning some of us landed to see the market, this being the great day when the natives come in from the country and surrounding villages, by sea and by land, in boats or on horseback, to sell their produce, and buy necessaries for the coming week. We walked through the shady streets to the two covered market buildings, partitioned across with great bunches of oranges, plantains, and many-colored vegetables, hung on strings. The mats, beds, and pillows still lying about suggested the idea that the salesmen and women had passed the night amongst their wares. The gayly attired, good-looking, flower-decorated crowd, of some seven or eight hundred people, all chatting and laughing, and some staring at us—but not rudely—looked much more like a chorus of opera-singers, dressed for their parts in some grand spectacle, than ordinary market-going peasants. Whichever way one turned, the prospect was an animated and attractive one. Here, beneath the shade of large, smooth, light-green banana leaves, was a group of earnest bargainers for mysterious-looking fish, luscious fruit, and vegetables; there, sheltered by a drooping mango, whose rich clusters of purple and orange fruit hung in tempting proximity to lips and hands, another little crowd was similarly engaged. Orange-trees were evidently favorite *rendezvous;* and a row of flower-sellers had established themselves in front of a hedge of scarlet hibiscus and double cape jasmine. Every vender carried his stock-in-trade, however small the articles composing it might be, on a bamboo pole, across his shoulder, occasionally with rather ludicrous effect, as, for instance, when the thick but light pole supported only a tiny fish six inches long at one end, and two mangoes at the other. Everybody seemed to have brought to market just what he or she happened to have on hand, however small the quantity. The women would have one, two, or three new-laid eggs in a leaf basket, one crab or lobster, three or four prawns, or one little trout. Under these circumstances, marketing for so large a party as ours was a somewhat lengthy operation, and I was much amused in watching our *proveedor*, as he went about collecting things by ones and twos, until he had piled a little cart quite full, and had had it pushed off to the shady quay.

We strolled about until six o'clock, at which hour the purchasers began to disperse, and were just preparing to depart likewise, when an old man, carrying half a dozen little fish and followed by a small boy laden with vegetables and fruit, introduced himself to us as the brother-in-law of Queen Pomare IV. and chief of Papiete, and, after a short talk, invited us to visit him at his house. We consented, and, following him, presently reached a break in the hedge and ditch that ran along the side of the road, beyond which was a track, bordered by pineapples and dracænas, leading to a superior sort of house, built in the native style, and surrounded, as usual, by bread-fruit, cocoanut, banana, mango, and guava trees. We were conducted into the one large room, which contained two four-post bedsteads and four mattresses, laid on the floor, two or three trunks, and a table in the corner, on which were writing materials and a few books. The chief himself spoke a very little English, his son an equally small amount of French; so the conversation languished, and after a decent interval we rose to depart. Our host asked if he might 'come and see my ship,' and procured pen, ink, and paper—not of the best quality—for me to write an order for him do so, 'in case lady not at home.' He also presented me with some pictures of soldiers, drawn by his son—a boy about eleven years old, of whom he seemed very proud, and expressed his regret that we could not prolong our stay, at the same time placing at our disposal the whole house and garden, including a fat sow and eleven little pigs.

Several other visitors had arrived by this time, one of whom was on horseback, and, as I was rather tired, he was asked if he would kindly allow me to ride down to the landing-place. He replied that he would lend the horse to a gentleman, but not to me, as the saddle was not suitable. I explained that this made no difference to me, and mounted, though I did not attempt to follow the fashion of the native ladies here, who ride like men. Our new friend was quite delighted at this, and volunteered himself to show us something of the neighborhood. Accordingly, leading my—or rather his—horse, and guiding him carefully over all the rough places, he took us through groves and gardens to the grounds belonging to the royal family, in which were plantations of various kinds of trees, and a thick undergrowth of guava. After an enjoyable little expedition we returned to the yacht at about half-past seven, accompanied by the small boy who had been carrying our special purchases from the market all this time, and by a little tail of followers.

At half-past eight we breakfasted, so as to be ready for the service at the native church at ten o'clock; but several visitors arrived in the interval, and we had rather a bustle to get off in time, after all. We landed close to the church, under the shade of an hibiscus, whose yellow and orange flowers dropped off into the sea and floated away amongst the coral rocks, peeping out of the water here and there. The building appeared to be full to overflowing. The windows and doors were all wide open, and many members of the congregation were seated on the steps, on the lawn, and on the grassy slope beyond, listening to a discourse in the native language. Most of the people wore the native costume, which, especially when made of black stuff and surmounted by a little sailor's hat, decorated with a bandana handkerchief or a wreath of flowers, was very becoming. Sailors' hats are universally worn, and are generally made by the natives themselves from plantain or palm leaves, or from the inside fiber of the arrowroot. Some rather elderly men and women in the front rows were taking notes of the sermon. I found afterwards that they belonged to the Bible class, and that their great pride was to meet after the service and repeat by heart nearly all they had heard. This seems to show at least a desire to profit by the minister's efforts, which, we must hope, were not altogether in vain.

After the usual service there were two christenings. The babies were held at the font by the men, who looked extremely sheepish. One baby was grandly attired in a book-muslin dress, with flounces, a tail at least six feet long dragging on the ground, and a lace cap with cherry-colored bows; the other was nearly as smart, in a white-worked long frock and cap, trimmed with blue bows. The christenings over, there was a hymn, somewhat monotonous as to time and tune, but sung with much fervor, followed by the administration of the sacrament, in which cocoanut milk took the place of wine, and bread-fruit that of bread. The proper elements were originally used, but experience proved that, although the bread went round pretty well, the cup was almost invariably emptied by the first two or three communicants, sometimes with unfortunate results.

After service we drove through the shady avenues of the town into the open country, past trim little villas and sugar-cane plantations, until we turned off the main road, and entered an avenue of mangoes, whence a rough road, cut through a guava thicket, leads to the main gate of Fautahua—a regular square Indian bungalow, with thatched roofs, verandas covered with creepers, windows opening to the ground, and steps leading to the gardens on every side, ample accommodation for stables, kitchens, servants, being provided in numerous outbuildings.

Soon after breakfast, Mrs. Brander dressed me in one of her own native costumes, and we drove to the outskirts of a dense forest, through which a footpath leads to the waterfall and fort of Fautahua. Here we found horses waiting for us, on which we rode, accompanied by the gentlemen on foot, through a thick growth of palms, orange-trees, guavas, and other tropical trees, some of which were overhung and almost choked by luxuriant creepers. Specially noticeable among the latter was a gorgeous purple passion-flower, with orange-colored fruit as big as pumpkins, that covered everything with its vigorous growth. The path was always narrow and sometimes steep, and we had frequently almost to creep under the overhanging boughs, or to turn aside to avoid a more than usually dense mass of creepers. We crossed several small rivers, and at last reached a spot that commanded a view of the waterfall, on the other side of a deep ravine. Just below the fort that crowns the height, a river issues from a narrow cleft in the rock, and falls at a single bound from the edge of an almost perpendicular cliff, 600 feet high, into the valley beneath. First one sees the rush of blue water, gradually changing in its descent to a cloud of white spray, which in its turn is lost in a rainbow of mist. Imagine that from beneath the shade of feathery palms and broad-leaved bananas through a network of ferns and creepers you are looking upon the Staubbach, in Switzerland, magnified in height, and with a background of verdure-clad mountains, and you will have some idea of the fall of Fautahua as we beheld it.

After resting a little while and taking some sketches, we climbed up to the fort itself, a place of considerable interest, where the natives held out to the very last against the French. On the bank opposite the fort, the last islander killed during the struggle for independence was shot while trying to escape. Situated in the center of a group of mountains, with valleys branching off in all directions, the fort could hold communication with every part of the coast, and there can be little doubt that it would have held out much longer than it did, but for the treachery of one of the garrison, who led the invaders, under cover of the night, and by devious paths, to the top of a hill commanding the position. Now the ramparts and earthworks are overrun and almost hidden by roses. Originally planted, I suppose, by the new-comers, they have spread rapidly in all directions, till the hillsides and summits are quite a-blush with the fragrant bloom.

Having enjoyed some strawberries and some icy-cold water from a spring, and heard a long account of the war from the *gardiens*, we found it was time to commence our return journey, as it was now getting late. We descended much more quickly than we had come up, but daylight had faded into the brief tropical twilight, and that again into the shades of night, ere we reached the carriage.

Dinner and evening service brought the day to a conclusion, and I retired, not unwillingly, to bed, to dream of the charms of Tahiti.

Sometimes I think that all I have seen must be only a long vision, and that too soon I shall awaken to the cold reality; the flowers, the fruit, the colors worn by every one, the whole scene and its surroundings, seem almost too fairylike to have an actual existence. I am in despair when I attempt to describe all these things. I feel that I cannot do anything like justice to their merits, and yet I fear all the time that what I say may be looked upon as an exaggeration.

> Long dreamy lawns, and birds on happy wings,
>   Keeping their homes in never-rifled bowers;
> Cool fountains filling with their murmurings
>   The sunny silence 'twixt the chiming hours.

At daybreak next morning, when I went on deck, it was a dead calm. The sea-breeze had not yet come in, and there was not a ripple on the surface of the harbor.

Outside, two little white trading schooners lay becalmed; inside, the harbor-tug was getting up steam. On shore, a few gayly dressed natives were hurrying home with their early market produce, and others were stretched lazily on the grass at the water's edge or on the benches under the trees. Our stores for the day, a picturesque-looking heap of fish, fruit, vegetables, and flowers, were on the steps, waiting to be brought off, and guarded in the meantime by natives in costumes of pink, blue, orange, and a delicate pale green they specially affect. The light mists rolled gradually away from the mountain tops, and there was every prospect of a fine day for a projected excursion.

I went ashore to fetch some of the fresh-gathered fruit, and soon we had a feast of luscious pineapples, juicy mangoes, bananas, and oranges, with the dew still upon them. The mango is certainly the king of fruit. Its flavor is a combination of apricot and pineapple, with the slightest possible suspicion of turpentine thrown in, to give a piquancy to the whole. I dare say it sounds a strange mixture, but I can only say that the result is delicious. To enjoy mangoes thoroughly you ought not to eat them in company, but leaning over the side of the ship, in the early morning, with your sleeves tucked up to your elbows, using no knife and fork, but tearing off the skin with your teeth, and sucking the abundant juice.

We breakfasted at half-past six, and, at a little before eight, went ashore, where we were met by a sort of *char-à-bancs*, or American wagon, with three seats, one behind the other, all facing the horses, and roomy and comfortable enough for two persons. Our Transatlantic cousins certainly understand thoroughly, and do their best to improve everything connected with, the locomotion they love so well. A Chinese coachman and a thin but active pair of little horses completed the turnout. Mabelle sat beside the coachman, and we four packed into the other two seats, with all our belongings.

The sun was certainly *very* powerful when we emerged from the shady groves of Papiete, but there was a nice breeze, and sometimes we got under the shade of cocoanut trees. We reached Papea at about half-past nine, and changed horses there. While waiting, hot and thirsty, under the shelter of some trees, we asked for a cocoanut, whereupon a man standing by immediately tied a withe of banana leaves round his feet and proceeded to climb, or rather hop, up the nearest tree, raising himself with his two hands and his feet alternately, with an exactly similar action to that of our old friend the monkey on the stick. People who have tasted the cocoanut only in England can have no idea what a delicious fruit it really is when nearly ripe and freshly plucked. The natives remove the outer husk, just leaving a little piece to serve as a foot for the pale brown cup to rest on. They then smooth off the top, and you have an elegant vase, something like a mounted ostrich-egg in appearance, lined with the snowiest ivory, and containing about three pints of cool sweet water. Why it is called milk I cannot understand, for it is as clear as crystal, and is always cool and refreshing, though the nut in which it is contained has generally been exposed to the fiercest sun. In many of the coral islands, where the water is brackish, the natives drink scarcely anything but cocoanut milk; and even here, if you are thirsty and ask for a glass of water, you are almost always presented with a cocoanut instead.

From Papea onwards the scenery increased in beauty, and the foliage was, if possible, more luxuriant than ever. The road ran through extensive coffee, sugar-cane, Indian corn, orange, cocoanut, and cotton plantations, and vanilla, carefully trained on bamboos, growing in the thick shade. Near Atemavao we passed the house of a great cotton planter, and, shortly afterwards, the curious huts, raised on platforms, built by some islanders he has imported from the Kingsmill group to work his plantations. They are a wild, savage-looking set, very inferior to the

Tahitians in appearance. The cotton-mills, which formerly belonged to a company, are now all falling to ruin; and in many other parts of the island we passed cotton plantations uncleaned and neglected, and fast running to seed and waste. So long as the American war lasted, a slight profit could be made upon Tahitian cotton, but now it is hopeless to attempt to cultivate it with any prospect of adequate return.

The sun was now at its height, and we longed to stop and bathe in one of the many fresh-water streams we crossed, and afterwards eat our lunch by the wayside; but our Chinese coachman always pointed onwards, and said, 'Eatee much presently; horses eatee too.' At last we arrived at a little house, shaded by cocoanut trees, and built in an inclosure near the sea-shore, with 'Restaurant' written up over the door. We drove in, and were met by the proprietor, with what must have been rather an embarrassing multiplicity of women and children about his heels. The cloth was not laid, but the rooms looked clean, and there was a heap of tempting-looking fish and fruit in a corner. We assured him we were starving, and begged for luncheon as soon as possible; and, in the meantime, went for a dip in the sea. But the water was shallow, and the sun made the temperature at least 90°, so that our bath was not very refreshing. On our return we found the table most enticingly laid out, with little scarlet crayfish, imbedded in cool green lettuce leaves, fruit of various kinds, good wine and fair bread, all arranged on a clean though coarse tablecloth. There was also a savory omelet, so good that Tom asked for a second; when, to our astonishment, there appeared a plump roast fowl, most artistic gravy, and fried potatoes. Then came a *biftek aux champignons*, and some excellent coffee to wind up with. On making the host our compliments, he said, 'Je fais la cuisine moi-même, madame.' In the course of our repast we again tasted the bread-fruit, but did not much appreciate it, though it was this time cooked in the native fashion—roasted underground by means of hot stones.

Our coachman was becoming impatient, so we bade farewell to our host, and resumed our journey. We crossed innumerable streams on our way, generally full not only of water, but also of bathers; for the Tahitians are very fond of water, and always bathe once or twice a day in the fresh streams, even after having been in the sea.

In many places along the road people were making hay from short grass, and in others they were weighing it preparatory to sending it into town. But they say the grass grown here is not at all nourishing for horses, and some people import it from Valparaiso.

The road round the island is called the Broom Road. Convicts were employed in its original formation, and now it is the punishment for any one getting drunk in any part of the island to be set to work to sweep, repair, and keep in order a piece of the road in the neighborhood of his dwelling. It is the one good road of Tahiti, encircling the larger of the two peninsulas close to the sea-shore, and surmounting the low mountain range in the center of the isthmus.

Before long we found ourselves close to the narrow strip of land connecting the two peninsulas into which Tahiti is divided, and commenced to ascend the hills that form the backbone of the island. We climbed up and up, reaching the summit at last, to behold a magnificent prospect on all sides. Then a short, sharp descent, a long drive over grass roads through a rich forest, and again a brief ascent, brought us to our sleeping-quarters for the night, the Hôtel de l'Isthme, situated in a valley in the midst of a dense grove of cocoanuts and bananas, kept by two retired French sailors, who came out to meet us, and conducted us up a flight of steps on the side of a mud bank to the four rooms forming the hotel. These were two sleeping apartments, a *salon,* and a *salle à manger,* the walls of which consisted of flat pieces of wood, their own width apart, something like Venetian shutters, with unglazed windows and doors opening into the garden.

We walked about four hundred yards along a grassy road to the sea, where Mabelle and I paddled about in shallow water and amused ourselves by picking up coral, shells, and *bêche-de-mer*, and watching the blue and yellow fish darting in and out among the rocks, until at last we found a place in the coral which made a capital deep-water bath. Dressing again was not such a pleasant affair, owing to the mosquitoes biting us in the most provoking manner. Afterwards we strolled along the shore, which was covered with cocoanuts and driftwood, washed thither, I suppose, from some of the adjacent islands, and on our way back to the hotel we gathered a handful of choice exotics and graceful ferns, with which to decorate the table.

The dinner itself really deserves a detailed description, if only to show that one may make the tour of Tahiti without necessarily having to rough it in the matter of food. We had crayfish and salad as a preliminary, and next an excellent soup, followed by delicious little oysters that cling to the boughs and roots of the guava and mangrove trees overhanging the sea. Then came a large fish, name unknown, the inevitable *bouilli* and cabbage, *côtelettes aux pommes*, *biftek aux champignons*, succeeded by crabs and other shell-fish, including *wurrali*, a delicate-flavored kind of lobster, an *omelette aux abricots*, and dessert of tropical fruit. We were also supplied with good wine, both red and white, and bottled beer.

I ought, in truth, to add that the cockroaches were rather lively and plentiful, but they did not form a serious drawback to our enjoyment. After dinner, however, when I went to see Mabelle to bed, hundreds of these creatures, about three inches long, and broad in proportion, scuttled away as I lighted the candle; and while we were sitting outside we could see troops of them marching up and down in rows between the crevices of the walls. Then there were the mosquitoes, who hummed and buzzed about us, and with whom, alas! we were doomed to make a closer acquaintance. Our bed was fitted with the very thickest calico mosquito curtains, impervious to the air, but not to the venomous little insects, who found their way in through every tiny opening in spite of all our efforts to exclude them.

Tuesday, December 5*th.*—The heat in the night was suffocating, and soon after twelve o'clock we both woke up, feeling half-stifled. There was a dim light shining into the room, and Tom said, 'Thank goodness, it's getting daylight;' but on striking my repeater we found to our regret that this was a mistake. In the moonlight I could see columns of nasty brown cockroaches ascending the bedposts, crawling along the top of the curtains, dropping with a thud on the bed, and then descending over the side to the ground. At last I could stand it no longer, and, opening the curtains cautiously, I seized my slippers, knocked half a dozen brown beasts out of each, wrapped myself in a poncho — previously well-shaken — gathered my garments around me, surmounted a barricade I had constructed overnight to keep the pigs and chickens out of our doorless room, and fled to the garden. All was still, the only sign of life being a light in a neighboring hut, and I sat out in the open air in comparative comfort, until driven indoors again by torrents of rain, at about half-past two o'clock.

I plunged into bed again, taking several mosquitoes with me, which hummed and buzzed and devoured us to their hearts' content till dawn. Then I got up and walked down to the beach to bathe, and returned to breakfast at six o'clock, refreshed but still disfigured.

It is now the depth of winter and the middle of the rainy season in Tahiti; but, luckily for us, it is nearly always fine in the daytime. At night, however, there is often a perfect deluge, which floods the houses and gardens, turns the streams into torrents, but washes and refreshes the vegetation, and leaves the landscape brighter and greener than before.

At half-past seven the horses were put to, and we were just ready for a start, when down came the rain again, more heavily than before. It was some little time before it ceased enough to allow us to start, driving along grassy roads and through forests, but progressing rather slowly, owing to the soaked condition of the ground. If you can imagine the Kew hot-houses magnified and multiplied to an indefinite extent, and laid out as a gentleman's park, traversed by numerous grassy roads fringed with cocoa-nut palms, and commanding occasional glimpses of sea, and beach, and coral reefs, you will have some faint idea of the scene through which our road lay.

Many rivers we crossed, and many we stuck in, the gentlemen having more than once to take off their shoes and stockings, tuck up their trousers, jump into the water, and literally put their shoulders to the wheel. Sometimes we drove out into the shallow sea, till it seemed doubtful when and where we should make the land again. Sometimes we climbed up a solid road, blasted out of the face of the black cliffs, or crept along the shore of the tranquil lagune, frightening the land-crabs into their holes as they felt the shake of the approaching carriage. Palms and passiflora abounded, the latter being specially magnificent. It seems wonderful how their thin stems can support, at a height of thirty or forty feet from the ground, the masses of huge orange-colored fruit which depend in strings from their summits.

At the third river, not far from where it fell into the sea, we thought it was time to lunch; so we stopped the carriage, gave the horses their provender, and sat down to enjoy ourselves after our long drive. It was early in the afternoon before we started again, and soon after this we were met by fresh horses, sent out from Paponoa; so it was not long before we found ourselves near Point Venus, where we once more came upon a good piece of road, down which we rattled to the plains outside Papiete.

We reached the quay at about seven o'clock, and, our arrival having been observed, several friends came to see us and to inquire how we had fared. Before we started on our excursion, instructions had been given that the 'Sunbeam' should be painted *white*, for the sake of coolness, and we were all very curious to see how she would look in her new dress; but unfortunately the wet weather has delayed the work, and there is still a good deal to do.

Wednesday, December 6th.—It was raining fast at half-past four this morning, which was rather provoking, as I wanted to take some photographs from the yacht's deck before the sea-breeze sprang up. But the weather cleared while I was choosing my position and fixing my camera, and I was enabled to take what I hope may prove to be some successful photographs.

Messrs. Brander's mail-ship, a sailing vessel of about 600 tons, was to leave for San Francisco at eight o'clock, and at seven Tom started in the 'Flash' to take our letters on board. The passage to San Francisco occupies twenty-five days on an average, and is performed with great regularity once a month each way. The vessels employed on this line, three in number, are well built, and have good accommodation for passengers, and they generally carry a full cargo. In the present instance it consists of fungus and tripang (*bêche-de-mer*) for China, oranges for San Francisco, a good many packages of sundries, and a large consignment of pearls, intrusted to the captain at the last moment.

So brisk is the trade carried on between Tahiti and the United States, that the cost of this vessel was more than covered by the freights the first year after she was built. In addition to these ships, there are those which run backwards and forwards to Valparaiso, and the little island-trading schooners; so that the Tahitians can boast of quite a respectable fleet of vessels, not imposing perhaps in point of tonnage, but as smart and serviceable-looking as could be desired. The trading schooners are really beautiful little craft, and I am sure that, if well kept and properly manned, they would show to no discredit among our smart yachts at Cowes. Not a day passes without one or more entering or leaving the harbor, returning from or bound to the lonely isles with which the south-west portion of the Pacific is studded. They are provided with a patent log, but their captains, who are intelligent men, do not care much about a chronometer, as the distances to be run are comparatively short and are easily judged.

Mr. Godfroi gave us rather an amusing account of the manner in which their negotiations with the natives are conducted. The more civilized islanders have got beyond barter, and prefer hard cash in American dollars for their pearls, shells, cocoanuts, sandal-wood, &c. When they have received the money, they remain on deck for some time discussing their bargains among themselves. Then they peep down through the open skylights into the cabin below, where the most attractive prints and the gaudiest articles of apparel are temptingly displayed, alongside a few bottles of rum and brandy and a supply of tobacco. It is not long before the bait is swallowed; down go the natives, the goods are sold, and the dollars have once more found their way back into the captain's hands.

I had a long talk with one of the natives, who arrived to-day from Flint Island—a most picturesque-looking individual, dressed in scarlet and orange-colored flannel, and a mass of black, shiny, curly hair. Flint Island is a place whose existence has been disputed, it having been more than once searched for by ships in vain. It was, therefore, particularly interesting to meet some one who had actually visited, and had just returned from, the spot in question. That islands do occasionally disappear entirely in these parts there can be little doubt. The Tahitian schooners were formerly in the habit of trading with a small island close to Rarotonga, whose name I forget; but about four years ago, when proceeding thither with the usual three-monthly cargo of provisions, prints, &c., they failed to find the island, of which no trace has since been seen. Two missionaries from Rarotonga are believed to have been on it at the time of its disappearance, and they seem to have shared its mysterious fate.

A Tahitian Lady.

Thursday, December 7th.—At eight o'clock I took Mabelle and Muriel for a drive in a pony-carriage which had been kindly lent me, but with a hint that the horse was rather *méchant* sometimes. He behaved well on the present occasion, however, and we had a pleasant drive in the outskirts of the town for a couple of hours.

Just as we returned, a gentleman came and asked me if I should like to see some remarkably fine pearls, and on my gladly consenting, he took me to his house, where I saw some pearls certainly worth going to look at, but too expensive for me, one pear-shaped gem alone having been valued at £1,000. I was told they came from a neighboring island, and I was given two shells containing pearls in various stages of formation.

It was now time to go on board to receive some friends whom we had invited to breakfast, and who arrived at about half-past eleven.

After breakfast, and a chat, and an examination of the photograph books, &c., we all landed, and went to see Messrs. Brander's stores, where all sorts of requisites for fitting out ships and their crews can be procured. It is surprising to find how plentiful are the supplies of the necessaries and even the luxuries of civilized life in this far-away corner of the globe. You can even get *ice* here, for the manufacture of which a retired English infantry officer has set up an establishment with great success. But what interested me most were the products of this and the neighboring islands. There were tons of exquisitely tinted pearl shells, six or eight inches in diameter, formerly a valuable article of commerce, but now worth comparatively little. The pearls that came out of them had unfortunately been sent away to Liverpool—£1,000 worth by this morning's, and £5,000 by the last mail-ship. Then there was vanilla, a most precarious crop, which needs to be carefully watered and shaded from the first moment it is planted, and which must be gathered before it is ripe, and dried and matured in a moist heat, between blankets and feather-beds, in order that the pods may not crack and allow the essence to escape. We saw also edible fungus, exported to San Francisco, and thence to Hong Kong, solely for the use of the Chinese; tripang, or *bêche-de-mer*, a sort of sea-slug or holothuria, which, either living or dead, fresh or dried, looks equally untempting, but is highly esteemed by the Celestials; coprah, or dried cocoa-nut kernels, broken into small pieces in order that they may stow better, and exported to England, and other parts, where the oil is expressed and oil-cake formed; and various other articles of commerce. The trade of the island is fast increasing, the average invoice value of the exports having risen from £8,400 in 1845 to £98,000 in 1874. These totals are exclusive of the value of the pearls, which would increase it by at least another £3,000 or £4,000.

I speak from personal experience when I say that every necessary for life on board ship, and many luxuries, can be procured at Tahiti. American tinned fruits and vegetables beat English ones hollow. Preserved milk is uncertain—sometimes better, sometimes worse, than what one buys at home. Tinned salmon is much better. Australian mutton, New Zealand beef, and South Sea pork leave nothing to be desired in the way of preserved meat. Fresh beef, mutton, and butter are hardly procurable, and the latter, when preserved, is uneatable. I can never understand why they don't take to potting and salting down for export the *best* butter, at some large Irish or Devonshire farm, instead of reserving that process for butter which is just on the turn and is already almost unfit to eat; the result being that, long before it has reached a hot climate, it is only fit to grease carriage-wheels with. It could be done, and I feel sure it would pay, as good butter would fetch almost any price in many places.. Some Devonshire butter, which we brought with us from England, is as good now, after ten thousand miles in the tropics, as it was when first put on board; but a considerable proportion is very bad, and was evidenty not in proper condition in the first instance.

We had intended going afterwards to the coral reef with the children to have a picnic there, and had accordingly given the servants leave to go ashore for the evening; but it came on to rain heavily, and we were obliged to return to the yacht instead. The servants had, however, already availed themselves of the permission they had received, and there was therefore no one on board in their department; so we had to unpack our basket and have our picnic on deck, under the awning, instead of on the reef, which I think was almost as great a treat to the children.

We have, I am sorry to say, had a good deal of trouble with some of our men here. One disappeared directly we arrived, and has never been seen since. Another came off suffering from delirium tremens and epileptic fits, brought on by drink. His cries and struggles were horrible to hear and witness. It took four strong men to hold him, and the doctor was up with him all last night. Nearly all the ships that come here have been at sea for a long time, and the men are simply wild when they get ashore. Some of the people know only too well how to take advantage of this state of things, and the consequence is that it is hardly safe for a sailor to drink a glass of grog, for fear that it should be drugged. No doubt there are respectable places to which the men could resort, but it is not easy for a stranger to find them out, and our men seem to have been particularly unfortunate in this respect. Tom talks of leaving two of them behind, and shipping four fresh hands, as our number is already rather short.

Friday, December 8th.—I persuaded Tom to make another excursion to the coral reef this morning, and at five o'clock he and Mabelle and I set off in the 'Flash,' just as the sun was rising. We had a delightful row, past the Quarantine Island, to the portion of the reef on the other side of the harbor, where we had not yet been, and where I think the coral plants and flowers and bushes showed to greater advantage than ever, as they were less crowded, and the occasional patches of sandy bottom enabled one to see them better. We were so engrossed in our examination of these marvels of the deep, and of the fish with which the water abounded, that we found ourselves aground several times, and our return to the yacht was consequently delayed.

After breakfast I had another visit from a man with war-cloaks, shell-belts, *tapa* and *reva-reva*, which he brought on board for my inspection. It was a difficult task to make him understand what I meant, but at last I thought I had succeeded in impressing on his mind the fact that I wished to buy them, and that they would be paid for at the store. The sequel unfortunately proved that I was mistaken. At nine o'clock we set out for the shore, and after landing drove along the same road by which we had returned from our excursion round the island.* After seeing as much of the place as our limited time would allow, we re-entered the carriages and drove over to 'Fautahua, where we found the children and maids had arrived just before us. The grand piano, every table, and the drawing-room floor, were spread with the presents we were expected to take away with us. There were bunches of scarlet feathers, two or three hundred in number, from the tail of the tropic bird, which are only allowed to be possessed and worn by chiefs, and which are of great value, as each bird produces only two feathers; pearl shells, with corals growing on them; red coral from the islands on the Equator, curious sponges and sea-weed, *tapa* cloth and *reva-reva* fringe, arrowroot and palm-leaf hats, cocoanut drinking-vessels, fine mats plaited in many patterns, and other specimens of the products of the island.

All the members of the royal family at present in Tahiti had been invited to meet us, and arrived in due course, including the heir-apparent and his brother and sister. All the guests were dressed in the native costume, with wreaths on their heads and necks, and even the servants—including our own, whom I hardly recognized—were similarly decorated. Wreaths had also been prepared for us, three of fragrant yellow flowers for Mabelle,

---

* We paid a brief visit to Point Venus, whence Captain Cook observed the transit of Venus on November 9th, 1769, and we saw the lighthouse and tamarind-tree, which now mark the spot. The latter, from which we brought away some seed, was undoubtedly planted by Captain Cook with his own hand.

Muriel, and myself, and others of a different kind for the gentlemen.

When the feast was ready the Prince offered me his arm, and we all walked in a procession to a grove of bananas in the garden through two lines of native servants, who, at a given signal, saluted us with three hearty English cheers. We then continued our walk till we arrived at a house, built in the native style, by the side of a rocky stream, like a Scotch burn. The uprights of the house were banana-trees, transplanted with their leaves on, so as to shade the roof, which was formed of plaited cocoanut palm-leaves, each about fifteen feet long, laid transversely across bamboo rafters. From these light green supports and the dark green roof depended the yellow and brown leaves of the *theve*, woven into graceful garlands and elegant festoons. The floor was covered with the finest mats, with black and white borders, and the center strewn with broad green plantain-leaves, to form the tablecloth, on which were laid baskets and dishes, made of leaves sewed together, and containing all sorts of native delicacies. There were oysters, lobsters, wurrali, and crayfish, stewed chicken, boiled sucking-pig, plantains, bread-fruit, melons, bananas, oranges, and strawberries. Before each guest was placed a half cocoanut full of salt water, another full of chopped cocoanut, a third full of fresh water, and another full of milk, two pieces of bamboo, a basket of *poi*, half a bread-fruit, and a platter of green leaves, the latter being changed with each course. We took our seats on the ground round the green table. An address was first delivered in the native language, grace was then said, and we commenced. The first operation was to mix the salt water and the chopped cocoanut together, so as to make an appetizing sauce, into which we were supposed to dip each morsel we ate, the empty salt-water bowl being filled up with fresh water with which to wash our fingers and lips. We were all tolerably successful in the use of our fingers as substitutes for knives and forks, though we could not manage the performance quite so gracefully as those more accustomed to it. The only drawback, as far as the dinner itself was concerned, was that it had to be eaten amid such a scene of novelty and beauty, that our attention was continually distracted. There was so much to admire around one, both in the house itself and outside, where we could see the mountain stream, the groves of palms and bread-fruit, and beyond them the bright sea and the surf-beaten coral reef. After we had finished, all the servants sat down to dinner, and from a daïs at one end of the room we surveyed the bright and animated scene, the gentlemen—and some of the ladies too—meanwhile enjoying their cigarettes.

When we got down to Papiete, at about half-past four, so many things had to be done that it seemed impossible to accomplish a start this evening. First of all the two Princes came on board, and were shown round, after which there were accounts to be paid, linen to be got on board, and various other preparations to be made. Presently it was discovered that the cloaks I had purchased—or thought I had purchased—this morning had not turned up, and that our saddles had been left at Fautahua on Sunday and had been forgotten. The latter were immediately sent for, but although some one went on shore to look after the cloaks, nothing could be heard of them; so I suppose I was not successful after all in making the man understand that he was to take them to the store and receive payment for them there.

At six o'clock the pilot sent word that it was no longer safe to go out; but steam was already up, and Tom therefore decided to go outside the reef and wait there for the people and goods that were still on shore. At this moment the saddles appeared in one direction, and the rest of the party in another. They were soon on board, the anchor was raised, and we began to steam slowly ahead, taking a last regretful look at Papiete as we left the harbor. By the time we were outside it was dark, the pilot went ashore, and we steamed full speed ahead. After dinner, and indeed until we went to bed, at half-past eleven, the lights along the shore were clearly visible, and the form of the high mountains behind could be distinguished.

Good-by, lovely Tahiti! I wonder if I shall ever see you again; it makes me quite sad to think how small is the chance of my doing so.

CHAPTER XV.

TAHITI TO SANDWICH ISLANDS—KILAUEA BY DAY AND BY NIGHT.

*Methinks it should have been impossible
Not to love all things in a world so filled,
Where the breeze warbles, and the mute still air
Is music, slumbering on her instrument.*

Saturday, December 9th.—After leaving the harbor of Papiéte we passed close to the island of Eimeo, on which we have gazed so often and with so much pleasure during the past week. It is considered the most beautiful island of the Georgian group, and we all regretted that we were unable to spare the time to visit it. From afar it is rather like the dolomite mountains in the Tyrol, and it is said that the resemblance is even more striking on a near approach. The harbor is a long narrow gorge between high mountains, clothed with palms, oranges, and plantains, and is one of the most remarkable features of the place. Huahine is the island of which the Earl and the Doctor speak, in 'South Sea Bubbles,' in terms of such enthusiasm, and Rarotonga is the head and center of all the missionary efforts of the present time in these parts.

The weather to-day was fine, though we had occasional squalls of wind and rain. We were close-hauled, and the motion of the vessel was violent and disagreeable. I was very sea-sick, and was consoled to find that several of the men were so too. A head sea—or nearly so—is quite a novel experience for us of late, and we none of us like the change.

Sunday, December 10*th.*—Another squally day. Still close-hauled, and even then not on our course. We had a short service at eleven, but it was as much as I could do to remain on deck.

Monday, December 11*th.*—Very like yesterday. We passed close to Flint and Vostok Islands, at the former of which I should have much liked to land. But it was a good deal to leeward of us; there is no anchorage, and the landing, which is always difficult and sometimes impossible, has to be effected in native surf-boats. It would have been interesting to see a guano island, of which this is a perfect specimen.

We had hoped to make the Caroline Islands before dark (not the Caroline Islands proper, but a group of low islets, whose position is very uncertainly indicated in the different charts and books); but the wind fell light, and as we could see nothing of them at sunset, although the view from the masthead extended at least fifteen miles in every direction, it was decided at eight o'clock to put the ship about, to insure not running on them or any of the surrounding reefs in the night. The currents run very swiftly between these islands, and it is impossible to tell your exact position, even a few hours after having taken an observation.

Tuesday, December 12*th.*—The wind freshened immediately after we had changed our course last night, and fell light directly we had put about again this morning, so that it was fully 9 a.m. before we had regained our position of yesterday evening.

Our compass-cards were getting worn out, and Tom gave out new ones before leaving Tahiti. I was very much amused to-night, when, as usual, just before going to bed, I went to have a look at the compass and see how the yacht was lying, and asked the man at the wheel what course he was steering. 'North and by west, half-east, ma'am,' he replied. 'That's a funny course,' I said; 'tell me again.' He repeated his statement; whereupon

I remarked that the course was quite a new one to me. 'Oh, yes, ma'am,' he answered, 'but them's the new compass-cards.' This man is one of the best helmsmen in the ship, but certainly seems to be an indifferent scholar.

Tattoo in the Tropics.

Friday, December 15*th.*—We crossed the line at half-past four this morning. Father Neptune was to have paid us another visit in the evening, but the crew were busy, and there were some difficulties about arranging the details of the ceremony. The children were obliged, therefore, to be content with their usual game of drilling every one that they were able to muster for soldiers, after the fashion of Captain Brown's 'rifle practice,' or marching up and down the deck to the strains of Jem Butt's fiddle playing 'Tommy make room for your uncle,' accompanied by the somewhat discordant noise of their own drums. These amusements after sunset, and scrubbing decks and working at the pumps before sunrise, give us all the much-needed exercise it is impossible to take in the heat of the day-time.

Saturday, December 16*th.*—At 1.30 a.m. I was awoke by

the strains of sweet music, and could not at first imagine where I could be, or whence the sounds came. It proved to be the performance of some 'waits' on board. I do not know who originated the idea, but it was a very good one, and was excellently carried out. Everybody assembled on deck by degrees, and the songsters enjoyed a glass of grog when their labors were finished, after which we all went to bed again.

It had fallen calm yesterday evening, and the funnel was raised at midnight, but the breeze sprang up again to-day, and at noon the fires were banked and the sails were set. Of course it then fell calm again, and at six o'clock we were once more proceeding under steam. There was one squall in the night, accompanied by the most tremendous rain I ever saw or heard. We talk of tropical rain in England, but the real thing is very different. It seemed just as if the bottom of an enormous cistern overhead had suddenly been removed, allowing the contents to fall exactly on the spot where we were. The water came down in sheets, and was soon three or four inches deep on the deck, though it was pouring out of the scuppers all the time as fast as possible.

Sunday, December 17*th.*—A showery morning. We had Communion Service and hymns at eleven. In the afternoon it was too rough for 'church,' and Tom was unable to deliver his intended address to the men.

Monday, December 18*th.*—We were close-hauled, with a strong north-east wind, and heavy squalls and showers at intervals. We saw several flying-fish and a good many birds, apparently hovering over a shoal of whales or grampuses. It is wonderful how little life we have seen on this portion of our voyage.

Tuesday, December 19*th.*—A fine day—wind rather more fair—sea still rough and disagreeable. I tried to work hard all day, but found it very difficult.

Thursday, December 21*st.*—Wind variable and baffling —sometimes calm, sometimes squally, sometimes a nice breeze. Sails were hoisted and lowered at least a dozen times, and fires were banked more than once.

Friday, December 22d.—At 6.30 a.m. we made the island of Hawaii, rather too much to leeward, as we had been carried by the strong current at least eighteen miles out of our course. We were therefore obliged to beat up to windward, in the course of which operation we passed a large bark running before the wind—the first ship we had seen since leaving Tahiti—and also a fine whale, blowing close to us. We could not see the high land in the center of the island, owing to the mist in which it was enveloped, and there was great excitement and much speculation on board as to the principal points which were visible. At noon the observations taken proved that Tom was right in his opinion as to our exact position. The wind dropped as we approached the coast, where we could see the heavy surf dashing against the black lava cliffs, rushing up the little creeks, and throwing its spray in huge fountain-like jets high above the tall cocoanut-trees far inland.

We sailed along close to the shore, and by two o'clock were near the entrance to the Bay of Hilo. In answer to our signal for a pilot a boat came off with a man who said he knew the entrance to the harbor, but informed us that the proper pilot had gone to Honolulu on a pleasure trip.

It was a clear afternoon. The mountains, Mauna Kea and Mauna Loa, could be plainly seen from top to bottom, their giant crests rising nearly 14,000 feet above our heads, their tree and fern clad slopes seamed with deep gulches or ravines, down each of which a fertilizing river ran into the sea. Inside the reef, the white coral shore, on which the waves seemed too lazy to break, is fringed with a belt of cocoanut palms, amongst which, as well as on the hill-sides, the little white houses are prettily dotted. All are surrounded by gardens, so full of flowers that the bright patches of color were plainly visible even from the deck of the yacht. The harbor is large, and is exposed only to one bad wind, which is most prevalent during the winter months. Still, with good ground-tackle, there is not much to be feared, and there is one particular spot, sheltered by the Blonde reef, which is almost always safe. Here, accordingly, we have taken up our station, though it is rather far from the town. Sometimes it is impossible to land at Hilo itself for days together, but there is fortunately a little creek behind Cocoanut Island which is always accessible.

This afternoon the weather was all that could be desired, and at three o'clock we landed and went straight to Mr. Conway's store to make arrangements for going to the volcano of Kilauea to-morrow. Mr. Conway sent a man off at once on horseback to warn the people at the 'Halfway House' and at 'Volcano House' to make preparations to receive our party—a necessary precaution, as visitors to the island are not numerous, and can only arrive by the monthly steamer from Honolulu.

Having arranged this matter, we went for a stroll, among neat houses and pretty gardens, to the suspension-bridge over the river, followed by a crowd of girls, all decorated with wreaths and garlands, and wearing almost the same dress that we had seen at Tahiti — a colored long-sleeved loose gown reaching to the feet. The natives here appear to affect duller colors than those we have lately been accustomed to, lilac, drab, brown, and other dark prints being the favorite tints. Whenever I stopped to look at a view, one of the girls would come behind me and throw a *lei* of flowers over my head, fasten it round my neck, and then run away laughing, to a distance, to judge of effect. The consequence was that, before the end of our walk, I had about a dozen wreaths, of various colors and lengths, hanging round me, till I felt almost as if I had a fur tippet on, they made me so hot; and yet I did not like to take them off for fear of hurting the poor girls' feelings.

We walked along the river bank, and crossed to the

other side just below the rapids, jumping over the narrow channels through which the water hurried and rushed. Some of our attendant girls carried Muriel and the dogs, and, springing barefooted from rock to rock, led us across the stream and up the precipitous banks on the other side. There is a sort of hotel here, kept by a Chinaman, where everything is scrupulously clean, and the food good, though plain. It is rather more like a lodging-house than a hotel, however. You hire your rooms, and are expected to make special arrangements for board. Before we got back to the yacht it had become dark, the moon had risen, and we could see the reflection in the sky of the fires in the crater of Kilauea. I do hope the volcano will be active to-morrow. It is never two days in the same condition, and visitors have frequently remained in the neighborhood of the crater for a week without seeing an eruption.

The starlit sky, the bright young moon, and the red cloud from Kilauea, floating far above our heads, made up a most beautiful scene from the deck of the 'Sunbeam.'

Saturday, December 23d.—The boatman who brought us off last night had told us that Saturday was market-day at Hilo, and that at five o'clock the natives would come in from the surrounding country in crowds to buy their Sunday and Christmas-Day provisions, and to bring their own produce for sale. We accordingly gave orders that the boat should come for us at a quarter to five, shortly before which we got up and went on deck. We waited patiently in the dark until half-past five, when, no boat appearing from the shore, the dinghy was manned and we landed. The lights in the town were all out, the day had hardly dawned, and there were no signs of life to be seen. At last we met two men, who told us we should find the market near the river, and offered to show us the way; but when we arrived at the spot they had indicated we found only a large butcher's shop, and were informed that the regular market for fish, fruit, and other things was held at five o'clock *in the afternoon* instead of in the morning. We had thus had all our trouble for nothing, and the non-appearance of the boat was fully explained.

Presently we met a friend who took us to his home. It was a pretty walk, by the side of the river and through numerous gardens, fresh with the morning dew. He gave us the latest news from the United States, and presented us with oranges and flowers, with which we returned to the yacht. We were on board again by seven, and, having packed up our things and sent them ashore, had an early breakfast, and landed, in readiness for our excursion to Kilauea. The baggage animals ought already to have started, but we found they had been kept back, in case we should happen to forget anything. Quite a crowd assembled to see us off, and a good deal of gossip had to be got through, so that it was half-past nine before we were all mounted and fairly off.

The first part of our way lay along the flat ground, gay with bright scarlet Guernsey lilies, and shaded by cocoa-nut-trees, between the town and the sea. Then we struck off to the right, and soon left the town behind us, emerging into the open country. At a distance from the sea, Hilo looks as green as the Emerald Isle itself; but on a closer inspection the grass turns out to be coarse and dry, and many of the trees look scrubby and half dead. Except in the 'gulches' and the deep holes, between the hills, the island is covered with lava, in many places of so recent a deposit that it has not yet had time to decompose, and there is consequently only a thin layer of soil on its surface. This soil being, however, very rich, vegetation flourishes luxuriantly for a time; but as soon as the roots have penetrated a certain depth, and have come into contact with the lava, the trees wither up and perish, like the seed that fell on stony ground.

The *ohia* trees form a handsome feature in the landscape, with their thick tall stems, glossy foliage, and light crimson flowers. The fruit is a small, pink, waxy-looking apple, slightly acid, pleasant to the taste when you are thirsty. The candle-nut trees attain to a large size, and their light green foliage and white flowers have a very graceful appearance. Most of the foliage, however, is spoiled by a deposit of black dust, not unlike what one sees on the leaves in a London garden. I do not know whether this is caused by the fumes of the not far-distant volcano, or whether it is some kind of mold or fungus.

After riding about ten miles in the blazing sun we reached a forest, where the vegetation was quite tropical, though not so varied in its beauties as that of Brazil, or of the still more lovely South Sea Islands. There were ferns of various descriptions in the forest, and many fine trees, entwined, supported, or suffocated by numerous climbing plants, amongst which were blue and lilac convolvulus, and magnificent passion-flowers. The protection from the sun afforded by this dense mass of foliage was extremely grateful; but the air of the forest was close and stifling, and at the end of five miles we were glad to emerge once more into the open. The rest of the way lay over the hard lava, through a sort of desert of scrubby vegetation, occasionally relieved by clumps of trees in hollows. More than once we had a fine view of the sea, stretching away into the far distance, though it was sometimes mistaken for the bright blue sky, until the surf could be seen breaking upon the black rocks, amid the encircling groves of cocoanut-trees.

The sun shone fiercely at intervals, and the rain came down several times in torrents. The pace was slow, the road was dull and dreary, and many were the inquiries made for the 'Half-way House,' long before we reached it. We had still two miles farther to go, in the course of which we were drenched by a heavy shower. At last we came to a native house, crowded with people, where they were making *tappa* or *kapa*—the cloth made from the bark of the paper-mulberry. Here we stopped for a few minutes until our guide hurried us on, pointing out the church and the 'Half-way House' just ahead.

We were indeed glad to dismount after our weary ride, and rest in the comfortable rocking-chairs under the veranda. It is a small white wooden building, overhung with orange-trees, with a pond full of ducks and geese outside it, and a few scattered outbuildings, including a cooking hut, close by. A good-looking man was busy broiling beef-steaks, stewing chickens, and boiling *taro*, and we had soon a plentiful repast set before us, with the very weakest of weak tea as a beverage. The woman of the house, which contained some finely worked mats and clean-looking beds, showed us some *tappa* cloth, together with the mallets and other instruments used in its manufacture, and a beautiful orange-colored *lei*, or feather necklace, which she had made herself. The cloth and mallets were for sale, but no inducement would persuade her to part with the necklace. It was the first she had ever made, and I was afterwards told that the natives are superstitiously careful to preserve the first specimen of their handiwork, of whatever kind it may be.

A woman dressed in a pink *holoku* and a light green apron had followed us hither from the cottages we had first stopped at, and I noticed at the time that, though she was chatting and laughing with a female companion, she did not seem very well. Whilst we were at lunch a sudden increase to her family took place, and before we were ready to start I paid her and her infant a visit. She was then sitting up, apparently as well as ever, and seemed to look upon the recent event as a very light matter.

Directly we had finished our meal—about three o'clock—the guide came and tried to persuade us that, as the baggage-mules had not yet arrived, it would be too late for us to go on to-day, and that we had better spend the night where we were, and start early in the morning. We did not, however, approve of this arrangement, so the horses were saddled, and, leaving word that the baggage-mules were to follow on as soon as posible, we mounted, and set off for the 'Volcano House.' We had not gone far before we were again overtaken by a shower, which once more drenched us to the skin.

The scene was certainly one of extreme beauty. The moon was hidden by a cloud, and the prospect lighted only by the red glare of the volcano, which hovered before and above us like the Israelites' pillar of fire, giving us hopes of a splendid spectacle when we should at last reach the long wished-for crater. Presently the moon shone forth again, and gleamed and glistened on the rain-drops and silver-grasses till they looked like fireflies and glowworms. At last, becoming impatient, we proceeded slowly on our way, until we met a man on horseback, who hailed us in a cheery voice with an unmistakable American accent. It was the landlord of the 'Volcano House,' Mr. Kane, who, fearing from the delay that we had met with some mishap, had started to look for us. He explained that he thought it was only his duty to look after and help ladies visiting the volcano, and added that he had intended going down as far as the 'Half-way House' in search of us. It was a great relief to know that we were in the right track, and I quite enjoyed the gallop through the dark forest, though there was barely sufficient light to enable me to discern the horse immediately in front of me. When we emerged from the wood, we found ourselves at the very edge of the old crater, the bed of which, three or four hundred feet beneath us, was surrounded by steep and in many places overhanging sides. It looked like an enormous caldron, four or five miles in width, full of a mass of cooled pitch. In the center was the still glowing stream of dark red lava, flowing slowly towards us, and in every direction were red-hot patches, and flames and smoke issuing from the ground. A bit of the 'black country' at night, with all the coal-heaps on fire, would give you some idea of the scene. Yet the first sensation is rather one of disappointment, as one expects greater activity on the part of the volcano; but the new crater was still to be seen, containing the lake of fire, with steep walls rising up in the midst of the sea of lava.

Twenty minutes' hard riding brought us to the door of the 'Volcano House,' from which issued the comforting light of a large wood fire, reaching half-way up the chimney. Native garments replaced Mabelle's and my dripping habits, and we sat before the fire in luxury until the rest of the party arrived. After some delay supper was served, cooked by our host, and accompanied by excellent Bass's beer, no wine or spirits being procurable on the premises. Mr. Kane made many apologies for shortcomings, explaining that his cook had run away that morning, and that his wife was not able to do much to assist him, as her first baby was only a week old.

Everything at this inn is most comfortable, though the style is rough and ready. The interior is just now decorated for Christmas, with wreaths, and evergreens, and ferns, and bunches of white plumes, not unlike *reva-reva*, made from the pith of the silver-grass. The beds and bedrooms are clean, but limited in number, there being only three of the latter altogether. The rooms are separated only by partitions of grass, seven feet high, so that there is plenty of ventilation, and the heat of the fire permeates the whole building. But you must not talk secrets in these dormitories or be too restless. I was amused to find, in the morning, that I had unconsciously poked my hand through the wall of our room during the night.

The grandeur of the view in the direction of the volcano increased as the evening wore on. The fiery cloud above the present crater augmented in size and depth of color; the extinct crater glowed red in thirty or forty different places; and clouds of white vapor issued from every crack and crevice in the ground, adding to the sulphurous smell with which the atmosphere was laden. Our room faced the volcano: there were no blinds, and I drew back the curtains and lay watching the splendid scene until I fell asleep.

Sunday, December 24th (Christmas Eve).—I was up at four o'clock, to gaze once more on the wondrous spectacle that lay before me. The molten lava still flowed in many places, the red cloud over the fiery lake was bright as ever, and steam was slowly ascending in every direction, over hill and valley, till, as the sun rose, it became difficult to distinguish clearly the sulphurous vapors from the morning mists. We walked down to the Sulphur Banks, about a quarter of a mile from the 'Volcano House,' and burned our gloves and boots in our endeavors to procure crystals, the beauty of which generally disappeared after a very short exposure to the air. We succeeded, however, in finding a few good specimens, and, by wrapping them at once in paper and cotton-wool and putting them into a bottle, hope to bring them home uninjured.

On our return we found a gentleman who had just arrived from Kau, and who proposed to join us in our expedition to the crater, and at three o'clock in the afternoon we set out, a party of eight, with two guides, and three porters to carry our wraps and provisions, and to bring back specimens. Before leaving the inn the landlord came to us and begged us in an earnest and confidential manner to be very careful, to do exactly what our guides told us, and especially to follow in their footsteps exactly when returning in the dark. He added, 'There never has been an accident happen to anybody from my house, and I should feel real mean if one did: but there have been a power of narrow escapes.'

First of all we descended the precipice, 300 feet in depth, forming the wall of the old crater, but now thickly covered with vegetation. It is so steep in many places that flights of zig-zag wooden steps have been inserted in the face of the cliff in some places, in order to render the descent practicable. At the bottom we stepped straight on to the surface of cold boiled lava, which we had seen from above last night. Even here, in every crevice where a few grains of soil had collected, delicate little ferns might be seen struggling for life, and thrusting out their green fronds towards the light. It was the most extraordinary walk imaginable over that vast plain of lava, twisted and distorted into every conceivable shape and form, according to the temperature it had originally attained, and the rapidity with which it had cooled, its surface, like half-molten glass, cracking and breaking beneath our feet. Sometimes we came to a patch that looked like the contents of a pot, suddenly petrified in the act of boiling; sometimes the black iridescent lava had assumed the form of waves, or more frequently of huge masses of rope, twisted and coiled together; sometimes it was piled up like a collection of organ-pipes, or had gathered into mounds and cones of various dimensions. As we proceeded the lava became hotter and hotter, and from every crack arose gaseous fumes, affecting our noses and throats in a painful manner; till at last, when we had to pass to leeward of the molten stream flowing from the lake, the vapors almost choked us, and it was with difficulty we continued to advance. The lava was more glassy and transparent-looking, as if it had been fused at a higher temperature than usual; and the crystals of sulphur, alum, and other minerals, with which it abounded, reflected the light in bright prismatic colors. In places it was quite transparent, and we could see beneath it the long streaks of a stringy kind of lava, like brown spun glass, called 'Pélé's hair.'

At last we reached the foot of the present crater, and commenced the ascent of the outer wall. Many times the thin crust gave way beneath our guide, and he had to retire quickly from the hot, blinding, choking fumes that immediately burst forth. But we succeeded in reaching the top; and then what a sight presented itself to our astonished eyes! I could neither speak nor move at first, but could only stand and gaze at the terrible grandeur of the scene.

We were standing on the extreme edge of a precipice, overhanging a lake of molten fire, a hundred feet below us, and nearly a mile across. Dashing against the cliffs on the opposite side, with a noise like the roar of a stormy ocean, waves of blood-red, fiery, liquid lava hurled their billows upon an iron-bound headland, and then rushed up the face of the cliffs to toss their gory spray high in the air. The restless, heaving lake boiled and bubbled, never remaining the same for two minutes together. Its normal color seemed to be a dull dark red, covered with a thin gray scum, which every moment and in every part swelled and cracked, and emitted fountains, cascades, and whirlpools of yellow and red fire, while sometimes one big golden river, sometimes four or five, flowed across it. There was an island on one side of the lake, which the fiery waves seemed to attack unceasingly with relentless fury, as if bent on hurling it from its base. On the other side was a large cavern, into which the burning mass rushed with a loud roar, breaking down in its impetuous headlong career the gigantic stalactites that overhung the mouth of the cave, and flinging up the liquid material for the formation of fresh ones.

It was all terribly grand, magnificently sublime; but no words could adequately describe such a scene. The precipice on which we were standing overhung the crater so much that it was impossible to see what was going on immediately beneath; but from the columns of smoke and vapor that arose, the flames and sparks that constantly drove us back from the edge, it was easy to imagine that there must have been two or three grand fiery fountains below. As the sun set, and darkness enveloped the scene, it became more awful than ever. We retired a little way from the brink, to breathe some fresh air, and to try and eat the food we had brought with us; but this was an impossibility. Every instant a fresh explosion or glare made us jump up to survey the stupendous scene. The violent struggles of the lava to escape from its fiery bed, and the loud and awful noises by which they were at times accompanied, suggested the idea that some imprisoned monsters were trying to release themselves from their bondage, with shrieks and groans, and cries of agony and despair, at the futility of their efforts.

Sometimes there were at least seven spots on the borders of the lake where the molten lava dashed up furiously against the rocks—seven fire-fountains playing simultaneously. With the increasing darkness the colors emitted by the glowing mass became more and more wonderful, varying from the deepest jet-black to the palest gray, from darkest maroon, through cherry and scarlet, to the most delicate pink, violet, and blue; from the richest brown, through orange and yellow, to the lightest straw-color. And there was yet another shade, only describable by the term 'molten-lava color.' Even the smokes and vapors were rendered beautiful by their borrowed lights and tints, and the black peaks, pinnacles, and crags, which surrounded the amphitheater, formed a splendid and appropriate background. Sometimes great pieces broke off and tumbled with a crash into the burning lake, only to be remelted and thrown up anew. I had for some time been feeling very hot and uncomfortable, and on looking round the cause was at once apparent. Not two inches beneath the surface, the gray lava on which we were standing and sitting was red-hot. A stick thrust through it caught fire, a piece of paper was immediately destroyed, and the gentlemen found the heat from the crevices so great that they could not approach near enough to light their pipes.

One more long last look, and then we turned our faces away from the scene that had enthralled us for so many hours. The whole of the lava we had crossed, in the extinct crater, was now aglow in many patches, and in all directions flames were bursting forth, fresh lava was flowing, and steam and smoke were issuing from the surface. It was a toilsome journey back again, walking as we did in single file, and obeying the strict injunctions of our head guide to follow him closely, and to tread exactly in his footsteps. On the whole it was easier by night than by day to distinguish the route to be taken, as we could now see the dangers that before we could only feel; and many were the fiery crevices we stepped over or jumped across. Once I slipped, and my foot sank through the thin crust. Sparks issued from the ground, and the stick on which I leaned caught fire before I could fairly recover myself.

Either from the effects of the unaccustomed exercise after our long voyage, or from the intense excitement of the novel scene, combined with the gaseous exhalations from the lava, my strength began to fail, and before reaching the side of the crater I felt quite exhausted. I struggled on at short intervals, however, collapsing several times and fainting away twice; but at last I had fairly to give in, and to allow myself to be ignominiously carried up the steep precipice to the 'Volcano House' on a chair, which the guides went to fetch for me.

It was half-past eleven when we once more found ourselves beneath Mr. Kane's hospitable roof; he had expected us to return at nine o'clock, and was beginning to feel anxious about us.

Monday, December 25th (Christmas Day).—Turning in last night was the work of a very few minutes, and this morning I awoke perfectly refreshed and ready to appreciate anew the wonders of the prospect that met my eyes. The pillar of fire was still distinctly visible when I looked out from my window, though it was not so bright as when I had last seen it; but even as I looked it began to fade, and gradually disappeared. At the same moment a river of glowing lava issued from the side of the bank we had climbed with so much difficulty yesterday, and slowly but surely overflowed the ground we had walked over. I woke Tom, and you may imagine the feelings with which we gazed upon this startling phenomenon, which, had it occurred a few hours earlier, might have caused the destruction of the whole party. If our expedition had been made to-day instead of yesterday, we should certainly have had to proceed by a different route to the crater, and should have looked down on the lake of fire from a different spot.

I cannot hope that in my attempt to give you some idea of Kilauea as we beheld it, I shall be successful in conveying more than a very faint impression of its glories. I feel that my description is so utterly inadequate, that, were it not for the space, I should be tempted to send you in full the experiences of previous visitors, as narrated in Miss Bird's 'Six Months in the Sandwich Islands,' and Mr. Bodham Whetham's 'Pearls of the Pacific.' The account contained in the former work I had read before arriving here; the latter I enjoyed at the 'Volcano House.' Both are well worth reading by any one who feels an interest in the subject.

It would, I think, be difficult to imagine a more interesting and exciting mode of spending Christmas Eve than yesterday has taught us, or a stranger situation in which to exchange our Christmas greetings than beneath the grass roof of an inn on the edge of a volcano in the remote Sandwich Islands. They were certainly rendered none the less cordial and sincere by the novelty of our position, and I think we are all rather glad not to have in prospect the inevitable feastings and ceremonies without which it seems to be impossible to commemorate this season in England. If we had seen nothing but Kilauea since we left home, we should have been well rewarded for our long voyage.

At six o'clock we were dressed and packed. Breakfast followed at half-past, and at seven we were prepared for a start. Our kind, active host, and his wife and baby, all came out to see us off. The canter over the dewy grass, in the fresh morning air, was most invigorating.

It was evident that no one had passed along the road since Saturday night, for we picked up several waifs and strays dropped in the dark on our way up—a whip, a stirrup, mackintosh hood, &c.

By half-past ten we had reached the 'Half-way House,' where we were not expected so early, and where we had ample opportunity to observe the native ways of living, while waiting for our mid-day meal—an uninteresting mess of stewed fowl and *taro*, washed down with weak tea. After it was over I made an unsuccessful attempt to induce the woman of the house to part with her orange-colored *lei*. I bought some *tappa* and mallets, however, with some of the markers used in coloring the cloth, and a few gourds and calabashes, forming part of the household furniture. While the horses were being saddled preparatory to our departure, Mabelle and I went to another cottage close by, to see the mother of the baby that had been born while we were here on Saturday. She was not at home; but we afterwards found her playing cards with some of her friends in a neighboring hut. Quite a large party of many natives were gathered together, not the least cheerful of whom was the young mother whose case had interested me so much.

The rest of the ride down to Hilo was as dull and monotonous as our upward journey had been, although, in order to enable us to get over it as quickly as possible, fresh horses had been sent to meet us. At last we reached the pier, where we found the usual little crowd waiting to see us off. The girls who had followed me when we first landed came forward shyly when they thought they were unobserved, and again encircled me with *leis* of gay and fragrant flowers. The custom of decorating themselves with wreaths on every possible occasion is in my eyes a charming one, and I like the inhabitants of Polynesia for their love of flowers. They are as necessary to them as the air they breathe, and I think the missionaries make a mistake in endeavoring to repress so innocent and natural a taste.

The whole town was *en fête* to-day. Natives were riding about in pairs, in the cleanest of bright cotton dresses and the freshest of *leis* and garlands. Our own men from the yacht contributed not a little to the gayety of the scene. They were all on shore, and the greater part of them were galloping about on horseback, tumbling off, scrambling on again, laughing, flirting, joking, and enjoying themselves generally after a fashion peculiar to English sailors. As far as we know the only evil result of all this merriment was that the doctor received a good many applications for diachylon plaster in the course of the evening, to repair various 'abrasions of the cuticle,' as he expressed it.

I think at least half the population of Hilo had been on board the yacht in the course of the day, as a Christmas treat. At last we took a boat and went off too, accompanied by Mr. Lyman. The appearance of the 'Sunbeam' from the shore was very gay, and as we approached it became more festive still. All her masts were tipped with sugar-canes in bloom. Her stern was adorned with flowers, and in the arms of the figure-head was a large bouquet. She was surrounded with boats, the occupants of which cheered us heartily as we rowed alongside. The gangway was decorated with flowers, and surmounted by a triumphal arch, on which were inscribed 'Welcome Home,' 'A Merry Christmas,' 'A Happy New Year,' and other good wishes. The whole deck was festooned with tropical plants and flowers, and the decorations of the cabins were even more beautiful and elaborate. I believe all hands had been hard at work ever since we left to produce this wonderful effect, and every garden in Hilo had furnished a contribution to please and surprise us on our return.

The choir from Hilo came out in boats in the evening, sang all sorts of songs, sacred and secular, and cheered everybody till they were hoarse. After this, having had a cold dinner, in order to save trouble, and having duly drunk the health of our friends at home, we all adjourned to the saloon, to assist in the distribution of some Christmas presents, a ceremony which afforded great delight to the children, and which was equally pleasing to the elder people and to the crew, if one may judge from their behavior on the occasion.

Then we sat on deck, gazing at the cloud of fire over Kilauea, and wondering if the appearance of the crater could ever be grander than it was last night, when we were standing on its brim.

So ended Christmas Day, 1876, at Hilo, in Hawaii. God grant that there may be many more as pleasant for us in store in the future!

CHAPTER XVI.

HAWAIIAN SPORTS.

In wrestling nimble, and in running swift,
In shooting steady, and in swimming strong,
Well made to strike, to leap, to throw, to lift,
And all the sports that shepherds are among.

Tuesday, December 26th.—We went ashore at eight o'clock, after an early cup of coffee, and found Mr. Lyman already waiting for us. Two baggage-mules were sent off with the photographic apparatus, and all the materials for breakfast, to the Rainbow Falls, where the children are looking forward with intense glee to boiling their own kettle, poaching their own eggs, and trying other cooking experiments.

Before setting out for the Falls ourselves, we went to see the national sport of surf-swimming, for their skill in which the Hawaiians are so justly famed.

The natives have many other games of which they are very fond, and which they play with great skill, including spear-throwing, transfixing an object with a dart, *kona*, an elaborate kind of draughts, and *talu*, which consists in hiding a small stone under one of five pieces of cloth, placed in front of the players. One hides the stone, and the others have to guess where it is; and it generally happens that, however dexterously the hider may put his arm beneath the cloth, and dodge about from one piece to another, a clever player will be able to tell, by the movement of the muscles of the upper part of his arm, when his fingers relax their hold of the stone. Another game, called *parua*, is very like the Canadian sport of 'tobogging,' only that it is carried on on the grass instead of on the snow. The performers stand bolt upright on a narrow plank, turned up in front, and steered with a sort of long paddle. They go to the top of a hill or mountain, and rush down the steep, grassy, sunburnt slopes at a tremendous pace, keeping their balance in a wonderful manner. There is also a very popular amusement, called *pahé*, requiring a specially prepared smooth floor, along which the javelins of the players glide like snakes. On the same floor they also play at another game, called *maita*, or *uru maita*. Two sticks, only a few inches apart, are stuck into the ground, and at a distance of thirty or forty yards the players strive to throw a stone between them. The *uru* which they use for the purpose is a hard circular stone, three or four inches in diameter, and an inch in thickness at the edge, but thicker in the middle.

Mr. Ellis, in his 'Polynesian Researches,' states that 'these stones are finely polished, highly valued, and carefully preserved, being always oiled or wrapped up in native cloth after having been used. The people are, if possible, more fond of this game than of the *pahé*, and the inhabitants of a district not unfrequently challenge the people of the whole island, or the natives of one island those of all the others, to bring a man who shall try his skill with some favorite player of their own district or island. On such occasions seven or eight thousand people, men and women, with their chiefs and chiefesses, assemble to witness the sport, which, as well as the *pahé*, is often continued for hours together.'

With bows and arrows they are as clever as all savages, and wonderfully good shots, attempting many wonderful feats. They are as swift as deer, when they choose, though somewhat lazy and indolent. All the kings and chiefs have been special adepts in the invigorating pastime of surf-swimming, and the present king's sisters are considered first-rate hands at it. The performers begin by swimming out into the bay, and diving under the huge Pacific rollers, pushing their surf-boards—flat pieces of wood, about four feet long by two wide, pointed at each end—edgewise before them. For the return journey they select a large wave; and then, either sitting, kneeling, or standing on their boards, rush in shorewards with the speed of a race-horse, on the curling crest of the monster, enveloped in foam and spray, and holding on, as it were, by the milk-white manes of their furious coursers. It looked a most enjoyable amusement, and I should think that, to a powerful swimmer, with plenty of pluck, the feat is not difficult of accomplishment. The natives here are almost amphibious. They played all sorts of tricks in the water, some of the performers being quite tiny boys. Four strong rowers took a whale-boat out into the worst surf, and then, steering her by means of a large oar, brought her safely back to the shore on the top of a huge wave.

After the conclusion of this novel entertainment, we all proceeded on horseback to the Falls, Baby going in front of Tom, and Muriel riding with Mr. Freer. After a couple of miles we dismounted, and had a short walk through grass and ferns to a pretty double water-fall, tumbling over a cliff, about 100 feet high, into a glassy pool of the river beneath. It fell in front of a fern-filled black lava cavern, over which a rainbow generally hangs. As it was too wet to sit on the grass after the rain, we took possession of the veranda of a native house, commanding a fine view of the bay and town of Hilo. The hot coffee and eggs were a great success eventually, though the smoke from the wood fire nearly suffocated us in the process of cooking. Excellent also was some gray mullet, brought to us alive, and cooked native fashion,—wrapped up in *ti* leaves, and put into a hole in the ground.

After taking a few photographs it was time to return; and we next went to a pretty garden, which we had seen on the night of our arrival, and, tying up our horses outside, walked across it to the banks of the river. Here we found a large party assembled, watching half the population of Hilo disporting themselves in, upon, and beneath the water. They climbed the almost perpendicular rocks on the opposite side of the stream, took headers, and footers, and siders from any height under five-and-twenty feet, dived, swam in every conceivable attitude, and without any apparent exertion, deep under the water, or upon its surface. But all this was only a preparation for the special sight we had come to see. Two natives were to jump from a precipice 100 feet high, into the river below, clearing on their way a rock which projected some twenty feet from the face of the cliff, at about the same distance from the summit. The two men, tall, strong, and sinewy, suddenly appeared against the sky-line, far above our heads, their long hair bound back by a wreath of leaves and flowers, while another garland encircled their waists. Having measured their distance with an eagle's glance, they disappeared from our sight, in order to take a run and acquire the necessary impetus. Every breath was held for a moment, till one of the men reappeared, took a bound from the edge of the rock, turned over in midair, and disappeared feet foremost into the pool beneath, to emerge almost immediately, and to climb the sunny bank as quietly as if he had done nothing very wonderful. His companion followed, and then the two clambered up to the twenty-feet projection, to clear which they had had to take such a run the first time, and once more plunged into the pool below. The feat was of course an easier one than the first; but still a leap of eighty feet is no light matter. A third native, who joined them in this exploit, gave one quite a turn as he twisted in his downward jump; but he also alighted in the water feet foremost, and bobbed up again directly, like a cork. He was quite a young man, and we afterwards heard that he had broken several ribs not more than a year ago, and had been laid up for six months in the hospital.

We now moved our position a little higher up the river, to the Falls, over which the men, gliding down the shallow rapids above, in a sitting posture, allowed themselves to be carried. It looked a pleasant and easy feat, and was afterwards performed by many of the natives in all sorts of ways. Two or three of them would hold each other's shoulders, forming a child's train, or some would get on the backs of their companions, while others descended singly in a variety of attitudes. At last a young girl was also persuaded to attempt the feat. She looked very pretty as she started, in her white chemise and bright garland, and prettier still when she emerged from the white foam beneath the fall, and swam along far below the surface of the clear water, with her long black hair streaming out behind her.

No description can give you any idea what an animated and extraordinary scene it was altogether. While our accounts were being settled, preparatory to our departure, I occupied myself in looking at some *kahilis* and feather *leis*. The yellow ones, either of Oo or Mamo feathers, only found in this island, are always scarce, as the use of them is a prerogative of royalty and nobility. Just now it is almost impossible to obtain one, all the feathers being 'tabu,' to make a royal cloak for Ruth, half-sister of Kamehameha V., and governess of Hawaii. Mamo feathers are generally worth a dollar apiece, and a good *lei* or loose necklace costs about five hundred dollars. *Kahilis* are also an emblem of rank, though many people use them as ornaments in their houses. They are rather like feather-brooms, two or three feet long, and three or four inches across, made of all sorts of feathers, tastefully interwoven. I bought one, and a couple of ordinary *leis*, which were all I could procure. But, alas! too soon all was over, and time for us to go on board.

On our way off to the yacht we met one of the large double canoes coming in under sail from a neighboring island. It consisted of two canoes lashed together, with a sort of basket dropped into the water between them, to enable them to carry their fish alive. They are not very common now, and we were therefore fortunate in meeting with one. Mr. Lyman made the men in charge turn her round, so as to afford us an opportunity of thoroughly examining her. In the time of Kamehameha there was a fleet of 10,000 of these canoes, and the king used to send them out in the roughest weather, and make them perform all sorts of manœuvres.

We found the yacht in the usual state of confusion incidental to a fresh departure, but everything was soon reduced to order, and off we started to steam and sail round the north end of the island, but we could not afford time to visit the place of Captain Cook's death and burial in Keelakeakua Bay. I believe there is not a great deal to see, however, and the spot is chiefly interesting from its associations. For many years a copper plate, fixed to a cocoanut-tree, marked the spot where Cook fell, but this has now been replaced by a monument, the cost of which was defrayed by subscriptions at Honolulu. Maui is, I believe, a charming place, containing many fine plantations, and several gentlemen's estates, laid out in the English style. Unfortunately, time forbids our accepting some invitations we have received to visit the island, where a great many interesting excursions may be made.

At Kahoolaue there does not seem much to be seen. It was purchased some years ago, and pays well as a sheep-run. Lauai, the next island, is scarcely inhabited, and its scenery is not remarkable.

A sad interest attaches to the island of Molokai, which is situated midway between Maui and Oahu. It is the leper settlement, and to it all the victims of this terrible, loathsome, and incurable disease, unhappily so prevalent in the Hawaiian archipelago, are sent, in order to prevent the spread of the contagion. They are well cared for and looked after in every way; but their life, separated as they inevitably are from all they hold most dear, and with no prospect before them but that of a slow and cruel death, must indeed be a miserable one. In Molokai there are many tiny children fatherless and motherless, parents without children, husbands without wives, wives without husbands, 'all condemned,' as Miss Bird says, 'to watch the repulsive steps by which each of their doomed fellows goes down to a loathsome death, knowing that by the same they too must pass.' A French priest has nobly devoted himself to the religious and secular instruction of the lepers, and up to the present time has enjoyed complete immunity from the disease; but even if he escapes this danger he can *never* return to his country and friends. When one thinks what that implies, and to what a death in life he has condemned himself for the sake of others, it seems impossible to doubt that he will indeed reap a rich reward hereafter.

At two o'clock we saw Diamond Head, the easternmost headland of Oahu, rising from the sea. By four o'clock we were abreast of it, and steaming along the coast. The cape itself rises grandly from the midst of a grove of cocoanuts, and the shore all along, with the sharp high mountains of the Pali as a background, is fine and picturesque. A coral reef stretches far into the sea, and outside this we lay waiting for a pilot to take us into Honolulu Harbor.

It was a long business mooring us by hawsers, from our stem and stern, but we were at last safely secured in a convenient place, a short distance from the shore, and where we should be refreshed by the sea breeze and the land breeze alternately. It was six o'clock, and nearly dark, when we reached the shore; the town seemed entirely deserted; all the little wooden houses were shut up, and there were no lights visible. The post-office was closed, but it was a terrible blow to hear there were no letters for us, though we still hoped that there might be some at the British Consulate.

After a short time we returned on board the yacht in time for a late dinner. The first lieutenant of H.M.S. 'Fantôme' came on board to pay us a visit during the evening, and told us all the latest English and American news, lending us some files of English papers—a great treat, but no compensation for our disappointment about the letters.

Thursday, December 28*th.*—Tom and I went ashore at seven o'clock to make arrangements for repairing our mizzen-sail. We soon found a sailmaker, who promised to set all hands to work and complete the job as quickly as possible. Being detained by a heavy shower of rain, we occupied the time in a gossip about Honolulu and its sayings and doings. When the shower was over, we walked through the town, which is clean and tidy, being laid out in squares, after the American style. The houses are all of wood, and generally have verandas overhanging the street. They are seldom more than one story high, and nearly all have a little greenery about them.

We returned to the yacht for breakfast, and, having heard that no sharks ever came into the long, narrow bay, were able to enjoy, in perfect peace of mind, the luxury of a bath overboard. It is a great pity that in the tropics, where bathing is such a delightful occupation, and where one might swim and paddle about for hours without fear of getting cold, it is often impossible even to enter the water for fear of the sharks. The natives are such expert swimmers that they do not seem to think much of this danger. As the shark turns on his back to take a bite at them, they dive underneath him, and he snaps his jaws on emptiness. In fact, sometimes the swimmer will take advantage of the opportunity to stab his enemy as he passes beneath him.

Scarcely was breakfast over when we were inundated with visitors, who kindly came to see what they could do for us to make our stay agreeable. We lunched on shore, and afterwards went to the new Government buildings and museum. From thence we strolled to the various shops where 'curios' and photographs are to be bought, and collected a goodly store, returning on board the yacht to find more visitors.

We lunched on shore, and afterwards went with Mr. Chambré, navigating-lieutenant of the 'Fantôme,' to the new Government buildings. There we found an excellent English library and an interesting collection of books printed in English and Hawaiian, on alternate pages, including alphabets, grammars, the old familiar nursery tales, &c. There is also a good, though small museum, containing specimens of beautiful corals, shells, seaweeds, and fossils; all the ancient native weapons, such as bows, arrows, swords and spears—now, alas! no longer procurable—sling-stones, and stones used in games, back-scratchers, hair-ornaments made of sharks' teeth, tortoise-shell cups and spoons, calabashes and bowls. There were some most interesting though somewhat horrible necklaces made of hundreds of braids of human hair cut from the heads of victims slain by the chiefs themselves; from these braids was suspended a monstrous hook carved from a large whale's tooth called a Paloola, regarded by the natives as a sort of idol. There are models of ancient and modern canoes — the difference between which is not very great—paddles inlaid with mother-of-pearl, old war-masks, and dresses still in use in the less frequented islands, anklets of human teeth, and many other things far too numerous to mention. The most interesting of all were, perhaps, the old feather war-cloaks, like the ancient *togas* of the Romans. They are made of thousands of yellow, red, and black feathers, of the *oo*, *mamo*, and *eine*, taken singly and fastened into a sort of network of strings, so as to form a solid fabric, like the richest velvet or plush, that glitters like gold in the sunlight. The helmets, made of the same feathers, but worked on to a frame of perfect Grecian shape, similar to those seen in the oldest statuary or on the Elgin marbles, are even more artistic and elegant. Whence came the idea and design? Untutored savages could scarcely have evolved them out of their own heads. Some element of civilization, and of highly artistic civilization too, must surely have existed among them at some remote period of their history.

Friday, December 29th.—We had a bathe overboard early this morning. The children were ashore at half-past nine, to go and spend the day at a friend's, at the top of the Nuuanu Avenue, on the road to the Pali.

The King's two sisters came to call on us in the morning with their respective husbands. We had a great many visitors all the morning, till it was time to go to lunch; after which we went to call on the Princess Likelike, who drove me to Waikiki, to see her sister, the Princess Kamakaeha, at her country residence, a very large native grass house, with an enormous veranda. Both ladies are married to Englishmen, and live partly in English style. Inside there is a spacious drawing-room, well furnished, with pictures and knickknacks, where we spent a pleasant half-hour in the gloaming. The sunset, over Diamond Head and the sea, which was just visible through the cocoanut-trees, was splendid. Both the Princesses were as kind as they could be. The royal family have formed quite a little colony here. The King's house is next door, and that of the Prince Leleiohoku is not far off. They all come here in the most unpretending way possible, and amuse themselves by fishing and bathing.

It had been quite dark for some time, when the Princess Likelike dropped me at the hotel at half-past seven, where I found Tom and Mr. Freer waiting for me. We had a quiet dinner, and then went for a stroll. It was a fine clear night, with an almost full moon. The streets were full of equestrians, riding about in pairs, for there was to be a great riding party up to the Pali to-night, the *rendezvous* for which was in Emma Square. Every lady had to select and bring with her an attendant cavalier.*

---

* The event was thus announced in the 'Hawaiian Gazette:'—'THE

There are no side-saddles in any of these islands ; all the ladies ride like men, and sit their horses very well. They wear long riding-dresses, cleverly and elegantly adapted to the exigencies of the situation, generally of some light material, and of *very* bright colors. The effect of a large party galloping along, with wreaths and garlands in their hats and necks, and with their long skirts floating in the wind, is therefore picturesque and strange in the extreme.

Saturday, December 30*th*.—Mabelle, Muriel, and I were up early, and went off to the coral-reef before seven in the 'Flash.' It is very beautiful, but not so fine as those we have already seen at Tahiti and other South Sea Islands. We collected four or five distinct varieties of coral, and saw many marvelous creatures swimming about or sticking to the rocks. There were several canoes full of natives fishing, who appeared highly amused when we ran aground on a coral-tree, as happened more than once. It was a pleasant way of spending the early morning in the bright sunshine, peering into the dark blue and light green depths below.

Breakfast was ready by the time we returned on board, and soon afterwards I went on shore to pay some visits and to do some shopping. We went first to the fish-market, which presented a most animated scene, owing not only to the abundance of the dead produce of air, earth, and sea, which it contained, but to the large number of gayly attired purchasers.

Saturday is a half-holiday in Oahu, and all the plantation and mill hands came galloping into Honolulu on horseback, chattering and laughing, dressed in the bright-

---

LAST CHANCE.—We are informed that a riding party will come off on Friday evening, when all the young ladies who desire to participate are expected to be on hand, each with the cavalier whom she may invite. As leap-year is drawing to a close it is expected that this opportunity will be extensively embraced. Place of rendezvous, Emma Square ; time, seven-thirty ; Luminary for the occasion, a full moon.'

est colors, and covered with flowers. The latter are not so plentiful nor so beautiful as in Tahiti, but still, to our English eyes, they appear very choice. For fruit, too, we have been spoiled in the South Seas. The fish-market here, however, is unrivaled.

Fish—raw or cooked—is the staple food of the inhabitants, and almost everybody we saw had half a dozen or more brilliant members of the finny tribe, wrapped up in fresh green banana-leaves, ready to carry home. Shrimps are abundant and good. They are caught both in salt and fresh water, and the natives generally eat them alive, putting them into their mouths, and either letting them hop down their throats, or crushing them between their teeth while they are still wriggling about. It looks a very nasty thing to do, but, after all, it is not much worse than our eating oysters alive.

From the fish-market we went to the prison, a large and apparently admirably managed establishment, built of stone, and overlooking the harbor. After a pleasant drive along shady fragrant roads, we returned to Emma Square, to hear the excellent performance of the Saturday afternoon band. There was a good assemblage of people, on horseback, in carriages, and on foot, and crowds of children, all more or less white, languid, and sickly-looking. Poor mites! I suppose the climate is too hot for European constitutions. Still, they abound among the foreigners, while the natives are gradually but surely dying out. Among the whole royal family there is only one child, a dear little girl of rather more than a year old. Princess Kauilani ('Sent from Heaven') she is always called, though she has a very long string of additional names. She is heiress-presumptive to the throne, and is thought a good deal of by everybody. Among twenty of the highest chiefs' families there is only one baby. On the other hand, all the foreign consuls, ministers, missionaries, and other white residents, appear to have an average of at least half a dozen in each family.

After the performance was over, we walked to the Princess Likelike's house, where we were entertained at a *poi* supper. The garden was illuminated, the band played and a choir sang alternately, while everybody sat out in the veranda, or strolled about the garden, or did what they liked best. Prince Leleiohoku took me in to supper, which was served in the native fashion, in calabashes and on leaves, laid on mats on the floor, in the same manner as the feast at Tahiti. The walls of the dining-room were made of palm-leaves and bananas, and the roof was composed of the standards of the various members of the royal family, gracefully draped. At one end of the long table, where the Prince and I sat, there was his special royal standard, as heir-apparent, and just behind us were stationed a couple of women, with two large and handsome *kahilis*, which they waved incessantly backwards and forwards. The viands were much the same as at Tahiti—raw seaweed, which was eaten with each mouthful, being substituted for the chopped cocoanut and salt water. The carved *koa* bowls, which were in constant requisition as finger-glasses, were specially elegant and useful-looking articles. *Poi* is generally eaten from a bowl placed between two people, by dipping three fingers into it, giving them a twirl round, and then sucking them. It sounds rather nasty; but, as a matter of fact, it is so glutinous a mixture that you really only touch the particles that stick to your fingers. The latter you wash after each mouthful, so that there is nothing so very dreadful about it, after all. There was a quantity of raw fish, which I did not touch, but which some of our party thought most excellent, besides dried and cooked fish, which seemed very good, fried candle-nuts, baked pig, and many other delicacies. We could get, however, nothing to drink. After supper we returned to the house, where we found an abundance of champagne and other wines, cakes, and biscuits.

At twelve o'clock we thought it was time to say good-by, as it was Saturday night. Beneath a brilliant full moon the drive to the wharf and row off in the boat were delightful.

Sunday, December 31*st*.—I was on deck at six o'clock, and saw what I had often heard about—a team of twenty oxen, driven by a man in a cart, drawing by means of a rope, about a quarter of a mile in length, a large ship through the opening in the reef, the man and cattle being upon the coral.*

About half-past eight Mabelle and I were just going overboard for a swim, when I thought I saw the upper fin of an old familiar enemy, and directly afterwards the cry was echoed all over the ship, 'A shark, a shark!' It was a ground shark, and very nearly aground in the shallow water. They say this is the worst kind of all, and on making inquiry I was told that the safest way to enjoy a dip here is to bathe with a number of other people. The splashing and noise made by a whole ship's company frighten the sharks away. This discovery puts an end therefore to our hopes of enjoying an occasional peaceful bath.

We went to eleven-o'clock service at the cathedral. It is a pleasant small building, beautifully cool, and well adapted to this climate. The Bishop was unfortunately away, but the service was well performed.

Later, Tom read the evening service to the men, and we afterwards landed and dined late at the hotel; so late, indeed, that we could hardly get anything to eat, and they began to shut up the room and put out the lights before we had half done. Luckily, we were a large party, and an indignant protest and threatened appeal to

---

* The following notice appeared in the 'Hawaiian Gazette' recently: 'TO BE REPAIRED.—That stanch little craft the 'Pele,' which Captain Brown has for so long a time successfully commanded, is now being hauled up for the purpose of repairs. She will probably be laid up for six or eight weeks, and in the meantime the antique plan of towing vessels in and out of the harbor with teams of oxen on the reef will be resumed.'

the landlord brought the Chinese waiters to their senses, and induced them to grant us half an hour's law. On our way back to the boat, the streets looked much more lively than they had hitherto done, being full of people returning from rides, drives, and excursions into the country. As a rule, directly after dark not a creature is to be seen about the streets, for every one disappears in the most mysterious manner.

We went on board, and sat in the calm moonlight, thinking and talking over the events of the year, whose end was so swiftly approaching, and wondering what its successor may have in store for us. So ends, with all its joys and sorrows, its pleasures and pains, its hopes and fears, for us, the now old year, 1876.

CHAPTER XVII.

HONOLULU—DEPARTURE FOR JAPAN.

Years following years, steal something every day;
At last they steal us from ourselves away.

Monday, January 1st, 1877.—At midnight we were awakened by our ship's bell, and that of the 'Fantôme,' being struck violently sixteen times. For the moment I could not imagine what it meant, and thought it must be an alarm of fire; indeed, it was not until Tom and I reached the deck, where we found nearly all the ship's company assembled at the top of the companion, and were greeted with wishes for 'A happy New Year, and many of them,' that we quite realized that nothing serious was the matter. Soon the strains of sweet music, proceeding from the Honolulu choirs, which had come out in boats to serenade us, fell upon our ears. The choristers remained alongside for more than an hour, singing English and American sacred and secular hymns and songs, and then went off to the 'Fantôme,' where they repeated the performance. The moon shone brightly; not a ripple disturbed the surface of the water; the cocoa-trees at Waikiki, and the distant mountains near the Pali, were all clearly defined against the dark blue sky. It was altogether a romantic and delicious scene, and we found it difficult to tear ourselves away from the sweet sounds which came floating over the sea.

When I again went on deck, at half-past six, there was a large double canoe close to the yacht, crowded with people. It was difficult to make out what they were doing, for they appeared to be sitting on a great heap of something, piled up between the two canoes. Our sailors suggested that it must be 'some sort of a New Year's set out.' I ordered the 'Flash' to be got ready, and went with the children to make a closer investigation; and, as we approached, we could see that the pile that had puzzled us was a huge fishing-net. The tide here is very uncertain; but as soon as the water is low enough, they stretch the long net right across the narrow mouth of the harbor, and so secure an enormous quantity of fish of various kinds. It was a really good New Year's haul, and provided a hearty meal for a great many people.

Mabelle and I went at twelve o'clock to the Queen's New Year's reception, held in the other wing of the palace. Having driven through the pretty gardens, we were received at the entrance by the Governor, and ushered through two reception-rooms into the royal presence. The Queen was dressed in a European court-dress, of blue and white material, with the Hawaiian Order of the Garter across her breast. Two maids of honor were also in court-dress. Of the other ladies, some were in evening, some in morning dress, some with bonnets and some without; but their costumes were all made according to the European fashion, except that of her Highness Ruth, the Governess of Hawaii, who looked wonderfully well in a rich white silk native dress, trimmed with white satin. She had a necklace of orange-colored *oo* feathers round her neck, and dark yellow alamanda flowers in her hair. This native costume is a most becoming style of dress, especially to the chiefs and chiefesses, who are all remarkably tall and handsome, with a stately carriage and dignified manner. The Queen stood in front of the throne, on which were spread the royal robes, a long mantle of golden feathers, without speck or blemish. On each side stood two men, dressed in black, wearing frock-coats, and capes of red, black, and yellow feathers over their shoulders, and chimney-pot hats on their heads. In their hands they held two enormous *kahilis* of black *oo* feathers, with handsome tortoise-shell and ivory handles. They were at least eight feet high altogether, and the feathers were about six inches across.

The Princess presented Mabelle and me to her Majesty, and we had a short conversation through a lady interpreter. It is always an embarrassing thing to carry on a conversation in this way, especially when you find yourself in the midst of a square formed by a large crowd of ladies, who you fancy are all gazing at you, the one stranger present, and I was glad when fresh people arrived, and her Majesty's attention was claimed elsewhere.

Queen Kapiolani is a nice-looking woman, with a very pleasing expression of countenance. She is the granddaughter of the heroic Princess Kapiolani, who, when the worship and fear of the goddess Pélé were at their height, walked boldly up to the crater of Kilauea, in defiance of the warnings and threats of the high-priestess of the idolatrous rites, proclaiming her confidence in the power of her God, the God of the Christians, to preserve her. This act did much to assist in the establishment of Christianity in the Island of Hawaii, and to shake the belief of the native worshipers of Pélé in the power of the fearful goddess.

The Princess showed me round the room which contains the portraits of the kings and queens of the Sandwich Islands for many generations, the early ones attired in their feather capes, the later ones dressed in European costumes. Most of them were the work of native artists, but the portraits of Kamehameha II. and his queen were painted, during their visit to England, by a good artist. Their Majesties are depicted in the height of the fashion of the day, the king wearing a blue coat and brass buttons, with many orders on his breast, the queen having on a very short-waisted, tight-fitting white satin dress, a turban surmounted by a tremendous plume of white feathers, and a pearl necklace and bracelets: rather a trying costume for a handsome woman with a dark complexion and portly figure. They both died in England, and their remains were brought back here for burial, in H.M.S. 'Blonde,' commanded by Lord Byron. There was also a portait of Admiral Thomas, whose memory is highly reverenced here for the happy way in which he succeeded in terminating the disputes arising out of our claim to the island in 1843, and in restoring King Kamehameha III. to his own again. The collection likewise included excellent portraits of Louis Philippe and Napoleon III. Curiously enough, each of these was sent off from France to the Sandwich Islands, by way of Cape Horn, while the original was in the zenith of his power and fame; and each reached its destination after the original had been deposed and had fled to England for refuge.

But the most interesting object of all was still to come—the real feather cloak, cape, and girdle of the Kamehamehas, not generally to be seen, except at a coronation or christening, but which the Princess Kamakaeha, in her capacity of Mistress of the Robes, had kindly ordered to be put out for my inspection. The cloak, which is now the only one of the kind in existence, is about eleven feet long by five broad, and is composed of the purest yellow, or rather golden, feathers, which, in the sunlight, are perfectly gorgeous, as they have a peculiar kind of metallic luster, quite independent of their brilliant color.

On leaving the palace I had intended to get some lunch at the hotel, but found that establishment was closed to the general public, and was in the possession of a native teetotal society; so I was obliged to return to the yacht. At half-past three, however, we all went ashore again, and set out on horseback, a large party, for an excursion to the Pali, the children, servants, and provisions preceding us in a light two-horse American wagon. We rode through the Nuuana Avenue, and then up the hills, along a moderately good road, for about seven miles and a half. This brought us into a narrow gorge in the midst of the mountains, from which we emerged on the other side of the central range of hills, forming the backbone of the island. The view from this point was beautiful, though I think that the morning would be a better time to enjoy it, as, with a setting sun, the landscape was all in shadow. The change of temperature, too, after the heat of Honolulu, was quite astonishing, considering the short distance we had come—about eight miles only. The carriage could not go quite to the top of the mountain, and after descending a short distance to where it had been left, we dismounted and spread our dinner on the ground; but darkness overtook us before we had finished. Matches and lamps had of course been forgotten; so that the business of packing up was performed under circumstances of great difficulty. The ride down, in the light of the almost full moon, was delightful.

We were on board by half-past seven, and went ashore to a ball at nine o'clock. The dance took place in the large room of the Hawaiian Hotel, and was a great success. The Royal band played for us, and there was neither stuffiness nor crowding, nor were there any regulations as to dress, gentlemen and ladies coming in evening or morning dress, as it suited them best. The Governor and most of the English present, including our own party, wore evening dress, and the officers of the 'Fantôme' were in uniform. Every door and window was open, there was a large veranda to sit in, a garden to stroll about in between the dances, and an abundance of delicious iced lemonade—very different from the composition thus named which is generally met with in London assemblies—to drink. At half-past twelve, when people were beginning to disperse, we took our departure, Captain Long taking us off to the yacht in his boat.

There is to be another ball on Thursday night, for which everybody is most anxious that we should stay, as it is to be rather a large affair. In order that you may see the Hawaiian fashion of sending out cards, I copy the form of invitation we received:—

The pleasure of the Company of Mr. and Mrs. Thos. Brassey is requested at a Subscription Ball, at the Hawaiian Hotel,

ON THURSDAY EVENING, JANUARY 4, 1877, AT 8 O'CLOCK.

Respectfully,   *H. A. Widemann,*

FOR THE COMMITTEE.

Mrs. Jas. Makee and Mrs. J. S. McGrew will kindly act as matrons of the evening.

Tuesday, January 2d.—At eleven o'clock, the King, who was rather better, went on board the 'Fantôme,' saw the men at quarters, and witnessed the firing of a couple of shots at a target, and shortly before twelve paid us a visit, accompanied by the Prince Leleiohoku and others. His Majesty is a tall, fine-looking man, with pleasant manners, and speaks English perfectly and fluently. He and the Prince visited and examined every corner of the yacht, and looked, I think, at almost every object on board. The pictures, curiosities, engines, and our various little contrivances for economizing space, seemed to interest them the most. The inspection occupied at least an hour and a half; and when it was over, we had a long chat on deck on various subjects. The Prince of Wales's visit to India, and the Duke of Edinburgh's voyage round the world, were much discussed. I think the King would like to use them as a precedent, and see a little more of the world himself. His voyage to, and stay in America, he thoroughly enjoyed.

It was two o'clock before our visitors left; and a quarter of an hour later the Queen and her sister arrived.

Her Majesty and her sister made quite as minute an inspection of the yacht as her royal consort and his brother had done before them. We had arranged to be 'at home' to all our kind friends in Honolulu at four o'clock, at which hour precisely the Governor sent the Royal band on board to enliven the proceedings. Soon our other visitors began to arrive; but the Queen appeared to be so well amused that she did not leave until five o'clock. By half-past six the last of our guests (over 150 in number) had said farewell, and there only remained the band to be shown round and feasted after their labors. Tom went on board the 'Fantôme' to dine, and to meet the British, French, German, and American representatives. We went to the hotel; and I must say that I never in my life felt more thoroughly worn out than I did that night, after standing about and receiving and entertaining all the day.

Wednesday, January 3d.—This was sure to be a disagreeable day, since it was to be the concluding one of our short stay in this pleasant place. The final preparations for a long voyage had also to be made; stores, water, and live stock to be got on board, bills to be paid, and adieux to be made to kind friends.

I was on deck at six o'clock, in order to take some photographs and to stow away the coral, shells, curiosities, and presents of various kinds, that the King, Queen, Prince, and Princess, as well as other kind friends, had sent us. Before seven the yacht was surrounded by boats, and the deck was quite impassable, so encumbered was it with all sorts of lumber, waiting to be stowed away, until the boats could be hoisted on board and secured for the voyage. The large mizzen-sail, which had just been repaired and sent on board, looked enormous as it lay on the deck, surrounded by hen-coops, sheep, geese, sacks of coal, and baskets and parcels of every size and shape. One really began to wonder whether space could possibly be found on board for such a miscellaneous collection.

Several visitors, who had been unable to come yesterday, arrived in the midst of the confusion. They must have carried away in their minds a different impression of the yacht from what they would have done had they seen her looking as trim and smart as she did yesterday. It could not, however, be helped; for the departure of a small vessel, with forty people on board, on a voyage of a month's duration, is a matter requiring considerable preparation.

At eleven o'clock we landed and went to see the interior of the Queen's Hospital. It is a fine and well-kept building, containing, at the time of our visit, about ninety patients, the men occupying the lower, the women the upper story. Each ward is tastefully decorated with bouquets, and the name is written up in bright mauve bougainvillea or scarlet hibiscus tacked on to white calico. Many of the convalescents wore wreaths and garlands of flowers, and even those in bed had a few beside them, or in some cases a single spray laid on the coverlet. The effect was bright and cheerful; and it seemed a kind and sensible idea to endeavor to gratify, instead of to repress, the instinctive love of flowers universally felt by the natives of these and of the South Sea Islands.

From the hospital we went to pay farewell visits, to lunch at the hotel, and to settle sundry bills. At three we were to go to the Royal Mausoleum. This was a special privilege, and, I believe, the greatest compliment that has been paid to us anywhere. No foreigners are allowed to enter, except admirals on the station; and very few inhabitants of Honolulu have ever seen the interior. The King has one key, the Dowager Queen Emma another, and the Minister of the Interior the third.

On our way up the hill to the Mausoleum, there was a funeral going on, very much after the style of an Irish wake in one of the dwellings of the poorer class. The house was decorated with flags, and was crowded with people, all dressed in black, and generally with bright yellow *leis* over their heads and necks. They had evidently come from some distance, judging by the number of carts and wagons drawn up outside the door. Several people were sitting in an upper veranda. The corpse was laid out in the lower room, facing the road, as we could see through the open windows and door. It was surrounded by mourners, and four women were waving large *kahilis* slowly backwards and forwards in front of it.

The Princess herself met us at the Mausoleum, which is a small but handsome stone Gothic building, situated above the Nuuanu Avenue, on the road to Pali. It commands a fine view over land and sea, and the gentle breezes waft through the open windows sweet scents from the many fragrant trees and flowers by which it is surrounded. There lay the coffins of all the kings of Hawaii, their consorts, and their children, for many generations past. The greater part were of polished *koa* wood, though some were covered with red velvet ornamented with gold. Many of them appeared to be of an enormous size; for, as I have already observed, the chiefs of these islands have almost invariably been men of large and powerful frames. The bones of Kamehameha I. were in a square oak chest. At the foot of the coffin of Kamehameha IV. there were two immense *kahilis* about twelve feet high, one of rose-colored, the other of black feathers, with tortoise-shell handles. The remains of King Lunalilo are not here, having been buried just outside the native church in the town. In the vestibule to the tombs of the kings rests the coffin of Mr. Wylie, described as 'the greatest European benefactor of the Hawaiian people.' A ship now in the harbor bears his name, and one constantly meets with proofs of the respect and reverence in which his name is held.

The Princess drove us down to the wharf, where we said good-by to her with feelings of the greatest regret. I cannot express the sorrow that we all feel at leaving the many kind friends we have met with in 'dear Honolulu,' as Muriel calls it. But the farewells were at last over, the anchor was weighed, and the yacht, which was by this time once more in apple-pie order, began to move slowly ahead. Suddenly we heard shouts from the shore, and saw a boat pursuing us in hot haste. We stopped, and received on board a basket of beautiful ferns and other parcels from different friends. A second boat was then seen coming off to us, which contained a fine dish of delicious honey and some flowers. The order to go ahead again was scarcely given before a third boat, in, if possible, hotter haste than the two previous ones, put off after us, bringing some things the laundress had forgotten.

Now we are fairly off; and now surely the last link that binds us to the shore is broken. But no! there are farewell signals and hearty cheers yet to come from the officers and men of the 'Fantôme;' and still farther out, on the top of the tiny lighthouse at the mouth of the narrow passage through the reef, stand other friends, cheering and waving their handkerchiefs. They had rowed out thither, being determined to give us really *the* parting cheer, and till the shades of twilight fell we could see their white handkerchiefs fluttering, and hear their voices borne on the evening breeze, as we meandered slowly through the tortuous channels into deep water.

Once outside we found there was plenty of wind and a heavy roll, which sent me quickly to bed.

CHAPTER XVIII.

HONOLULU TO YOKOHAMA.

As slow our ship her foamy track
Against the wind was cleaving,
Her trembling pennant still look'd back
To that dear isle 'twas leaving.

Thursday, January 4th.—It was very rough, but fortunately the wind came from a favorable quarter. Sorry as we all were to bid farewell to these charming islands, I could not help rejoicing that we had picked up a fresh fair wind so unexpectedly soon.

While we were at Honolulu a regular epidemic of influenza prevailed in the place, affecting both man and beast. This is often the case during the prevalence of the south wind, which blew, more or less, during the whole of our stay. We none of us suffered from the malady at the time, but now nearly everybody on board is affected, and some very severely.

Friday, January 5th.—The fresh fair breeze still continues. At noon we had sailed 240 knots. The head-sea we could dispense with, as it makes us all very uncomfortable. Muriel, Baby, the three maids, and several of the crew, are ill to-day with influenza, and I have a slight touch of it, so I suppose it will go right through the ship. Towards the evening the breeze increased to a gale.

Saturday, January 6th.—The gale increased during the night, and the head-sea became heavier. There was a good deal of rain in the course of the day. The wind dropped about sunset, and was succeeded by intervals of calm, with occasional sharp squalls. Baby was very poorly all day, but seemed better at night. We have now regularly settled down to our sea life again, and, if only the children recover, I hope to get through a good deal of reading and writing between this and Japan. At present they occupy all my time and attention, but I think, like the weather, they have now taken a turn for the better.

Sunday, January 7th.—A very rough and disagreeable day, with much rain. All the morning we rolled about, becalmed, in a heavy swell. Steam was ordered at half-past twelve, but before it was up the fair wind had returned, so the fires were put out. We had the Litany at eleven, and a short service, without a sermon, at four.

Baby was *very* ill all night. Everything was shut up on account of the torrents of rain, so that the heat was almost insufferable, and we tossed and tumbled about in the most miserable manner.

Monday, January 8th.—All the early part of the morning we were in the greatest anxiety about Baby; she could hardly draw her breath, and lay in her cot, or on her nurse's lap, almost insensible, and quite blue in the face, in spite of the application of mustard, hot water, and every remedy we could think of. The influenza with her has taken the form of bronchitis and pleurisy. The other children are still ailing. Heavy squalls of wind and rain, and continuous rolling, prevailed throughout the day.

Tuesday, January 9th.—The wind fell light, and the weather improved; but we tumbled about more than ever. The thermometer in the nursery stood at 90°. The children are a shade better.

Wednesday, January 10th.—Very hot, and a flat calm. Steam was up at 7.30 a.m. Mabelle is convalescent; Muriel not so well; Baby certainly better. In the afternoon one of the boiler-tubes burst. It was repaired, and we went on steaming. In the evening it burst again, and was once more repaired, without causing a long stoppage.

(*Thursday, January* 11*th,* had no existence for us, as,

in crossing the 180th parallel of latitude, we have lost a day.)

Friday, January 12th.—Wednesday morning with us was Tuesday evening with people in England, and we were thus twelve hours in advance of them. To-day the order of things is reversed, and we are now twelve hours behind our friends at home. Having quitted one side of the map of the world (according to Mercator's projection) and entered upon the other half, we begin to feel that we are at last really 'homeward bound.'

At 4 a.m. Powell woke us with the announcement that the boiler-tube had again burst, and that we had consequently ceased steaming. Letting off steam, and blowing out the boiler, made a tremendous noise, which aroused everybody in the ship. It was a lovely morning, but a flat calm, and the sun rose magnificently. The few light clouds near the surface of the water caught and reflected the rays of light most brilliantly before the sun itself appeared, and assumed all manner of fanciful shapes.

About six o'clock a very light breeze sprang up, which increased during the day; but the sea remained perfectly calm. We think we must have got into the trade again. This weather is indeed a luxury after all the knocking about we have lately gone through; and I feel as if I could never rest enough. The constant effort to maintain one's balance, whether sitting, standing, or moving about, has been most fatiguing, and the illness of the children has made matters worse. Baby is, I hope, now quite out of danger.

Saturday, January 13th.—The engineers made up their minds that we were in the trade winds again yesterday, and that we should not want the engines for some days. They therefore did not hurry on with the repairs as they should have done. This morning there was a calm, and when Tom ordered steam to be got up at once, the reply was, 'Please, sir, the engine won't be ready till night.' This was annoying; but they worked extra hard all day, and by 4 p.m. steam was raised. At six a nice little breeze sprang up, which freshened during the evening, and at midnight orders were given to stop steaming.

We had another bad night of it—a head wind, the sea washing over the decks, everything shut up, and the thermometer standing at 90°.

Sunday, January 14*th.*—I was on deck at 4 a.m. The Southern Cross, the Great Bear, and the North Star were shining with a brilliancy that eclipsed all the other stars.

During the day the wind freshened to a squally gale. Sometimes we were going ten, sometimes thirteen, and sometimes fifteen knots through the water, knocking about a good deal all the while. Service was an impossibility; cooking and eating, indeed, were matters of difficulty. It rained heavily, and the seas came over the deck continually.

Many of the sailors and servants were ill. I was hopelessly so. Nothing annoys me more than to find that, after having sailed tens and tens of thousands of miles, I cannot cure myself of sea-sickness. I can stand a good deal more rolling than I once could; but still, many are the days when nothing but the firmest determination not to think about it, but to find something to do, and to do it with all my might, keeps me on my feet at all. Fewer, happily, are the days when struggling is of no avail, when I am utterly and hopelessly incapacitated, ignominiously and literally laid flat on my back, and when no effort of will can enable me to do what I most wish to accomplish. If only some physician could invent a sovereign remedy for sea-sickness, he would deserve well of his country, and of mankind in general.

Monday, January 15*th.*—I woke once or twice in the night, and felt exactly as if I were being pulled backwards through the water by my hair. We were rushing and tearing along at such a pace, against a head-sea, that it almost took one's breath away. But at noon we were rewarded for all discomfort by finding that we had run 298 sea, or 343 land miles, in 24 hours, and that between 8.14 yesterday and 8.15 to-day we had made 302 knots, or 347 land miles—nearly 350 miles in the 24 hours—under very snug canvas, and through a heavy sea. The wind still continued fair and fresh, but the sea was much quieter, and we all felt comparatively comfortable. More sails were set during the afternoon. Some albatrosses and long-tailed tropic birds were seen hovering about us. The moon begins to give a good light now, and we found it very pleasant on deck this evening.

Wednesday, January 17*th.*—It was a fine warm morning, and we got the children on deck for the first time for ten days.

Thursday, January 18*th.*—Between breakfast and lunch we sailed over the spot where Tarquin Island is marked on the chart, and, between lunch and dinner, over a nameless reef, also marked on the chart. A good lookout had been kept at the masthead and in the bows, but not a trace could be seen of either of these objects in any direction. The weather kept clear and bright, and the sea was much calmer.

During the last five days we have covered 1,221 sea miles.

Monday, January 22*d.*—At daylight Asuncion Island was still visible. It is of volcanic origin, and is in the form of a perfect sugar-loaf, 2,600 feet high, rising out of the sea, exactly as I had expected the Peak of Teneriffe to appear. I should like to have landed on the islands Agrigan or Tinian, so as to see the interesting remains left by the ancient inhabitants. Some people say that they resemble Aztec remains; others, that they are like those of the more modern Peruvians. All authorities, however, seem to agree that they are like those on Easter

Island, the south-east extremity of Polynesia, this being the north-west.

Amateur Navigation.

We were close-hauled all day; the wind was strong, and the sea rough and disagreeable.

Tuesday, January 23d. — Still close-hauled, and still a heavy swell. I felt very ill, and could scarcely move my head for neuralgia. The galley boiler burst to-day, so we are now dependent on the one in the forecastle. During the night we passed the Euphrosyne rock. It looks like a ship in full sail, and abounds with turtle, fish, and sea-elephants.

Wednesday, January 24th.—Very much colder, though we are only just outside the tropics. The wind was rather freer, and we had a beautiful moonlight night.

Friday, January 26th.—During the night the breeze freshened, and in the morning increased to a gale. Steam was therefore let off. It has been a miserable day; so cold, wet, and rough, that it was impossible to do anything, or to sit anywhere, except on the floor.

About 9 p.m. I was sitting in the deck-house, when I heard a tremendous crash, and looking out, saw that the fore gig davits had been carried away, taking with them a piece of the rail, stanchion, and cavil. The gig was hanging from the after davits, one might say, by a thread, splashing and dashing in and out of the water, and crashing and splintering against the side of the yacht. All hands were speedily on deck; and in spite of the risk they ran, and of the remonstrances of their comrades, two of the gig's crew jumped into her with a rope, which they tried to pass round her. It was a difficult task in that heavy sea, and many times they failed, and we constantly feared that men, boat, and all were gone. Half a dozen of the crew caught hold of the rigging outside, put their backs against the yacht, and with legs outstretched tried to keep the gig off the ship's side, while all the loose gear was floating away out of her. At last there was a shout of triumph. The rope was round her, the men jumped on board the yacht again, whilst sailors, stewards, and passengers proceeded to hoist and drag the boat in, with all their might and main. Alas! she was only a wreck. Her sides were stove in, her planks were started, there was a hole in her bottom, and the moon shone through her many cracks.

Saturday, January 27th.—About two o'clock this morning the yacht plunged so heavily into a deep sea, that the jibboom, a beautiful spar, broke short off, and the foretopgallant mast and topgallant yard were carried away almost at the same moment, with a terrible noise. It took about eight hours to clear the wreck, all hands working all night; and a very forlorn appearance the deck presented in the morning, lumbered up with broken spars, ropes, &c. The jibboom fell right across the forefoot of the yacht, and now looks as if it had been cut at for weeks with some blunt tool.

The weather cleared a little to-day, but there was still a heavy sea and nearly a head wind. The crew were busily engaged in repairing damages. Unfortunately, two of them are ill, and so is the carpenter, a specially important person at this juncture. No men could have behaved better than they all did after the accident. It was frightful to see them aloft in such weather, swinging on the ends of the broken spars, as the yacht rolled and pitched about. When it comes to a pinch they are all good men and true: not that they are perfection, any more than other men are.

Sunday, January 28th.—It is finer, but bitterly cold. Several of my tropical birds are already dead. The little pig from Harpe Island, and the Hawaiian geese, look very wretched, in spite of all my precautions.

We had the Litany at eleven, and prayer and a sermon at four; after which Tom addressed the men, paying them some well-deserved compliments on their behavior on Friday night.

The decks were very slippery, and as we kept rolling about a good deal there were some nasty falls among the passengers. We had a splendid though stormy sunset, which did not belie its promise, for the wind shortly afterwards became stiffer and stronger, until at last we had two reefs down, and were tumbling about in all directions, as we rushed through the water. The dining-tables tilted till they could go no further, and then paused to go back again; but not quickly enough, for the glasses began to walk up-hill and go over the edge in the most extraordinary manner. On deck the night looked brilliant but rather terrible. The full moon made it as light as day, and illuminated the fountains of spray blown from the waves by which we were surrounded. Without her heavy jibboom, and with her canvas well reefed down, the 'Sunbeam' rode through it all, dipping her head into the sea, shivering from stem to stern, and then giving herself a shake, preparatory to a fresh start, just like a playful water-bird emerging from a prolonged dive.

At midnight a tremendous sea struck her, and for a minute you could not see the yacht at all, as she was completely enveloped in spray and foam. Tom said it was just like being behind the falls of Niagara, with the water coming over you from every quarter at once. It was only loose stuff, however, for not a green sea did she take on board the whole night through. Our old engineer, who has been with us so long, made up his mind that we had struck on a rock, and woke up all the servants and told them to go on deck. I never felt anything like it before, and the shock sent half of us out of our beds.

Monday, January 29th.—At four o'clock I was called to go on deck to see the burning mountain. The wind was still blowing hard, but we were among the islands, and in comparatively smooth water. The full moon still rode high in the heavens, her light being reflected in rainbow hues from the spray and foam that drifted along the surface of the water. On every side were islands and rocks, among which the sea boiled, and seethed, and swirled, while the roaring breakers dashed against the higher cliffs, casting great columns of spray into the air, and falling back in heavy rollers and surf. Just before us rose the island of Vries, with its cone-shaped volcano, 2,600 feet high, emitting volumes of smoke and flame. It was overhung by a cloud of white vapor, on the under side of which shone the lurid glare of the fires of the crater.

Sometimes this cloud simply floated over the top of the mountain, from which it was quite detached; then there would be a fresh eruption; and after a few moments' quiet great tongues of flame would shoot up and pierce through the overhanging cloud to the heavens above, while the molten lava rose like a fountain for a short distance, and then ran down the sides of the mountain. It was wondrously beautiful; and, as a defense against the intense cold, we wrapped ourselves in furs, and staid on deck watching the scene, until the sun rose glorious from the sea, and shone upon the snow-covered sides of Fujiyama, called by the Japanese 'the matchless mountain.' It is an extinct crater, of the most perfect form, rising abruptly from a chain of very low mountains, so that it stands in unrivaled magnificence. This morning, covered with the fresh-fallen snow, there was not a spot nor a fleck to be seen upon it, from top to bottom. It is said to be the youngest mountain in the world, the enormous mass having been thrown up in the course of a few days only 862 years B.C.

We reached the entrance to the Gulf of Yeddo about nine o'clock, and passed between its shores through hundreds of junks and fishing boats. I never saw anything like it before. The water was simply covered with them; and at a distance it looked as though it would be impossible to force a passage. As it was, we could not proceed very fast, so constantly were the orders to 'slow,' 'stop,' 'port,' 'starboard,' given; and I began at last to fear that it would be impossible to reach Yokohama without running down at least one boat.

The shores of the gulf, on each side, consist of sharp-cut little hills, covered with pines and cryptomerias, and dotted with temples and villages. Every detail of the scene exactly resembled the Japanese pictures one is accustomed to see in England; and it was easy to imagine that we were only gazing upon a slowly moving panorama, unrolling itself before us.

It was twelve o'clock before we found ourselves among the men-of-war and steamers lying near the port of Yokohama, and two o'clock before the anchor could be dropped. During this interval we were surrounded by a swarm of boats, the occupants of which clamored vociferously to be allowed on board, and in many cases they succeeded in evading the vigilance of the man at the gangway, by going round the other side and climbing over the rail. A second man was put on guard; but it was of no use, for we were invaded from all directions at once. We had a good many visitors also from the men-of-war, Japanese and English, and from the reporters of newspapers, full of curiosity, questions, and astonishment.

Having at last managed to get some lunch, Tom went to bed to rest, after his two hard nights' work, and the rest of us went on shore. Directly we landed at the jetty we were rushed at by a crowd of *jinrikisha* men, each drawing a little vehicle not unlike a Hansom cab, without the seat for the driver—there being no horse to drive. The man runs between the shafts, and is often preceded by a leader, harnessed on in front, tandem fashion. Each of these vehicles holds one person, and they go along at a tremendous pace.

We went first to the Consul's, where we got a few letters, and then to the Post Office, where many more awaited us. We had then to go to various places to order stores, fresh provisions, coals, and water, all of which were urgently needed on board, and to give directions for the repair of boats, spars, &c., with as little delay as possible. All this business, including the inevitable search for a good laundress, lay in the European quarter of the town, the appearance of which was not remarkable. But the people we met in the streets were a study in themselves. The children said they looked 'like fans walking about;' and it was not difficult to understand their meaning. The dress of the lower orders has remained precisely the same for hundreds of years; and before I had been ashore five minutes I realized more fully than I had ever done before the truthfulness of the representations of native artists, with which the fans, screens, and vases one sees in England are ornamented.

While we were going about, a letter was brought me containing the sad news (received here by telegram) of the death of Tom's mother. It was a terrible shock, coming, too, just as we were rejoicing in the good accounts from home which our letters contained. I went on board at once to break the bad news to Tom. This sad intelligence realized a certain vague dread of something, we knew not what, which had seemed to haunt us both on our way hither.

CHAPTER XIX.

YOKOHAMA.

Heavily plunged the breaking wave,
And foam flew up the lea,
Morning and evening the drifted snow
Fell into the dark gray sea.

Tuesday, January 30th.—When we awoke from our slumbers this morning, it was very cold and dark, and we heard noises of a strange kind. On going on deck to ascertain the cause of this state of things, we discovered that the skylights and portholes were all covered and blocked up with snow, and that the water froze as it came out of the hose, forming a sheet of ice on the deck. Masses of snow and ice were falling from the rigging, and everything betokened that our welcome to Japan would not be a warm one.

After breakfast we had many visitors, and received letters from Sir Harry and Lady Parkes, inviting us to go up to Yeddo to-morrow for a long day, to settle our future plans.

Having landed, we went with the Consul to the native town, to see the curio shops, which are a specialty of the place. The inhabitants are wonderfully clever at making all sorts of curiosities, and the manufactories of so-called 'antique bronzes' and 'old china' are two of the most wonderful sights in Yokohama. The way in which they scrape, crack, chip, mend, and color the various articles, cover them with dust, partially clean them, and imitate the marks and signatures of celebrated makers, is more creditable to their ingenuity than to their honesty. Still, there are a good many genuine old relics from the temples, and from the large houses of the reduced Daimios, to be picked up, if you go the right way to work, though the supply is limited. Dealers are plentiful, and travelers, especially from America, are increasing in numbers. When we first made acquaintance with the shops we thought they seemed full of beautiful things, but even one day's shopping, in the company of experienced people, has educated our taste and taught us a great deal; though we have still much to learn. There are very respectable-looking lacquer cabinets ranging in price from 5s. to £20. But they are only made for the foreign market. No such things exist in a Japanese home. A really good bit of old lacquer (the best is generally made into the form of a small box, a portable medicine-chest, or a chow-chow box) is worth from £20 to £200. We saw one box, about three inches square, which was valued at £45; and a collection of really good lacquer would be costly and difficult to procure even here. The best specimens I have ever seen are at Lady Alcock's; but they are all either royal or princely presents, not to be bought with money. The tests of good lacquer are its exquisite finish, its satiny, oily feel, and the impossibility of making any impression on it with your thumb-nail. It is practically indestructible, and will wear forever. All the poor as well as the rich people here use it, and have used it for centuries, instead of china and glass, for cups, saucers, dishes, bowls, which would need to be often washed in the hottest of water. It is said that the modern Japanese have lost the art of lacquer making; and as an illustration I was told that many beautiful articles of lacquer, old and new, had been sent from this country to the Vienna Exhibition in 1873, but the price put on them was so exorbitant that few were sold, and nearly all had to be sent back to Japan. Just as the ship with these things on board reached the Gulf of Yeddo, she struck on a rock and sank in shallow water. A month or two ago a successful attempt was made to raise her, and to recover the cargo, when it was found that the new lacquer had been reduced to a state of pulp, while the old was not in the least damaged. I tell you the tale as it was told to me.

After a long day's shopping, we went to dine, in real Japanese fashion, at a Japanese tea-house. The establishment was kept by a very pleasant woman, who received us at the door, and who herself removed our exceedingly dirty boots before allowing us to step on her clean mats. This was all very well, as far as it went; but she might as well have supplied us with some substitute for the objectionable articles, for it was a bitterly cold night, and the highly polished wood passages and steep staircase felt very cold to our shoeless feet. The apartment we were shown into was so exact a type of a room in any Japanese house, that I may as well describe it once for all. The woodwork of the roof and the framework of the screens were all made of a handsome dark polished wood, not unlike walnut. The exterior walls under the veranda, as well as the partitions between the other rooms, were simply wooden lattice-work screens, covered with white paper, and sliding in grooves; so that you could walk in or out at any part of the wall you chose, and it was, in like manner, impossible to say whence the next comer would make his appearance. Doors and windows are, by this arrangement, rendered unnecessary, and do not exist. You open a little bit of your wall if you want to look out, and a bigger bit if you want to step out. The floor was covered with several thicknesses of very fine mats, each about six feet long by three broad, deliciously soft to walk upon. All mats in Japan are of the same size, and everything connected with house-building is measured by this standard. Once you have prepared your foundations and woodwork of the dimensions of so many mats, it is the easiest thing in the world to go to a shop and buy a house, ready made, which you can then set up and furnish in the scanty Japanese fashion in a couple of days.

On one side of the room was a slightly raised daïs, about four inches from the floor. This was the seat of honor. On it had been placed a stool, a little bronze ornament, and a china vase, with a branch of cherry-blossom and a few flag-leaves gracefully arranged. On the wall behind hung pictures, which are changed every month, according to the season of the year. There was no other furniture of any sort in the room. Four nice-looking Japanese girls brought us thick cotton quilts to sit upon, and braziers full of burning charcoal, to warm ourselves by. In the center of the group another brazier was placed, protected by a square wooden grating, and over the whole they laid a large silk eider-down quilt, to retain the heat. This is the way in which all the rooms, even bedrooms, are warmed in Japan, and the result is that fires are of very frequent occurrence. The brazier is kicked over by some restless or careless person, and in a moment the whole place is in a blaze.

Presently the eider-down and brazier were removed, and our dinner was brought in. A little lacquer table, about six inches high, on which were arranged a pair of chop-sticks, a basin of soup, a bowl for rice, a *saki* cup, and a basin of hot water, was placed before each person, whilst the four Japanese maidens sat in our midst, with fires to keep the *saki* hot, and to light the tiny pipes with which they were provided, and from which they wished us to take a whiff after each dish. *Saki* is a sort of spirit, distilled from rice, always drunk hot, out of small cups. In this state it is not disagreeable, but we found it exceedingly nasty when cold.

Everything was well cooked and served, though the ingredients of some of the dishes, as will be seen from the following bill of fare, were rather strange to our ideas. Still they were eatable, and most of them really palatable.

Soup.

Shrimps and Seaweed.

Prawns, Egg Omelet, and Preserved Grapes.

Fried Fish, Spinach, Young Rushes, and Young Ginger.

Raw Fish, Mustard and Cress, Horseradish, and Soy.

Thick Soup, of Eggs, Fish, Mushrooms, and Spinach; Grilled Fish.

Fried Chicken, and Bamboo Shoots.

Turnip Tops and Root Pickled.

Rice ad libitum in a large bowl.

Hot Saki, Pipes and Tea.

The meal concluded with an enormous lacquer box of rice, from which all our bowls were filled, the rice being thence conveyed to our mouths by means of chop-sticks. We managed very well with these substitutes for spoons and forks, the knack of using which, to a certain extent, is soon acquired. The long intervals between the dishes were beguiled with songs, music, and dancing, performed by professional singing and dancing girls. The music was somewhat harsh and monotonous; but the songs sounded harmonious, and the dancing was graceful, though it was rather posturing than dancing, great use being made of the fan and the long trailing skirts. The girls, who were pretty, wore peculiar dresses to indicate their calling, and seemed of an entirely different stamp from the quiet, simply dressed waitresses whom we found so attentive to our wants. Still they all looked cheery, light-hearted, simple creatures, and appeared to enjoy immensely the little childish games they played amongst themselves between whiles.

After dinner we had some real Japanese tea, tasting

exactly like a little hot water poured on very fragrant new-mown hay. Then, after a brief visit to the kitchen, which, though small, was beautifully clean, we received our boots, and were bowed out by our pleasant hostess and her attentive handmaidens.

On our return we had considerable difficulty in procuring a boat, our own boats being all ashore under repair. It was a beautiful moonlight night, but bitterly cold. The harbor being so full of shipping, our boatmen were at first puzzled how to find the yacht, till we pointed to the lights in the deck-house—always a good beacon at night in a crowded harbor.

Wednesday, January 31*st.*—We left the yacht soon after eight o'clock, and started by the 9.34 a.m. train for the city formerly called Yeddo, but latterly, since the Mikado has resided there, Tokio, or eastern capital of Japan. The ground was covered with snow, and there were several degrees of frost, but the sun felt hot, and all the people were sunning themselves in the doorways or wide verandas of their houses.

Yokohama has been so completely Europeanized, that it was not until we had left it that we caught our first glimpse of Japanese life; and the whole landscape and the many villages looked very like a set of living fans or tea-trays, though somehow the snow did not seem to harmonize with it.

We crossed several rivers, and reached Tokio in about an hour, when we at once emerged into the midst of a clattering, chattering crowd, amongst whom there did not seem to be a single European. The reverberation, under the glass roof of the station, of the hundreds of pairs of wooden clogs, pattering along, was something extraordinary. Giving up our tickets, and following the stream, we found ourselves surrounded by a still more animated scene, outside the station. We were just deliberating what to do next, when a smart little Japanese, with a mail-bag over his shoulder, stepped forward and said something about Sir Harry Parkes. He then popped us all into several double and treble manned *jinrikishas*, and started off himself ahead at a tremendous pace, shouting and clearing the way for us.

Tokio is a genuinely Japanese town. Not a single foreigner resides within its limits, with the exception of the foreign Ministers. There is no hotel nor any place of the kind to stay at; so that, unless you have friends at any of the Legations, you have no choice but to return to Yokohama the same day, which makes a visit rather a fatiguing affair.*

Our first halting-place was at the Temple of Shiba, not far from the station, where most of the Tycoons have been buried. It is a large inclosure, many acres in extent, in the center of the city, with walls overgrown with creepers, and shadowed by evergreen trees, amid whose branches rooks caw, ravens croak, and pigeons coo, as undisturbedly as if in the midst of the deepest woodland solitude. I had no idea there was anything so beautiful in Japanese architecture as this temple. The primary idea in the architecture of Japan is evidently that of a tent among trees. The lines of the high, overhanging, richly decorated roofs, with pointed gable ends, are not straight, but delicately curved, like the suspended cloth of a tent. In the same way, the pillars have neither capital nor base, but seem to run through the building perpendicularly, without beginning or end. The principal temple was burned down a few years ago; but there are many smaller ones remaining, built in exactly the same style, and all the tombs are perfect. Some people say the bodies are inclosed in coffins, filled with vermilion, but I need hardly say we had no opportunity of ascertaining the correctness of this statement. We entered several of the temples, which are perfect marvels of carving, gild-

---

* I have since heard that there are two hotels at Tokio, such as they are.

ing, painting, and lacquer work. Their style of decoration may be somewhat barbaric; but what a study they would form for an artist! Outside, where no color is used, the overhanging roofs and the walls are carved with a depth and boldness, and yet a delicacy, I have seldom seen equaled; the doors and railing being of massive bronze, brought from the Corea. Within, a dim religious light illumines and harmonizes a dazzling mass of lacquer, gold, and painting. It is the grandest burial-place imaginable; too good for the long line of men who have tyrannized over Japan and its lawful sovereigns for so many centuries past.

The streets of Tokio were crowded with a motley throng up to the very gates of the citadel, where, within the first moat, stand all the *yashgis*, or residences of the Daimios. Each *yashgi* is surrounded by a blank wall, loopholed, and with a tower at each of the four corners. Within this outer wall is the court of the retainers, all of them 'two-sworded' men; then comes a second wall, also loopholed, inside which dwell distant relations of the Daimio; and then again a third inclosure, guarding the Daimio himself, with his immediate belongings. After crossing the third moat we reached the Mikado's gardens and pâlace, the public offices, and the residences of the foreign Ministers, all of which were formerly occupied by the Tycoon, or Shogun, and his ministers. On the waters of the inner moat were thousands of wild ducks and geese. Nobody is allowed to harm them, and the birds seem to be perfectly aware of this fact, for they disport themselves with the greatest confidence.

The English Embassy is a nice red brick house, built in the center of a garden, so as to be as secure as possible from fire or attack. After a most pleasant luncheon we looked over the nucleus of a second collection which Lady Parkes is beginning to form. Her former beautiful collection was burned a few years ago, a most disheartening misfortune, especially as the opportunities for obtaining really old and good things in Japan are diminishing day by day.

A little later we started in great force, some in carriages and some on horseback, attended by running grooms, to see something more of the city. These men think nothing of running by the side of a horse and carriage some forty miles a day. They form a distinct class, and when working on their own account wear little clothing. When in the service of private individuals they are dressed in tight-fitting dark blue garments, with short capes, fastened to their arms, and large hats.

Just outside the Embassy we passed two of the finest of the still existing *yashgis*, the larger one being used as the Home Office, the other as the Foreign Office.

There is always a festival going on in some part of Tokio. To-day there had been a great wrestling-match, and we met all the people coming away. Such crowds of *jinrikishas*, full of gayly dressed and painted women and children, with their hair plastered into all sorts of inconceivable shapes, and decorated with artificial flowers and glittering pins! We met six of the wrestlers themselves, riding in *jinrikishas*—big men, prodigiously fat, and not at all, according to our ideas, in fighting or wrestling condition. One of their *jinrikisha* men stumbled and fell, just as they passed us, and the wrestler shot out, head over heels, and lay, a helpless ball of fat, in the middle of the road, till somebody came and picked him up. He was not in the least hurt, and, as soon as he was set on his feet again, began to belabor the poor *jinrikisha* man most unmercifully. After a long and delightful drive we arrived at the station just in time to catch the train.

The return journey to Yokohama, in the omnibus-like railway carriages, was very cold, and the *jinrikisha* drive to the Grand Hotel colder still; but a roaring fire and a capital dinner soon warmed and comforted us.

After dinner we looked over a fine collection of photographs of Japanese scenery and costumes, and then returned to the yacht in the house-boat belonging to the hotel, which was prettily decorated with bright-colored lanterns, and which afforded welcome shelter from the biting wind.

Thursday, February 1st.—Careful arrangements have been made for our excursion to the Island of Inoshima, to see the great figure of Daibutz. By eight o'clock we had landed, and packed ourselves into a funny little shaky carriage, drawn by four horses. We drove quickly through the town, past the station, along the Tokaido, or imperial road, running from one end of the Island of Niphon to the other, and on which so many foreigners have been murdered even within the last ten years. Now, however, it is perfectly safe. The houses are one story high, and their walls are made of the screens I have already described. These screens were all thrown back, to admit the morning air, cold as it was. We could consequently see all that was going on within, in the sitting-room in front, and even in the bedrooms and kitchen. At the back of the house there was invariably a little garden to be seen, with a miniature rockery, a tree, and a lake; possibly also a bridge and a temple. Even in the gardens of the poorest houses an attempt at something of the sort had been made. The domestic occupations of the inhabitants being conducted in this public manner, a very good idea might be obtained, even at the end of a few miles' drive, of how the lower class of Japanese wash and dress themselves and their children, how very elaborate the process of hair-dressing is, to say nothing of a bird's-eye view of the ground plan of the houses, the method of cooking food, &c.

As we emerged into the open country the landscape became very pretty, and the numerous villages, nestling in the valleys at the foot of the various small hills, had a most picturesque appearance. At a stone-quarry that we passed, on the side of a mountain, there were about seventy men at work, without any clothing, though the thermometer was far below freezing point. The Japanese are a sensitive nation, and finding that foreigners were astonished and shocked at the habits of the people, in going about without clothes, and in bathing in public and at their house-doors, they passed a law prohibiting these customs in towns. In the country, however, the more primitive customs are still in force, and every dwelling has its half-open bath-house, whilst the people do as they like in the matter of clothing.

After stopping twice on the road, to drink the inevitable tea, we changed from our carriage to *jinrikishas*, each drawn and pushed by four strong men, bowling along at a merry pace. The sun was very warm in the sheltered valleys, and the abundance of evergreens of all kinds quite deluded one into the belief that it was summer time, especially as camellias grew like forest trees, covered with red and white bloom, amidst a dense tangle of bamboos and half-hardy palms. There were many strange things upside down to be seen on either hand—horses and cows with bells on their tails instead of on their necks, the quadrupeds well clothed, their masters without a scrap of covering, tailors sewing from them instead of to them, a carpenter reversing the action of his saw and plane. It looked just as if they had originally learned the various processes in 'Alice's Looking-glass World' in some former stage of their existence.

We had not long left the town before our men began to undress each other; for their clothes were so tight that it required no inconsiderable effort to remove them. Some of them were beautifully tattooed. My wheeler had the root of a tree depicted on one foot, from which sprang the trunk and branches, spreading gradually, until on his back and chest they bore fruit and flowers, amongst which birds were perched. On his other leg was a large stork, supposed, I imagine, to be standing under the shadow of the same tree. Another man had human figures tattooed all over him, in various attitudes.

In less than an hour we reached the narrow strip of land which at low water connects the island or peninsula of Inoshima with the mainland. This isthmus was covered with natives gathering shells and seaweed, casting their nets, and pushing off or dragging up their boats; whilst an island rose fresh and green from the sea, with a background of snowy mountains, stretching across the bay, above which Fujiyama towered grandly. This name signifies 'not two, but one mountain,' the Japanese thinking it impossible that there can be another like it in the world. The lovely little island is called Inoshima, and is conical in shape and covered with evergreens and Buddhist temples, with a few small fishing villages scattered on its shores. We walked right across it in about an hour; so you may imagine it is not very large. The sea teems with curiously shaped fish and beautiful shells. The staple food of the inhabitants seems to be those lovely 'Venus's ears,' * as they are called—a flattish univalve, about as big as your hand, with a row of holes along the edge, and a lining of brilliant black mother-of-pearl. These were lying about in heaps everywhere, mixed with white mother-of-pearl shells, as big as your two fists, and shaped like a snail-shell.

Our *jinrikisha* men deposited us at the bottom of the main street of the principal village, to enter which we passed through a simple square arch of a temple. The street was steep and dirty, and consisted principally of shell-fish and seaweed shops.

An old priest took us in hand, and, providing us with stout sticks, marched us up to the top of the hill to see various temples, and splendid views in many directions. The camellias and evergreens on the hillside made a lovely framework for each little picture, as we turned and twisted along the narrow path. I know not how many steps on the other side of the island had to be descended before

---

* The generic name 'Haliotis.'

the sea-beach was reached. Here is a cavern stretching 500 feet straight below high-water mark, with a shrine to Benton Sama, the Lucinda of Japan; and having been provided with candles, we proceeded a few hundred feet through another cave, running at right angles to the first.

As it would have been a long steep walk back, and I was very tired, we called to one of the numerous fishing boats near the shore, and were quickly conveyed round to our original starting place. Before we said good-by, one of the old priests implored to be allowed to dive into the water for half a dollar. His request was complied with, and he caught the coin most successfully.

We lunched at a tea-house, our meal consisting of fish of all kinds, deliciously cooked, and served, fresh from the fire, in a style worthy of Greenwich; and as we had taken the precaution to bring some bread and wine with us, we were independent of the usual rice and *saki*.

After this we proceeded on our way towards the Daibutz, or Great Buddha, situated within the limits of what was once the large city of Kama-kura, now only a collection of small hamlets. As all Japanese cities are built of wood, it is not wonderful that they should in time entirely disappear, and leave no trace behind them. But there still remain some of the columns of the temple which once existed in the gardens surrounding the idol. Now he is quite alone; and for centuries has this grand old figure sat, exposed to the elements, serenely smiling on the varying scene beneath him. The figure is of bronze, and is supposed to have been cast about the year 1250 or 1260. It is some 50 feet high, with golden eyes and a silver spiral horn on the forehead. It is possible to sit or stand on the thumb, and within the hollow body an altar is erected, at which the priests officiate. Sitting there, amidst a grove of enormous cryptomerias and bamboos, there is an air of ineffable silent strength about that solitary figure, which affords a clue to the tenacity with which the poorer classes cling to Buddhism. The very calmness of these figures must be more suggestive of relief and repose to the poor weary worshipers than the glitter of the looking-glass and crystal ball to be found in the Shintoo temples. The looking-glass is intended to remind believers that the Supreme Being can see their innermost thoughts as clearly as they can perceive their own reflection; while the crystal ball is an emblem of purity. Great store is set by the latter, especially if of large size and without flaw; but to my mind the imperfect ones are the best, as they refract the light and do not look so much like glass.

In another village close by—also part of the ancient Kama-kura—there is a fine temple, dedicated to the God of War; but we were pressed for time, and hurried back to the little carriages. The homeward drive was long and cold; but the Tokaido looked very pretty lighted up, the shadows of the inmates being plainly visible on the paper walls, reminding one of a scene in a pantomime. On our way down a very steep hill we met the men carrying a *cango*. It is a most uncomfortable-looking basket-work contrivance, in which it is impossible to sit or lie with ease. These *cangos* used formerly to be the ordinary conveyance of Japan, but they are now replaced by the *jinrikishas*, and they are seldom met with, except in the mountains or in out-of-the-way places.

Friday, February 2d.—I was called at five o'clock, and at half-past six Mabelle and I started for the market. It was blowing a gale, and our four oarsmen found it as much as they could do to reach the shore. The Shanghai mail-boat was just in, and I pitied the poor passengers, who were in all the misery of being turned out into the cold of the early morning, with the spray breaking over them as they sat in the small boats.

The market at Yokohama is one of the sights of the place. There were large quantities of birds and game of all kinds—pheasants with tails six feet long, of a rare copper-colored variety, ducks, pigeons, small birds, hares, deer, rabbits. The fish-market was well supplied, especially with cuttle-fish. They are not inviting-looking, but are considered a delicacy here. A real octopus, in a basket, with its hideous body in the center, and its eight arms, covered with suckers, arranged in the form of a star, is worth from a dollar to a dollar and a half, according to its size. I was not tempted, however, to make any purchases.

From the market we went to one or two small shops in back streets, and thence over the bluffs, in the teeth of a bitterly cold wind, to a nursery garden, to examine the results of the Japanese art of dwarfing and distorting trees. Some of the specimens were very curious and some beautiful, but most were simply hideous. We saw tiny old gnarled fruit-trees, covered with blossom, and Scotch firs and other forest trees, eight inches high, besides diminutive ferns and creepers.

It being now half-past nine o'clock, we went to the hotel to meet the rest of the party for breakfast, and at one o'clock we returned to the yacht. At half-past one Lady Parkes and several other friends from Tokio came on board to luncheon. They told of three disastrous fires that had taken place in Tokio yesterday, by which the Home Office—one of the finest old Tartar *vashgis*—and several smaller edifices had been destroyed.

After the departure of our guests we paid another visit to the shore, and saw the foxhounds. They are a nice pack, and have good kennels outside the foreign settlement. They were out this morning at 6.30, but unfortunately we did not know of it. There are plenty of foxes, and some very fair country not far from here; so they expect to have good sport.

We weighed anchor at 8.30 p.m. and proceeded under steam. At 11.30, when off Touraya-saki, we set some of the head canvas. It was a cold night, with sleet and snow, though it was not blowing as hard as during the day.

CHAPTER XX.

KIOTO, LATE MIACO.

*Manners with fortunes, humors change with climes,
Tenets with books, and principles with times.*

Saturday, February 3d.—The occasional glimpses of the coast scenery through the sleet and snow were very fine. We passed Rocky Island, Lady Inglis rocks, and Matoya. But Mabelle and I spent most of the day in bed; she suffering from a blow from the boom, which had produced slight concussion of the brain, and I having a wretched cold, which has been gradually getting worse the last few days, and which has quite taken away my voice.

Sunday, February 4th.—It was blowing hard all day, raining, snowing, and sleeting. The scenery appeared to be pretty, and we passed through crowds of picturesque junks.

At 4.25 we rounded Tomamgai Smia, and at 9 p.m. anchored off the town of Kobe, or Hiogo.

These constant changes of names are very puzzling. Miaco and Yeddo, which we did know something about, are quite cut out, and replaced by Kioto and Tokio. Oddly enough, the same syllables, reversed, mean capital of the Western Empire and capital of the Eastern Empire respectively.

Monday, February 5th.—By seven o'clock a boat was alongside with letters from the Consul and Sir Harry Parkes, who had kindly made all the necessary arrangements for us to see the opening of the railway from Kobe to Kioto, and for the presentation of the gentlemen to the Mikado.

It certainly was a great opportunity for seeing a Japanese holiday crowd, all dressed in their best. Thousands and thousands of people were in the streets, who, though naturally anxious to see as much as possible, behaved in the most quiet and orderly manner. The station was beautifully decorated with evergreens, camellias, and red berries. Outside there was a most marvelous pavilion, the woodwork of which had been entirely covered with evergreens, and ornamented with life-sized dragons and phenixes (the imperial insignia of Japan), all made in flowers. The roof was studded with large chrysanthemums—the private device of the Mikado, that of the Tycoon being three hollyhock leaves. The sides of the pavilion were quite open, the roof being simply supported on pillars; so that we could see everything that went on, both inside and out. The floor was covered with red cloth; the daïs with an extremely ugly Brussels carpet, with a large pattern. On this the Mikado's throne was placed, with a second canopy above it. Tom in R.N.R. uniform, the other gentlemen in evening dress, accompanied the Consul on to the platform to receive the Mikado; while the children and I went with Mrs. Annesley to seats reserved for the foreign representatives. There were not many Europeans present; but the platform was densely crowded with Japanese, sitting on their heels, and patiently waiting to see the extraordinary sight of their hitherto invisible spiritual Emperor brought to them by a steam engine on an iron road. The men had all had their heads fresh shaven, and their funny little pigtails rearranged for the occasion. The women's hair was elaborately and stiffly done up with light tortoise-shell combs and a large pin, and decorated with artificial flowers. Some of the children were gayly dressed in red and gold under-garments, the prevailing color of the costumes being dark blue, turned up with red. They also wore gay embroidered *obis*, or large sashes, which are put on in a peculiar fashion. They are of great width, and are fastened tightly round the waist, while an enormous bow behind reaches from between the shoulders to far below the hips. The garments fit tightly in front, while at the back they form a sort of huge bunch. On their high-heeled clogs the women walk with precisely the same gait as ladies in high-heeled boots. In fact, so exactly do the Japanese women (you never see Japanese *ladies* walking about in the streets) caricature the present fashionable style of dress in Europe, that I have formed a theory of my own on the subject, and this is it.

Some three or four years ago, among other proposed reforms in Japan, the Ministers wished the Empress and her court to be dressed in European fashion. Accordingly a French milliner and dressmaker, with her assistants, was sent for from Paris, and in due time arrived. The Empress and her ladies, however, would not change their style of dress. They knew better what suited them, and in my opinion they were very sensible. This is what I hear. Now what I think is, that the Parisienne, being of an enterprising turn of mind, thought that she would not take so long a journey for nothing—that if the Japanese ladies would not follow European fashions, at least European ladies should adopt the Japanese style. On her return to Paris I am convinced that she promulgated this idea, and gradually gave it effect. Hence the fashions of the last two years.

Watching the crowd occupied the time in a most interesting manner, till the firing of guns and the playing of bands announced the arrival of the imperial train. The Mikado was received on the platform, and after a very short delay he headed the procession along the covered way on to the daïs.

He is a young, not very good-looking man, with rather a sullen expression, and legs that look as though they did not belong to him—I suppose from using them so little, and sitting so much on his heels; for until the last few years the Mikado has always been considered far too sacred a being to be allowed to set foot on the earth. He was followed by his highest Minister, the foreign Ministers, and a crowd of Japanese dignitaries, all, with one or two exceptions, in European official dress, glittering with gold lace. I believe it was the first time that many of them had ever worn it. At any rate, they certainly had never learned to put it on properly. It would have driven to distraction the tailor who made them, to see tight-fitting uniforms either left unbuttoned altogether, or hooked askew from top to bottom, and to behold the trousers turned up and disfigured by the projecting tags of immense side-spring boots, generally put on the wrong feet. Some of the visitors had no gloves, while others wore them with fingers at least three inches too long. Certainly a court dresser as well as a court tailor ought to be appointed to the Mikado's establishment, before the European costume becomes generally adopted.

I could not help thinking that the two or three old conservative Ministers who had stuck to their native dress must have congratulated themselves on their firmness, when they saw the effect of the unaccustomed garments upon their *confrères*. The old court dress of the Daimios is very handsome, consisting of rich silks and brocades, with enormously long loose trousers trailing two or three feet on the ground, and with sleeves, like butterfly wings, of corresponding dimensions. A small high-peaked black cap is worn on the head, to accommodate the curious little cut-off pigtail, set up like a cock's comb, which appears to be one of the insignia of a Daimio's rank in Japan.

As soon as the people had arranged themselves into three sides of a square, Sir Harry Parkes read an address, and presented his five compatriots to the Mikado, who replied in inaudible but no doubt suitable terms. Then the Governor of Kobe had to read an address, and I pitied the poor man from the bottom of my heart. His knees shook, his hands trembled, and his whole body vibrated to such an extent, that his cocked hat fell and rolled on the floor of the daïs, and finally hopped down the steps, while the address nearly followed its example. How thankful he must have felt when it was over!

The proceedings in the pavilion being now at an end, the Mikado walked down the middle of the assembly, followed by all his Ministers in single file, on his way to the luncheon tent. After they had gone, we inspected the imperial railway carriage, the soldiers, guns, &c., and just as we were leaving the station yard, to look at the daylight fireworks they were letting off in honor of the occasion, a salute announced the departure of the Mikado for Kioto.

We lunched at the Consulate, our gentlemen changed to more comfortable attire, and then we went to see a Buddhist temple, supposed to be rather a fine specimen of woodwork. It is specially curious on account of some monkeys and a white horse, each kept in a sort of side shrine. Every worshiper at the temple stopped before these shrines, and for a small coin bought rice or beans to feed them with, through the priest. Whether it was an act of worship, or simply of kindness, I could not discover, though I paid several visits to the spot during our stay at Kobe.

From the temple we went to the shops in the main street of Hiogo, and full of interest and temptation we found them. The town itself is quite Japanese, and consists, as usual, of wooden houses, narrow streets, and quaint shops. To-day all was *en fête*, in preparation for the illuminations to-night.

Kobe, the foreign settlement, is, on the contrary, brand-new, spick and span, with a handsome parade, and grass and trees, planted boulevard fashion, along the edge of the sea. It is all remarkably clean, but quite uninteresting. To-night, however, it looked very well, illuminated by thousands and thousands of colored paper lanterns, arranged in all sorts of fanciful devices. It was dark and clear, and there was no wind, so that everything went off well.

Tuesday, February 6th.—My cold being still bad, Mabelle by no means well yet, and Tom very busy, we at first thought of keeping quiet to-day. But our time is so short, that we could not afford to waste it; so half our party started early for Kioto, it being arranged that Tom and Mabelle should follow us by an early train to-morrow. It was a wet, cheerless day, and the country did not look its best. Still, the novelty of the scenes around could not fail to make them interesting. The Japanese have an intense horror of rain, and it was ludicrous to see the peasants walking along with scarcely any clothes on except a pair of high clogs, a large hat, and a paper umbrella. We crossed several large bridges, stopped at a great many stations, where heaps of native travelers got in and out, and finally reached Kioto at half-past two o'clock. It was still raining, and all the *jinrikisha* men wore their large rain hats and rain cloaks, made either of reeds or of oiled paper. Most of the *jinrikishas*, too, had oiled paper hoods and aprons.

The drive to our hotel, through long, narrow, crowded, picturesque streets, seemed long and wearisome. It was still a holiday, and remains of the previous night's illuminations were to be seen on all sides. The large paper lanterns still remained fastened to the high poles, with an open umbrella at the top to afford protection from the rain.

Kioto is a thoroughly Japanese town. I do not suppose it contains a single European resident; so that the manners and customs of the natives may be seen in perfection. Its theaters and jugglers are famous throughout Japan. In the suburb, where the two hotels are situated, stand numberless tea-houses and other places of entertainment. Our hotel is situated half-way up the hill called Maruyama.

After about three-quarters of an hour's ride in the *jinrikisha*, we were deposited at the bottom of a flight of steps, which appeared to lead to a temple, but by which we reached the hotel in about five minutes. We were received by servants, who bowed to the ground, but who did not speak a word which we could understand.. The rooms looked clean and comfortable, and the dining-room boasted a table and six chairs, besides several screens and *hibatchis*. The bedrooms, too, had beds, screens, and washstands ; quite an unexpected luxury. Still more so was a strip of glass about half-way up the screens, through which we could admire the fine prospect. Anything in the shape of a transparent window is a complete novelty in a Japanese house, where, in winter, you feel as if you were imprisoned. The view from the veranda of the hotel over the pretty fantastic garden, the Temple grounds, the town of Kioto, and the mountains in the distance was an endless source of delight to me.

The servants soon produced a luncheon, excellently well cooked ; and directly we had finished it we sallied forth again to see what we could before dark. First we went to the temple of Gion, a fine building, standing in extensive grounds, and surrounded by smaller temples and houses for the priests. The Dutch envoys used to stay here when they were brought through the country, like prisoners, to pay their annual tribute for being allowed to trade with Japan. They were subjected to all kinds of indignities, and used to be made to dance and sing, pretend to be drunk, and play all sorts of pranks, for the amusement of the whole court as well as for the Mikado and the Empress, hidden behind a grating.

From Gion we went to see other temples, and wandered about under the large conifers of all kinds, trying to find out the quarters of the British Legation for some time, until Sir Harry Parkes returned. The rooms at his residence were comfortable, but cold-looking, for mats and paper screens do not look nice in a frost. There were tables and chairs and paraffin lamps, but no bedsteads, only about a dozen cotton and silk quilts, some of which were supposed to serve as a couch, while others were to be used as coverings.

Sir Harry has had, I fear, a great deal of trouble about the yacht. She is the first vessel of the kind ever seen in Japan, with the exception of the one sent out in 1858 as a present from the Queen to the then Tycoon, and now used by the Mikado. The officials, it seems, cannot make the 'Sunbeam' out. 'Is she a man-of-war? We know what that is.' 'No.' 'Is she a merchant ship?' 'No; she is a yacht.' But what can be the object of a vessel without guns is quite beyond their comprehension. At last it has been settled that, in order to be like other nations, the Japanese officials will not force us to enter at the Custom House, or to pay a fine of sixty dollars a day for not doing so. As a matter of precedent, it was important that the point should be settled, though I hardly imagine that many yachts will follow our example, and come out to Japan through the Straits of Magellan and across the Pacific.

As it was now growing late, we returned to the hotel for dinner. The night was cold, and *hibatchis* and lamps alike failed to warm the thinly walled and paper-screened room.

Sir Harry Parkes came and spent the evening with us, and taught us more about Japan in two or three hours than we could have learned by much study of many books. The fact is, that in this fast-changing country guide-books get out of date in two or three years. Besides which, Sir Harry has been one of the chief actors in many of the most prominent events we have recently been reading about. To hear him describe graphically the wars of 1868, and the Christian persecutions in 1870, with the causes that led to the revolution, and the effect it has had on the country, was indeed interesting. Still more so was his account of his journey hither to force the newly emerged Mikado and his Ministers to sign the treaty, which had already received the assent (of course valueless) of the deposed Tycoon.

Wednesday, February 7th.—A misty but much warmer morning succeeded a wet night. At 8.30 Sir Harry Parkes and two other gentlemen arrived, and we all started at once in *jinrikishas* to see what could be seen in the limited time at our disposal. We went first to the temple of Gion Chiosiu, described elaborately in books by other travelers. It is specially interesting to Europeans, as it was the temple assigned to the foreign envoys when they paid their first visit to the Mikado in 1868. Sir Harry Parkes showed us all their apartments, and the large though subsidiary temple once used as a hospital, and we afterwards went to see the service performed in the temple. A dozen bonzes, or priests, were sitting round in a circle, chanting monotonously from ponderous volumes, with an occasional accompaniment from a gong or drum. Incense was being burned, vestments worn, processions formed, and prayers offered to Buddha to intercede with the Supreme Being. The accessories and surroundings were of course different, but the ceremonial struck me as being much the same as that in use at Roman Catholic places of worship.

I was only a month in Japan, and that is far too short a time for anything like serious study; but I was much struck by the temples, and I find I have some notes in my book comparing them with the Jewish. How any direct connection could possibly exist, is far beyond my powers of conjecture; but I will state the points of resemblance, and leave others to inquire further and collect additional information.

Wood and bronze to this day furnish the material of which temples are constructed in Japan, with stone as a base. Such also were the materials of Solomon's temple. There are inclosures round each court or shrine, and sometimes these courts are three in number. Hills or groves are usually sites for a temple, the ascent to which is by a long flight of steps; usually two flights give access to the shrine. One is long, straight, and steep, for the men; the other, less steep, but curved, is for the women. It will be remembered that it was the great stairs at Solomon's temple that so impressed the Queen of Sheba. Small shrines or miniature temples, called Tenno Samma, or 'Heaven's Lord,' are carried on staves, like the Ark of the Covenant, at their religious ceremonies. The inner shrine, or Holy of Holies, is small, and a cube, or nearly so, in proportion. It is usually detached behind the other portions of the temple, the door being closed, so that it cannot be seen into, and it generally contains, not an image, but a tablet, or what the Japanese call a 'Gohei,' or piece of paper, cut so that it hangs down in folds on each side. In the early days of writing, a tablet was a book, a stylus the pen. The stone on which the law was inscribed was only a form of the book, and the Chinese ancestral tablet, or other tablet, in a temple, is only a variety of this book form. These 'Goheis' are so common in Japan, and occupy so important a place in all their temples, that I had a great desire to know what they originally meant; but as on many questions of this kind I could get no information, the only suggestion which presented itself to me was, that it might be some form of the book, for the book was a very sacred thing in past time, and that which is yet called the 'Ark,' in a Jewish synagogue, contains now nothing but a book. There is a distinct priesthood who wear vestments, and they use incense, music, and bells. There are two religions in Japan, Buddhism and Shintooism; the latter being the primitive faith, and the former an importation from China. The forms of the two have become slightly mixed, both in the construction of their temples and in the ceremonial; but the remarks I have just made apply particularly to the Shintoo religion.

One of the late acts of the government has been to declare the Shintoo, as the old religion of the country, to be the only state faith. This is the disestablishment of Buddhism, but it does not imply its suppression. The Buddhist priests complain very much, saying that their temples are not now so popular, and many are being closed. Speculators are buying up their fine bronze bells, and sending them home to be coined into English pennies and half-pennies. Changes in faith present many strange aspects, and this is certainly a curious one.

We strolled about the temple grounds, and ascended the hill to see the famous bell, which is the second biggest in Japan. The immense beam which strikes it was unlashed from the platform for our edification, and the bell sent forth a magnificent sound, pealing over the city and through the woods. At one of the gates there is a curious staircase, leading up to the top, and there, over the gate, is seated a figure of Buddha, surrounded by twelve disciples, all carved in wood and colored. They are quite worth a scramble up to see.

From Chiosiu we went right across the city to the temple of Nishni Hongangi. On our way we were more than once stopped and turned off the direct road, which was kept by soldiers for the passage of the Mikado to worship at the tombstone of his innumerable ancestors, real or imaginary. Being a spiritual Emperor, he has to be well kept up to his religious duties, and is always being sent off to worship at some shrine or another, in order to maintain his popularity with the people, his Ministers meanwhile managing the affairs of state. Tanjo and Ikawura went off in haste to-day to Tokio, as there are rumors of a rebellion in the south.

Nishni Hongangi is one of the largest and finest temples we have yet seen, even in spite of a large portion having been destroyed by the disastrous fire of 1864. The gates are splendidly ornamented, with carved chrysanthemum flowers. The center temple is very fine, and is surrounded by smaller rooms, all decorated by the best Japanese artists of about two hundred years ago. Notice had been sent that the English Minister was coming with a party of friends, and everything had accordingly been prepared for our reception. In some places they had even put down carpets, to obviate the necessity of our having to take off our boots. The Abbot was out, which I much regretted, for he belongs to the Montos, the most advanced sect of Buddhism, and has more than once remarked to English visitors that he thought their own principles were so enlightened that they were paving the way for a higher form of religion, in the shape of Christianity—rather a startling confession to come from the lips of a Buddhist priest.

After spending a long time among the paintings, wood-carvings, lacquers, bronzes, and gardens, we left the temple, and crossed several courtyards, before the main street was reached. Then after a short walk, we came to another beautiful garden, laid out like a miniature park, with lakes, bridges, rocks, streams, canals, pavilions, &c. All these surround a house built by the celebrated Tycoon, Tako Sama, in the fifteenth century. Here, again, everything was prepared for our reception. Fires were lighted, flowers arranged, carpets laid down, and fruit and cakes placed in readiness, with *hibatchis* to warm each and all of us. We went all over the house, which differs little from a Japanese house of the present day, except that a higher style of art was employed in its construction and decoration.

From here we went to quite another quarter of the city, to see what was formerly the Tycoon's palace, now used as a sort of police office. It is built on the same plan of three inclosures as all the *yashgis*, though on a very different scale from the one at Tokio. There, the Tycoon reigns in undisturbed sovereignty. Here, he appears as a humble servant of his rightful master—really his prisoner. The late Tycoon, after the last battle, fought at this place, fled to his castle at Osaka, where, though he might have held out for an indefinite period, he preferred to surrender. Two of his Ministers came to him and represented that he must not only think of himself, but of the party who supported the Shogunate, and that as he had betrayed them by false hopes he had no choice but to perform Hara-kiru. This he refused to do, although they set him the example; and he is now living as a private individual on an estate in the country, not far from Tokio, where he amuses himself with hunting, shooting, and fishing. It is said that it is possible he may one day join the ministry of the present Mikado.

From the Tycoon's palace we drove to the 'Toshio,' or court quarter of the town, where the Mikado and all his relatives live, in palaces, surrounded by large gardens, inclosed in whitewashed walls. We saw the whole of Tako Sama's household furniture and wearing apparel, the celebrated swords of Yoritiome, called the 'knee-cutter' and the 'beard-cutter,' from their wonderful sharpness, and many other interesting objects.

Here we said good-by to Sir Harry Parkes, and returned across the town by another route to our hotel to lunch, after which we made another expedition to one or two more temples, and then to a pawnbroker's shop, in the heart of the city, which had been strongly recommended to us. The exterior did not look promising; the shop itself was small and dirty; and they had to take some very filthy garments out of the way before we could enter. Once inside, however, it was a very different story. They showed us splendid old embroideries, and quantities of second-hand court dresses, embroidered in gold, silver, and colors, with exquisite designs. The Empress has thirteen ladies of honor, who wear their best dresses only twice, and then sell them: hence the pawnbroker's abundant stock.

Wherever we went a large but perfectly civil crowd followed us, and people ran on before to tell others to come to their doors and look at us, though we were under the charge of an officer and two men. It was now getting dark, and we were very tired; so we at last turned back, and once more climbed those weary steps to our hotel. To-night there is some *fête* going on in this suburb, and the whole place is alive with lights, dancing, music, and tum-tums.

After dinner all our purchases arrived, each accompanied by at least four or five men. Other people had heard of our visit, and had brought more things for us to look at; so that the room soon resembled a bazaar. At last we got rid of them, having settled that they should pack our things and take them down to Kobe, where they would be paid for. The Japanese shopkeepers, though difficult to deal with, are incorruptible when once the bargain is made. They pack most carefully, frequently adding boxes, bags, and baskets, not originally included in the purchase, in order that the articles may travel more safely. The smallest article is sure to be put in, and the greatest care is taken of everything, even if they know you do not mean to open the cases for months.

If it were only warmer, how delightful it would all be! The cold spoils everything to a certain extent. At night we have to choose whether to be half frozen in our beds, or stifled with the fumes of charcoal from the *hibatchis*.

Thursday, February 8th.—The sunrise over the city, with the river and mountains beyond, was superb. We breakfasted at eight; but even by that hour the courtyard and passage were crowded with venders of curiosities of all sorts, and no doubt great bargains might have been picked up. But we had no time to lose, for our train started at 9.30, and we had a delightfully rapid drive to the station through the sunny streets of Kioto.

Arrived at Kobe, we went first to lunch with some friends, and immediately after hastened on board to receive the foreign Ministers and other friends; and did not land again that evening.

Friday, February 9th.—We left by ten o'clock train for Osaka, which has been called the Venice of Japan. It is intersected by innumerable rivers and canals, and boats were continually making their appearance at points where they were least expected, as our *jinrikisha* men hurried us along the narrow and not very sweet-smelling streets. We went so fast that, more than once before we reached the Mint, I thought we should have been tipped into one of the canals, as we turned a sharp corner. Our men upset the baskets and stalls that encroached on the road, in the most unceremonious manner; but their proprietors did not seem to mind, many of them quietly moving their wares out of the way as they heard the shouts that announced our approach. The smell in the fish-market was disgusting, and enough to poison the air for miles around, but the people did not seem to mind it in the least.

At last we left the river and town, and, climbing a slight eminence, crossed the first moat by a stone bridge, and reached the guard-house on the other side. There was some hesitation at first about admitting us; but it was soon overcome. This castle, the last stronghold of the Tycoon, is built on exactly the same plan as the *yashgis* we had already visited, but much stronger, being composed of enormous blocks of stone. One wonders how human labor could ever have transported them from their quarry to this place, for some measured 40 feet long by 20 feet high. We crossed the three moats and the three inclosures, now all full of barracks and soldiers. In the very center, the old well and a little square tower are still standing, part of the Tycoon's original residence, which was destroyed by fire. The view from the top over the town and surrounding country is very fine. You can see countless streams coming from the mountains, and flowing into Odawarra, on which Osaka is situated. The course of the river itself could be traced to the bay; and the line of coast to Kobe, and the far-off mountains in the Inland Sea, were plainly visible.

On returning to the Mint we found luncheon awaiting us, and afterwards spent a pleasant time looking at a wonderful collection of curios.

The Imperial Mint of Japan is a large handsome building, in great force just now, for the whole of the old money is being called in and replaced by the government. The contrast between the two moneys is very great. The ancient coinage consisted of long thin oval obangs and shobangs, worth from two dollars to eighteen pounds each, square silver itzeboos, and square copper pieces, with a hole in the center; while that which is taking its place is similar to European coinage, and is marked in English characters, and ornamented with Japanese devices, such as the phenix and the dragon. It did not seem worth while to go minutely over the Mint, as it is arranged on exactly the same principle as the one in London, and the processes are carried out in the same manner.

Osaka used to be the emporium of all the inland commerce, and was considered the pearl of Japanese cities. After the revolution, and when the Mint was built, there was some intention of making it the capital of the empire. That idea was, however, abandoned; and the inconvenience of having the Mint so far away from the seat of government is greatly felt, all the bullion having to be sent backwards and forwards at great expense by sea. Commerce has now almost deserted Osaka, owing to the difficulty experienced by large ships in anchoring near the town, and the impossibility of their crossing the bar. The foreign consuls and representatives have all left the place for the newly established settlement at Kobe, where they feel safer, with men-of-war at anchor just under their windows.

There was just time to go round some o the old

streets, and to some of the shops, before the hour by which we were due at the station. Osaka is famous for its waxworks and theaters. Five of the best of these have, however, been burned down within the last eighteen months, with terrible loss of life. We heard that a short time ago there was nearly being serious trouble, in consequence of one of the managers having produced on the stage, in a most objectionable manner, a representation of the cruel and unprovoked assassination of an officer and two men, part of a boat's crew of a French ship. The English and French consuls went to the governor of the town, who promised that the piece should be stopped, and the obnoxious placards announcing the performance removed at once. But his instructions were not complied with, for the next day the piece was again performed, and the placards were still there. Some French sailors, luckily accompanied by their officers, saw the latter, and wanted to tear them down; but they were persuaded to wait while the consuls were telegraphed for. They came at once, and again saw the governor, who sent some soldiers to stop the play and remove the bills; and so the affair ended peaceably.

We reached Kobe about seven o'clock, and went on board at once to dinner.

Saturday, February 10*th.*—We were to have gone early this morning to Arrima, a village in the mountains, situated among groves of bamboos, where there are mineral springs and a hot-water bath, in which people bathe in the old style. But the weather was impossibly bad for our intended expedition, with showers of snow and sleet. We waited till half-past eleven, and then landed and talked of going to Osaka again by train; but finally decided that even this was not practicable, and that we had better stay and potter about at Kobe and Hiogo. The children set out to buy toys, whilst I went with a lady to pay another visit to the white horse and monkeys at the temple, and then walked on to a waterfall, prettily situated in a ravine, a little way behind the town. We afterwards visited several pawnbrokers' shops, at all of which there was something interesting to be seen. Many are perfect museums; but their proprietors never seem to care much to show you what they have, unless you are accompanied by a resident or some one they know. Then they invite you into the iron fire-proof 'godown' or store, at the back, and out of funny little boxes and bags and parcels produce all sorts of rare and curious things which have been sent to them to be sold, or which they may possibly have bought themselves. It is not of the slightest use to go to the large shops, full of things, if you want anything really good, for you will only find there articles specially prepared for the European and American market.

I am very glad to hear that Dr. Dresser is here, collecting, lecturing, and trying to persuade the Japanese to adhere to their own forms and taste in art and decoration. It is a great pity to observe the decadence of native art, and at the same time to see how much better the old things are than the new. A true Japanese artist never repeats himself, and consequently never makes an exact pair of anything. His designs agree generally, and his vases are more or less alike, without being a precise match. He throws in a spray of flowers, a bird, or a fan, as the fancy strikes him, and the same objects are therefore never placed in exactly the same relative position. Modern articles are made precisely alike, not only in pairs, but by the dozen and the hundred.

There are beautiful bantams to be seen in some of the shops here; but they cannot be bought, as they are private pets. They seem generally very small, and one I saw to-day had his head far behind his tail, which divided in the middle outwards, and fell forward on either side of his neck in the most extraordinary way. How he picked up his food and got through life, I am sure I don't know. There are plenty of little Japanese dogs; but they are not seen to advantage this cold weather, and there would be great difficulty in getting them home.

I bought some fine bantams at Yokohama, and a whole cage full of rice-birds. They are the dearest little things, and spend most of the day bathing and twittering, occasionally getting all together into one nest, with their twenty-five heads peeping out. They are exactly like a magnified grain of rice, with legs and a bill. I hope I shall take them home alive, as they have borne the cold very well so far. We have also some mandarin ducks on board, and some gold and silver fish with two tails. Our sailors have over a hundred birds of their own, which never appear on deck, except on very sunny days. I don't know where they can keep them, unless they stow them away in their Japanese cabinets.

We went on board about dark, and a few friends came to dinner.

Sunday, February 11*th.*—About 7 a.m., two Japanese officers came on board with a message which nobody could understand. When we went on deck, we saw that all the ships were dressed, and concluded that we had been asked to do the same; but we thought it better to send ashore to ascertain positively. The next difficulty was to get a Japanese flag. Tom went on board the 'Thabor,' a Japanese ship, to borrow one, and found everything was in bustle and confusion, news having arrived from Kiusiu that the rebels were mustering in great force, and that they had seized some ships. The 'Thabor,' 'Mihu Maru,' and three others, are therefore to go through the Inland Sea to Nagasaki this afternoon.

The Japanese admiral sent word early this morning that he would come on board at two o'clock with some of his captains, and the French admiral also expressed a hope that it would be convenient to receive him and his captains at three. Their visits occupied nearly all the afternoon. We afterwards landed with the French admiral, paid some farewell visits, and went to look at a collection of old lacquer and Satsuma china, before we returned to the yacht.

CHAPTER XXI.

THE INLAND SEA.

Dipped in the lines of sunset, wreathed in zones,
The clouds are resting on their mountain thrones;
One peak alone exalts its glacier crest,
A golden paradise above the rest.
Thither the day with lingering steps retires,
And in its own blue element expires.

Monday, February 12*th.*—Fires were lighted at 4 a.m., and by six we were steaming slowly out of the beautiful bay of Kobe. It was a cold bright morning, with a strong head wind, increasing every moment as we proceeded; until, in the straits of Akashi, it became almost impossible to make any way against it. There was not much sea, but the wind impeded our progress so much that it was at last reduced to one mile instead of nine an hour. The straits are very fine, and the old castle presents an admirable specimen of the architecture of a Daimio's residence.

We proceeded across the Harima Nada, where we were more or less exposed to the open sea, and where we took more water on board than we had done in the gale before arriving at Yokohama. There were no big waves, but we rolled tremendously, and the spray came over us, though the mere force of the wind seemed to keep the sea down.

After struggling until twelve o'clock, and having done but little good for the last three hours, Tom determined to run back, and in a short time we found ourselves once more at anchor in the harbor of Kobe. It was a work of considerable difficulty, owing to the strong wind and tide, to steer safely among the numerous vessels, and for a few minutes we thought we were aground, as we did not make the slightest progress, though the engines were working ahead full speed. The proveedor's boat came out to us as soon as we were perceived, and we landed in her; but it was as much as the six stout oarsmen could do to make way against the wind.

We went for a walk, or rather a scramble, to the waterfall, half-way up to the Temple of the Moon. Much of the ground was covered with snow, the streams were frozen at the sides, and there were hanging icicles to be seen, six feet in length; and yet on either side were camellias and tea-trees covered with red and white blossoms, orange-trees laden with fruit; gold-fish swimming about in ponds, overhung with maidenhair fern, besides pteris and hot-house ferns, shaded by bamboos, palms, and castor-oil plants. The order of vegetation seems to be as much reversed as everything else in this strange country. In England all those plants would require conservatories, or at least sheltered spots, and the greatest care, instead of being exposed to frost and snow.

Getting on board again was even a more difficult business than landing had been; but we arrived at last without mishap.

Tuesday, February 13*th*.—The wind dropped at sunset, and as it continued calm all night, Tom ordered fires to be lighted at 4 a.m. By six o'clock, however, it was blowing harder than ever, and we therefore decided to make an excursion to Arrima instead of attempting another start.

We went ashore to make the necessary arrangements, and it was settled that we should start at ten o'clock, which we did, with the Consulate constable as our guide.

We had three men to each *jinrikisha*, and went along at a merry pace through the long straggling towns of Kobe and Hiogo. The cold was intense, and before we started our poor *jinrikisha* men were shivering until they nearly shook us out of the vehicles. Soon they were streaming with perspiration, and at our first halting-place they took off almost all their garments, though it was as much as we could do to keep warm in our furs and wraps. We waited while they partook copiously of hot tea and bowls of rice, and bought new straw shoes, or rather sandals, for less than a farthing a pair.

To-day being the Japanese New Year's Day, all the little shrines in the houses and along the road were prettily decorated, and had offerings of rice, *saki*, and fruit deposited upon them. The spirits of the departed are supposed to come down and partake, not of the things themselves, but of the subtle invisible essence that rises from them. The road now became very pretty, winding through the valleys, climbing up and dipping down the various hills, and passing through picturesque villages, where all the people, leaving their meals or their games, came out to look at us, while some of the children scampered on to secure a good view of the foreigners, and others ran away frightened and screaming. They were all dressed in dark blue clothes, turned up with red, with bright embroidered *obis* and flowers in their elaborately dressed hair. I have managed to get some dolls' wigs, which give a good idea of the various styles of hair-dressing.

In rather more than three hours we reached Arrima, a village far more beautifully situated than any we had seen, in the very center of the mountains, where a dozen valleys converge into one center. On one side are mineral springs, on the other a river. Bamboos grow luxuriantly on all sides, and the inhabitants of the various valleys obtain their livelihood by manufacturing from them all sorts of articles: boxes for every conceivable purpose; baskets, fine and coarse, large and small, useful and ornamental, colored and plain; brushes, pipes, battledores and shuttlecocks, sticks, spoons, knives and forks, sauce ladles, boats, lamps, cradles, &c.

The first glimpse of the village is lovely; that from

the bridge that crosses the river is still more so. We clambered up narrow streets, with quaint carved houses and overhanging balconies, till we reached a tea-house, kept by a closely shaven bonze, or priest. He seemed very pleased to see us, and bowed and shook hands over and over again. He placed his whole house at our disposal, and a very clean, pretty, and well-arranged house it was, with a lovely little formal garden, ornamented with mimic temples and bridges of ice, fashioned by the hard frost, with but little assistance from the hand of man. Bits of wood and stone, a few graceful fern-leaves and sprays of bamboo, and a trickling stream of water produced the most fairy-like crystalline effects imaginable. If only some good fairy could, with a touch of her wand, preserve it all intact until a few months hence, what a delight it would be in the hot summer weather!

To-day the paper house was indeed cold; but even so slight a shelter from the bitter wind was acceptable, though we regretted the screens could not be opened to enable us to admire the prospect on all sides. The luncheon basket being quickly unpacked, the good priest warmed our food and produced a bottle of port wine, which he mulled for our benefit. Cheered and refreshed we proceeded on our way, leaving him much delighted with what seemed to us but a small recompense for his courtesy.

Every house and shop in those narrow picturesque streets was a study in itself, and so were the quaint groups of people we met, and who gazed eagerly at us. We looked into the public baths, two oblong tanks, into which the mineral springs came bubbling up, thick and yellow, and strongly impregnated with iron, at a temperature of 112°. They are covered in, and there is a rough passage round them. Here, in the bathing season, people of both sexes stand in rows, packed as tight as herrings in a barrel, and there are just as many outside waiting their turn to enter. To-day there were only two bathers, immersed up to their chins in the steaming water. They had left all their clothes at home, and would shortly have to pass through the streets without any covering, notwithstanding the cold.

From the baths we went to some of the best basket shops, where the beauty and cheapness of the articles exposed for sale offered great temptations. We had to disturb our *jinrikisha* men, who were enjoying their frugal meal at a separate tea-house. It was beautifully served, and as clean and nicely cooked as possible, though consisting of viands which we might not have fancied, such as various kinds of fish, seaweed, sea-snails (*bêche de mer*), and rice. Each man had his own little table and eight or ten separate dishes, a bottle of *saki*, tea-pipe, and *hibatchi*, arranged exactly as ours had been at the tea-house at Yokohama. How well they managed their chop-sticks, how quickly they shoveled the food down, and how clean they left each dish! Habit is everything.

We were anxious to make the best of our way home, and starting at four, with but a short stop at the half-way tea-house, we reached the hotel soon after seven, having taken less than an hour to come five miles over a very bad road, an inch deep in mud. So much for a 'man-power carriage,' the literal translation of the word *jinrikisha*.* Soon after an excellent dinner we returned on board, so as to be ready for an early start to-morrow morning.

Wednesday, February 14*th.*—We were called at 4 a.m. Fires were lighted, but before steam was up the wind had risen; so our start was once more postponed to the afternoon. We steamed out to the buoy, from among the shipping, in order to be able to get away more easily at night. The wind generally goes down at sunset, and Tom hoped that, by taking our departure then, we should get through the worst part of the Inland Sea before the wind again rose with the sun.

---

* Or pull-man-car, as it is sometimes called.

After breakfast we went ashore, and dispersed in different directions, to meet again at the hotel for luncheon. Then we all again separated, the children going to the circus, whilst I took a drive, with a pair of black and white Hakodadi ponies, to the foot of the hills behind the town.

It was a pleasant circuit by pretty valleys, and brought us back to the town by a different road. I went to pick up the children at the circus, and found them just coming out, with delighted faces, having most thoroughly enjoyed themselves. They went on board to tea, but Mabelle and I went with the Consul in *jinrikishas* to a Japanese theater at Hiogo. The streets were crowded with holiday-makers; for to-day is the first of the Chinese new year, as yesterday was the first of the Japanese new year. The floor of the theater was crowded with people, all squatting on their heels, each with his or her chow-chow box and *hibatchi* or brazier of burning charcoal to keep themselves warm. The performance frequently goes on for ten or twelve hours, with short intervals, and whole families come and take up their abode at the theater for twelve hours at a time. The acting was not at all bad, and the performers were beautifully dressed.

We did not stay very long at the theater, but were soon tearing back again through the streets to the Consulate. These quick rides in a *jinrikisha*, especially at night, are very amusing. You have the pleasure of going at a high speed, and yet, being on a level with the people, you can see much more of them and of their manners than would be possible in a carriage.

When we reached the Consulate we found the chief of the police of the foreign settlement waiting for the Consul, to inform him that Japanese soldiers were patrolling the town with fixed bayonets, alleging that information had been sent to the Governor that some of the rebels were in the hills at the back of the town, and might appear at any moment. The ships-of-war were to be communicated with at once for the protection of the inhabitants. They do not expect a general attack here, but seem to think the rebels' plan is to creep up by degrees to Ôsaka, where the Mikado is shortly expected to stay, and take possession of his person and the imperial treasure at one blow.

When I got on board the 'Sunbeam' again, I found that steam was up and all was ready for starting; but the wind was still strong against us, and it was evidently necessary again to wait until four o'clock to-morrow morning.

We were rolling a good deal, and, coming along the engine-room passage, my foot slipped, a door banged to, and my thumb was caught in the hinge and terribly crushed. Dressing it was a very painful affair, as the doctor had to ascertain whether the bone was broken, and I fainted during the operation. At last I was carried to my cabin and put to bed, after taking a strong dose of chloral to soothe the agonizing pain.

Thursday, February 15*th*.—I wonder if anybody who has not experienced it can realize the stupefying, helpless sensation of being roused up from a sound sleep, in the middle of the night, on board ship, by the cry of 'Fire!' and finding one's self enveloped in a smoke so dense as to render everything invisible.

At 2.30 a.m. I was awakened by a great noise and a loud cry of 'The ship is on fire!' followed by Mr. Bingham rushing into our cabin to arouse us. At first I could hardly realize where we were, or what was happening, as I was half stupid with chloral, pain, and smoke, which was issuing from each side of the staircase in dense volumes. My first thought was for the children, but I found they had not been forgotten. Rolled up in blankets, they were already in transit to the deck-house. In the meantime Mr. Bingham had drenched the flames with every available jug of water, and Tom had roused the crew, and made them screw the hose on to the pump. They were afraid to open the hatches, to discover where the fire was, until the hose and *extincteurs* were ready to work, as they did not know whether or not the hold was on fire, and the whole ship might burst into a blaze the moment the air was admitted. Allen soon appeared with an *extincteur* on his back, and the mate with the hose. Then the cupboard in Mr. Bingham's room was opened, and burning cloaks, dresses, boxes of curios, portmanteaus, &c., were hauled out, and, by a chain of men, sent on deck, where they were drenched with sea-water or thrown overboard. Moving these things caused the flames to increase in vigor, and the *extincteur* was used freely, and with the greatest success. It is an invaluable invention, especially for a yacht, where there are so many holes and corners which it would be impossible to reach by ordinary means. All this time the smoke was pouring in volumes from the cupboard on the other side, and from under the nursery fire-place. The floors were pulled up, and the partitions were pulled down, until at last the

The Yacht on Fire.

flames were got under. The holds were next examined. No damage had been done there; but the cabin floor was completely burned through, and the lead from the nursery fireplace was running about, melted by the heat.

The explanation of the cause of the fire is very simple. Being a bitterly cold night, a roaring fire had been made up in the nursery, but about half-past ten the servants thought it looked rather dangerous and raked it out. The ashpan was not large enough, however, to hold the hot embers, which soon made the tiles red-hot. The woodwork caught fire, and had been smoldering for hours, when the nurse fortunately woke and discovered the state of affairs. She tried to rouse the other maids, but they were stupefied with the smoke, and so she rushed off at once to the doctor and Mr. Bingham. The former seized a child under each arm, wrapped them in blankets, and carried them off to the deck-house, Mabelle and the maids following, with more blankets and rugs, hastily snatched up. The children were as good as possible. They never cried nor made the least fuss, but composed themselves in the deck-house to sleep for the remainder of the night, as if it were all a matter of course. When I went to see them, little Muriel remarked, 'If the yacht is on fire, mamma, had not Baby and I better get our ulsters, and go with Emma in the boat to the hotel, to be out of the way?' It is the third time in their short lives that they have been picked out of bed in the middle of the night and carried off in blankets away from a fire, so I suppose they are getting quite used to it.

There can be no doubt that the preservation of the yacht from very serious damage, if not from complete destruction, was due to the prompt and efficient manner in which the *extincteurs* were used. It was not our first experience of the value of this invention; for, not very long before we undertook our present expedition, a fire broke out in our house in London, on which occasion the *extinc-*

teurs we fortunately had at hand rendered most excellent service in subduing the flames.

By half-past three all danger was past, and we began to settle down again, though it took a long time to get rid of the smoke.

At four o'clock we weighed anchor, and once more made a start from Kobe, and passed through the Straits of Akaski. The wind was dead ahead, but not so strong as when we made our previous attempts. It was bitterly cold, the thermometer, in a sheltered place, being only one degree above freezing, and the breeze from the snowy mountains cutting like a knife.

We were all disappointed with our sail to-day; perhaps because we had heard so much of the extreme beauty of the scenery, and this is not the best time of year for seeing it. The hills are all brown, instead of being covered with luxuriant vegetation, and all looked bleak and barren, though the outlines of the mountain ranges were very fine. We were reminded of the west coast of Scotland, the Lofoden Islands in the Arctic Circle, and the tamer portions of the scenery of the Straits of Magellan.

After passing through the Straits, we crossed the Harima Nada—rather a wider portion of the sea—and then entered the intricate channels among the islands once more. There are three thousand of them altogether, so one may take it for granted that the navigation is by no means easy. The currents and tides are strong, sunken rocks are frequent, and the greatest care is requisite. Indeed, many people at Yokohama urged Tom to take a pilot.

We had one lovely view in the afternoon of the island of Yoken San, with its snowy mountain at the back, and a pretty little village, with a few picturesque junks in the foreground. The yacht passed between Oki Sama and Le Sama, steering straight for the cone-shaped little island of Odutsi. Towards dusk we made the light of Nabae Sinaon Yo Sina, and, steering past it, had to take several sharp and awkward turns, to avoid two reefs off Siyako and Usi Suria. Thus we threaded the St. Vincent's Channel, and, avoiding the Conqueror bank by another sharp turn, dropped anchor at Imo Ura, in Hurisima, precisely at 8.30 p.m. Tom had been on the lookout since 5 a.m., and we were all more or less worn out with the fatigue and excitement of last night.

Friday, February 16*th.*—Off again at 4 a.m. The scenery was much finer than yesterday, and the wind not quite so bitterly cold.

About 11 a.m. I heard a hurrying to and fro, and once more the cry of 'Fire!' This time it was in the store-room that it broke out. The iron plates on which the saloon and galley grates are fixed had become red-hot, and the wooden deck below had consequently caught fire. The boxes on both sides, containing the stores, were in flames; but they were quickly removed, water was poured down, and the second and third fires were thus soon extinguished.

Saturday, February 17*th.*—At 3.15 a.m. we began to slow; at 3.45 the anchor was dropped near the lighthouse of Isaki, and we waited until daylight before proceeding through the Straits of Simono-seki. About nine o'clock a fresh start was made, under steam, but before long the wind freshened, and as soon as the anchorage near the town was reached we let go once more, near two men-of-war, who had preceded us from Kobe, but who were now wind-bound, like ourselves.

To our astonishment, we also saw a large ship from Nova Scotia at anchor, the 'Mary Fraser,' although this is not a free port, nor within treaty limits. The gig was lowered at once, and we rowed alongside to gain what intelligence could be learned, as well as to ascertain what likelihood there might be of our obtaining fresh supplies here. The captain was very civil and kind, and volunteered to go on shore with us and act as our interpreter. We landed opposite a large tea-house, where we were immediately surrounded by a crowd of Japanese, who stared at us eagerly and even touched us, only through curiosity. They pursued us wherever we went, and when we entered a tea-house or shop the whole crowd immediately stopped, and if we retired to the back they surged all over the front premises, and penetrated into the interior as far as they could. A most amusing scene took place at one of the tea-houses, where we went to order some provisions for the yacht. It was rather a tedious process, and when we came out of the back room we found the whole of the front of the place filled by a gaping, curious crowd. The proprietor suggested that they should retire at once, and an abrupt retreat immediately took place, the difficulties of which were greatly augmented by the fact that every one had left his high wooden shoes outside, along the front of the house. The street was ankle deep in mud and half-melted snow, into which they did not like to venture in their stockings; but how the owners of two or three hundred pairs of clogs, almost exactly alike, ever found their own property again I do not understand, though they managed to clear out very quickly. I believe Muriel and I were the chief objects of attraction. They told us that no European lady or child had ever been at Simono-seki before. It is not a treaty port, so no one is allowed to land, except from a man-of-war, without special permission, which is not often given; it is, besides, the key to the Inland Sea, and the authorities are very jealous about any one seeing the forts. There is only one European resident here, connected with the telegraph; and a dull time he must have of it. The wire crosses the Straits a few miles higher up.

The streets appeared to be full of soldiers, patrolling singly and in pairs, with fixed bayonets. The temples were being used as barracks, and the principal buildings seemed to be strongly guarded; but otherwise everything appeared to go on as usual.

We waded through the mud and snow to the proverbial end of all things, always followed by the same crowd, and stared at by all the inhabitants of the houses we passed. They seemed very timid, and inclined to run away directly we turned round. Still, their curiosity, especially respecting my sealskin jacket and serge dress, was insatiable, and I constantly felt myself being gently stroked and touched.

We returned to the yacht, and whilst we were at lunch some officers came on board to say that, this not being a treaty port, we could not purchase any provisions, except through them, and with special permission. This was soon arranged, and our visitors were rewarded for their trouble by being shown over the yacht.

Sunday, February 18th.—We were awakened in the night by a heavy gale, with snow and sleet beating furiously on the deck. In the morning the land was covered with snow, the water froze as it was pumped on deck, and the bitter wind howled and whistled through the rigging. In the afternoon the wind even increased in violence, the snowstorms became more frequent, and the sky was dark and overcast.

We had service at eleven and again at four. The sun set cold and stormy, promising a wild night. At times the shore was quite hidden by the snowstorms, though only a few cables' lengths off.

Monday, February 19th.—The wind and weather became worse than ever, and, as time was precious, Tom decided to retrace our steps for a short distance and go through the Bungo Channel, between the islands of Sikok and Kiusiu, instead of going out to sea through the Simono-seki Straits, as, in the latter case, the gale would be right in our teeth, and we should make but little progress. Now we shall be under the shelter of Kiusiu and the Linschoten and Luchu islands for at least two days, and so make a fair wind of it. Steering due south, too, we may hope to be soon out of this horrid weather. The only drawback to this plan is that we shall miss seeing Nagasaki, which I much regret. There are no great sights there, but the scenery is pretty, and the place is interesting owing to the fact that it was the first, and for many years the only, port open to foreigners, and also the scene of the cruel murders of Christians and the site of the beautiful island of Pappenberg. Shanghai I do not think I regret so much, though Tom would have been interested to talk with the merchants about their commerce, and to see their houses, many of which are, I am told, perfect palaces. It would be very cold there, too, at this time of year; and I do so long to lose my cough and feel warm once more.

At 8.30 p.m. we weighed and proceeded under steam. The views of the mountains, between the snowstorms, were lovely, with the fresh-fallen snow shining in an occasional gleam of sunshine. We soon passed the Isaki light, with wind and tide in our favor, and at sunset found ourselves in the open waters of the North Pacific.

Tuesday, February 20th. — A lovely day; the thermometer already twenty degrees higher than it was yesterday. The wind had dropped, and at 10 a.m. it had become so calm that fires were lighted.

It was delightful to see everybody and everything on board — people, children, animals, and birds, all and each sunning themselves, and trying to get thawed after the freezing they have had. We have unfortunately lost one of the Hawaiian geese, which I much regret, as it is irreplaceable. None have, I believe, ever been exported before. The pig from Harpe Island is very well. We have not seen him all the cold weather, as he has been buried in straw in a box, but they say that the cold has stopped his growth.

We were continually passing islands throughout the day, sometimes six or seven being in sight at one time, some with active and more with extinct volcanoes. We saw smoke issuing from three of the cones, but by night we were too far off to notice the flames.

Wednesday, February 21st.—The calm still continues. The sun is bright, the sky blue, and the atmosphere warm. During the night we passed Suwa Sima, Akuisi Sima, and Yoko Sima.

In the afternoon a light breeze sprang up; we stopped steaming, and before nightfall were bowling along smoothly at the rate of ten knots.

Thursday, February 22d.—The same delightful breeze continued throughout the night and most of the day. By noon we had done 220 miles. Everybody had on summer clothes, and we all felt ourselves gradually expanding after being shriveled up by the cold of the last month.

I should never recommend anybody to come to Japan in the winter. You do not see it at its best, I am sure, and the scanty protection afforded by houses and carriages makes traveling a penance rather than a pleasure. Travelers, however, who wish to see Japan should do so at once; for the country is changing every day, and in three years more will be so Europeanized that little will be left worth seeing; or a violent anti-foreign revulsion of feeling may have taken place, and then the ports will be closed more strictly than they were even before the execution of the first treaty. Nothing that we can give them do they really want; their exports are not large; and they have learned nearly all they care to know from the foreigner. We have seen many of the European engineers of Japanese vessels, and they all agree in declaring that the natives learn to imitate anything they see done with wonderful quickness. These men also averred that in a few years there will not be a single foreigner employed in Japan, as the Japanese will be quite in a position to dispense with such aid; and although the government pays foreigners in a high position exceedingly well, their service offers no career to a young man. His engagement is for so many years, and when his subordinates have learned to do the work, he may go where he likes. I am bound to add that I have heard the contrary opinion equally strongly expressed; but the facts I have mentioned make me lean rather to the former than to the latter side of the story.

Friday, February 23d.—Another pleasant day. The wind dropped, fires were lighted, and at 4.30 p.m. we proceeded under steam. Soon after seven, whilst we were at dinner, the table gave a sudden lurch, which was followed by the sound of rain on the deck above. We found that a breeze had sprung up all at once, and had carried away some of our head-sails before they could possibly be taken in. Even under close-reefed canvas we had a most uneasy night, racing along at from ten to twelve knots an hour.

Saturday, February 24th.—We were rushing along, literally *through* the water all day, for there was plenty of it on deck—not really any great quantity, but sufficient to make everything wet and uncomfortable.

At 1.35 we made the island of Ockseu, a capital landfall, and very satisfactory in every way; for the sky was too much overcast to get an observation, and the currents hereabouts are strong and variable. During the night the wind fell light, but we maintained a speed of from nine to ten knots.

Sunday, February 25th.—A much finer day. At 8 a.m. we had run 299 knots since the same time yesterday. We met a large steamer and pased a brigantine; also several Chinese junks. About twelve o'clock we saw a flag being waved frantically from a junk not far from us. At first we thought something was wrong with them; but soon a small boat put off with three men, and we found on its arrival alongside that it contained a pilot anxious for a job. He was very disappointed that we would not let him come on board; but Tom always likes doing the pilotage himself. The boat was a rough wash-tub kind of affair, not much better than those used by the inhabitants of Terra del Fuego and Patagonia.

About two o'clock we entered the tropics; but the weather is now colder again, and not nearly so pleasant as it was two days ago. I suppose it is owing to the north-east monsoon.

In the course of the afternoon we received several more offers of pilotage, all of which were declined; and at 7.45 we got up steam and lay-to all night, ready to go into Hongkong harbor at daylight.

Monday, February 26*th.*—At 4 a.m. we found ourselves close under the light on the eastern end of the island of Hongkong. We were surrounded by islands, and the morning was dark and thick; so we waited till 5.30, and then steamed on through the Kowloon passage up to the city of Victoria, as it is really named, though it is generally called Hongkong. The channel is long, and in some places so narrow that it is like going through a mountain pass, with barren hills and rocks on either hand; but the combined effect of the blue waters, and red, brown, and yellow hills, is very fine.

Off the town of Victoria the crowd of shipping is immense, and it became a difficult task to thread our way between the fleets of sampans and junks. The latter are the most extraordinary-looking craft I ever saw, with high, overhanging sterns, and roll, or rather draw, up sails, sometimes actually made of silk, and puffed like a lady's net ball-dress. Then their decks are so crowded with lumber, live and dead, that you wonder how the boats can be navigated at all. But still they are much more picturesque than the Japanese junks, and better sea boats. The sampans are long boats, pointed at both ends, and provided with a small awning. They have deep keels; and underneath the floor there is one place for a cooking fire, another for an altar, and a third where the children are stowed to be out of the way. In these sampans whole families, sometimes five generations, live and move and have their being. I never shall forget my astonishment when, going ashore very early one morning in one of these strange craft, the proprietor lifted up what I had thought was the bottom of the boat, and disclosed three or four children, packed away as tight as herrings, while under the seats were half a dozen people of larger growth. The young mother of the small family generally rows with the smallest baby strapped on to her back, and the next-sized one in her arms, whom she is also teaching to row. The children begin to row by themselves when they are about two years old. The boys have a gourd, intended for a life-preserver, tied round their necks as soon as they are born. The girls are left to their fate, a Chinaman thinking it rather an advantage to lose a daughter or two occasionally.

Many of these sampan people have never set foot on shore in their lives, and this water-life of China is one of the most extraordinary features of the country. It is what strikes all travelers, and so has tempted me to a digression.

A lieutenant from the flag-ship came on board and piloted us into a snug berth, among the men-of-war, and close to the shore, where we were immediately surrounded by sampans, and pestered by pertinacious Chinese clambering on board. The donkey-engine, with well-rigged hose, soon, however, cleared the decks, bulwarks, and gangways, and we were not bothered any more.

After breakfast we landed on the Praya, a fine quay, extending the whole length of the town. On it are situated many of the large stores, offices, and markets of the city. The streets are wide and handsome, and the buildings in European style, with deep verandas and arcades, all built of stone. The town is built on the side of a hill, with ferny, moss-covered banks, overhung by tropical trees, close to some of the principal offices. At the back are the mountains, the peak overhead, with the signal station on the top, always busily at work, making and answering signals with flags as ships and junks enter or leave the harbor. Soldiers and sailors abound in the streets; and if it were not for the sedan-chairs and palanquins, in which everybody is carried about by Chinese coolies with enormous hats, one might easily fancy one's self at dear old Gib., so much do these dependencies of the Crown in foreign countries resemble one another, even in such opposite quarters of the globe.

We were very anxious to leave the yacht here and to go up to Canton; but we find there is no possible hotel at the latter place. This is rather unfortunate, as, after our long residence on board, and all the knocking about at sea, the yacht requires repairing and refitting. She looks very well painted white, and the change is a great comfort in hot weather; but white paint does not wear well, and in order to maintain her good looks she ought to receive a fresh coat at every port. We can only go up the Pearl River at the very top of the tide, for in several places there are not fourteen feet of water over the shoals. It will, therefore, take us two or three days to accomplish what the steamers do in six hours, and a great waste of time will be involved.

To-day, for the first time, we have heard 'pidgin English' seriously spoken. It is very trying to one's composure to hear grave merchants, in their counting-houses, giving important orders to clerks and compradors in what sounds, until one gets accustomed to it, like the silliest of baby-talk. The term really means 'business English;' and certain it is that most Chinamen you meet understand it perfectly, though you might just as well talk Greek as ordinary English to them. 'Take pieccy missisy one piecey bag topside,' seems quite as difficult to understand as 'Take the lady's bag upstairs' would be; but it is easier to a Chinaman's intellect.

From the Praya we went up the hill to write our names in the Governor's book. It was a beautiful road all the way, running between lovely gardens and beneath shady trees. Government House is a fine building, situated on a high point of land, commanding extensive views in every direction. After a pleasant chat we descended the hill again, and proceeded to the Hongkong hotel for tiffin. It does not seem a very desirable abode, being large, dirty, and ill-kept. At one o'clock a bell rang, and the visitors all rushed in and took their places at various little tables, and were served with a 'scrambly' sort of meal by Chinese boys.

After this, a carriage was sent for us, and we drove to the race-course. This is the fourth and last day of the races, and there is to be a ball to-night to wind up with, to which everybody seems to be going. The drive was a very pleasant one, the road presenting a most animated appearance, with crowds of soldiers, sailors, Chinamen, Parsees, Jews, all hurrying along by the side of the numerous sedan-chairs and carriages. We were puzzled to imagine where, on this rocky, hilly island, there could possibly be found a piece of ground flat enough for a race-course. But the mystery was solved when we reached a lovely little valley, about two miles from the town, where we found a very fair course, about the size of that at Chester, but not so dangerous. The grand stand is a picturesque object, with its thatched roof, verandas, and sun-blinds. The interior, too, looks comfortably arranged, and certainly contains the most luxurious basket-chairs one could possibly desire. There are a lawn and a paddock attached, and very good temporary stables, over many of which are private stands and tiffin-rooms.

Hongkong races are a great event, and people come down from Canton, Shanghai, Macao, and all sorts of places for them. Everybody knows everybody, and it seems to be altogether a most pleasant social meeting. Many ladies were present. Some of the races were capital, the little Chinese ponies scuttling along at a great pace under their big riders, whose feet seemed almost to touch the ground. There also was a race for Australian horses. But the most amusing event of all was the last scramble for Chinese ponies ridden by Chinese boys, in which horses and riders seemed to be exactly suited to one another.

The sun went down, and it grew cold and dark before all was over. The gentlemen walked back to the town, and I went down to the landing-place in solitary state, in a carriage driven by an Indian coachman, attended by a Chinese footman. I was immediately surrounded by a vociferating crowd, each individual member of which was anxious to extol the merits of his own sampan. The carriage having driven off, I was quite alone, and had some difficulty in dispersing them, and being allowed to enter the sampan I had selected. However, I did succeed at last, and making my boatmen understand that they were to take me to 'the white ship,' as the yacht is generally called, returned on board to rest.

CHAPTER XXII.

TO CANTON UP THE PEARL RIVER.

Sails of silk and ropes of sandal
Such as gleam in ancient lore,
And the singing of the sailors,
And the answer from the shore.

Tuesday, February 27th.—Until half-past ten we were occupied in the pleasant task of reading news from home —all good this time, I am happy to say. At 10.30 we landed and went up the hill to breakfast with Sir Arthur and Miss Kennedy, and heard a good deal about the colony. It is wonderful to think that thirty years ago it scarcely existed, and now it is a large and flourishing place, with splendid houses, institutions, roads, and gardens. We were also most agreeably surprised by the beauty of the scenery. It is really lovely, and, though the hills around are barren, wherever cultivation has been attempted, vegetation appears to flourish luxuriantly. The climate cannot be very bad, judging by the healthy look of the residents and troops. Typhoons seem to be the greatest drawback. They come without any warning, and it is impossible to guard against them and their disastrous effects. Thousands of lives, and millions of pounds' worth of property, are destroyed in a few hours. We have been shown some of the effects of a very severe typhoon that occurred in 1874. It seems almost incredible that the mere force of the wind can snap iron posts in two, break granite columns, and blow off heavy roofs.

After breakfast the ceremony of presenting the departing Governor with a state umbrella took place. It was a token of respect from ten thousand Chinese inhabitants of Hongkong, and is the greatest compliment that can be paid to any official. It arrived in a large camphor-wood box, and the address, beautifully embroidered in gold thread and silk, was inclosed in a magnificent sandal-wood box about four feet long, covered with the richest carving. Precisely at twelve some forty vermilion-colored visiting cards were handed in, with the name of each member of the deputation written in Chinese and English characters. The visitors were all received in a large drawing-room, whilst we ladies observed the proceedings through the doors leading from a smaller room. It is not considered etiquette by the Chinese for ladies to appear at these public ceremonies.

After it was all over, a stroll through the town, and a look at the shops, filled up the rest of the time in the morning, until we went on board to fetch the children for an expedition up the Peak to the signal station. As usual many visitors came on board the yacht, and it was later than we had intended before we could make a start. I had to be carried up the steep ascent in a chair, but the children and dogs thoroughly enjoyed themselves scampering about. The little ones picked heaps of flowers and ferns. The dogs had not been allowed to land before, as everybody told me they would be sure to be stolen directly. We returned on board before sunset, and had time for a little rest before some friends arrived to dinner. We have shipped two Chinese boys here to work in the pantry and kitchen. They are excellent servants as a rule, but how they will get on with the others, and how they will like the sea-life, remains to be proved.

Wednesday, February 28th.—I was up and off at half-past six to the market, and returned to a late breakfast on board; after which a large party of China merchants came as a deputation to invite Tom to fix a day to dine with them. I think they proposed to pay him what is for them an unusual compliment, partly because they were pleased with some remarks he made yesterday at Government House, and partly because they think so much of his enterprise in making a voyage round the world in a yacht with his wife and family. They examined everything on board, and seemed to be specially interested in Tom's Board of Trade certificate, which one of their number translated in full for the benefit of the rest.

Later in the afternoon we drove through the Chinese town to the native theater.

The Chinese part of the town stands quite away from the foreign settlement. It is dirty and crowded in spite of its wide streets, and the large, gayly colored houses have the names and advertisements of their proprietors painted all across them. The theater is in the middle of the city, and was densely crowded. A box had been reserved for us, for the ordinary seats are like a carpenter's bench. On the floor of the house men and women sat together, but in the galleries the men sat apart, and there were separate boxes for the women. The acting was rough, and accompanied by the most discordant music. The scenery seemed of an excessively rudimentary description, as you may imagine when I tell you that a steep hill up which the hero and heroine climbed with great difficulty was composed of five kitchen chairs arranged in a pyramid on the top of three kitchen tables, held in position by men in their ordinary dress. The fugitives were supposed to be a Tartar general and his wife, escaping from their enemies after a great battle. The fighting was renewed at intervals with great noise and spirit. Some of the costumes were very fine, and cost from £30 to £40 apiece.

From the theater we drove to the Chinese hospital, and thence to the Chinese recreation ground, where we saw sundry itinerant quacks and venders of all sorts of rubbish. As we were walking along, having left our chairs for a few minutes to look at the Chinese shops, a man picked my pocket of a one-dollar note. Mr. Freer and the Doctor saw, pursued and caught him. He vehemently protested his innocence, but to no avail. They proceeded to strip him, found the note, gave him a good shaking, and told him to go.

Thursday, March 1st.—A most lovely morning ushered in the new month, which, having come in like the most peaceable of lambs, will, we hope, not end like a roaring lion just as we expect to be in the middle of the Bay of Bengal. We left the yacht at 7.30, and went on board the 'Kin-Shan,' which is a regular American river steamer with beam engines and many deck-houses, which are painted white. The lower deck is crowded with the most inferior class of Chinese, some eight hundred of them being on board. It gave us rather a turn to see them all padlocked in under the hatchways and iron gratings. At each opening is posted an armed sentinel, ready to fire among the crowd in case of any disturbance. In the saloon, also, is a stand of pistols, and rifles with fixed bayonets, ready for the European passengers to defend themselves with, in case of emergency. These are very necessary precautions, on account of the numerous pirates who occasionally ship in disguise among the crowd, murder the passengers and crew, and take possession of the steamer. Not quite two years ago a vessel belonging to this same company was assailed in that way. Every one on board was murdered, and the ship taken to Macao.* But this voyage was more prosperous, the captain was most kind and polite, and the boat clean and comfortable. An excellent breakfast was served at nine o'clock, and an elaborate tiffin at noon, all for the sum of four dollars a head, including wine, beer, and spirits *ad libitum*.

On first leaving Hankow the course lies between islands and through fine mountain passes. Later on, the country becomes flat and uninteresting till the Bogue

---

* I have since been told that only the captain and one or two passengers were killed, and the vessel run ashore *near* (not *at*) Macao.

Forts are reached. Here are to be seen the remains of the old forts knocked down by the French and English guns.

About one o'clock we reached Whampoa, the leading port of Canton. The Pearl River is too shallow for large steamers to go up any higher; so we stopped here only a few minutes to disembark some of the Chinese passengers, and from this point the interesting part of the voyage began. The river, as well as all the little supplementary creeks, was alive with junks and sampans—masts and sails stuck up in every direction, gliding about among the flat paddy-fields. Such masts and sails as they are! The mandarins' boats, especially, are so beautifully carved, painted, and decorated, that they look more as if they were floating about for ornament than for use. Just about two o'clock our large steamer was brought up close alongside the wooden pier as easily as a skiff, but it must require some skill to navigate this crowded river without accident. On the shore was an excited, vociferating crowd, but no one came to meet us; and we had begun to wonder what was to become of us—what we should do, and whither we should go in a strange city, where we did not know a soul—when we were relieved from our embarrassment by the appearance of the Vice-Consul, who came on board to meet a friend. He told us that, owing to an expected ball, all the houses were unusually full, and that not one of the people who had been written to could take us in. This was rather bad news, but we felt sure that something would turn up.

We landed, and after proceeding a short distance along the dirty street, came to a bridge with iron gates, which were thrown open by the sentry. After crossing a dirty stream we found ourselves in the foreign settlement—Shameen it is called—walking on nice turf, under the shade of fine trees. The houses of the merchants which line this promenade are all fine, handsome stone buildings, with deep verandas. At the back there are compounds with kitchen gardens, and under the trees dairy cows are grazing. Every household appears to supply itself with garden and farm produce, and the whole scene has a most English, home-like appearance. We went first to the Vice-Consul, and then to the Jardine Hong. All the business houses retain the names of the firms to which they originally belonged, even when they have passed into entirely different hands. After a little chat we went on to the Deacon Hong, where we found they had just done tiffin, and where we met some old friends.

By the kindness of various people, to whom we were introduced, we all found ourselves gradually installed in luxurious quarters. As for us, we had a large room comfortably furnished in English fashion, with a bath-room attached. All the houses are very much alike, and are fitted up in an equally comfortable style.

About three o'clock we started in five chairs, with Man-look-Chin for our guide. Tom vigorously protested against not being allowed to use his own legs, but everybody assured him that it was impossible in the crowded streets of the city, so he had to submit to being carried. No Chinaman, except those employed by foreigners, is allowed to cross any of the bridges over the stream, which completely surrounds the foreign settlement, and makes the suburb of Shameen a perfect island. There are iron gates on each bridge, guarded by sentries. The contrast in the state of things presented by the two sides of the bridge is most marvelous. From the quiet country park, full of large villas and pretty gardens, you emerge into a filthy city, full of a seething, dirty population, and where smells and sights of the most disgusting description meet you at every turn. People who have seen many Chinese cities say that Canton is the cleanest of them all. What the dirtiest must be like is therefore beyond my imagination. The suburbs of the city, where all sorts of cheap eating-shops abound—where the butchers and fishmongers expose the most untempting-looking morsels for sale, and where there are hampers of all sorts of nasty-looking compounds, done up ready for the buyer of the smallest portion to take home—are especially revolting. The Chinese, however poor, like several courses to their meals, which are served in little bowls on a small table to each person, and eaten with chop-sticks, as in Japan. It is to gratify this taste that what we should think a very minute fish, or a tiny chicken, is cut up into half a dozen pieces and sold to several purchasers.

The Chinese are very fond of fish, and are most ingenious in propagating, rearing, and keeping them. The dried-fish and seaweed shops are not at all picturesque or sweet-smelling, especially as all the refuse is thrown into the streets in front. Men go about the streets carrying pails of manure, suspended on bamboo poles across their shoulders, and clear away the rubbish as they go. I was very glad when we got through all this to the better part of the town, and found ourselves in a large shop, where it was cool, and dark, and quiet.

The streets of the city are so narrow, that two chairs can scarcely pass one another, except at certain points. The roofs of the houses nearly meet across the roadway, and, in addition, the inhabitants frequently spread mats overhead, rendering the light below dim and mysterious. Every shop has a large vermilion-colored board, with the name of its occupant written in Chinese characters, together with a list of the articles which he sells, hung out in front of it, so that the view down the narrow streets is very bright and peculiar. These highways and byways are not unlike the bazaars at Constantinople and Cairo, and different wares are also sold in different localities after the Eastern fashion. This is, in some respects, a great advantage, as, if you are in search of any particular article, you have almost an unlimited choice of whatever the town has to offer. But, on the other hand, if you want a variety of articles, it is an inconvenient arrangement, as you have to go all over the place to find them, and probably have to visit the most opposite quarters. We saw thousands of china vases, and bowls, and tea and dinner services, some very handsome, but many extremely poor. There were a few specially made for the French Exhibition next year, which were exceedingly handsome. We visited an ivory shop, and saw some splendid specimens of carving. One man had been for fifteen months employed in carving on one side of an enormous elephant's tusk the representation of a battle scene, and on the other that of a thanksgiving procession. It will take him at least another year to finish the job. It is for the Paris Exhibition. It will be quite interesting to look for our old Japanese and Chinese friends and their products on that occasion.

From ivory carving, we went to a black-wood furniture shop, where we saw some very handsome things, by no means dear considering the amount of time and labor bestowed upon them. We finished up with the Temple of the Five Hundred Genii, whose five hundred carved wooden statues, thickly gilt, all very ugly, and all in different attitudes, stand round the statue of a European in sailor's costume, said to be meant for Marco Polo, but, whoever it may be, evidently considered an object at least of veneration, if not of worship.

We now returned through the dirty city to Shameen, and the relief, after crossing the bridge into an open space where one could breathe freely and see the blue sky, was indescribable.

Friday, March 2d.—Before we had finished breakfast the other gentlemen strolled in from their various quarters, and the drivers and guides arrived from the Vice-Consul's. A long morning's work had been mapped out for us—thirteen sights before luncheon, then a visit to the French Consulate, followed by eight more objects of interest to be seen before we finally crossed the Pearl River to visit the Honan Temple. Quitting the pretty, cool suburb by another bridge, we passed through streets quite as dirty as those of yesterday, until the heart of the city had been reached. We went first to the wedding-chair shop, where they keep sedan-chairs, of four qualities, for hire whenever a wedding occurs. Even the commonest are made gorgeous by silver gilding and lacquer, while the best are really marvels of decorative art, completely covered with the blue lustrous feathers of a kind of kingfisher. In shape they are like a square pagoda, and round each tier are groups of figures. The dresses are also made of expensive feathers, but then they last for generations. There are no windows to these strange conveyances, in which the bride is carried to her future home, closely shut up, with joss-sticks burning in front of her. Recently there have been two sad accidents. In one case the journey was long, there was no outlet for the smoke of the joss-sticks, and when they arrived and opened the chair, the bride was found dead from suffocation. The other accident occurred through the chair catching fire while it was passing through some narrow street under an archway. The bearers became frightened, put down their burden, and ran away, leaving the poor bride locked up inside to be burned to death.

From the chair shop we went to the embroiderers, to see them at work. Their productions are exquisite, and it is a pity that better specimens are not seen in England. The process of lacquer-making, too, is very interesting. We had, however, to go from house to house to witness it, as only one portion of the process is carried on at each —from the gradual coating of the roughest wood with three coatings of varnish, until it is finally ornamented with delicate designs, and polished ready for sale. In appearance, price, and length of wear there is a vast difference.

The next thing to see was the weaving of silk, which is done in the most primitive manner. One man throws the shuttle, while another forms the pattern by jumping on the top of the loom and raising a certain number of threads, in order to allow the shuttle to pass beneath them.

Then came a visit to the Temple of Longevity, a large Buddhist temple, with a monastic establishment of about ninety priests attached to it. It contains three shrines with large figures, but nothing specially interesting. There is a large pond in the midst of the garden, covered with duckweed, and full of beautiful gold and silver fish of many kinds. The Chinese certainly excel in producing gold and silver and red fish; they are the pets of every household, and are of all colors, some being striped and spotted, and boasting any number of tails from one to five.

Outside the temple stands the Jadestone Market, where incredible quantities of this valuable stone change hands before ten o'clock every morning, both in its rough and its polished state. The stalls are the simplest wooden stands, and the appearance of the venders is poor in the extreme. The contents of the stalls, however, are worth from £500 to £1,000 (not dollars), and there are hundreds of these stalls, besides an entire jadestone street which we afterwards visited. We saw several of the shops, and asked the prices, as we wished to take home a small specimen; but they had no good carved cups, which were what we wanted, and for what they had they asked an enormous price. Jadestone is a material very difficult to work, and in many cases the result attained is not worth the labor expended upon it. It is more a *tour de force* than a work of art. For a good stone, green as grass (as it ought to be), they ask from 2,500 to 3,000 dollars; for a necklace of beads, 5,000 dollars; a set of mandarin's buttons, one large and one small, 50 to 150 dollars.

After looking in at the goldbeaters at work, we next made our way to the Temple of the Five Genii who are supposed to have founded the city of Canton. Being a Tartar temple, all the gods have a totally different cast of features, and are represented as Tartars with long beards. It is much frequented by women of all classes, and up and down the numerous flights of steps leading from one shrine to another, poor little women tottered and tumbled on their crippled feet, holding on to one another or leaning on a stick. This temple is interesting as having been the headquarters of the allied forces during their occupation of Canton from 1858 to 1861. The great bell in front of its principal shrine has been broken by a shot.

We then went to see the Flowery Pagoda, built A.D. 512, but now deprived of many of its decorations. The Brilliant Pagoda too, so called from having once been covered with snow-white porcelain, is now only a tall brick-pointed tower nine stories high.

By this time we all felt hungry, and began to wend our way towards the *yamun*. On the outskirts may be seen prisoners in chains, or wearing the *cangue*, imprisoned in a cage, or else suffering one of the numerous tortures inflicted in this country. I did not go to see any of these horrors, neither did I visit the execution ground; but some of the party did, and described it as a most horrible sight. Skulls were lying about in all directions, one of which had been quite recently severed from its trunk, the ground being still moist and red.

Whilst luncheon was being prepared we were taken over many of the rooms and through several of the inclosures within the fortified gate. The meal was excellently served by Chinese servants in a charmingly picturesque Tartar room, and after it we wandered about the park, looked at the deer, and admired the Nagasaki bantams. Then it was time to start on a fresh sight-seeing expedition, armed with fresh directions. We set out first to the Temple of the Sleeping Buddha, where there is a large, fat, reclining figure; then to the Temple of Horrors —most rightly named, for in a suite of rooms built round three sides of a large yard are represented all the tortures of the Buddhist faith, such as boiling in oil, sawing in pieces, and other horrible devices. The yard itself is crowded with fortune-tellers, charm-sellers, deputy prayer-sayers, beggars, and all sorts of natural horrors, exhibiting various deformities. Altogether it is a most unpleasant place, but still it is one of the characteristic sights of Canton.

We saw the hotel to-day for the first time. It certainly looks very hopeless. We were anxious to get in there if possible, as we were such a large party, but everybody assured us it was quite out of the question. One gentleman told me he never could fancy using his portmanteau again after even laying it down on the floor for a few minutes. The absence of a decent hotel renders Canton an inconvenient place to visit. The European inhabitants are so very kind, however, that you are sure to find somebody who knows somebody else who will hospitably take you in.

From the Temple of the Sleeping Buddha we went up the height to breathe a little fresh air, and to see the five-storied pagoda at the spot where the allied forces had encamped, the Chinese groves in the White Cloud Mountains beyond, and to gain a general view of the densely crowded city beneath. It is all too flat, however, to be picturesque. The three *yamuns* at our feet, with their quaint towers, grand old trees, flags, and the broad Pearl River on the other side of the city, are the only elements of positive beauty in the landscape.

We soon descended the heights again, and, passing the Cantonese Viceroy's *yamuns*, paid our promised visit to the French Consul. His residence is, if possible, more quaint and beautiful than that of the English representative. The trees are finer, especially one grand avenue leading from the outer gates to the private apartments. We were most kindly received, and shown a wonderful collection of embroideries and china. It was a delightful visit, but we could not remain so long as we wished, for we had to see the water clock. The tower in which it stands is approached by a flight of steps, and was built between the years A.D. 624 and 907; and it has been repaired, destroyed, and repaired again, several times, having suffered in the bombardment of the town by the allied fleets in 1857.

In the next street, Treasury Street (said to be the finest in Canton), you can buy burning-sticks measured to mark the time. They are extremely cheap, but perfectly accurate, and there seems little doubt that they have been used by the Chinese for thousands of years before the Christian era. Here, too, were the large spectacles so much worn; opium pipes, with all the paraphernalia for cleaning and smoking them; water pipes in pretty little shagreen cases, and many other curious articles in common use, of which we purchased specimens.

In the Feather Street are innumerable shops containing nothing but feathers of all kinds for mandarins, actors, and ordinary mortals; but the great ambition of every Chinaman is to have a feather from the Emperor. They are all called peacocks' feathers, one-eyed, two-eyed, or three-eyed; but, in reality, many are pheasants' feathers. Some of these are from six to eight feet in length, beautifully marked. I bought two pairs over seven feet long. They are rather rare, as each bird has only two long feathers, and these are in perfection for but one month in the year. In this part of the town stands a Chinese restaurant where only cats' and dogs' flesh is served.

We passed through innumerable streets, and at last reached the site of the old factories, now only occupied by a large and comfortable house. We were to have embarked in the Consul's boat to visit the Temple of Honan across the river, but it was getting late, and every one felt tired; so we went back through more crowded streets to rest awhile, before dressing to go out to dinner at eight o'clock. The dinner was quite English in its style, and the table looked bright with tea roses, heliotrope, and mignonette. The tables had been charmingly decorated by the Chinese servants, and even the *menu* had been arranged by them. They seem to save their employer all trouble, even that of thinking, provided the services of really good ones can be secured. We have had one for only a few days, and he does everything for Tom and me. He appears to know exactly what we want to do or to wear, and to foresee all our requirements.

But to return to this famous repast. It began with mandarin bird's-nest soup, with plover's eggs floating about in it. This is a most delicious and dainty dish, and is invariably given to strangers on their first arrival. I had no idea how expensive the nests were—54 dollars a 'pice,' weighing something under a pound, and it takes two or three ounces to make enough soup for ten people. We had a very pleasant evening, talking over our experiences, and exchanging news as to our mutual friends.

CHAPTER XXIII.

CANTON AND MACAO TO SINGAPORE.

I remember the black wharves and the slips,
And the sea-tides tossing free;
And Spanish sailors with bearded lips,
And the beauty and mystery of the ships,
And the magic of the sea.

Saturday, March 3d.—After our long day yesterday, I did not feel capable of acceding to our guide's proposition of being ready at half-past six for further explorations before breakfast; besides, I wanted to see Tom off by the nine-o'clock boat to Hongkong, whither he is obliged to return in order to keep various engagements. The rest of our party have been persuaded to stay and see a little more of Canton, and to go with some friends to a picnic in the White Cloud Mountains. A man brought home to-day some carved tortoise-shell brushes Tom has given me, with my name carved on them in Chinese. It was no good writing it down for the engraver's guidance, and after hearing it several times he wrote down two characters; but, as the 'r' is always a great difficulty with the Chinese, I much doubt whether the name is really spelled rightly.

It was a most lovely day, and after some little delay we started about eleven o'clock, a party of seventeen, in chairs. There were five ladies and twelve gentlemen—a most unusual proportion for Canton. A few weeks ago they wanted to get up a fancy ball, but there were only five available ladies to be found in the city. At present one or two more are staying here on a visit, and it is hoped that another ball may be arranged during this week, which may boast of at least ten ladies. We made quite a procession, with all the servants, bearers, &c., and excited much commotion in the narrow streets, where everybody had to make room and squeeze up to the side as best they could. Men ran before to clear the way for us, shouting, yet we were more than an hour going right across the city. On our way we passed through the egg market, saw the pork-fat market, and the poulterers' and fowlers' shops.

We managed to visit several shops for the sale of real Chinese furniture. It is very handsome, but curious in form, and, unless it is specially ordered, is made only for native use. Every Chinese reception-room is furnished in precisely the same manner, with very stiff high arm-chairs, arranged in two rows. A small four-legged square table stands between every two chairs, a larger table in the center, and at the end an enormous sofa, big enough for six or eight people to lie full length across. The sofa and all the chairs have marble seats and backs, and the tops of the tables are also made of marble, or a sort of soap-stone, on which may be distinguished natural landscapes slightly assisted by art.

In the bird market I saw numbers of little birds for sale, for the Chinese are very fond of pets, and often take their birds out in a cage with them when they go for a walk, just as we should be accompanied by a dog. They manage to tame them thoroughly, and when they meet a friend they will put the cage down, let the bird out, and give him something to eat while they have their chat. I saw this done several times.

Our road next led us through part of the butchers' quarter, where rats were hung up by their tails, and what looked very like skinned cats and dogs dangled beside them. Whole cages full of these animals were exposed for sale alive. Some travelers deny that the Chinese eat cats and dogs and rats, but there can be no question that they do so, though they may be the food only of the lower classes. Nor do 'puppy dogs' appear on the tables of the rich, except on one particular day in the year, when to eat them is supposed to bring good luck. We passed a restaurant where I was shown the bill of fare in Chinese, of which this is a translation :—

BILL OF FARE FOR THE DAY.

One tael of black dog's flesh	eight cash.
One tael weight of black dog's fat . .	three kandareems of silver.
One large basin of black cat's flesh .	one hundred cash.
One small basin of black cat's flesh .	fifty cash.
One large bottle of common wine . .	thirty-two cash.
One small bottle of common wine . .	sixteen cash.
One large bottle of dark rice wine . .	sixty-eight cash.
One small basin of cat's flesh . . .	thirty-four cash.
One large bottle of plum wine . . .	sixty-eight cash.
One small bottle of plum wine . . .	thirty-four cash.
One large basin of dog's flesh . . .	sixty-eight cash.
One small bottle of pear wine . . .	thirty-four cash.
One large bottle of timtsin wine . .	ninety-six cash.
One small bottle of timtsin wine . .	forty-eight cash.
One basin of congee	three cash.
One small plate of pickles	three cash.
One small saucer of ketchup or vinegar	three cash.
One pair of black cat's eyes	three kandareems of silver.

The fish here, as at Hongkong, are almost always kept alive in large tubs of water, with a fountain playing over them. They even keep some sea-fish alive in salt water. But it is in the north of China that they excel in rearing fish in large quantities. At Foo-chow cormorant fishing may be seen to great perfection, and it is said to be a very amusing sight.

At last the city gates were reached, and we once more found ourselves outside the walls, and able to breathe again. Here a halt was made, and several of the party got out of their chairs and walked, and we were able to chat, whilst we wended our way by a narrow path through nursery gardens and graveyards. In fact the whole of the White Cloud Mountain is one vast cemetery—it is the

Chinese Holy of Holies, whither their bodies are sent, not only from all parts of China, but from all parts of the world. Frequently a shipload of 1,500 or 1,600 bodies arrives in one day. The Steamboat Company charges 40 dollars for the passage of a really live Chinaman, as against 160 dollars for the carriage of a dead Celestial. The friends of the deceased often keep the bodies in coffins above ground for several years, until the priests announce that they have discovered a lucky day and a lucky spot for the interment. This does not generally happen until he—the priest—finds he can extract no more money by divination, and that no more funeral feasts will be given by the friends. We passed through what they call the city of the dead, where thousands of coffins waiting for interment were lying above ground. The coffins are large and massive, but very plain, resembling the hollowed-out trunk of a tree. The greatest compliment a Chinese can pay his older relatives is to make them a present of four handsome longevity boards for their coffins. Outside the city of the dead were the usual adjuncts of a large burying-place—coffin-makers and stone-carvers, all living in dirty little cottages, surrounded by pigs, ducks, and young children.

Leaving the cemetery and cottages behind, a too short drive brought us to a lovely valley, where we were to lunch at the temple of San Chew, in one of its fairest gorges. The meal was spread in a large hall in a most luxurious manner, and as the wind changed almost immediately, and it came on to rain, we felt ourselves fortunate indeed in having reached shelter. We had plenty of wraps, and the bearers ran us down the hill again very quickly, so that we suffered no discomfort.

By the time the city walls were reached the rain had ceased, and a glorious red sunset glowed over the roofs, glinting through the holes in the mats, and lighting up all the vermilion boards and gold characters with which the houses and shops are decorated. The shadowy streets were now full of incense or rather joss-stick smoke, for every house and every shop has a large altar inside, and a small one without, before which joss-sticks are burned more or less all day long.

The streets seemed more crowded even than usual. Each of our bearers struck out a line of his own, and it was not until we reached Shameen that we all met again. Some of the ladies had been rather frightened at finding themselves alone in the dark, crowded city. We were only just in time to dress and go to dinner, after which we examined an interesting collection, chiefly of coins, in process of formation for the French Exhibition. They are carefully arranged, and will be most valuable and interesting when complete. The knife-and-fork coins are particularly curious and rare, some of them being worth as much as 5,000 dollars each, as curiosities. All the coins have holes in the center for convenience of carriage.

Sunday, March 4th.—There is a fine cathedral at Shameen, in which the services are beautifully performed. A lady kindly lent us her house-boat, and after service we rowed across to Fa-ti, to see the gardens of Canton. They are laid out on an island a very short way up the river. The gardens are very wonderful, and contain plants cut into all sorts of shapes, such as men, birds, beasts, fishes, boats, houses, furniture, &c. Some are full-sized, others only in miniature. But almost all must have required considerable time and patience to reach their present growth, for their ages vary from 10 to 150 years. There are other plants not so elaborately trained, but the effect of the whole is rather too formal to be pretty. I managed to bring home some euphorbias, cut into the form of junks, and some banyan-trees, one 100 and one 50 years old. I believe they are the first that have ever reached England alive and have flourished. Not far from Fa-ti are the duck-hatching establishments, and still farther up the river are the duck sampans, where the crowds of ducks are reared. They are sent out every morning to get their own living and return at night. Until they learn to obey their keeper's call quickly the last duck is always whipped. I am told it is most ridiculous to see the hurry of the last half-dozen birds of a flock of some thousands of ducks. I was most anxious to see them, but it is not the right time of year now. The young ducks are only just beginning to hatch, and the old ones are numerous, and are mostly laying.

There was no time to go and see the temple of Honan, for we were more anxious to avail ourselves of a chance of visiting some interesting places in the Chinese city. We went through a street, consisting entirely of fruiterers' shops, to which the name of Kwohlaorn, or fruit-market, is applied. In this market, which is of great extent, there is for sale at all seasons of the year an almost countless variety of fruit.

A silkworm establishment was pointed out to us in the distance, but we did not go over it, as we had seen many before, and it is not the best season of the year. The silkworms are most carefully tended, the people who look after them being obliged to change their clothes before entering the rooms where they are kept, and to perform all sorts of superstitious ceremonies at every stage of the insect's growth. No one at all ailing or deformed is allowed to approach a building where they are kept. The worms are supposed to be very nervous, and are guarded from everything that can possibly frighten them, as well as from all changes of temperature or disturbances of the atmosphere. Thunder and lightning they are supposed specially to dread, and great pains are taken to shelter them by artificial means, and keep them from all knowledge of the storm.

The next place we visited was a bird's-nest-soup-shop street, where we went into one of the best and most extensive establishments. There were three or four well-dressed assistants behind the counter, all busily occupied in sorting and packing birds' nests. Some of the best were as white as snow, and were worth two dollars each, while a light brown one was worth only one dollar, and the black dirty ones, full of feathers and moss, could be purchased at the rate of a quarter-dollar.

Certainly the Chinese seem an exception to the rule laid down by some writers, that no people can flourish who do not rest every seventh day. In many ways they are an abnormal people, one striking point in their condition being the state of dirt and filth in which they not only exist, but increase and multiply. The children look healthy and happy too, in spite of these apparent drawbacks, and notwithstanding the fact that in many cases their poor little feet must be cruelly tortured by the practice of bandaging them tightly to make them small.

When we got back to Shameen there was time for a stroll along the Bund. It is very pleasant, for the river runs close under the parapet, and its surface is always covered with junks, sampans, and boats and ships, going swiftly up or down with the strong tide. The walk is shaded with trees, and seats stand at intervals all along it.

An agreeable saunter was followed by a quiet, pleasant little dinner, and though we have been here only a few days we feel quite sorry that this is to be our last night in Canton, so kind has everybody been to us.

Monday, March 5th.—I was awake and writing from half-past four this morning, but before I got up, a woman who comes here every day to work brought me some small ordinary shoes which I had purchased as curiosities, and took the opportunity of showing me her feet. It really made me shudder to look at them, so deformed and cramped up were they, and, as far as I could make out, she must have suffered greatly in the process of reducing them to their present diminutive size. She took off her own shoes and tottered about the room in those she had brought, and then asked me to show her one of mine. Having most minutely examined it, she observed, with a melancholy shake of the head, 'Missisy foot much more good, do much walky, walky; mine much bad, no good for walky.'

Having said farewell to our kind hostess, we went off in the house-boat to the steamer. There was a great crowd on the lower deck—at least 900 Chinamen—to struggle through in order to reach the European quarters. We found other friends on board, who had come to see us off.

A few minutes before nine o'clock the bell rang as a signal for our friends' departure, and we steamed ahead, among such a crowd of sampans and junks that it was more like moving through a town than along a river. No accident, however, occurred, though one junk and one sampan had the very narrowest escape.

The voyage down took much longer than our voyage up, on account of the tide being against us, and in consequence we did not reach Hongkong until 3.30 p.m., when the gig with the children was soon alongside. We got off as soon as we could, for we expected some friends to afternoon tea on board the yacht. There was just time to dress before the first visitors arrived, and by half-past six at least two hundred had come. At one time quite a flotilla of boats lay around us, looking very pretty with all their flags flying. I think the people enjoyed it very much as something new, and we only wanted a band to enliven the proceedings.

Tuesday, March 6th.—The little girls and I went ashore at 7.30, to collect all our purchases with the help of a friend. We glanced at the museum too, which contains some curious specimens of Chinese and Japanese arms and armor, and the various productions of the two countries, besides many strange things from the Philippine and other islands. I was specially interested in the corals and shells. There were splendid conch shells from Manilla, and a magnificent group of Venus flower-baskets, dredged from some enormous depth near Manilla. There were also good specimens of reptiles of all sorts, and of the carved birds' heads for which Canton is famous. They look very like amber, and are quite as transparent, being carved to a great depth. I believe the bird is a kind of toucan or hornbill, but the people here call it a crane.

It was now time to say good-by to Hongkong and to our kind friends, for we had to go on board the 'Flying Cloud,' which starts for Macao at two o'clock precisely, and our passages had been taken in her. Tom could not go with us, as he had fixed to-night for the dinner at which the Chinese gentlemen proposed to entertain him; but he came to see us off. We went out of the harbor by a different way, and passed along a different side of the island of Hongkong, but the scenery was not particularly interesting. Off Choolong a heavy ground-swell, called 'Pon choughai,' made us roll about most unpleasantly. In bad weather, or with a top-heavy ship, this passage could not be attempted. Sometimes there are very heavy fogs, and always strong currents, so that the short voyage of forty-two miles is not absolutely free from danger.

The town of Macao is situated on a peninsula at the end of the island of the same name. It was the first foreign settlement in China belonging to the Portuguese, and was once a fine, handsome town, with splendid buildings. Unfortunately Macao lies in the track of the typhoons, which at times sweep over it with a resistless force, shattering and smashing everything in their career. These constantly recurring storms, and the establishment of other ports, have resulted in driving many people away from the place, and the abolition of the coolie traffic has also tended to diminish the number of traders. Now the town has a desolate, deserted appearance, and the principal revenue of the government is derived from the numerous gambling-houses.

We landed at the pier soon after five o'clock, and were carried across the peninsula through the town to the

Praya on the other side. Here we found a large unoccupied mansion, situated in a garden overlooking the sea, and, having delivered our Chinese letters, were received with the greatest civility and attention by the comprador and the servants who had been left in charge of our friend's house. The rooms upstairs, to which we were at once shown, were lofty and spacious, opening into a big veranda. Each room had a mosquito room inside it, made of wire gauze and wood, like a gigantic meat-safe, and capable of containing, besides a large double bed, a chair and a table, so that its occupant is in a position to read and write in peace, even after dark. This was the first time we had seen one of these contrivances. By the direction of the comprador the house chairs were prepared, and coolies were provided to take us for an expedition round the town, while our things were being unpacked, and the necessary arrangements made for our comfort. Macao is a thoroughly Portuguese-looking town, the houses being painted blue, green, red, yellow, and all sorts of colors. It is well garrisoned, and one meets soldiers in every direction. We passed the fort, and went up to the lighthouse, which commands a fine view over land and sea; returning home by a different way through the town again, which we entered just as the cathedral bell and the bells of all the churches were pealing the Ave Maria. On our return we found a fire lighted and everything illuminated, and by half-past eight we had a capital impromptu dinner served. Chinese Tommy, who waited on us, had decorated the table most tastefully with flowers. Macao is a favorite resort for the European residents of Hongkong who are addicted to gambling. The gentlemen of our party went to observe the proceedings, but to-night there were only a few natives playing at fan-tan—a game which, though a great favorite with the natives, appears very stupid to a European. The croupier takes a handful of copper cash and throws it upon the table; he then with chop-sticks counts the coins by fours, the betting being upon the possible number of the remainder. It takes a long time to count a big handful, and you have only one, two, three, or four to back—no colors or combinations, as at *rouge-et-noir*, or *trente-et-quarante*.

At Macao the sleep-disturbing watchman, unlike those of Canton, come round every hour and beat two sharp taps on a drum at intervals of half a minute, compelling you to listen against your will, until the sound dies away in the distance for a brief interval.

Wednesday, March 7th.—We started soon after ten o'clock on another exploring expedition, going first in chairs through the town, and across the peninsula to where we left the steamer yesterday. Here we embarked —chairs, bearers, and all, in a junk, evidently cleaned up for the occasion, for it was in beautiful order, and mats were spread under an awning upon deck.

All along beneath the deck was a cabin, between two and three feet high, which contained the altar, the kitchen, and the sleeping and living apartments of the family. There was also a dear little baby, two months old, which seemed to take life very quietly, while its mother assisted its grandfather to row.

We soon reached the island of Chock-Sing-Toon, and disembarked at a small pier near a village, which looked more like sampans pulled up on the shore than huts or cottages. The children and I rode in chairs, while the gentlemen walked, first over a plain covered with scrubby palms, then through miles of well-cultivated plots of vegetable ground, till we reached a temple, built at the entrance to the valley for which we were bound. Thence the path wound beside the stream flowing from the mountains above, and the vegetation became extremely luxuriant and beautiful. Presently we came to a spot where a stone bridge spanned the torrent, with a temple on one side and a joss-house on the other. It was apparently a particularly holy place, for our men had all brought quantities of joss-sticks and sacred paper with them to burn. There was a sort of eating-house close by, where they remained whilst we climbed higher up to get a view. The path was well made, and evidently much used, judging from the large number of natural temples we found adapted and decorated among the rocks. As usual, our descent was a comparatively quick affair, and we soon found ourselves on board the junk on our way back to Macao, beating across the harbor.

Just before tiffin the yacht made her appearance, causing great excitement in the minds of the natives. The gig was soon lowered and came as close as she could. There was not water enough for her to come within four miles of the shore, but we went out to meet her occupants. Tom, who was one of them, looked so ill and miserable that I felt quite alarmed for a few minutes, till the Doctor comforted me by assurances that it was only the effect of the Chinese dinner last night—an explanation I had no difficulty in accepting as the correct one after perusing the bill of fare. In their desire to do him honor, and to give him pleasure, his hosts had provided the rarest delicacies, and of course he felt obliged to taste them all. Some of the dishes were excellent, but many of them were rather trying to a European digestion, especially the fungus and lichen. One sort had been grown on ice in the Antarctic Sea, the whale's sinews came from the Arctic Ocean, the shark's fins from the South Sea Islands, and the birds' nests were of a quality to be found only in one particular cave in one particular island. To drink, they had champagne in English glasses, and arrack in Chinese glasses. The whole dinner was eaten with chop-sticks, though spoons were allowed for the soup. After dinner there were some good speeches, the chief host expressing his deep regret that their manners and customs did not permit them to ask ladies, as they were particularly anxious to invite me, and had only abandoned the idea of doing so after considerable discussion. I append the bill of fare :—

A CHINESE BANQUET.

March 6, 1877.

BILL OF FARE.

4 courses of small bowls, one to each guest, viz.—

Bird's-nest Soup
Pigeon's Eggs
Ice Fungus (said to grow in ice)
Shark's Fins (chopped)

8 large bowls, viz.—

Stewed Shark's Fins
Fine Shell Fish
Mandarin Bird's Nest
Canton Fish Maw
Fish Brain
Meat Balls with Rock Fungus
Pigeons stewed with Wai Shan (a strengthening herb)
Stewed Mushroom

4 dishes, viz.—

Sliced Ham
Roast Mutton
Fowls
Roast Sucking Pig

1 large dish, viz.—

Boiled Rock Fish

8 small bowls, viz.—

Stewed Pig's Palate
Minced Quails
Stewed Fungus (another description)
Sinews of the Whale Fish
Rolled Roast Fowl
Sliced Teals
Stewed Duck's Paws
Peas stewed

We went all round the town, and then to see the ruins of the cathedral, and the traces of the destruction caused by the typhoon in 1874. Next we paid a visit to the garden of Camoëns, where he wrote his poems in exile.*

---

* Luis de Camoëns, a celebrated Portuguese poet, born about 1520; fought against the Moors, and in India; but was often in

The garden now belongs to a most courteous old Portuguese, with whom I managed, by the aid of a mixture of Spanish and French, to hold a conversation. The place where Camoëns's monument is erected commands, however, an extensive prospect, but we had already seen it, and as Tom was anxious to get clear of the islands before dark we were obliged to hasten away.

On reaching the yacht, after some delay in embarking, we slipped our anchor as quickly as possible, and soon found ourselves in a nasty rolling sea, which sent me to bed at once. Poor Tom, though he felt so ill that he could hardly hold his head up, was, however, obliged to remain on deck watching until nearly daylight; for rocks and islands abound in these seas, and no one on board could undertake the pilotage except himself.

Thursday, March 8th.—When I went on deck at half-past six o'clock there was nothing to be seen but a leaden sky, a cold gray rolling sea, and two fishing junks in the far distance, nor did the weather improve all day.

Friday, March 9th.—Everybody began to settle down to the usual sea occupations. There was a general hair-cutting all round, one of the sailors being a capital barber, and there is never time to attend to this matter when ashore. The wind was high and baffling all day. At night the Great Bear and the Southern Cross shone out with rivaling brilliancy: 'On either hand an old friend and a new.'

Saturday, March 10th.—A fine day, with a light fair breeze. Passed the island of Hainan, belonging to China, situated at the entrance of the Gulf of Tonquin, which, though very barren-looking, supports a population of 150,000.

---

trouble, and was frequently banished or imprisoned. During his exile in Macao he wrote his great poem 'The Lusiad,' in which he celebrates the principal events in Portuguese history.

Repacked the curiosities and purchases from Canton and Hongkong, and made up our accounts.

About noon we passed a tall bamboo sticking straight up out of the water, and wondered if it were the topmast of some unfortunate junk sunk on the Paranella Shoal. There were many flying-fish about, and the sunset was lovely.

Sunday, March 11th.—We feel that we are going south rapidly, for the heat increases day by day. The services were held on deck at eleven and four.

About five o'clock I heard cries of 'A turtle on the starboard bow,' 'A wreck on the starboard bow.' I rushed out to see what it was, and the men climbed into the rigging to obtain a better view of the object. It proved to be a large piece of wood, partially submerged, apparently about twenty or thirty feet long. The exposed part was covered with barnacles and seaweed, and there was a large iron ring attached to one end. We were sailing too fast to stop, or I should have liked to have sent a boat to examine this 'relic of the sea' more closely. These waifs and strays always set me thinking and wondering, and speculating as to what they were originally, whence they came, and all about them, till Tom declares I weave a complete legend for every bit of wood we meet floating about.

Tuesday, March 13th.—About 2.30 a.m. the main peak halyards were carried away. Soon after we gybed, and for two or three hours knocked about in the most unpleasant manner. At daybreak we made the island of Pulu Lapata, or Shoe Island, situated on the coast of Cochin China, looking snowy white in the early morning light.

The day was certainly warm, though we were gliding on steadily and pleasantly before the north-east monsoon.

Wednesday, March 14th.—The monsoon sends us along at the rate of from six to seven knots an hour, without the slightest trouble or inconvenience. There is an unexpected current, though, which sets us about twenty-five miles daily to the westward, notwithstanding the fact that a 'southerly current' is marked on the chart.

March 16*th*.—There was a general scribble going on all over the ship, in preparation for the post to-morrow, as we hope to make Singapore to-night, or very early in the morning. About noon Pulo-Aor was seen on our starboard bow. In the afternoon, being so near the Straits, the funnel was raised and steam got up. At midnight we made the Homburgh Light, and shortly afterwards passed a large steamer steering north. It was a glorious night, though very hot below, and I spent most of it on deck with Tom, observing the land as we slowly steamed ahead half speed.

CHAPTER XXIV.

SINGAPORE.

Betwixt them lawns, or level downs, and flocks
Grazing the tender herb, were interpos'd,
Or palmy hillock, or the flow'ry lap
Of some irriguous valley spread her store,
Flow'rs of all hues, and without thorn the rose.

Saturday, March 17*th.*—We were off Singapore during the night. At 5 a.m. the pilot came on board and took us into Tangong Pagar to coal alongside the wharf. We left the ship as soon as possible, and in about an hour we had taken forty-three tons of coal on board and nearly twenty tons of water. The work was rapidly performed by coolies. It was a great disappointment to be told by the harbor-master that the Governor of the Straits Settlement and Lady Jervoise were to leave at eleven o'clock for Johore. We determined to go straight to the Government House and make a morning call at the unearthly hour of 8 a.m. The drive from the wharf was full of beauty, novelty, and interest. We had not landed so near the line before, and the most tropical of tropical plants, trees, flowers, and ferns, were here to be seen, growing by the roadside on every bank and dustheap.

The natives, Malays, are a fine-looking, copper-colored race, wearing bright-colored sarongs and turbans. There are many Indians, too, from Madras, almost black, and swathed in the most graceful white muslin garments, when they are not too hard at work to wear anything at all. The young women are very good-looking. They wear not only one but several rings, and metal ornaments in their noses, and a profusion of metal bangles on their arms and legs, which jingle and jangle as they move.

The town of Singapore itself is not imposing, its streets, or rather roads of wooden huts and stone houses, being mixed together indiscriminately. Government House is on the outskirts of the city, in the midst of a beautiful park, which is kept in excellent order, the green turf being closely mown and dotted with tropical trees and bushes. The House itself is large and handsome, and contains splendid suites of lofty rooms, shaded by wide verandas, full of ferns and palms, looking deliciously green and cool. We found the Governor and his family did not start until 11.30, and they kindly begged us to return to breakfast at half-past nine, which we did. Before finally leaving, Sir William Jervoise sent for the Colonial Secretary, and asked him to look after us in his absence. He turned out to be an old schoolfellow and college friend of Tom's at Rugby and Oxford; so the meeting was a very pleasant one. As soon as the Governor and his suite had set off for Johore we went down into the hot dusty town to get our letters, parcels, and papers, and to look at the shops. There are not many Malay specialties to be bought here; most of the curiosities come from India, China, and Japan, with the exception of birds of Paradise from New Guinea, and beautiful bright birds of all colors and sizes from the various islands in the Malay Archipelago.

The north-east monsoon blows fresh and strong, but it was nevertheless terribly hot in the streets, and we were very glad to return to the cool, shady rooms at Government House, where we thoroughly appreciated the delights of the punkah.

There are very few European servants here, and they all have their own peons to wait on them, and carry an umbrella over them when they drive the carriage or go for a walk on their own account. Even the private soldier in Singapore has a punkah pulled over his bed at night. It is quite a sight to meet all the coolies leaving barracks at 5 a.m., when they have done punkah-pulling.

At four o'clock Mr. Douglas called to take us for a drive. We went first to the Botanical Gardens, and saw sago-palms and all sorts of tropical produce flourishing in perfection. There were many beautiful birds and beasts, Argus pheasants, Lyre birds, cuckoos, doves, and pigeons, more like parrots than doves in the gorgeous metallic luster of their plumage. The cages were large, and the inclosures in front full of Cape jasmine bushes (covered with buds) for the birds to peck at and eat.

From the gardens we went for a drive through the pretty villas that surround Singapore in every direction. Every house outside the town is built on a separate little hill in order to catch every breath of fresh air. There is generally rather a long drive up to the houses, and the public roads run along the valleys between them.

It was now dark, and we returned to dine at Government House.

Sunday, March 18*th*.—At six o'clock this morning Mabelle and I went ashore with the steward and the comprador to the market. It is a nice, clean, octagonal building, well supplied with vegetables and curious fruits. The latter are mostly brought from the other islands, as this is the worst season of the year in Singapore for fruit. I do not quite understand why this should be, for, as it is only a degree above the line, there is very little variation in the seasons here. The sun always rises and sets at six o'clock all the year round; for months they have a north-east monsoon, and then for months together a south-west monsoon.

We tasted many fruits new to us—delicious mangosteens, lacas, and other fruits whose names I could not ascertain. Lastly, we tried a durian, *the* fruit of the

East, as it is called by people who live here, and having got over the first horror of the onion-like odor, we found it by no means bad.

The fish market is the cleanest, and best arranged, and sweetest smelling that I ever went through. It is situated on a sort of open platform, under a thick thatched roof, built out over the sea, so that all the refuse is easily disposed of and washed away by the tide. From the platform on which it stands, two long jetties run some distance out into the sea, so that large fishing boats can come alongside and discharge their cargoes from the deep at the door of the market with scarcely any exposure to the rays of the tropical sun.

The poultry market is a curious place. On account of the intense heat everything is brought alive to the market, and the quacking, cackling, gobbling, and crowing that go on are really marvelous. The whole street is alive with birds in baskets, cages, and coops, or tied by the leg and thrown down anyhow. There were curious pheasants and jungle-fowl from Perak, doves, pigeons, quails, besides cockatoos, parrots, paroquets, and lories. They are all very tame and very cheap; and some of the scarlet lories, looking like a flame of fire, chatter in the most amusing way. I have a cage full of tiny parrots not bigger than bullfinches, of a dark green color, with dark red throats and blue heads, yellow marks on the back, and red and yellow tails. Having bought these, everybody seemed to think that I wanted an unlimited supply of birds, and soon we were surrounded by a chattering crowd, all with parrots in their hands and on their shoulders. It was a very amusing sight, though rather noisy, and the competition reduced the prices very much. Paroquets ranged from twelve to thirty cents apiece, talking parrots and cookatoos from one to five dollars. At last the venders became so energetic that I was glad to get into the gharry again, and drive away to a flower shop, where we bought some gardenias for one penny a dozen, beautifully fresh and fragrant, but with painfully short stalks.

Towards the end of the south-west monsoon, little native open boats arrive from the islands 1,500 to 3,000 miles to the southward of Singapore. Each has one little tripod mast. The whole family live on board. The sides of the boat cannot be seen for the multitude of cockatoos, parrots, paroquets, and birds of all sorts, fastened on little perches, with very short strings attached to them. The decks are covered with sandal-wood. The holds are full of spice, shells, feathers, and South Sea pearl shells. With this cargo they creep from island to island, and from creek to creek, before the monsoon, till they reach their destination. They stay a month or six weeks, change their goods for iron, nails, a certain amount of pale green or Indian red thread for weaving, and some pieces of Manchester cotton. They then go back with the north-east monsoon, selling their goods at the various islands on their homeward route. There are many Dutch ports nearer than Singapore, but they are over-regulated, and preference is given to the free English port, where the simple natives can do as they like so long as they do not transgress the laws.

As we were going on board, we met the Maharajah of Johore's servant, just going off with invitations to dinner, lunch, and breakfast for the next two days for all our party, and with all sorts of kind propositions for shooting and other amusements.

Some of our friends came off before luncheon to see the yacht, and we returned with them to tiffin at Government House. At four o'clock the carriage came round to take us to Johore. We wished good-by to Singapore and all our kind friends, and started on a lovely drive through the tropical scenery. There is a capital road, fifteen miles in length, across the island, and our little ponies rattled along at a good pace. There was a pleasant breeze and not much dust, no sun, and a stream ran the whole way by the side of the road. The acacia flamboyante—that splendid tree which came originally from Rangoon and Sumatra—was planted alongside the road, and produced a most charming effect. It is a large tree, with large leaves of the most delicate green; on its topmost boughs grow gorgeous clusters of scarlet flowers with yellow centers, and the effect of these scarlet plumes tossing in the air is truly beautiful. As we were driving along we espied a splendid butterfly, with wings about ten inches long. Mr. Bingham jumped out of the carriage and knocked it down with his hat; but it was so like the color of leaves in grass that in the twilight nobody could distinguish it, and, to our great disappointment, we could not find it. We were equally unsuccessful in our attempted capture of a water-snake a couple of feet long. We threw sticks and stones, and our syce waded into the stream, but all to no purpose; it glided away into some safe little hole under the bank.

We reached the sea-shore about six o'clock, and found the Maharajah's steam-launch waiting to convey us across the Straits to the mainland. These Straits used to be the old route to Singapore, and are somewhat intricate. Tom engaged a very good pilot to bring the yacht round, but at the last moment thought that he should like to bring her himself; the result being that he arrived rather late for dinner. The Maharajah and most of the party were out shooting when we arrived; but Sir William Jervoise met us and showed us round the place, and also arranged about rooms for us to dress in. Johore is a charming place; the Straits are so narrow and full of bends that they look more like a peaceful river or inland lake in the heart of a tropical forest than an arm of the mighty ocean. As we approached we had observed a good deal of smoke rising from the jungle, and as the shades of evening closed over the scene, we could see the lurid glare of two extensive fires.

We sat down thirty to dinner at eight o'clock. There were the Maharajah's brothers, the Prime Minister, Harkim, or Judge, and several other Malay chiefs, the Governor of the Straits Settlements, his family and suite, and one or two people from Singapore. The dinner was cooked and served in European style; the table decorated with gold and silver épergnes full of flowers, on velvet stands, and with heaps of small cut-flower glasses full of jasmine. We were waited on by the Malay servants of the establishment, dressed in gray and yellow, and by the Governor's Madras servants, in white and scarlet. The Maharajah and his native guests were all in English evening dress, with white waistcoats, bright turbans, and sarongs. The room was large and open on all sides, and the fresh evening breeze, in addition to the numerous punkahs, made it delightfully cool. The Maharajah is a strict Mohammedan himself, and drinks nothing but water. I spent the three hours during which the dinner lasted in very pleasant conversation with my two neighbors. We returned on board soon after eleven o'clock.

Monday, March 19*th.*—Mabelle and I went ashore at six o'clock for a drive. It was a glorious morning, with a delightfully cool breeze, and the excursion was most enjoyable. We drove first through the old town of Johore, once of considerable importance, and still a place of trade for opium, indigo, pepper, and other tropical products. Nutmeg and maize used to be the great articles of export, but latterly the growth has failed, and, instead of the groves we had expected to see, there were only solitary trees. After leaving the town we went along a good road for some distance, with cottages and clearings on either side, until we came to a pepper and gambir plantation. The two crops are cultivated together, and both are grown on the edge of the jungle, for the sake of the wood, which is burned in the preparation of the gambir. I confess that I had never heard of the latter substance before, but I find that it is largely exported to Europe, where it is occasionally employed for giving weight to silks, and for tanning purposes.

The pepper garden we saw was many acres in extent. Some of the trees in the forest close by are very fine, especially the camphor-wood, and the great red, purple, and copper-colored oleanders, which grow in clumps twenty and thirty feet in height. The orchids with which all the trees were covered, hanging down in long tassels of lovely colors, or spread out like great spotted butterflies and insects, were most lovely of all. By far the most abundant was the white phalænopsis, with great drooping sprays of pure white waxy blossoms, some delicately streaked with crimson, others with yellow. It was a genuine jungle, and we were told that it is the resort of numerous tigers and elephants, and that snakes abound.

On our way back through the town we stopped to see the process of opium-making. This drug is brought from India in an almost raw state, rolled up in balls, about the size of billiard balls, and wrapped in its own leaves. Here it is boiled down, several times refined, and prepared for smoking. The traffic in it forms a very profitable monopoly, which is shared in Singapore between the English Government and the Maharajah of Johore.

We also saw indigo growing; the dye is prepared very much in the same way as the gambir. That grown here is not so good as that which comes from India, and it is therefore not much exported, though it is used by the innumerable Chinese in the Malay peninsula to dye all their clothes, which are invariably of some deep shade of blue. We saw sago-palms growing, but the mill was not working, so that we could not see the process of manufacture; but it seems to be very similar to the preparation of tapioca, which we had seen in Brazil.

On our passage through the town we went to look at a large gambling establishment; of course no one was playing so early in the morning, but in the evening it is always densely crowded, and is a great source of profit to the proprietor. I could not manage to make out exactly from the description what the game they play is like, but it was not fan-tan. We now left the carriage, and strolled to see the people, the shops, and the market. I bought all sorts of common curiosities, little articles of everyday life, some of which will be sure to amuse and interest my English friends. Among my purchases were a wooden pillow, some joss candles, a two-stringed fiddle, and a few preserved eggs, which they say are over a hundred years old. The eggs are certainly nasty enough for anything; still it seems strange that so thrifty a people as the Chinese should allow so much capital to lie dormant —literally buried in the earth.

At half-past nine o'clock the Maharajah, with the Governor and all his guests, came on board. His Highness inspected the yacht with the utmost minuteness and interest, though his Mohammedan ideas about women were considerably troubled when he was told that I had had a great deal to do with the designing and arrangement of the interior. At half-past eleven the party left, and an hour afterwards we went to make our adieux to the Maharajah.

On our departure the Maharajah ordered twenty coolies to accompany us, laden with fragrant tropical plants. He also gave me some splendid Malay silk sarongs, grown, made, and woven in his kingdom, a pair of tusks of an elephant shot within a mile of the house, besides a live little beast, not an alligator, and not an armadillo or a lizard; in fact I do not know what it is; it clings round my arm just like a bracelet, and it was sent as a present by the ex-Sultan of Johore. Having said farewell to our kind host and other friends, we pushed off from the shore, and embarked on board the yacht; the anchor was up, and by five o'clock a bend in the Straits hid hospitable and pleasant Johore from our view, and all we could see was the special steamer on her way back to Singapore with the Maharajah's guests on board. At Tanjore we dropped our funny little pilot, and proceeded on our course towards Penang. The Straits are quite lovely, and fully repaid the trouble and time involved in the detour made to visit them. The sun set and the young moon arose over as lovely a tropical scene as you can possibly imagine.

Tuesday, March 20th.—At 5.30, when we were called, the Doctor came and announced that he had something very important to communicate to us. This proved to be that one of our men was suffering from small-pox, and not from rheumatic fever, as had been supposed. My first thought was that Muriel had been with the Doctor to see him yesterday evening; my next, that many men had been sleeping in the same part of the vessel with him; my third, that for his greater comfort he had been each day in our part of the ship; and my fourth, what was to be done now? After a short consultation, Tom decided to alter our course for Malacca, where we arrived at half-past nine; the Doctor at once went on shore in a native prahu to make the best arrangements he could under the circumstances. He was fortunate enough to find Dr. Simon, nephew of the celebrated surgeon of the same name, installed as head physician at the civil hospital here. He came off at once with the hospital boat, and, having visited the invalid, declared his illness to be a very mild case of small-pox. He had brought off some lymph with him, and recommended us all to be re-vaccinated. He had also brought sundry disinfectants, and gave instructions about fumigating and disinfecting the yacht. All the men were called upon the quarter-deck, and addressed by Tom, and we were surprised to find what a large proportion of them objected to the operation of vaccination. At last, however, the prejudices of all of them, except two, were overcome. One of the latter had promised his grandfather that he never would be vaccinated under any circumstances, while another would consent to be inoculated, but would not be vaccinated. We had consulted our own medical man before leaving England, and knew that for ourselves the operation was not necessary, but we nevertheless underwent it *pour encourager les autres.* While the Doctor was on shore we had been surrounded by boats bringing monkeys, birds, ratan and Malacca canes, fruit, rice, &c., to sell, and as I did not care to go ashore, thinking there might be some bother about quarantine, we made bargains over the side of the yacht with the traders, the result being that seven monkeys, about fifty birds, of sorts, and innumerable bundles of canes, were added to the stock on board. In the meantime Dr. Simon had removed our invalid to the hospital.

Malacca looks exceedingly pretty from the sea. It is a regular Malay village, consisting of huts, built on piles close to the water, overshadowed by cocoa palms and other forms of tropical vegetation. Mount Ofia rises in the distance behind; there are many green islands, too, in the harbor. By one o'clock we were again under way, and once more *en route* for Penang.

Wednesday, March 21st.—During the night we had heavy thunderstorms. About 11 a.m. we passed a piece of drift-wood with a bird perched on the top, presenting a most curious effect. Several of the men on board mistook it for the back fin of a large shark. About 5 p.m. we made the island of Penang. After sunset it became very hazy, and we crept slowly up, afraid of injuring the numerous stake nets that are set about the Straits most promiscuously, and without any lights to mark their position. Before midnight we had dropped our anchor.

Thursday, March 22d.—At 5 a.m., when we were called, the whole sky was overcast with a lurid glare, and the atmosphere was thick, as if with the fumes of some vast conflagration. As the sun rose in raging fierceness, the sky cleared, and became of a deep, clear, transparent blue. The island of Penang is very beautiful, especially in the early morning light. It was fortunate we did not try to come in last night, as we could now see that we must inevitably have run through some of the innumerable stake nets I mentioned. As we approached Georgetown, the capital of the province, we passed many steamers and sailing ships at anchor in the roads. A pilot offered his services, but Tom declined them with thanks, and soon afterwards skillfully brought us up close in shore in the crowded roadstead. The harbor-master sent off, as did also the mail-master, but no Board of Health officials appeared; so after some delay, the Doctor went on shore to find the local medical man, promising shortly to return. He did not, however, reappear, and after waiting a couple of hours, we landed without opposition. We packed off all the servants for a run on shore, and had all the fires put out in order to cool the ship. Our first inquiry was for a hotel where we could breakfast, and we were recommended to go to the Hôtel de l'Europe.

Our demands for breakfast were met at first with the reply that it was too late, and that we must wait till one-o'clock tiffin; but a little persuasion induced the manager to find some cold meat, eggs, and lemonade. We afterwards drove out to one or two shops, but anything so hopeless as the stores here I never saw. Not a single curiosity could we find, not even a bird. We drove round the town, and out to the Governor's house; he was away, but we were most kindly received by Mrs. Anson and his daughter, and strongly recommended by them to make an expedition to the bungalow at the top of the hill. In about an hour and a half, always ascending, we reached the Governor's bungalow, situated in a charming spot, where the difference of 10° in the temperature, caused by being 1,500 feet higher up, is a great boon. After tiffin and a rest at the hotel, a carriage came to take us to the foot of the hill, about four miles from the town. We went first to a large Jesuit establishment, where some most benevolent old priests were teaching a large number of Malay boys reading, writing, and geography. Then we went a little farther, and, in a small wooden house, under the cocoa-trees, at last found some of the little humming-birds for which the Malay Archipelago is famous. They glisten with a marvelous metallic luster all over their bodies, instead of only in patches, as one sees upon those in South America and the West Indies. The drive was intensely tropical in character, until we reached the waterfall, where we left the carriage and got into chairs, each carried by six coolies. The scenery all about the waterfall is lovely, and a large stream of sparkling, cool, clear water tumbling over the rocks was most refreshing to look at. Many people who have business in Penang live up here, riding up and down morning and evening, for the sake of the cool, refreshing night air. One of the most curious things in vegetation which strikes our English eyes is the extraordinary abundance of the sensitive plant. It is interwoven with all the grass, and grows thickly in all the hedgerows. In the neatly kept turf, round the Government bungalow, its long, creeping, prickly stems, acacia-like leaves, and little fluffy mauve balls of flowers are so numerous, that, walking up and down the croquet lawn, it appears to be bowing before you, for the delicate plants are sensible of even an approaching footstep, and shut up and hide their tiny leaves among the grass long before you really reach them.

From the top of the hill you can see ninety miles in the clear atmosphere, far away across the Straits of Perak to the mainland. We could not stay long, and were carried down the hill backwards, as our bearers were afraid of our tumbling out of the chairs if we traveled forwards. The tropical vegetation is even more striking here, but, alas! it is already losing its novelty to us. Those were indeed pleasant days, when everything was new and strange; it seems now almost as if years, not months, had gone past since we first entered these latitudes. We found the carriage waiting for us when we arrived at the bottom of the hill about seven o'clock, and it was not long before we reached the town.

The glowworms and fireflies were numerous. The natives were cooking their evening meal on the ground beneath the tall palm-trees as we passed, with the glare of the fires lighting up the picturesque huts, their dark figures relieved by their white and scarlet turbans and waist-cloth. The whole scene put us very much in mind of the old familiar pictures of India, the lithe figures of the natives looking like beautiful bronze statues, the rough country carts, drawn by buffaloes without harness, but dragging by their hump, and driven by black-skinned natives armed with a long goad. We went straight to the jetty, and found to our surprise that in the roads there was quite a breeze blowing, and a very strong tide running against it, which made the sea almost rough.

Mrs. and Miss Anson, Mr. Talbot, and other friends, dined with us. At eleven they landed, and we weighed anchor, and were soon gliding through the Straits of Malacca, shaping for Acheen Head, *en route* to Galle.

It seems strange that an important English settlement like Penang, where so many large steamers and ships are constantly calling, should be without lights or quarantine laws. We afterwards learned on shore that the local government had already surveyed and fixed a place for two leading lights. The reason why no health officers came off to us this morning was probably that, small-pox and cholera both being prevalent in the town, they thought that the fewer questions they asked, and the less they saw of incoming vessels, the better.

Friday, March 23*d.*—A broiling day, everybody panting, parrots and paroquets dying. We passed a large bark with every sail set, although it was a flat calm, which made us rejoice in the possession of steam-power. Several people on board are very unwell, and the engineer is really ill. It is depressing to speculate what would become of us if anything went wrong in the engine-room department, and if we should be reduced to sail-power alone in this region of calmness. At last even I know what it is to be too hot, and am quite knocked up with my short experience.

Saturday, March 24th.—Another flat calm. The after-forecastle having been battened down and fumigated for

How the Journal was written.

the last seventy-two hours, was to-day opened, and its contents brought up on deck, some to be thrown overboard, and others to be washed with carbolic acid. I never saw such quantities of things as were turned out; they covered the whole deck, and it seemed as if their cubic capacity must be far greater than that of the place in which they had been stowed. Besides the beds and tables of eight men, there were forty-eight birds, four monkeys, two cockatoos, and a tortoise, besides Japanese cabinets and boxes of clothes, books, china, coral, shells, and all sorts of imaginable and unimaginable things. One poor tortoise had been killed and bleached white by the chlorine gas.

Sunday, March 25th.—Hotter than ever. It was quite impossible to have service either on deck or below. We always observe Sunday by showing a little extra attention to dress, and, as far as the gentlemen are concerned, a little more care in the matter of shaving. On other days I fear our toilets would hardly pass muster in civilized society. Tom set the example of leaving off collars, coats, and waistcoats; so shirts and trousers are now the order of the day. The children wear grass-cloth pinafores and very little else, no shoes or stockings, Manilla or Chinese slippers being worn by those who dislike bare feet. I find my Tahitian and Hawaiian dresses invaluable; they are really cool, loose, and comfortable, and I scarcely ever wear anything else.

We passed a large steamer about 7.30 a.m., and in the afternoon altered our course to speak the 'Middlesex,' of London, bound to the Channel for orders. We had quite a long conversation with the captain, and parted with mutual good wishes for a pleasant voyage. It was a lovely moonlight night, but very hot, though we found a delightful sleeping-place beneath the awning on deck.

Monday, March 26th.—The sun appeared to rise even fiercer and hotter than ever this morning. I have been very anxious for the last few days about Baby, who has been cutting some teeth and has suffered from a rash. Muriel has been bitten all over by mosquitoes, and Mabelle has also suffered from heat-rash. Just now every little ailment suggests small-pox to our minds.

About noon, when in latitude 6.25 north, and in longitude 88.25 east, we began to encounter a great deal of drift-wood, many large trees, branches, plants, leaves, nautilus shells, backbones of cuttlefish, and, in addition, large quantities of yellow spawn, evidently deposited by some fish of large size. The spawn appeared to be of a very solid, consistent character, like large yellow grapes, connected together in a sort of gelatinous mass. It formed a continuous wide yellow streak perhaps half a mile in length, and with the bits of wood and branches sticking up in its midst at intervals, it would not have required a very lively imagination to fashion it at a little distance into a sea serpent. Where does all this *débris* come from? was the question asked by everybody. Out of the Bay of Bengal probably, judging from the direction of the current. We wondered if it could possibly be the remains of some of the trees uprooted by the last great cyclone.

At 1.30 p.m. a man cried out from the rigging, 'Boat on the starboard bow!' a cry that produced great excitement immediately; our course was altered and telescopes and glasses brought to bear upon the object in question. Every one on board, except our old sailing-master, said it was a native boat. Some even said that they could see a man on board waving something. Powell alone declared it to be the root of a palm from the Bay of Bengal, and he proved right. A very large root it was, with one single stem and a few leaves hanging down, which had exactly the appearance of broken masts, tattered sails, and torn rigging. We went close alongside to have a good look at it; the water was as clear as crystal, and beneath the surface were hundreds of beautifully colored fish, greedily devouring something—I suppose small insects, or fish entangled among the roots.

Tuesday, March 27th.—It requires a great effort to do anything, except before sunrise or after sunset, owing to the intense heat; and when one is not feeling well it makes exertion still more difficult. At night the heat below is simply unbearable; the cabins are deserted, and all mattresses are brought up on deck.

CHAPTER XXV.

CEYLON.

> *Thus was this place*
> *A happy rural seat of various views,*
> *Groves whose rich trees wept odorous gums and balm,*
> *Others, whose fruit, burnish'd with golden rind,*
> *Hung amiable, Hesperian fables true.*

Wednesday, March 28th.—At midnight the wind was slightly ahead, and we could distinctly smell the fragrant breezes and spicy odors of Céylon. We made the eastern side of the island at daylight, and coasted along its palm-fringed shores all day. I had been very unwell for some days past, but this delightful indication of our near approach to the land seemed to do me good at once. If only the interior is as beautiful as what we can see from the deck of the yacht, my expectations will be fully realized, brilliant as they are.

As the sun set, the beauty of the scene from the deck of the yacht seemed to increase. We proceeded slowly, and at about nine o'clock were in the roads of Galle and could see the ships at anchor. Tom did not like to venture farther in the dark without a pilot, and accordingly told the signal-man to make signals for one; but being impatient, he sent up a rocket, besides burning blue lights, a mistake which had the effect of bringing the first officer of the P. and O. steamship 'Poonah' on board, who thought perhaps we had got aground or were in trouble of some sort. He also informed us that pilots never came off after dark, and kindly offered to show us a good anchorage for the night.

Thursday, March 29th.—The pilot came off early, and soon after six we dropped anchor in Galle harbor. The entrance is fine, and the bay one of the most beautiful in the world. The picturesque town, with its old buildings, and the white surf dashing in among the splendid cocoa-trees which grow down to the water's edge, combined to make up a charming picture. We went on board the 'Poonah' to breakfast as arranged, and afterwards all over the ship, which is in splendid order. Thence we went ashore to the Oriental Company's Hotel, a most comfortable building, with a large, shady veranda, which to-day was crowded by passengers from the 'Poonah.' At tiffin there was a great crowd, and we met some old friends. At three o'clock we returned to the yacht, to show her to the captain of the 'Poonah' and some of his friends, and an hour later we started in two carriages for a drive to Wockwalla, a hill commanding a splendid view. The drive was delightful, and the vegetation more beautiful than any we have seen since leaving Tahiti, but it would have been more enjoyable if we had not been so pestered by boys selling flowers and bunches of mace in various stages of development. It certainly is very pretty when the peach-like fruit is half open and shows the network of scarlet mace surrounding the brown nutmeg within. From Wockwalla the view is lovely, over paddy-fields, jungle, and virgin forest, up to the hills close by and to the mountains beyond. There is a small refreshment-room at the top of the hill, kept by a nice little mulatto woman and her husband. Here we drank lemonade, ate mangoes, and watched the sun gradually declining, but we were obliged to leave before it had set, as we wanted to visit the cinnamon gardens on our way back. The prettiest thing in the whole scene was the river running through the middle of the landscape, and the white-winged, scarlet-bodied cranes, disporting themselves along the banks among the dark green foliage and light green shoots of the crimson-tipped cinnamon-trees. We had a glorious drive home along the sea-shore under cocoanut-trees, among which the fireflies flitted, and through which we could see the red and purple afterglow of the sunset. Ceylon is, as every one knows, celebrated for its real gems, and almost as much for the wonderful imitations offered for sale by the natives. Some are made in Birmingham and exported, but many are made here and in India, and are far better in appearance than ours, or even those of Paris. More than once in the course of our drive, half-naked Indians produced from their waist-cloths rubies, sapphires, and emeralds for which they asked from one to four thousand rupees, and gratefully took fourpence, after a long run with the carriage, and much vociferation and gesticulation. After *table-d'hôte* dinner at the hotel we went off to the yacht in a pilot boat; the buoys were all illuminated, and boats with four or five men in them, provided with torches, were in readiness to show us the right way out. By ten o'clock we were outside the harbor and on our way to Colombo.

Friday, March 30th.—It rained heavily during the night, and we were obliged to sleep in the deck-house instead of on deck. At daylight all was again bright and beautiful, and the cocoanut-clad coast of Ceylon looked most fascinating in the early morning light. About ten o'clock we dropped our anchor in the harbor at Colombo, which was crowded with shipping. 175,000 coolies have been landed here within the last two or three months; consequently labor is very cheap this year in the coffee plantations.

The instant we anchored we were of course surrounded by boats selling every possible commodity and curiosity, carved ebony, ivory, sandal-wood, and models of the curious boats in use here. These boats are very long and narrow, with an enormous outrigger and large sail, and when it is very rough, nearly the whole of the crew of the boat go out one by one, and sit on the outrigger to keep it in the water, from which springs the Cingalese saying,

'One man, two men, four men breeze.' The heat was intense, though there was a pleasant breeze under the awning on deck; we therefore amused ourselves by looking over the side and bargaining with the natives, until our letters, which we had sent for, arrived. About one o'clock we went ashore, encountering on our way some exceedingly dreadful smells, wafted from ships laden with guano, bones, and other odoriferous cargoes. The inner harbor is unsavory and unwholesome to the last degree, and is just now crowded with many natives of various castes from the South of India.

Colombo is rather a European-looking town, with fine buildings and many open green spaces, where there were actually soldiers playing cricket, with great energy, under the fierce rays of the midday sun. We went at once to a hotel and rested; loitering after tiffin in the veranda, which was as usual crowded with sellers of all sorts of Indian things. Most of the day was spent in driving about, and having made our arrangements for an early start to-morrow, we then walked down to the harbor, getting drenched on our way by a tremendous thunderstorm.

Saturday, March 31st.—Up early, and after rather a scramble we went ashore at seven o'clock, just in time to start by the first train to Kandy. There was not much time to spare, and we therefore had to pay sovereigns for our tickets instead of changing them for rupees, thereby receiving only ten instead of eleven and a half, the current rate of exchange that day. It seemed rather sharp practice on the part of the railway company (*alias* the Government) to take sovereigns in at the window at ten rupees, and sell them at the door for eleven and a half, to speculators waiting ready and eager to clutch and sell them again at an infinitesimally small profit.

The line to Kandy is always described as one of the most beautiful railways in the world, and it certainly deserves the character. The first part of the journey is across jungle and through plains; then one goes climbing up and up, looking down on all the beauties of tropical vegetation, to distant mountains shimmering in the glare and haze of the burning sun. The carriages were well ventilated and provided with double roofs, and were really tolerably cool.

About nine o'clock we reached Ambepussa, and the scenery increased in beauty from this point. A couple of hours later we reached Peradeniya, the junction for Gampola. Here most of the passengers got out, bound for Neuera-ellia, the sanitarium of Ceylon, 7,000 feet above the sea. Soon after leaving the station, we passed the Satinwood Bridge. Here we had a glimpse of the botanical garden at Kandy, and soon afterwards reached the station. We were at once rushed at by two telegraph boys, each with a telegram of hospitable invitation, whilst a third friend met us with his carriage, and asked us to go at once to his house, a few miles out of Kandy. We hesitated to avail ourselves of his kind offer, as we were such a large party; but he insisted, and at once set off to make things ready for us, whilst we went to breakfast and rest at a noisy, dirty, and uncomfortable hotel. It was too hot to do anything except to sit in the veranda and watch planter after planter come in for an iced drink at the bar. The town is quite full for Easter, partly for the amusements and partly for the Church services; for on many of the coffee estates there is no church within a reasonable distance.

About four o'clock the carriage came round for us, and having dispatched the luggage in a gharry, we drove round the lovely lake, and so out to Peradeniya, where our friend lives, close to the Botanic Gardens. Many of the huts and cottages by the roadside have 'small-pox' written upon them in large letters, in three languages, English, Sanskrit, and Cingalese, a very sensible precaution, for the natives are seldom vaccinated, and this terrible disease is a real scourge among them. Having reached the charming bungalow, it was a real luxury to lounge in a comfortable easy-chair in a deep cool veranda, and to inhale the fragrance of the flowers, whilst lazily watching the setting of the sun. Directly it dipped below the horizon, glowworms and fireflies came out, bright and numerous as though the stars had come down to tread, or rather fly, a fairy dance among the branches of the tall palm-trees high overhead. Our rooms were most comfortable, and the baths delicious. After dinner we all adjourned once more to the veranda to watch the dancing fireflies, the lightning, and the heavy thunder-clouds, and enjoy the cool evening breeze. You in England who have never been in the tropics cannot appreciate the intense delight of that sensation. Then we went to bed, and passed a most luxurious night of cool and comfortable sleep, not tossing restlessly about, as we had been doing for some time past.

Sunday, April 1st.—I awoke before daylight. Our bed faced the windows, which were wide open, without blinds, curtains, or shutters, and I lay and watched the light gradually creeping over the trees, landscape, and garden, and the sun rising glorious from behind the distant mountains, shining brightly into the garden, drawing out a thousand fresh fragrances from every leaf and flower.

By seven o'clock we found ourselves enjoying an early tea within the pretty bungalow in the center of the Botanic Gardens, and thoroughly appreciating delicious fresh butter and cream, the first we have tasted for ages. We went for the most delightful stroll afterwards, and saw for the first time many botanical curiosities, and several familiar old friends growing in greater luxuriance than our eyes are even yet accustomed to. The groups of palms were most beautiful. I never saw anything finer than the tallipot-palm, and the areca, with the beetle-vine climbing round it; besides splendid specimens of the kitool or jaggery-palm. Then there was the palmyra, which to the inhabitant of the North of Ceylon is what the cocoanut is to the inhabitant of the South—food, clothing, and lodging. The pitcher-plants and the rare scarlet amherstia looked lovely, as did also the great groups of yellow and green stemmed bamboos. There were magnolias, shaddocks, hibiscus, the almost too fragrant yellow-flowered champac, sacred to Hindoo mythology; nutmeg and cinnamon trees, tea and coffee, and every other conceivable plant and tree, growing in the wildest luxuriance. Through the center of the gardens flows the river Ambang Ganga, and the whole 140 acres are laid out so like an English park that, were it not for the unfamiliar foliage, you might fancy yourself at home.

We drove back to our host's to breakfast, and directly afterwards started in two carriages to go to church at Kandy. The church is a fine large building, lofty, and cool, and well ventilated. This being Easter Sunday, the building was lavishly decorated with palms and flowers. The service was well performed, and the singing was excellent. The sparrows flew in and out by the open doors and windows. One of the birds was building a nest in a corner, and during the service she added to it a marabout feather, a scrap of lace, and an end of pink ribbon. It will be a curious nest when finished, if she adds at this rate to her miscellaneous collection.

After church we walked to the Government House. Sir William Gregory is, unfortunately for us, away in Australia, and will not return till just after our departure. The entrance to it was gay with gorgeous scarlet lilies, brought over by some former Governor from South America. It is a very fine house, but unfinished. We wandered through the ' banquet halls deserted,' and then sat a little while in the broad, cool, airy veranda looking into the beautiful garden and on to the mountain beyond.

At half-past eleven it was time to leave this delightfully cool, retired spot, and to drive to a very pleasant luncheon, served on a polished round walnut-wood table, without any tablecloth, a novel and pretty plan in so hot a climate. As soon as it became sufficiently cool we went on round the upper lake and to the hills above, whence we looked down upon Kandy, one of the most charmingly placed cities in the world. As we came back we stopped for a few minutes at the Court, a very fair specimen of florid Hindoo architecture, where the judges sit, and justice of all kinds is administered, and where the Prince of Wales held the installation of the Order of St. Michael and St. George during his visit. We also looked in at some of the bazaars, to examine the brass chatties and straw-work. Then came another delicious rest in the veranda among the flowers until it was time for dinner. Such flowers as they are! The Cape jessamines are in full beauty just now, and our host breaks off for us great branches laden with the fragrant bloom.

Monday, April 2d.—Before breakfast I took a stroll all round the place, with our host, to look at his numerous pets, which include spotted deer, monkeys, and all sorts of other creatures. We also went to the stables, and saw first the horses, and the horsekeepers with their pretty Indian wives and children. Then we wandered down to the bamboo-fringed shores of the river, which rises in the mountains here, and flows right through the island to Trincomalee.

At eleven o'clock Tom and I said 'good-by' to the rest of the party, and went by train to Gampola, to take the coach to Neuera-ellia, where we were to stay with an old friend. We went only a dozen miles in the train, and then were turned out into what is called a coach, but is really a very small rough wagonette, capable of holding six people with tolerable comfort, but into which seven, eight, and even nine were crammed. By the time the vehicle was fully laden, we found there was positively no room for even the one box into which Tom's things and my own had all been packed; so we had to take out indispensable necessaries, and tie them up in a bundle like true sailors out for a holiday, leaving our box behind, in charge of the station-master, until our return. The first part of the drive was not very interesting, the road passing only through paddy-fields and endless tea and coffee plantations. We reached Pusillawa about two o'clock, where we found a rough and ready sort of breakfast awaiting us. Thence we had a steep climb through some of the finest coffee estates in Ceylon, belonging to the Rothschilds, until we reached Rangbodde. Here there was another delay of half an hour; but although we were anxious to get on, to arrive in time for dinner, it was impossible to regret stopping amidst this lovely scenery. The house which serves as a resting-place is a wretched affair, but the view from the veranda in front is superb. A large river falls headlong over the steep wall of rock, forming three splendid waterfalls, which, uniting and rushing under a fine one-arched bridge, complete this scene of beauty and grandeur.

We were due at Neuera-ellia at six, but we had only one pair of horses to drag our heavy load up the steep mountain road, and the poor creatures jibbed, kicked over the traces, broke them three times, and more than once were so near going over the edge of the precipice that I jumped out, and the other passengers, all gentlemen, walked the whole of that stage. The next was no better, the fresh pair of horses jibbing and kicking worse than ever. At last one kicked himself free of all the harness, and fell on his back in a deep ditch. If it had not been so tiresome, it really would have been very laughable, especially as everybody was more or less afraid of the poor horse's heels, and did not in the least know how to extricate him.

In this dilemma our hunting experiences came in usefully, for with the aid of a trace, instead of a stirrup leather, passed round his neck, half a dozen men managed to haul the horse on to his legs again; but the pitchy darkness rendered the repair of damages an exceedingly difficult task. The horses, moreover, even when once more in their proper position, declined to move, but the gentlemen pushed and the drivers flogged and shouted, and very slowly and with many stops we ultimately reached the end of that stage. Here we found a young horse, who had no idea at all of harness; so after a vain attempt to utilize his services, another was sent for, thus causing further delay.

It was now nine o'clock, and we were all utterly exhausted. We managed to procure from a cottage some new-laid eggs and cold spring water, and these eaten raw, with a little brandy from a hunting flask, seemed to refresh us all. There was again a difficulty in starting, but, once fairly under way, the road was not so steep and the horses went better. I was now so tired, and had grown so accustomed to hairbreadth escapes, that, however near we went to the edge of the precipice, I did not feel capable of jumping out, but sat still and watched listlessly, wondering whether we should really go over or not. After many delays we reached Head-quarter House, where the warmth of the welcome our old friend gave us soon made us forget how tired we were. They had waited dinner until half-past seven, and had then given us up. There were blazing wood fires both in the drawing-room and in our bedroom, and in five minutes a most welcome dinner was put before us. Afterwards we could have staid and chatted till midnight, but we were promptly sent off to bed, and desired to reserve the rest of our news until morning.

Tuesday, April 3d.—A ten-o'clock breakfast afforded us ample opportunity for a delicious rest and letter-writing beforehand. Afterwards we strolled round the garden, full of English flowers, roses, carnations, mignonnette, and sweet peas. Tom and the gentlemen went for a walk, whilst we ladies rested and chatted and wrote letters.

After lunch we all started—a large party—to go to the

athletic sports on the race-course, where an impromptu sort of grand-stand had been erected—literally a stand, for there were no seats. There were a great many people, and the regimental band played very well. To us it appeared a warm, damp day, although the weather was much cooler than any we have felt lately. This is *the* week of the year, and everybody is here from all parts of the island. People who have been long resident in the tropics seem to find it very cold; for the men wore great-coats and ulsters, and many of the ladies velvet and sables, or sealskin jackets. On the way back from the sports we drove round to see something of the settlement; it cannot be called a town, for though there are a good many people and houses, no two are within half a mile of one another. There are two packs of hounds kept here, one to hunt the big elk, the other a pack of harriers. The land-leeches, which abound in this neighborhood, are a great plague to horses, men, and hounds. It rained last night, and I was specially cautioned not to go on the grass or to pick flowers, as these horrid creatures fix on one's ankle or arm without the slightest warning. I have only seen one, I am thankful to say, and have escaped a bite; but everybody seems to dread and dislike them.

After dinner we went to a very pleasant ball, given by the Jinkhana Club, at the barracks. The room was prettily decorated with the racing jackets and caps of the riders in the races, and with scarlet wreaths of geranium and hibiscus mingled with lycopodium ferns and selaginella. We did not remain very late at the ball, as we had to make an early start next morning; but the drive home in the moonlight was almost as pleasant as any part of the entertainment.

Wednesday, April 4th.—We were called at four o'clock, and breakfasted at five, everybody appearing either in dressing-gowns or in habits to see us set off. They all tried to persuade us to stay for the meet of the hounds at the house to-day. Another ball to-night, and more races, and another ball to-morrow; but we are homeward bound, and must hurry on. It was a lovely morning, and we waited with great patience at the post-house for at least an hour and a half, and watched the hounds come out, meet, find, and hunt a hare up and down, and across the valley, with merry ringing notes that made us long to be on horseback.

We saw all the race-horses returning from their morning gallop, and were enlightened by the syces as to their names and respective owners. There were several people, a great deal of luggage, and, though last not least, Her Majesty's mails, all waiting, like us, for the coach. About a quarter to seven a message arrived, to the effect that the horses would *not* come up the hill, they had been jibbing for more than an hour, so would we kindly go down to the coach. A swarm of coolies immediately appeared from some mysterious hiding-place, and conveyed us all, bag and baggage, down the hill, and packed us into the coach. Even this concession on our part did not induce the horses to make up their minds to move for at least another quarter of an hour. Then we had to stop at the hotel to pick up somebody else; but at last we had fairly started, eleven people in all, some inside and some perched on a box behind. The horses were worse than ever, tired to death, poor things; and as one lady passenger was very nervous and insisted on walking up all the acclivities, we were obliged to make up our pace down the hills. The Pass looked lovely by daylight, and the wild flowers were splendid, especially the white datura and scarlet rhododendron trees, which were literally covered with bloom.

By daylight, the appearance of the horses was really pitiable in the extreme—worn-out, half-starved wretches, covered with wounds and sores from collars and harness, and with traces of injuries they inflict on themselves in their struggles to get free. When once we had seen their shoulders, we no longer wondered at their reluctance to start; it really made one quite sick to think even of the state they were in.

If some of the permanent officials were to devote a portion of their time to endeavors to introduce American coaches, and to ameliorate the condition of the horses on this road, they would indeed confer a boon on their countrymen. The coachman, who was as black as jet, and who wore very little clothing, was a curious specimen of his class, and appeared by no means skilled in his craft. He drove the whole way down the steep zigzag road with a loose rein; at every turn the horses went close to the precipice, but were turned in the very nick of time by a little black boy who jumped down from behind and pulled them round by their traces without touching the bridle. We stopped at Rangbodde to breakfast, and again at Pusillawa. This seemed a bad arrangement, for we were already late; it resulted in the poor horses having to be unmercifully flogged in order to enable us to catch the train at Gampola, failing which, the coach proprietors would have had to pay a very heavy penalty.

From Gampola we soon arrived at Peradeniya, where we met Mr. Freer, who was going down to Colombo. Tom had decided previously to go straight on, so as to have the yacht quite ready for an early start to-morrow. I in the meantime went to our former hosts for one night to pick up Mabelle and the waifs and strays of luggage.

On my way from the station to the house, going over the Satinwood Bridge, from which there is a lovely view of the Peacock Mountain, I saw an Englishman whom we had observed before, washing stones in the bed of the river for gems. He has obtained some rubies and sapphires, though only of small size, and I suppose he will go on washing forever, hoping to find something larger and more valuable. On one part of the coast of the island near Managgan the sands on the side of one of the rivers are formed of rubies, sapphires, garnets, and other precious stones washed down by the current, but they are all ground to pieces in the process, not one being left as big as a pin's head. The effect in the sunlight, when this sand is wet with the waves, is something dazzling, and proves that the accounts of my favorite Sindbad are not so fabulous as we prosaic mortals try to make out. The island must be rich in gems, for they seem to be picked up with hardly any trouble. At Neuera-ellia it is a favorite amusement for picnic parties to go out gem-hunting, and frequently they meet with very large and valuable stones by the riverside or near deserted pits, large garnets, cinnamon-stone, splendid cat's-eyes, amethysts, matura diamonds, moonstone, aqua marine, tourmaline rubies, and sapphires.

On my arrival at the house I found that Mabelle had just returned with some friends, who had kindly taken charge of her during our absence, and that a very old friend had arrived almost directly we left on Monday, and had departed early this morning to climb Adam's Peak, the ascent of which is a long and tedious affair, but it cannot be difficult, as thousands of aged and infirm pilgrims go every year to worship at the Buddhist or Mohammedan temples at the summit. The giant footprint has been reverenced alike by both religions from the earliest ages. Its existence is differently accounted for, however, by the two sects. The Buddhists say it is the footprint of Buddha, and that an account of its origin was written 300 or 400 years B.C. The Mohammedans say that it is the first step Adam took when driven out of Paradise. They do not quarrel about it, however, but live very happily close beside one another in their respective temples on the very small summit of the mountain. The iron chains, still used by the pilgrims and visitors to assist them up the last weary flight of steps, are said to have been placed there in the time of Alexander the Great, and are mentioned by successive historians.

After lunch I went to rest, thoroughly tired out with

the hard work of the last two days, whilst the gentlemen went into Kandy, to see Buddha's tooth and a Brahmin temple.

Just before sunset we went to have a last look at those lovely Botanical Gardens. They were more beautiful than ever in the afternoon light, and I saw many things which had escaped my notice before. I have made acquaintance with the taste of all sorts of new fruits while here, more than in our former journey; but this is to be explained by the proximity of the Botanical Gardens. I expected to revel in fruit all through the tropics, but, except at Tahiti, we have not done so at all. There is one great merit in tropical fruit, which is, that however hot the sun may be, when plucked from the tree it is always icy cold; if left for a few minutes, however, it becomes as hot as the surrounding atmosphere, and the charm is gone.

On my return, when I went to dress for dinner, I found on my table a nasty-looking black beast about six inches long. It looked very formidable in the half-light, like a scorpion or centipede. It turned out, however, to be quite harmless, and a sort of millipede, and rather handsome, with jet-black rings, and hundreds of orange-colored legs. There are a great many venomous snakes in Ceylon, but they always get out of the way as fast as they can, and never bite Europeans. All the roofs of the thatched bungalows swarm with rats, and in every house is kept a rat-snake, which kills and eats these rats. I more than once heard a great scuffle going on over my bedroom, which generally ended in a little squeak, indicating that the snake had killed, and was about to eat, his prey. One of the snakes came out one day in front of my window, and hung down two or three feet from the roof. If I had not been previously assured that he was perfectly harmless, it would have been rather an alarming apparition in the dark, and even as it was, I must confess that for a moment I did feel rather frightened as I watched him spying about, darting his forked tongue in and out, and looking quite ready for a spring at my face.

Thursday, April 5th.—Another early start by the seven o'clock train to Colombo. We were very sorry to say good-by to our kind host, and when we took our departure, we were quite laden with flowers, good wishes, and messages for mutual friends in England. It was rather a hot journey down, and the train seemed full, but the scenery was lovely. As we approached Colombo the heat became greater, and in the town itself it was almost insupportable.

We breakfasted at the hotel in the fort, where we were joined by Tom. There is one very curious thing about the hotels here. The sitting-rooms are all two stories high, with pointed raftered roofs. The bedrooms are only screened off from each other, and from the central room, by partitions eight or ten feet high, so that you can hear everything going on from end to end of the building. I am not at all sure that the larger amount of ventilation secured by this plan compensates for the extra amount of noise and want of privacy, especially when, as was the case to-day, there is a crying baby who refuses to be pacified in one of the rooms, a poor little girl ill with whooping-cough in another, and some very noisy people, who are making themselves both unhappy and cross over some lost keys, in a third.

While we were at breakfast the crows were most amusing and impertinent. Every door and window was open, and they were perched on the top of the punkah, or on the iron crossbars supporting the roof, watching their opportunity to pounce down and carry off the bits left on our plates. They did not seem to mind the waiters a bit, and with their heads cocked on one side, looked as droll and saucy as possible. People tell you all sorts of funny stories about them; but though they are very entertaining to watch, and apparently perfectly tame, it appears to be impossible to capture one alive.

By the time breakfast was over we found that the 'Sunbeam' was already under way, and steaming about the anchorage; so it was not long before we were once more on board. Going out of harbor we passed a large steamer whose passengers and crew cheered us and waved their handkerchiefs until we were out of sight, and with that pleasant, homely sound ringing in our ears we bade a last farewell to Colombo, and started on another stage of our homeward voyage. The heat was intense, and there was a roll outside which at once made me feel very uncomfortable. There was no wind all the afternoon, and the sun sank into the sea, glorious and golden, as we took our last look at the lovely island of Ceylon, the land of spice and fragrance and beauty.

CHAPTER XXVI.

TO ADEN.

Heaven speed the canvas, gallantly unfurled
To furnish and accommodate a world,
To give the Pole the produce of the sun,
And knit the unsocial climates into one.

Friday, April 6th.—Our visit to Ceylon has been so delightful that I wish it could have been prolonged for a month, instead of lasting only a week; but in that case I should have preferred to select a cooler season of the year, when traveling is more practicable. A most interesting journey could be made through the center of the island to see the ancient cities, temples, and tanks, over the road from Matelle to Nalandi Senadoora, to the curious rock temple at Dambool, near which is the fortified rock of Sigiri, and a few miles farther are the vast ruins of Topari, or Ponamira, the mediæval capital of Ceylon. It is full of wonderful ruins, some of them among the oldest in the world. The Ranhol Dagoba, the Jayti Wana Rama, and the Galle Wihara and rock temple, carved out of the living rock, are alone worth a long journey to see. Then think of visiting Anajapoora, the city of rubies, the sacred capital of the kingdom of ruins; on whose splendors even the Chinese travelers of the early ages used to expatiate with fervor. From this point it would be easy to reach the peninsula of Jaffna, which has been peopled with Tammils for more than two thousand years. It is the country *par excellence* of gardens exquisitely kept, and skillfully irrigated on the old Moorish system. Here are grown all the ingredients for the making of curry, which are sent to all parts of this island and to Southern India. The most important crop of all, however, is tobacco, whose excellence is famed throughout India, and of which the Rajah of Travancore holds the monopoly.

Then one might go southward from Jaffna, past Aripo, and the Gulf of Calpentyn, until the curious reef of Adam's Bridge was reached, which almost connects Ceylon with India. People say it has been separated by some convulsion of nature in former days, and that the passage is gradually deepening; but recent examinations have shown that instead of being a remnant of the original rock by which Ceylon is supposed to have been once connected with the Indian continent, it is in reality a comparatively recent ridge of conglomerate and ironstone, covered with alluvial deposits carried by the current and heaped up at this particular point; whilst the gradual rising of the coast has contributed to give the reef its present altitude.

Balchus tells a most improbable story of fifteen Portuguese frigates escaping through the passages of Panupam, when pursued by some Dutch cruisers in 1557. Formerly the Straits were only thirty-five yards wide, with a maximum depth of six feet of water, but lately they have been widened and deepened by ten feet, and a little government steamer frequently passes through on a tour round the island. At present a sailing ship going from Bombay to Madras has to make a curve of five thousand miles in order to weather the Maldives and Ceylon. It seems a long course for any vessel drawing over ten feet of water to be obliged to take.

In the center of the channel there is a little island where a Dutch establishment for horse-breeding formerly stood, the original stud having been imported from Arabia. The horses were all turned into corrals and caught by means of lassos, and then conquered by domidores, exactly as they are at the present day in South America. Now the stud is dispersed, the buildings are in ruins, and all that remains is the Indian pagoda, where religious ceremonies, curious processions, and dances of nautch-girls occasionally take place and are attended by great crowds. To the southward again of Adam's Bridge is the celebrated Gulf of Manar, from which the best pearls come.

This is an exceptionally good year for pearls, and the price of the shells went up many rupees per thousand in the first week. The pearl fishery can be reached in about eight hours by steam from Colombo, and it would have been delightful to have visited it, had time permitted. We were shown an oyster with some beautiful pearls in it, all found in the one shell. When a boat with pearls reaches the shore, the shells are divided into equal heaps, one-fourth going to the boat's crew, and three-fourths to the Government Inspector. They keep whichever heap he chooses to kick; so that, being uncertain which they will get for themselves, the boat's crew are sure to make a fair division. These heaps are then divided and sold by auction in thousands, and then subdivided again and again. Of course it is always a matter of speculation as to whether you get good pearls, bad pearls, or no pearls at all, though this last misfortune seldom happens.

The love of gambling is inherent in every Oriental mind, and the merest beggar with but a few pice in his wallet to buy his daily food will invest them in a small number of oyster shells, hoping to find a pearl of great value; and, should he fail to do so, he contents himself with eating the oyster and hoping for better luck next time. The shells are generally left on the sand in carefully guarded heaps till they die and open, when the pearls are extracted, and the fish left to decay. Some of the oysters are taken in sealed-up sacks to Colombo, Kandy, and other inland places, in order to enable people to indulge their love of gambling and speculation, without the trouble of a journey to Manaar. Though called oysters, they are not the proper oyster, but a sort of avicula (*Melea-*

grina margaritifera being the name given by Samarik), very different from the large mother-of-pearl shells in which the South Sea pearls are found.

I have not been able to keep my mind from running incessantly on Sir Emerson Tennent's delightful book on Ceylon, which describes places we have not ourselves visited, but which I wanted very much to see, and I have been so interested reading about them that I cannot help thinking other people will share my feelings. It seems wonderful that so much which is strange, beautiful, and interesting should be so easy of access from England, and yet that so few English travelers know comparatively anything of Ceylon, except Galle and Colombo, and perhaps Kandy and Trincomalee.

Saturday, April 7th.—To-day we passed close to the island of Minnikoy, between the groups of islands called the Laccadives and Maldives, some of which we saw dotting the horizon; and still farther to the south stretches the Chagos Archipelago. It was very hot all day, with hardly a breath of air, and we have all returned to our former light and airy costumes: the gentlemen to their shirts and trousers, the children to their pinafores and nothing else, and I to my beloved Tahitian dresses.

Before we left England we could not make ourselves believe what we were told about heat in the tropics; so we started with very few windsails and without any punkahs or double awnings. It was all very well in the Atlantic or Pacific, but between Hongkong and Singapore the state of things became simply unbearable. The carpenter has rigged up a punkah, and the men have improvised some double awnings. At Colombo they made some windsails, so we are now better off than on our last hot voyage. It has been really hotter than ever to-day, but a pleasant breeze sprang up in the afternoon.

Sunday, April 8th.—A delightful fresh morning after a cool night. Everybody looks quite different, and we begin to hope we shall carry the north-east monsoon right across, which would be an exceptional piece of good fortune. We had service in the saloon at eleven o'clock and at four, and though there was an unusually full attendance it was cool and pleasant even without the punkah. The thermometer registers nearly the same as it did on Friday, when we were all dead with the heat. The apparently nice cool breeze that refreshes our heated bodies does not produce any corresponding effect on the glassy surface of the ocean; for we find to-day, as on previous occasions, that the temperature, both of the water and of the air, registered by the thermometer, does not by any means correspond with the effect on the human frame.

The two Chinese servants we shipped at Hongkong are a great success, as every one on board agrees. Even the old sailing-master is obliged to confess that the two 'heathen Chinee' keep the mess-rooms, ships' officers' and servants' berths much cleaner and more comfortable than his own sailors ever succeeded in doing. At Galle we shipped three black firemen, two from Bombay and one from Mozambique, a regular nigger, with his black woolly hair clipped into the shape of Prince of Wales feathers. Their names are Mehemet, Abraham, and Tom Dollar. They live in a little tent we have had pitched for them on deck, cook their own food, and do their work in the engine-room exceedingly well. In the intervals they are highly amused with the children's picture books. The picture of the durbar at Delhi delighted them, especially as they recognized the figures, and learned a little English through them. They can say a few words already, and have told me all about their wives and children at Mozambique and Bombay, and have shown me the presents they are taking home to them. They have been nearly a year on board the P. and O. steamship 'Poonah,' and appear to have saved nearly all their earnings. I do not suppose our own men could have stood the fearful heat below in the engine-room for many days together, so it was fortunate we met with these amiable salamanders.

Monday, April 9th.—No wind. We passed through a large shoal of porpoises, and at dusk we saw the light of a distant ship. At all the places we have recently visited we have found excellent ice-making machines, and have been able to get a sufficient supply to last us from port to port, which has been a great comfort. The machine at Colombo unfortunately broke down the day before we left, so that in the very hottest part of our voyage we have had to do without our accustomed luxury; and very much we miss it, not only for cooling our drinks, but for keeping provisions, &c. As it is, a sheep killed overnight is not good for dinner next day; butter is just like oil, and to-day in opening a drawer my fingers touched a sticky mess; I looked and discovered six sticks of sealing-wax running slowly about in a state resembling treacle.

Wednesday, April 11th.—Hotter than ever. We could see a steamer in the far distance. About sunset we passed through a shoal of flying-fish; the night was intensely hot, and everybody slept on deck.

Friday, April 13th.—At 6 a.m. we made the island of Sokotra, and about seven o'clock saw 'The Brothers,' two islands where large quantities of turtle and ambergris are found. Though generally uninhabited, they are sometimes visited by the natives for the purpose of collecting articles of commerce.

One of our large pigs took it into his head to jump overboard to-day. The helm was put round as quickly as possible, but the most anxious spying could not discover any trace of poor piggy's whereabouts; so we proceeded on our original course for a few minutes, when suddenly, to our great astonishment, we saw him alongside, having been nearly run down, but still gallantly swimming along. The dinghy was lowered and two men sent in pursuit. They had, however, no easy task before them, for as soon as they approached, piggy swam away faster than they could row, and bit and fought most furiously when they tried to get him into the boat. It was a good half-hour's work before he was secured, yet when he arrived he did not appear to be in the least exhausted by his long swim, but bit and barked at everybody so furiously that he was condemned to death, to prevent the possibility of further accidents. It is quite clear from the foregoing incident that some pigs can swim, and swim very well too, without cutting their own throats in the process.

All the afternoon a large steamer had been gradually gaining on us. We exchanged signals and made out that she was the 'Calypso' (?) of Glasgow. About half-past five she altered her course and came alongside to speak us. The fore-deck was crowded with the crews. On the bridge were many of the officers; and sitting bolt upright on a stool, 'looking out forward' in the most amusing manner, was the captain's little Skye terrier. The stern was crowded with passengers, of every shade of color. To our surprise a voice from among them shouted out 'Three cheers for Mr. Brassey!' which was responded to by ringing shouts from all on board, and taken up again by some of our own men. It was a very pleasant and unexpected greeting to hear in the middle of the Indian Ocean. The ship soon drew ahead again, but handkerchiefs and caps were waved till their owners faded away into the distance. Meeting and passing thousands of people as you at home do daily, you can hardly understand the excitement a little incident like this causes on board ship, where even a distant sail in these lonely oceans makes everybody leave his occupation and crowd to look at her. Soon after sunset we saw the island of Abd-al-Kuri, with its fantastic peaks, melting into orange, gold, and purple tints, beneath the gorgeous Arabian afterglow.

Saturday, April 14*th.*—We made Cape Rasalhir, formerly called Guardafui, about nine o'clock yesterday evening, and passing it during the night entered the

Gulf of Aden.* All to-day we have been going along the Somali coast. There is a good deal of trade carried on in native boats. Passing all these strange and comparatively unknown and little-visited islands and coasts, from which all sorts of things in daily use at home are brought, one dimly realizes what commerce means, and how necessary one part of the world is to the other.

Sunday, April 15*th.*—Still intensely hot. The usual services were held on deck at eleven and four o'clock. The land, both in Arabia and in Africa, could be seen the whole day, with precipitous mountains. In the afternoon we could make out the rock of Aden, and at sunset it stood grandly forth, looming in purple darkness against the crimson and blood-red sky, which gradually faded to tenderest tints of yellow and green, before it finally blazed forth into a radiant afterglow. At half-past eight a gun from the fort at Aden summoned us to show our colors, or rather lights. At nine o'clock we dropped our anchor in the roads; a boat came off with a bag of newspapers and to ask for orders in the morning. It was sent by the great Parsee merchants here, who undertake to supply us with coals, provisions, water, and everything we want, and spare us all trouble. For the last three or four days we have had a nice little breeze astern, and if we had not been in a hurry to cross the Indian Ocean before the south-west monsoon set in, we should certainly have been contented with four or five knots an hour under sail instead of eight and a half under steam. We have averaged over 200 miles a day under steam alone, ever since we left Penang, and have burned only four tons of coal for every fifty miles.

Monday, April 16*th.*—At 1.30 a.m. I heard the signal gun fired, and shortly afterwards a great splash of boats

---

* We found considerable difficulty in making the light, and since our return there have been several wrecks, and many lives lost, on this dangerous point.

and oars, and a vast chattering and shouting of tongues, announced the arrival of a P. and O. steamer. She dropped her anchor just outside us, so we had the benefit of the noise all night. I got up at daylight and found the pilot just coming off. He took us to a buoy, a little closer in, and soon the business of coaling and watering commenced.

We reached the shore about 7.30, and, landing at the pier, had our first near view of the natives, who are most curious-looking creatures. They have very black complexions, and long woolly hair, setting out like a mop all round, and generally dyed bright red, or yellow by the application of lime. Mr. Cowajee had sent his own private carriage to meet us. It was a comfortable open barouche, with a pair of nice horses, and two servants in Eastern liveries, green vests and full trousers, and red and orange turbans. We went first to his store, which seemed to be an emporium for every conceivable article. There was carved sandal-wood, and embroidered shawls from China, Surat, and Gujerat, work from India, English medicines, French lamps, Swiss clocks, German toys, Russian caviare, Greek lace, Havana cigars, American hides and canned fruits, besides many other things. The feathers did not look very tempting; there was a great deal of feather and very little stem about most of them, and only a few were white, the majority being a pretty sort of brown and drab. But this general store is only a very small part of their business, for about 60,000 tons of coal pass through their hands every year.

We went on to the Hôtel de l'Europe, which was by no means in first-rate order, but allowances must be made for a new house. A delightful breeze was blowing in through the open windows, and although the thermometer registered 85° in the dining-room, it did not seem at all hot. The view over the bay is very pretty, and the scene on shore thoroughly Arabian, with the donkeys and camels patiently carrying their heavy loads, guided by the true Bedaween of the desert, and people of all tinges of complexion, from jet black to pale copper-color. A pair of tame ostriches, at least seven feet high, were strolling about the roadway, and a gazelle, some monkeys, parrots, and birds lived happily together beneath a broad veranda. After a little while we went for a drive to see the camp and town of Aden, which is four or five miles from the Point where everybody lands. On the way we met trains of heavily-laden camels bringing in wood, water, grain, and fodder, for garrison consumption, and coffee and spices for exportation. After driving for about four miles we reached a gallery pierced through the rock, which admits you into the precincts of the fort. The entrance is very narrow, the sides precipitous, and the place apparently impregnable. We went all through the town, or rather towns, past the Arab village, the Sepoy barracks, and the European barracks, to the water tanks, stupendous works carved out of the solid rock, but until lately comparatively neglected, the residents depending entirely on distillation for their supply of water. There is a pretty little garden at the foot of the lowest tank, but the heat was intense in the bottom of the deep valley amongst the rocks, where every sun-ray seemed to be collected and reflected from the white glaring limestone, and every breath of air to be excluded. We saw a little more of the town and the market crowded with camels, the shops full of lion, leopard, and hyæna skins. We went to the officers' mess-house, visited the Protestant and Roman Catholic churches and the Mohammedan mosque, and then passing through two long tunnels, bored and blasted in the solid rock, we looked over the fortifications. Finally we returned to the Point again, by way of the Isthmus, and went to Government House, which gets a fresh breeze from every quarter. They say that to-day is hotter than usual, but it is never really very oppressive here unless there is an exceptionally hot wind blowing from the desert, but even that is partially cooled before it arrives. To us it appears delightful after our sultry voyage and the heat at Penang and Singapore.

We were all agreeably disappointed with Aden, and find that it is by no means the oven we expected; it is prettier, too, than I thought, the mountains and rocks are so peaked and pointed, and although the general effect is one of barrenness, still, if you look closely, every crack and crevice is full of something green. The soil, being of volcanic origin, is readily fertilized by moisture, and at once produces some kind of vegetation. This adds of course greatly to the effect of color, which in the rocks themselves is extremely beautiful, especially at sunrise and sunset. The sea, too, is delightfully blue on one side of the peninsula, and pale green on the other, according to the wind, and the white surf curls and breaks on the sandy shore beyond the crisp waves.

We went back to the hotel a little before one, and found many friends had called during our absence. After superintending the children's dinner, I went with Tom to luncheon at Government House. It was very pleasant; General and Mrs. Sneider were more than kind, and the house felt deliciously cool and airy.

We are told that thirty miles inland the country is sometimes very beautiful. There are exquisitely green valleys, with a stream running through them, amongst peaks and rocky mountains, which one rarely sees in the desert. Here the natives cultivate their crops of corn— such corn as it is too, reaching six feet above a man's head! All sorts of useful vegetables grow abundantly, besides roses, fruits, and fragrant flowers, large supplies of which are brought daily into Aden. About ten miles from the town there are acres of the most fertile garden ground, which is cultivated to supply the garrison with vegetables. Sometimes a party of seventy or eighty men, and ten or twenty Arab guides, goes out for three weeks or a month at a time surveying. The natives are much more friendly than they used to be a few years ago, when people were afraid even to ride outside the town. Now, pleasant excursions lasting a few days may be made, especially as there is very fair shooting to be got. After luncheon I was shown some lovely feathers. The contrast between these and the steamer-feathers is ludicrous; the price, too, is proportionately cheaper, for the feathers are infinitely better. Long, white, full, and curly feathers can be bought for much less than you give for them in England. We drove down to the town, finished our business transactions, and then went in the 'Vestal's' steam launch on board the 'Gamma,' one of the new Chinese gunboats on her way out to China.

After afternoon tea we all adjourned to the 'Sunbeam,' where we found many other friends already arrived or arriving. We had only just time to look round before the sun set, and the short twilight was succeeded by the swift tropical darkness. All too soon good-by had to be said; the anchor was raised, and we were actually drifting slowly along under our head canvas before our friends took their departure. It was a lovely evening, with a light fair breeze, and although there appeared hardly any wind, it was wonderful how swiftly we crept out of the harbor, and, as sail after sail was spread, how rapidly we glided past the land.

Our visit to Aden has been short but very agreeable; it is not by any means such a dreadful place as we had always fancied. Most of the people we have seen to-day seem rather to like it; there is good boating, excellent sea fishing, moderate shooting, and many rides and excursions. A vehicle of some sort is an absolute necessity, however, if you want to see anything of your friends, for the three divisions of the settlement are at least four miles apart, and the heat is far too great for driving or riding in the middle of the day, except on business. I cannot say, however, that we ourselves found it intolerably hot to-day.

CHAPTER XXVII.

TO SUEZ.

*Round the decay
Of that colossal wreck; boundless and bare
The lone and level sands stretch far away.*

Tuesday, April 17th.—The breeze still continued and freshened, and we sailed along pleasantly before it, finding it a great relief to be rid of the thud and beat of the engine. There is no vibration, but the noise is unpleasant. About eleven o'clock we passed the island of Perim, a most desolate-looking place. I do not wonder that officers so much dislike being quartered there. It is an important position though, and is shortly to be strengthened, when water-tanks will be built, and attempts made to cultivate the soil. At present there does not appear to be a blade of vegetation, and on the side we passed, between the island and the coast of Arabia, nothing is to be seen but the little white lighthouse and the path leading up to it. On the southern side there is a very fair harbor and a moderate town. On the shore all round the island turtles are caught at the season when they land to deposit their eggs. To pass the island of Perim we sailed through the Straits of Bab-el-Mandeb, or 'Gate of Tears,' thus called on account of the numerous wrecks which took place there in former years. Once through the straits, we were fairly in the Red Sea. The color of the Red Sea is certainly the bluest of ultramarines. In the afternoon the town of Mocha Yamen, celebrated alike for its breed of Arab horses and its coffee, was visible from the masthead. It is a large white town, full of cupolas and minarets, surrounded with green as far as irrigation extends, and looking like a pearl set in emeralds on the margin of the deep blue sea against a background of red and yellow sand-mountains. Later in the afternoon we passed Great and Little Hamish, where the P. and O. boat, 'Alma,' was wrecked some fifteen years ago, and during the night sailed by Jebel Zibayar and Tukar.

Wednesday, April 18*th.*—In the morning, at daylight, we were off Jebel Teir, Mussawa Island, Annesley Bay lying 60 miles to the west. Our position was about 60 miles to the south-west of Mussawa Zoulia, where the expedition under Lord Napier of Magdala landed in 1867. At noon we had sailed 221 miles, a most unexpected run in the Red Sea. In the afternoon it fell calm, but the wind freshened again, and we went on sailing until after midnight.

Thursday, April 19*th.*—We commenced steaming at 1 a.m., stopped, however, at 5 a.m., and sailed all day. Yesterday we were surrounded by some beautiful blue birds, who hovered about us and settled at intervals on the masts and yards. During the night two were caught napping by the men, and in the course of to-day two more, hotly pursued by a hawk, took refuge on board and were also captured. One was given to me. It appears to be a very beautiful kind of jay, with feathers of the most brilliant shades of blue. The men have killed their birds for the sake of the skins, but I mean to try and keep mine alive. At Colombo several birds and two curiously starred tortoises were added to our collection; and we took on board at Aden a gazelle, a black cockatoo, and a green monkey.

We passed Souakim to-day, the port of Nubia. It is about 275 miles, or 25 days' camel-journey, from thence to Berber on the Nile. The road passes through Korib, and among fine red granite and black basalt mountings, 4,000 feet high. We left one of the firemen, Tom Dollar, behind at Aden by mistake, and only found out yesterday that we had done so. It appears that he has a brother living there, whom he was most anxious to go and see directly the anchor was let go, in the morning. Unfortunately, he did not speak to us on the subject. He had never been in anything but a regular steamer before, and could not believe it possible that the 'Sunbeam' could spread her wings and be off without any preliminary 'fire-worshiping.' I am very sorry for the poor man, as he has left all his clothes and the wages he had earned on board the P. and O. steamer behind him. We must send them back from Suez, and telegraph to some one to look out for him. The heat is intense, and we all sleep on deck at night; the sunrises and sunsets are magnificent.

Friday, April 20th.—A little hotter still; there is no wind at all, and we are obliged to steam. In the morning we passed to the southward of Jeddo, the port of Mecca. Unfortunately it was so hazy that we could not distinguish anything whatever of the town or country, only a line of mountains rearing their heads above the clouds. We had hoped to be at Suez early on Sunday, but now I fear we shall not arrive until Monday.

Saturday, April 21st.—Hotter and still hotter every day, says the thermometer, and so we say also. Everybody told us these would be our two hottest days, and certainly the prediction has been verified. We did not see a single ship all day, but in the afternoon passed Zambo, the port of Medina. A little before midnight we made the light on the Dædalus shoal on the starboard bow.

This being Muriel's fifth birthday, Mabelle and the Doctor and the men have been arranging a surprise for her all day, and none of us were allowed to go on the port side of the deck, but after dinner we were taken to a hastily fitted-up theater, very prettily decorated with flags and Japanese lanterns. On a throne covered with the Union-Jack, Muriel was seated, the two pugs being on footstools on either side of her to represent lions *couchant.* Some of the men had blackened their faces, and gave us a really very excellent Christy Minstrel entertainment, in which undreamed-of talent came to light. It is very odd and interesting how one is perpetually finding out something new about the men. Some of the crew we thought the most unpromising when we started, have turned out among our best men, always ready and willing for everything, while others, who at first appeared the best, have not proved so good. Many we knew well beforehand. On the whole, however, we have very little cause to complain of our crew; all pull well together when they are kept up to their work and have plenty to do.

Sunday, April 22d.—Clouds veiled the sunrise this morning, which was a welcome relief; still it was too hot for service in the saloon, and it was therefore held on deck. A light breeze sprang up ahead during its performance, which cooled and refreshed us immensely. About twelve o'clock we passed another pair of 'Brothers,' a couple of odd-looking rocks or islands, like tables, rising straight out of the sea; there is a beacon on the northernmost one. While we were at lunch, the breeze freshened so much that we were all glad to add some wraps to our light and airy costumes. A little later, a summer gale was blowing ahead, making some of us feel very uncomfortable and long for the halycon days of the past, even with the accompaniment of the inevitable heat. Such is mankind, and womankind too for that matter, 'never blessed, but always to be blessed.' The gale freshened, the screw was raised, the yacht pitched and rolled, and we were obliged to put her off her course and under sail before night fell. The spray came over the decks, and there was a strong wind dead ahead. We all felt cold and miserable, though the thermometer still registered 75°. The poor monkeys and parrots looked most wretched and unhappy, and had to be packed away as speedily as possible. Nine monkeys in an empty wine case seemed very happy and cuddled together for warmth, but the two larger and more aristocratic members of the party required a box to themselves. The gazelle had a little tent pitched for him specially in a sheltered corner, and the birds were all stowed away and battened over in the smoking fiddle. Dinner was rather a lame pretense, and it was not long before we all retired, and certainly no one wished to take his or her mattress on deck to-night. It is the first night I have slept in a bed on board the yacht for many weeks, and a very disturbed night it was, for the waves ran high, and we have lately been sailing so steadily over smooth seas, that we did not know what to make of this.

Monday, April 23d.—The gale blew as hard as ever, and quite as dead ahead. About noon we made the island of Shaduan, or isle of Seals, so named by the ancients, when the sea and gulf abounded with seals. There are still a few occasionally to be seen to the northward by the fishermen, and their skins are brought to Suez for sale. We are making tacks backwards and forwards across the narrow sea, an exciting amusement for a yachtsman, as it requires constant attention. The sailing directions say that this sea is ill surveyed, except in the direct channel. There are many coral reefs and sunken rocks, and on whichever side you may happen to be wrecked, the natives are ready to rob, ill-treat, and kill you, or sell you as slaves in the interior. It was on two projecting coral reefs from the island of Shaduan that the 'Carnatic' was wrecked in 1869. She ran ashore at four o'clock in the morning of the 13th of September, soon after having made the light on Rhas Garril. We were at Suez in October of the same year, and everybody was then full of the sad particulars of the wreck, the soldiers being especially useful in bringing in the passengers' luggage, which had been recovered from the Arabs. One of our firemen, Abraham, was on board the 'Carnatic' at the time of the disaster, and lost all his worldly goods (not many, I should think, judging by what he has brought on board here).

The sea was very rough and disagreeable all day. To us the temperature appears quite cool, indeed cold, though the thermometer still remains at 75°. Our friends at Aden, who prophesied that I should want my sealskin jacket before leaving the Gulf of Suez, were not so far wrong in their prognostications as I imagined at the time.

Tuesday, April 24th.—We are still beating to windward against a head gale, and by noon had made sixty-five miles to the good, right in the wind's eye—not a bad performance, considering that the gale was blowing with a force of nine or ten. It has the merit of novelty too, for I suppose that for years no sailing ships have been seen in the Gulf of Suez. The winds blow so steadily for months together, that for six months in the year you cannot get into the Red Sea, and for the other six months you cannot get out of it.

We passed the island of Rhas Garril, and soon afterwards a steamer went by, altering her course a good deal to inspect us. She evidently thought we were a broken-down steamer, and intended to come to our rescue. All yesterday and to-day we have been making flannel coats for the monkeys, and covers for bird-cages, and improvising shelters and snug corners for our pets. At night especially the wind is quite crisp. If this gale continues, it will be Thursday or Friday before we reach Suez; but it may possibly change to-night, and it looks now as if it were breaking.

Wednesday, April 25th.—At last the gale *has* broken. There was not much wind when I went on deck at 4 a.m., and by seven o'clock it was so nearly calm that the funnel could be raised and fires lighted, and we were soon steaming straight for our destination. We could not see Mount Sinai on account of the mist, but made out the place where the Israelites are said to have crossed the

Red Sea, and by four o'clock the town of Suez lay right ahead. The shores are very barren, not a blade of grass nor a scrap of vegetation being visible. Nothing is to be seen save mountain peaks, rocks, stones, and sand. But even this barren scene has a special beauty of its own, particularly at sunrise and sunset. The shapes of mountain and rock are alike striking, the sharp shadows are lovely, and the contrast of reds, yellows, and browns, with the bright blue sea and crisp white waves, is very beautiful. Even when the sun has set, and the rich tints have faded away, the full moon adds another charm to the landscape.

This afternoon, as we were steaming up towards Suez, I had a chat with Mehemet, one of our Indian firemen, who was fringing a piece of muslin for a turban. I asked him if it was English. 'No, Missy; no English—Switzerland; English no good; all gum and sticky stuff; make fingers dirty; all wash out; leave nothing.' In the South Sea and Sandwich Islands, and in the Malay Peninsula, the natives make the same complaints as to the Manchester cottons. At Hongkong some of the large shops had fifty expensive English ships' compasses on hand; they were all quite unsalable owing to the liquid having gone bad, in consequence of its not having been properly prepared. Some American compasses of the same quality were in good order and not in the least affected by the climate. It will be a bad day when the confidence in England's honesty as a nation throughout the world, and consequently her well-earned supremacy in commerce, have passed away. The burden, unfortunately, will not fall on the heads of the offenders alone, but, as usual, the innocent will suffer with and for the guilty.

After four o'clock we came near two steamers lying at anchor, and were shortly afterwards boarded by the captain of the port, the health officer, and sundry other functionaries. After a short delay we dropped anchor, and just as the sun was setting in 'purple and gold' behind the mountains of Arabia, we went ashore in the steam launch. We landed at the Canal Company's Office, in front of which there is a bust of Lieutenant Waghorn, the inaugurator of the overland route.

At the office, the 'Sunbeam' was entered on the Company's books, and arrangements were made with the chief pilot for to-morrow, while the children amused themselves by riding a pony up and down, and jumping over the little brooks, and I strolled about admiring the enormous growth of the vegetation since we were here last in 1869. We next steamed five miles farther on to the town of Suez, and landed opposite the big hotel, which is more uncomfortable than ever. The rooms are dirty, and the cooking execrable.

There is nothing to see at Suez, but still we went for a ramble to see that nothing. We cleared our boxes and our letters, and then went on ankle deep in sand to the one European house, the railway station, the Arab quarter and the bazaars, where it is occasionally possible to pick up rather interesting little curiosities brought by the pilgrims from Mecca and Medina.

Thursday, April 26th.—Such a sunrise as this morning's you could only see in Arabia or Egypt. There is a peculiarity about desert coloring at sunrise and sunset that can never be seen anywhere else. We had sundry visitors during the early morning, and before ten o'clock we were in the Canal and steaming on at regulation speed. As the sun rose the heat became intense, 96° in the shade under double awnings. So far from there being a cool breeze to temper it, a hot wind blew from the desert, like the blast from a furnace. I stood on the bridge as long as I could bear the heat, to look at the strange desert view, which could be seen to great advantage in going through at the top of high water. Sand, sand everywhere; here a train of camels, there a few Arab tents, now a whole party shifting their place of abode; a group of women washing, or a drove of buffaloes in a small tributary stream. After going about eight miles we stopped at a *gare* (as the stopping-places are called) to allow three vessels to pass. One was a fine steamer belonging to the Ducal Line; the others were a Dutch and a German boat (one, the 'Friesland,' has been since wrecked off Cape Finisterre, in December, 1877). The cleanliness and general smartness of the former presented a great contrast to her companions, on which the passengers looked very hot and uncomfortable. The center part of each vessel was crowded with a large number of Dutch or German boys, going out as soldiers to Acheen, who certainly did not appear to be enjoying their voyage.

We passed Chaloux and reached Ismailia just at nine o'clock, not without considerable effort on the part of the pilot. A steam launch came off from the shore, and we (children and all) landed at once; and, after a moonlight donkey-ride, dined at the excellent Hôtel de Paris, kept by an old Frenchman. *Table-d'hôte* was over, but they gave us a capital little dinner by ourselves. The children and I, and some of the gentlemen, start to-morrow, overland *viâ* Cairo, to join the yacht at Alexandria, in order that they may see the Pyramids. It was a glorious night as we rowed off to the yacht under the bright beams of the full moon, and the air, too, was quite fresh and cool—a most refreshing change from the noontide heat.

The traffic on the Canal has increased during the last few years, and especially during the last few months; on an average four or five ships pass through every day. To-day they took £6,000 at the Suez office alone. They have an excellent plan of the Canal there, and little models of ships, which are arranged according to the telegrams constantly received, so that the chief officers at each end of the Canal know exactly where every ship is. Instant information is of course sent of any stoppage or any accident, but these occur comparatively seldom. Some time ago M. Lesseps bought a small canal partially stopped up leading from the Nile at Cairo to Ismailia. It has been widened and deepened, and was opened a few weeks ago with great ceremony and grand doings. Now any vessel not drawing more than fourteen feet can go direct from Suez or Port Said to Cairo. If we had had time, we might have done it in the yacht, and lain at anchor almost under the shadow of the Pyramids of Cheops. The special object of the new canal is to make Cairo and Ismailia Egyptian ports as well as Alexandria, thereby saving much land carriage and labor of shifting. Already several ships laden with grain, from Upper Egypt, have availed themselves of this new means of communication.

Friday, April 27th.—Another glorious sunrise. The pilot was on board at 5 a.m., and the Dhebash with fish, strawberries and fresh vegetables. This is a beautiful climate, though there is scarcely any rain; only one very slight shower has occurred during the last three years at Suez, but the soil of the desert after the Nile overflow brings forth tenfold.

The 'Sunbeam' was to start at eight o'clock, as soon as a large vessel had passed up from Port Said. There are only certain places in the Canal where vessels can pass one another, so one ship is always obliged to wait for another. We landed at half-past seven. The sun was already blazing with a burning fury, and we found it very hot riding up to the hotel on donkeys. We had an excellent breakfast at the same comfortable hotel, paid a very moderate bill, and left by the eleven o'clock train for Cairo. We stopped at Zag-à-zig for an hour for luncheon in a nice cool dark room, and started again about three o'clock. The change in the face of the country since we were here eight years ago is something extraordinary. A vast desert of sand has been transformed into one large oasis of undulating fields of waving corn, where there used to be nothing but whirlwinds of sand. All this has been effected by irrigation. The wealth of Egypt ought greatly to increase. How the people managed to live before is a mystery. Now every field is full of laborers reaping and stacking the corn, women gleaning, and in some places the patient, ugly, black buffaloes plowing the stubble for fresh crops.

At half-past six we reached Cairo, and were conveyed in a large *char-à-bancs* to what was formerly Shepherd's Hotel, now partly rebuilt and much altered for the better. Even in that short drive we could see that the face of the capital of Egypt had altered as much as the country, though I am not sure that it is so greatly improved. After a refreshing dip in cool marble baths and a change of garments, we went down to the large *table-d'hôte*. Then we sat in the veranda looking on the street until we became tired of doing nothing, after which we started for a stroll in the Ezkebieh gardens close by. They are beautifully laid out for evening promenade; but although the flowers are lovely, and the turf, thanks to constant waterings, is deliciously green, all the large trees have been cut down. There is no seclusion, no shade, which seems a pity in a country where the greatest desire of life is shelter from the noonday heat. To-night both Arab and French bands were playing within the inclosure, and it was pleasant enough listening to Offenbach's music under the beams of the full moonlight. Few people appeared to appreciate it, however, for the gardens were nearly empty; but then the season is over, and every one has fled before the coming heat.

Saturday, April 28th.—We had settled to start at six o'clock this morning to visit the Pyramids, an excursion which had been for some little time eagerly looked forward to and talked about by the younger members of our party. The morning was cold and gray, a strong northerly wind was blowing, and the change from the weather which had prevailed but a few hours previously was altogether most striking and unexpected. We drove rapidly through the streets and the outskirts of the town, where old houses are being pulled down and new ones rapidly built up, and where a general air of new bricks and old rubbish pervades the scene. Then we crossed the Nile by a handsome iron bridge, and saw the Palace of Gezireh, where the Prince of·Wales and his suite were lodged. We passed the railway extension works, and, to the great delight of the children, saw two elephants busily employed, one of which was being made to lie down to enable his mahout to dismount. Soon the little ones gave a shout of 'The Pyramids!' and there before us stood those grand monuments of a nameless founder, which for centuries have stood out in the sands of the desert, while the burning African sun and the glorious African moon have risen and set on their heavenward-pointing summits for countless days and nights. Even the earth has changed her position so much since they were erected that the pole star no longer sheds its light in a direct line through the central passages, as it did when first they were designed.

We drove along under avenues of now leafless trees to the foot of the hill on which the Pyramids are situated. Here everybody was turned out to walk except Muriel and me, and a tremendous tug the horses had to drag even us two up to the real foot of the Pyramids. On arriving we were at once surrounded by a crowd of Arabs. They are certainly a fine-looking lot of men, rather clamorous for backshish, and anxious to sell their curiosities, real or imitation. They were, however, good-natured, civil, and obliging, and amused me much during the hour I spent alone with them while the rest of the party were ascending and descending the Pyramids. Many could speak several languages quite fluently, and almost all of them took a good deal of interest in the war, and the prospects of success on either side; while many had a fair knowledge of the geography of Europe. While all the rest were on the top of the one large Pyramid, a man ran down from the summit and up to the top of the next smaller one (which is, however, more difficult to ascend) in 'eight minutes for a franc.' This feat was repeated several times by different men, but it really occupied nearer ten minutes.

We ate some bread and wine, bought a few curiosities, and then drove back to the city, feeling very cold and shivery, and regretting the wraps we had left behind. We reached the hotel just in time for twelve o'clock *table-d'hôte* breakfast, and, after an acceptable rest, sallied forth again, this time on donkeys, to see the bazaars and the sunset from the citadel. We went across squares and gardens and through wide streets, for, alas! Cairo is being rapidly Haussmannized. For the capitalist or resident Cairo may be improved, but for the traveler, the artist, the lover of the picturesque, the quaint, and the beautiful, the place is ruined. Cairo as a beautiful and ancient Oriental city has ceased to exist, and is being rapidly transformed into a bad imitation of modern Paris, only with bluer skies, a more brilliant sun, and a more serene climate than it is possible to find in Europe. Only a few narrow streets and old houses are still left, with carved wooden lattices, where you can yet dream that the 'Arabian Nights' are true.

We went to the gold and silver bazaar, and bought some quaint silver jewelry from Assouan, Soudan, and Abyssinia; then through the Turkish bazaar, the saddlery bazaars, past mosques and old houses, till at length we emerged into new squares and new streets, before climbing the hill to the citadel, the Viceroy's palace, and the splendid Mosque of Mehemet Ali, built of Egyptian alabaster. The view from the terrace is superb, over city, desert, river, palm-trees, and Pyramids. The sunset this evening was a disappointment; yellow, cold, and watery, a strong north wind bringing up all the sand from the desert. We returned to the hotel for dinner, and were all glad to go early to bed.

Sunday, April 29*th.*—The children and I went to the English church, a semi-Gothic building, without a single window which could open. Though the church was nearly empty, the air felt like that of an exhausted receiver, and made one gasp. In the cool of the afternoon we drove through Roulai, where the museum stands, in a beautiful garden close by the riverside, amid flowers in full bloom.

After an early meal (hardly to be called dinner) we went to the station, just as all the people were going for a drive to Shoubrah in the smartest carriages and the prettiest toilets.

Our journey to Alexandria in the evening was cool and pleasant. A huge break met us, and we drove to Abbat's Hotel—considerably improved since our last visit in 1869.

Monday, April 30th.—Got up at 5 a.m. After a deliciously soft but very muddy bath, I went for a donkey ride before breakfast with Mabelle. Tom arrived from the yacht in time for twelve o'clock breakfast, and announced the voyage from Port Said to have been rough and unpleasant.

We called on the Consul, the Vice-Consul, and our old friend, Consul Burton of Trieste, Haj Abdullah. He has just returned from a journey through the ancient land of Midian, undertaken at the special request of the Viceroy. He describes the expedition as having been most successful; the climate is almost perfect from September to May; the land is well watered by little streams flowing through fertile valleys, and full of fragrant flowers and luscious fruits. The corn reaches above the camel-men's heads, which means a height of fourteen or fifteen feet. But the mineral wealth of the country is its most extraordinary feature. He found traces of gold in the sand of the river-beds, in spots pointed out to him by his fellow-pilgrims on the way to Mecca twenty years ago, to say nothing of tin, iron, &c. Perhaps the most interesting part of his discovery was the remains of eight ruined cities, with traces in the dry river-beds of stone-crushing and gold-seeking apparatus, which must have been used centuries ago. He is writing a book on the subject, which you may perhaps see before you read this.

The Consul kindly sent a janizary with us to show us the Sultan's palace. It is large and bare of furniture; and the general style of decoration is like that of the palaces at Cherniga and Dolma Batcher. Thence we went to see Pompey's Pillar and Cleopatra's Needle, the dahabeas ready to go up the Nile, &c.; and returned to the hotel in time for dinner and a chat afterwards in the cool courtyard.

Tuesday, May 1st.—I wrote from 3 a.m. to 6.30 a.m., in order to send letters off by the French mail, and at seven Mabelle and I sallied forth on donkeys to visit the market. There was not much to see, however, everything being so crowded and jammed up, meat, fish, vegetables, and fruit, all close together. The crowd was amusing, as all the European householders had negroes or Arabs following them, laden with their purchases. We found some lovely flowers in a street near the market, and then we went on to the big gold and silver bazaar, and to the Turkish and Syrian bazaars, where we saw all the specialties of Constantinople, and Broussa, Damascus, and Jerusalem laid out before us. After breakfast, the antics of two enormous apes, who came round on a donkey, accompanied by a showman and a boy, amused the children much. They were hideously ugly, but the cleverest monkeys I ever saw. They went through a regular little play, quarreled with one another; the man and the boy rode the ape, and made him kick; at last the ape was hurt, and lay fainting in the man's arms, limp and languid, just able to sip a little water; then he died, and dropped down stiff, with his eyes shut. His tail was pulled, his lips and eyelids were forced open, but he never winked an eyelid or moved a hair of his whiskers. He was thrown about from side to side, remaining perfectly motionless till, at a sign from his master, he jumped up as well as ever, shouldered his gun, and mounted his ass to take his departure. He was promptly ordered to dismount and ask for backshish, which he did, cap in hand. Some of the crowd round about not contributing to his master's satisfaction, the ape took a nasty venomous-looking little snake out of a bag which he carried over his shoulder, and threw it among the by-standers, to their great consternation.

At two o'clock we went to lunch with the Consul, and what a pleasant lunch it was, prepared by a French cook, and eaten in a cool, airy, and shady room free from flies, which were kept out by fine wire gauze placed in front of each well-shaded door and window! The table was one mass of the roses for which Alexandria is so famous. Everybody had wandered about the world more or less, everybody was in good spirits, and we laughed and chatted and talked sense or nonsense as the fancy took us, till it was time to go on board the yacht *en masse*, and receive some visitors at tea. A few had arrived before us, but the children and some others of the party were on board and had been doing the honors and showing them round. About 5.30 p.m. our last guests departed, and all was ready for a start; but, alas! we had to wait for an absent steward, who had gone in search of the always late linen, that plague of the poor yachtsman's life when he has a large party on board. The sun was sinking fast, the wind was blowing fresh and fair, and if we did not start soon it would be impossible to do so at all, and a night's work of more than 120 miles would be lost. At last the welcome boat was seen coming from the shore; we unmoored, and went ahead for about an hour. But the light gradually faded away; it became impossible to distinguish the beacon; the sandbanks are numerous, and there are no lights. It was only endangering the ship and the lives of all on board to proceed; so the order was reluctantly given, 'Hard a-port.' Round she went in her own length almost, and very soon we let go the anchor just outside our old moorings, and spent the night, after all, in the harbor of Alexandria.

CHAPTER XXVIII.

'HOME.'

She comes, majestic with her swelling sails,
The gallant bark along her watery way ;
Homeward she drives before the favoring gales.
Now flitting at their length the streamers fly,
And now they ripple with the ruffling breeze.

Wednesday, May 2d.—Steam was up at five o'clock, the wind being still fair but light. Soon it dropped to a calm, and then went round and blew with great force exactly in the opposite direction, dead ahead. The fires had to be put out, for it was so rough we could do no good steaming against the gale. The screw kept racing round and shaking the vessel terribly. Of course I was very ill; but the maids did not mind, and the children rather enjoyed the tumbling about and the water on deck. We continued scudding along through the water, but not making much progress on our course.

Thursday, May 3d.—The wind kept on increasing, and at last blew quite a gale. We have gone a long way out of our course to the northward, ready for a favorable change, but we can scarcely make any way to the westward.

Friday, May 4th.—A repetition of yesterday—

> Beating, beating all the day,
> But never a bit ahead.

Saturday, May 5th.—A lull at last, and we are able to have the fires lighted and to steam on our course. We made the Island of Scarpanto in the morning. All the afternoon and evening we have been steaming along ten miles to the southward of Crete. Its outline was very beautiful, surmounted by the snow-capped mountains. I was up on deck just in time to behold the most lovely sunset, with exquisite rosy, purple, and crimson tints on sea and sky.

I have not quite got over my attack in Cairo yet, and for the last three days have been completely laid up with a various mixture of land illness and sea-sickness. We stopped steaming late in the day, but fires were lighted again in the middle of the night, as the wind was still ahead. There was a discussion whether or not to go round the north side of the Island of Kandia, so as to have a glimpse of the British Fleet at anchor in Suda Bay, if they have already arrived there.

Sunday, May 6th, and Monday, May 7th.—Early in the morning the snowy mountains of Crete were still in sight. Service was held as usual at eleven, but it was too rough in the afternoon for it to be repeated.

Sail and steam, wind and calm, alternated with one another all day. Tom is anxious to sail every mile he can, and yet not to lose any unnecessary time, and finds it exceedingly difficult to combine these two objects.

Tuesday, May 8th.—A fine morning, with a cold strong head breeze. At noon we rejoiced to think that Malta was not more than a few miles ahead, or we should assuredly have failed to reach our port before nightfall. About three we closed in with the land about Marsa Scirocco and Delamara Point, and, after one or two tacks, rounded the Point of Ricasole, and leaving Port St. Elmo on our right, we swiftly glided into the grand harbor of Valetta. We have been here so often that it feels quite like reaching home. We soon found ourselves in our old quarters in the Dockyard Creek, and had scarcely moored before one of the officers came on board with the usual complimentary offers of assistance, whilst directly afterwards came an invitation to a farewell ball at the Palace, given to the Duke of Edinburgh. Our old boatman, Bubbly Joe, took us ashore to dinner, and we found everything looking as bright and cheerful and steep as it always does and always will do; not the least bit altered or modernized. The landlord of the Hôtel d'Angleterre was delighted to see us again, and so were his servants, who came flocking from all parts of the house, nearly pulling the children to pieces, and plying our own servants with questions in their anxiety to know all about us.

We had to go back on board the yacht to dress, and then return for the ball, by which time I was so thoroughly tired, and had so bad a headache, that I could not enjoy it much, pleasant as it was. Very soon after supper we came away and had a charming row across the harbor to our snug quarters on board the 'Sunbeam.' These sudden bursts of dissipation on shore are a delightful change after days and weeks at sea.

Wednesday, May 9th.—I was up soon after sunrise and admired this often-abused creek as much as I always do. The stone houses, the carved and colored verandas of bright flowers, the water lapping the very door-steps, the gayly painted boats with their high prows at either end, the women in their black dresses and faldettas, and black-robed priests, all helped to carry the imagination over the Mediterranean and up the Adriatic to lovely Venice. At this hour in the morning there were not many English soldiers or sailors to spoil the illusion.

Malta is essentially a border-land—African by geographical configuration, European politically, and assuredly Asiatic in its language, its buildings, and in the manners and customs of the natives. We gave everybody on board a holiday, and the chance of a run ashore to-day to stretch their legs after their long sea voyage. Tom went on board the 'Sultan' to see the Duke of Edinburgh and his splendid ship. Whilst at breakfast I received an intimation that the Duke of Edinburgh wished to come and examine the yacht. His Royal Highness arrived soon afterwards, quite unattended, in a beautiful ten-oared barge, and paid us a long visit, inspecting the yacht minutely and looking at all the pets. He took a great interest in our voyage and courses, as well as in the numerous curiosities, knowing at once from what place each had been procured. The Duke, who had taken very nearly the same cruise himself in the 'Galatea' a few years ago, inquired very kindly after all his old friends at Tahiti, Hilo, Honolulu, and many other places. The Duke is very kind to everybody here. He is much liked by his brother officers in the squadron, and both H.R.H. and the Duchess seem to have made themselves most popular here during the winter. The officers of the 'Sultan,' several of whom are old friends of ours, appear to think themselves fortunate indeed in having such a commanding officer, whilst on shore his approaching departure is universally regretted. Everybody seems full of their Royal Highnesses' winter ball, which must have been a most brilliant affair.

After the Duke's departure we went ashore again, called on various friends before luncheon, and went over the palace and through the armory. Then we took a walk down the Strada Reale, the shopping street of Valetta, until it was time to go on board to receive some friends to tea. The shops are full of coral, lace, gold and silver filigree work, and a new sort of lace they make in Gozo, of white silk, in beautiful patterns. It has been manufactured only during the last few years, and varies much in quality and design. Some forty or fifty friends came on board and amused themselves looking at our curiosities and photographs until long past the dinner hour. We had to hurry on shore to dine, and go afterwards to the Opera Manoel. The new Grand Opera House is not to be opened until next October. It had been blowing fresh and strong from the westward all day, but to-night, as we rowed across the harbor, the breeze had dropped to a flat calm, and Tom is most anxious to be off at daybreak.

Thursday, May 10*th.*—I was up before sunrise. A fresh fair wind was blowing, and as soon as the children could be got ready we all went ashore to the market, which was crowded with people, and full of fish, meat, and all spring vegetables and fruit. We were to start at 6.30, so there was no time to lose, and laden with lovely bouquets of flowers we hastened on board; but it was nine o'clock, after all our haste, before we were fairly off, through some mistake about the bill of health.

Malta is certainly the most delightful place for yachting winter quarters, with its fine healthy harbor, charming society, very cheap living, and abundance of everything good. It is in proximity to many pleasant places, and most interesting excursions can easily be made to Sicily and Italy, or the coast of Africa. To-day we glided along the coast, passed the strongly fortified little island of Consino, standing boldly out in mid-channel between Malta and Gozo. The Mediterranean appears to us a highway after the lonely oceans and seas we have been sailing over. Within one hour this morning, we saw more ships than in the whole of our passage from Valparaiso to Tahiti and Yokohama. Towards the evening we could see the island of Pantellaria in the distance. We retain a lively remembrance of it from having been becalmed just off it in the 'Albatross' for three weary days and nights. It was after this and a long series of other vexations and delays that Tom and I registered a vow never to go a long voyage again in a yacht without at least auxiliary steam power.

Friday, May 11*th.*—At 2.30 a.m. Pantellaria was abeam. At five the homeward-bound P. and O. steamer passed us quite close, and at six we met the outward-bound P. and O. steamer. At eight we passed Cape Bon and sailed across the mouth of the Bay of Tunis, in the center of which is Goletta, the port of Tunis, the site of the ancient city of Carthage. Once we anchored close by that place for two or three days, and on that occasion I collected enough varieties of marble and mosaic from the old palaces to make some beautiful tables when we got home. In the afternoon and evening we made the Fratelli and the Sorelle Rocks, and still later the little Island of Galita. There were many steamers going in all directions, and it struck one very forcibly how much this little islet in mid-channel stands in need of a light.

Sunday, May 13th.—The wind was dead ahead, and the sea of that remarkably confused character for which the Mediterranean is famous. It seemed as if the wind of yesterday, the wind of to-morrow, and the wind of to-day, had all met and were bent on making a night of it. We had service at eleven and four. The chart, now a good old friend, for it has been used by us on so many Mediterranean voyages, showed that this is the fourth noontide we have spent within a radius of thirty miles of this particular spot; within a radius of sixty miles we have spent at least three weeks of our lives at various periods. This does not of course include voyages in steamers, which are not recorded in the chart.

Monday, May 14th.—About breakfast time to-day we crossed the meridian of Greenwich; and this virtually completed our voyage round the world, our original point of departure having really been Rochester, which is a few minutes to the east of Greenwich. The wind changed in the middle of the day, and we passed through a large fleet of merchantmen hove-to under shelter of Cape de Gat, where they had collected, I suppose, from various ports in Spain and Italy.

Tuesday, May 15th.—This was a somewhat sad day, many of our pets dying from the effects of the cold wind or from accidents. The steward's mocking-bird from Siam, which talked like a Christian and followed him about like a dog, died of acute bronchitis early this morning; and his monkey, the most weird little creature, with the affectionate ways of a human friend, died in the afternoon, of inflammation and congestion of the lungs. Two other monkeys and several birds also expired in the course of the day.

This evening 'Beau Brummel,' the little pig I brought from Bow Island, in the South Pacific, died of a broken spine, as the doctor, who made a post-mortem examination in each case, discovered. A spar must have dropped upon poor piggy accidentally whilst he was running about on deck, though of course no one knew anything about it. I am very sorry; for though I must confess he was somewhat greedy and pig-like in his habits, he was extremely amusing in his ways. He ran about and went to sleep with the pugs, just like one of themselves. Besides, I do not think any one else in England could have boasted of a pig given to them by a South Sea Island chief. Probably 'Beau Brummel' was a lineal descendant of the pigs Captain Cook took out in the 'Endeavor.'

The bodies were all placed together in a neat little box and committed to the deep at sunset, a few tears being shed over the departed pets, especially by the children.

Cape de Gat was abeam early this morning. The wind fell light, but Tom hoped it would freshen again; otherwise, with steam we might easily have got into Gibraltar to-night. As it was, fires were not lighted until ten o'clock.

Wednesday, May 16th.—At 3 a.m. I was called to see the light on Europa Point, and staid on deck to watch the day dawn and the rising of the sun. It was not, however, a very agreeable morning; the Levanter was blowing, the signal station was enveloped in mist, the tops of the mountains of Africa were scarcely discernible above the clouds, and Ceuta and Ape's Hill were invisible. Algeciras and San Roque gleamed white on the opposite shore of the bay, while the dear old Rock itself looked fresher and cleaner than usual, exhaling a most delicious perfume of flowers. As the sun rose, the twitterings of the birds in the Alameda sounded most homelike and delightful.

We had dropped our anchor inside the New Mole about 4.30, and before six the familiar sounds of English martial music could be heard from all the different barracks, as the regiments came marching down the hill and along the Alameda to the north front with all their baggage, military trains, tents, and ambulances, for a day's camping out. We were anxious to get on shore to see about coals, water, and provisions, but no health-boat came near us. About seven o'clock we started in despair, first to hail a policeman on shore (at a most respectful distance), to inquire where we could get *pratique;* then we procured it, and sent word back to the 'Sunbeam' that she was out of quarantine, and might hoist the yellow flag. We landed, went to the market, bought some lovely carnations stuck in a prickly-pear leaf to keep them fresh, and then went to the Hôtel Royal—kept by the landlord of the old Club House Hotel, where we had so often staid—to order breakfast. Our old friends the servants greeted us at every step from the house-door to the coffee-room, and we were taken special care of by a waiter who remembered us. After breakfast we went to pay some visits. We thought we ought to go and look at the galleries and Signal Station, as one or two of our party had never been here before; so we started, some on foot, and some on donkeys. All the way up the steep streets to the Moorish castle, girls met us, selling lovely scarlet carnations and yellow roses. The galleries have not changed in the least since our last visit, but our soldier-guide told us they were daily expecting some big guns to come out, and he gave us a minute explanation how they were to be mounted. It was a pleasant ride, neither too hot nor too cold. Every crevice and interstice between the rocks was full of wild flowers, looking bright and pretty, though somewhat insignificant after the gorgeous tropical blossoms our eyes have been lately accustomed to. The fog had cleared off, and the view was beautiful; ships lay in the bay below us from all parts, including a Portuguese gun-boat. We saw also one of the two old eagles sitting near her nest in the accustomed place; this year she has only one young one. We did not see the monkeys, on account of the Levanter, but their number has increased to twenty-four, so that there is no immediate fear of their becoming extinct.

At half-past six p.m. we weighed anchor and steamed out of the anchorage inside the New Mole. In the straits the wind was fair, so the funnel was soon lowered, and the screw feathered, and we were racing along under sail alone. Off Tarifa we found quite a gale blowing, and the wind continued fresh and fair throughout the night.

Thursday, May 17*th.*—The strong fair wind dropped, and then came dead ahead, and off Cadiz we had to get up steam. There was a strong wind off the mountains near Cape Sagres, and while Tom was below and the men were busy reefing the sails, we nearly ran ashore. Luckily I noticed our danger and called Tom, who came up just in time to alter the helm, when the yacht went round like a top, though the shore was too close to be pleasant. It only shows how easily an accident may occur. Both our fishermen-mates could not bear to be idle, and always considered looking out an insignificant occupation, and so neglected that important duty to assist with the sails.

Off Cape St. Vincent it blew so hard that we were afraid we should be obliged to bring up in the bay of Sagres; but we found that it was only a land breeze, and that it was much smoother outside than we had expected.

Friday, May 18*th.*—Fresh breeze. We met many steamers going down the coast with all sail set. After passing Cape Espichel the wind increased to a northerly gale, against which it was impossible to proceed. We therefore put into Lisbon. The mountains at the mouth of the Tagus, the tower and church of Belem, and the noble river itself looked even more beautiful in the sunset than my recollection led me to expect. We soon landed and had an excellent dinner at the Hôtel Braganza, where we had staid before, and where we were at once recognized and cordially received by the same landlord and landlady we remembered in 1861.

After dinner we went for a walk. One of the things we saw during our stroll was the fine statue of Luis de Camoëns, specially interesting to us, as we had so recently seen the place where he passed many of the weary years

Vasco de Gama.

of his exile. Rolling Motion Square was as giddy as ever. It was a curious fancy to pave it in such a way as to make it look like the waves of the sea, perpetually moving; and it must be a severe trial to the peripatetic powers of those who have not quite recovered their sea legs.

Saturday, May 19th. — We were off early; it was a lovely day, and we had a pleasant drive to Cintra. On our arrival we mounted donkeys and went to Peña, the beautiful palace of the ex-King Ferdinand, situated at the top of the mountains. It is an extraordinary-looking place, the different parts being built in every imaginable style of architecture, with exquisite carving and old tiles, that would delight the heart of a connoisseur. One of the most prominent objects near the Palace of Peña is the statue of Vasco de Gama, nobly placed on a pedestal of natural rocks, piled on the summit of a mountain peak, and worthy of the adventurous traveler it is erected to commemorate. The gardens are full of camellias, roses, bougainvillea, &c. We lunched at the excellent hotel, and came to the conclusion that Cintra is the place, not only 'to spend a happy day,' but many happy months. It is always pleasant to revisit places of which you have agreeable reminiscences, and to find your expectations surpassed instead of disappointed.

We had a hot drive back to Lisbon, and then went by tram to Belem, where we spent some time in the church and in wandering through its exquisite cloisters. The first stone was laid in 1500, and the name changed from Bairro de Restello to Belem, or Bethlehem, by Prince Henry of Portugal, the great promoter of maritime discovery in that century. It was built specially to commemorate the successful voyage of Vasco de Gama, who returned from the discovery of India in 1499.

Tom met us with the yacht, and we went on board with the intention of proceeding straight to sea. But after passing through the Canal del Norte a heavy gale obliged us to anchor in Cascaes Bay for the night, not far from a small schooner yacht with three ladies on board. It was rather rough, and we were very tired, or I think we should have ventured to pay them a visit even at that late hour. It is absurd to stand upon ceremony when traveling; but I scarcely know what the strict etiquette would be on such an occasion—whether they, as first anchored in the bay, should call on us, or we on them, as probably the greater travelers and out longer at sea.

Sunday, May 20th.—Weighed at 5 a.m. There was a dense fog off Cape del Roca, and the steam-whistle, fog-horns, and bell were constantly kept going, with lugubrious effect. We had service at eleven and 4.30. Passed the Burlings at 1.30. Heavy swell all day.

Monday, May 21st.—Rough and disagreeable. Off Viana at noon. Passed Oporto and Vigo in the course of the afternoon.

Tuesday, May 22d.—If yesterday was bad, to-day was worse. We hove-to for some time under the shelter of Cape Finisterre, then went on again for a short distance; but at 1.30 a.m. on the 23d we were obliged to put round and wait for daylight.

Wednesday, 23d, and Thursday, 24th.—In the course of the day the weather mended, though the sea still continued rough, and our course was really in the direction of America rather than England. In the evening of the 24th we were able to light fires, and, with the assistance of steam, to keep nearly on our proper course.

Saturday, May 26th.—Saw the first English land, the Start, at 2.30 a.m. Wind continued fresh and fair, but at noon dropped calm, and we had to steam through the Needles instead of sailing, as we had done on our way out. We reached Cowes about 3 p.m., and were immediately welcomed by several yachts, who dipped their ensigns and fired their guns. We landed, and were warmly greeted by many friends, and, after sending off telegrams and letters, re-embarked and proceeded towards Hastings. We were anxious to land by daylight, but this was not to be. So it turned out to be midnight before we reached Beachy Head and could discern the lights of Hastings shining in the distance. As we drew near to our anchorage we could see two boats coming swiftly towards us from the shore. The crews were members of the Royal Naval Artillery Volunteers, and as they came alongside they raised a shout of welcome. Hastings had been expecting us all the afternoon, and late as was the hour,

1.30 a.m., we were immediately surrounded by a fleet of boats, and many willing hands seized our heterogeneous cargo and multitudinous packages, and before daylight all had been safely landed on the pier. We committed ourselves to the care of the R. N. A. V., and landed in their boats, and at 4.30, proceeding to the Queen's Hotel, we had a joyous meeting with T. A. B. and Maud.

How can I describe the warm greetings that met us everywhere, or the crowd that surrounded us, not only when we landed, but as we came out of church; how, along the whole ten miles from Hastings to Battle, people were standing by the roadside and at their cottage doors to welcome us; how the Battle bell-ringers never stopped ringing except during service time; or how the warmest of welcomes ended our delightful year of travel and made us feel we were home at last, with thankful hearts for the providential care which had watched over us whithersoever we roamed?

Home at Last.

I travel'd among unknown men,
  In lands beyond the sea,
Nor, England! did I know till then
  What love I bore to thee.

APPENDIX.

SUMMARY OF THE ENTIRE VOYAGE,

COMPILED FROM THE LOG-BOOK.

JULY, 1876.

July	Remarks	Temp. of water	Temp. of air	Latitude	Longitude	Course	Since previous noon Distance Steam	Sail	Wind and weather
6	Left Cowes, I. of W.	...	...	...	...	Various	...	...	...
7	Arrived at Torbay at 8.30 a.m.	...	...	...	...	"	...	113	...
8	Left Torbay at noon	...	...	...	...	"	8	8	...
9	...	...	...	...	...	"	...	107	...
10	...	...	...	48 45 N	4 46 W	...	...	62	...
11	Cape Villano, 69 miles, at noon	...	...	46 27 N	6 50 W	SW. ¾° W	99	164	...
12	Madeira, 513; Torbay, 672 miles	...	...	44 16 N	9 10 W	SW by S	...	227	NNE 26 c.
13	Madeira, 375 miles	...	67	40 29 N	11 1 W	SW	98	36	SE 2
14	Madeira, 246 miles	...	69	38 24 N	12 21 W	SW. ¾° W	40	90	NNE 2, Foggy
15	Porto Santo, 90 miles	72	70	36 36 N	13 58 W	S. 33° W	29	123	NE 3
16	Arrived at Madeira (Funchal) at noon	73	...	34 25 N	15 35 W	S. 31° W	79	57	...
19	Left Madeira at 9.25 p.m.	70	...	...	...	...	...	...	...
20	Teneriffe, 165 miles	72	70	31 11 N	16 45 W	S. 30° E	20	67	NE 3 to 5
21	Arrived at Puerto Orotava, at 2.30 p.m.	72	75	28 38 N	16 42 W	S. 2° E	144	15	...
24	Left Puerto Orotava, Teneriffe, at noon	72	74	...	...	...	...	...	...
25	...	73	71	26 53 N	19 11 W	S. 37° W	20	173	...
26	...	...	77	24 45 N	21 0 W	S. 39° W	...	161	...
27	...	...	75	22 27 N	23 4 W	S. 29° W	...	180	...
28	...	75	73	19 48 N	24 14 W	S. 22° W	...	172	...
29	Arrived at Tarafal Bay, St. Antonio, 9 a.m.; left 6 p.m.	78	...	17 26 N	24 55 W	S. 16° W	15	148	...
30	...	...	...	...	...	Various	120	52	...
31	...	...	...	14 45 N	25 26 W	...	...	12	NE 3
	Average temperature for the month	73.2°	72.33°						

AUGUST, 1876.

Aug.	Remarks	Temp. of water	Temp. of air	Latitude	Longitude	Course	Since previous noon			Wind and weather
							Steam	Distance	Sail	
		F	F	° ′	° ′					
1	...	79°	74°	11 59 N	25 9 W	S, 5° E	159		13	Calm
2	...	78	74	9 10 N	24 46 W	S, 7° E	163		...	SW by W 2
3	...	79	75	7 42 N	21 38 W	S, 57° E	160		27	SSW 7
4	Sierra Leone, 289 miles	79	74	7 16 N	18 34 W	S, 84° E	...		241	S to SSE 6-7
5	The warm Guinea and Equatorial currents extend to	79	75	5 48 N	20 30 W	S, 53° W	...		139	S 4
6	about 7° N, and the latter to about 5° S, of the Equator									
7	...	79	74	3 58 N	22 6 W	S, 42° W			156	S by E 5 to 6
8	St. Paul's Rock, 250 miles. Crossed Equator at 10.30 a.m.	74	71	1 52 N	24 5 W	S, 43° W			179	S, 4 to 5
9	...	75	72.3	0 56 S	26 34 W	S, 42° W			225	SE 6 to 7
10	Pernambuco, 270 miles	78	74	4 23 S	28 42 W	S, 32° W			243	SSE, ESE 7
11	...	78	73.8	7 35 S	30 19 W	S, 24° W			211	SE 6
12	Bahia, 300 miles	77	71.5	10 11 S	32 26 W	S, 39° W			200	SE 4 to 5
13	...	74	71.3	13 1 S	33 51 W	S, 28° W			196	SE 5
14	...	74.3	71	15 42 S	35 51 W	S, 37° W			202	SE by S 5
15	...	73	70.7	17 25 S	37 31 W	S, 43° W			141	NNE 4
16	...	66	69.5	19 58 S	38 1 W	S, 11° W			155	NEly 5
17	Arrived at Rio de Janeiro at 6.15 p.m.	64.5	65	22 37 S	40 39 W	S, 45° W			225	NE 5
				23 53 S	42 50 W	...	87		82	WSW 6 to 9
	Average temperature for the month	75.3°	71.94°							

SEPTEMBER, 1876.

Sept.	Remarks	Temp. of water	Temp. of air	Latitude	Longitude	Course	Since previous noon - Distance Steam	Since previous noon - Distance Sail	Wind and weather
		F.°	F.°	° ′	° ′				
5	Left Rio de Janeiro at 6 a.m.	...	...	...	...	...	36	...	SSW 2 to 3
6	...	70	64	24 56 S	45 40 W	...	120	32	NE 5
7	...	67	65	26 39 S	47 34 W	...	...	136	NE 8
8	...	68	67	30 39 S	49 4 W	S. 16° W	...	243	NE 8 to 9
9	Lobos, WSW, 160 miles	57	57.5	34 18 S	51 43 W	S. 31° W	...	270	SW 4
10	...	57	58	34 48 S	54 13 W	S. 72° W	119	31	S by E 6 to 7
11	Arrived at Monte Video at 4.30 a.m.	60.3	60	...	...	...	115	...	NE 2 to 3
12	Left Monte Video at 6 a.m.	...	...	...	...	...	119	...	...
13	Arrived off Buenos Ayres at 10 p.m.	...	...	...	...	...	...	...	...
27	Left Buenos Ayres at 11.30 a.m.	62	60.3	...	...	Various down R. Plate	...	...	...
28	Rescued crew of 'Monkshaven'	53	57.5	36 57 S	55 44 W	...	119	50	WSW to NW 3, WNW 7 to 8
29	...	51.3	57	38 50 S	57 5 W	S. 40° W	83	53	NW by W 6
30	...	52	51.5	41 20 S	59 50 W	...	...	196	
	Average temperature for the month	59.7°	59.78°						

OCTOBER, 1876.

Oct.	Remarks	Temp. of water	Temp. of air	Latitude	Longitude	Course	Since previous noon			Wind and weather
							Distance			
							Steam	Sail		
		°F	°F	° ′	° ′					
1	...	50.7	53°	43 33 S	62 28 W	S. 45° W	103	64		NW by W 6
2	...	49	51	45 33 S	64 0 W	S. 39° W	139	31		SW 7 to 8
3	...	46	49	48 31 S	65 9 W	S. 15° W	65	116		W by S 6
4	...	43.5	42.5	49 25 S	67 17 W	...	122	14		SE by S 6
5	Off Cape Virgin at noon. Arrived at Possession Bay at 7.45 p.m.	43.5	44	52 20 S	68 17 W	...	185	...		N by E 4
6	Left Possession Bay at 6 a.m. Arrived at Sandy Point at 2.30 p.m.	...	...	52 45 S	70 20 W	...	95	...		Light airs, SW 6
8	Left Sandy Point at 6 a.m. Arrived at Borja Bay, Straits of Magellan, at 6.30 p.m.	46	46.2	53 53 S	71 17 W	Various	105	...		SE and E 3 to 4
9	Left Borja Bay at 6.30 a.m. Arrived at Otter Bay at 6.55 p.m.	45.8	45.8	52 22 S	73 40 W	"	105	...		...
10	Left Otter Bay at 5 a.m. Arrived at Puerto Bueno at 5.30 p.m.	49	48.7	51 0 S	74 12 W	"	95	...		...
11	Left Puerto Bueno at 5 a.m. Arrived at Port Grappler at 7 p.m.	49	50	49 26 S	74 20 W	"	105	...		Calm and light southerly winds
12	Left Port Grappler at 5 a.m.	51	51	...	...	...	60	...		NEly 5 to 3
13	...	52	51.8	46 0 S	76 23 W	N. 14° W	150	25		SW 2 to 3
14	...	53.7	52.8	44 55 S	76 46 W	N. 14° E	...	67		Calm, S by E 1-2
15	...	56	55	42 47 S	76 3 W	N. 20° E	100	32		S by E 2 to 3
16	...	57.8	57.5	39 52 S	74 42 W	N. 52° E	152	37		NW by W 4 to 5
17	...	59	58.2	39 0 S	74 38 W	Various	28	63		Calm & light airs
18	Arrived at Lota, Chili, at 9 a.m.	...	...	...	...	...	144	...		NW by W 6
19	Left Lota at 2 p.m.	57	57.9	36 5 S	72 59 W	...	...	...		S by W 5 to 6
20	Valparaiso, 195 miles	60.2	...	33 18 S	72 19 W	...	...	65		S by W 6
21	Arrived at Valparaiso at 4 p.m.	...	...	...	...	...	...	211		Light airs and calms
30	Left Valparaiso at 3 p.m.	62.1	61	32 34 S	72 58 W	N. 73° W	...	81		NW by N 5
31	Average temperature for the month	51.7°	51.5°							

NOVEMBER, 1876.

Nov.	Remarks	Temp. of water Noon	Temp. of water 6 p.m.	Temp. of air Noon	Temp. of air 6 p.m.	Latitude	Longitude	Course	Distance Steam	Distance Sail	Wind and weather
1	In S. Pacific Ocean	63.9	...	61.2	...	31 30 S	72 55 W	N. 64° W	...	112	W by N 3 to 4
2	Ditto	65.6	...	62.3	...	30 54 S	74 9 W	N. 61° W	...	111	S 3
3	Ditto	67.3	...	63.5	...	29 11 S	76 15 W	N. 46° W	...	151	SSE 6
4	Ditto	68.1	...	64.2	64	27 45 S	80 5 W	N. 59° W	...	167	SE 3
5	Ditto	71.8	68.2	66	65.3	26 54 S	83 10 W	N. 63° W	...	113	SE 3
6	Ditto	71.5	69.3	68	65	25 52 S	86 5 W	N. 64° W	...	140	ESE 3
7	Ditto	71	69.7	68.8	66.3	24 47 S	86 58 W	N. 69° W	...	163	NE by E 3
8	Ditto	...	70	...	...	23 47 S	88 27 W	N. 46° W	...	107	NNW 2. Calms
9	Ditto	72	72.3	68	68.2	21 28 S	89 48 W	N. 31° W	...	18	ESE 4
10	Ditto	72.3	72	74	69	19 12 S	91 42 W	N. 29° W	144	166	E by S 6
11	Ditto	73	71.3	69.5	68.8	17 19 S	94 43 W	N. 44° W	...	156	ESE 6
12	Ditto	73	72.3	71	70	16 53 S	98 17 W	S. 82° W	...	178	ESE 4 to 6
13	Ditto	74.3	73.2	71.3	70.5	16 56 S	102 11 W	S. 89° W	...	215	ESE 7
14	Ditto	73.5	73.8	72.8	71	17 6 S	105 57 W	S. 87° W	...	217	E 6
15	Ditto	76	76	73	71.7	16 44 S	109 16 W	N. 86° W	...	217	ENE 6
16	Ditto	77	75.8	73	73	17 16 S	112 0 W	S. 85° W	...	199	ENE
17	Ditto	77.8	77.5	76.2	75.0	16 18 S	114 52 W	N. 70° W	...	159	E to N 5
18	Ditto	79	77.8	75.2	73.5	15 38 S	117 52 W	N. 77° W	...	173	E 5
19	Ditto	79	78.2	76	76	15 19 S	120 17 W	S. 87° W	...	180	...
20	Ditto	80.2	79.3	77	76.3	15 25 S	122 18 W	N. 88° W	...	139	ENE 3
21	Ditto	80	79.8	78.2	77	15 4 S	124 20 W	S. 87° W	...	121	ENE 3 to 4
22	Ditto	81	80.2	78	77	15 15 S	126 40 W	N. 83° W	...	123	NE by E 3 to 4
23	Ditto	81.2	81	79.2	77.8	15 25 S	129 12 W	S. 85° W	...	141	NE 3
24	Ditto	81	80.2	79	78.3	15 27 S	132 12 W	S. 86° W	...	153	NNE 3
25	Ditto	81	81.5	80.7	78	15 47 S	135 20 W	...	...	21	E 2
26	Ditto	82.2	80.5	79	...	16 54 S	138 9 W	...	...	35	ESE 4
27	Ditto	81	...	...	...	...	...	...	...	32	...
28	Stopped at Bow Island, Low Archipelago, for three hours	81.8	81.6	80	79.6	17 55 S	140 43 W	S. 56° W	20	148	ESE 4 to 5
29	...	81.7	81	79.5	77	18 41 S	143 7 W	...	10	152	SE 4 to 5
30	...	81.3	81	80	79.3	18 20 S	145 57 W	N. 79° W	...	162	NE 4 to 5
	Average temperature for the month	76.3°		73.3°							

DECEMBER, 1876.

Dec.	Remarks	Temp. of water		Temp. of air		Latitude	Longitude	Since previous noon				
		Noon	6 p.m.	Noon	6 p.m.			Course	Distance		Wind and weather	
									Steam	Sail		
		° F	° F	° F	° F	° ′	° ′					
1	Landed at Maitea at 10 a.m. Left at 3.30 p.m.	...	...	...	...	17 53 S	147 55 W	W, ¼° N	...	139	NE 4 to 3,	
2	Arrived at Tahiti at 8 a.m.	...	...	...	...	...	...	...	17	98	NE to NW, 5 to a calm	
8	Left Tahiti at 6 p.m.	...	...	...	...	...	...	...	...	...		
9	...	82.3	82	80	79	15 28 S	149 24 W	N, 10° W	101	24	ENE and E 5	
10	...	82.5	82	80.3	79	13 31 S	149 45 W	...	...	124	NE by E 3 to 7	
11	...	83.3	82.5	81	79.2	11 0 S	150 3 W	N, 8° W	...	155	NE and NE 5	
12	...	83.6	81	79.4	79	9 10 S	149 48 W	N, 15° W	...	151	NE 4 to 5	
13	...	81.5	82	80.2	78.5	5 34 S	150 45 W	N, 24° W	...	224	NE 5	
14	Crossed Equator at 4.30 a.m.	81.5	80	80	77.8	2 12 S	152 18 W	N, 4° E	...	221	NE by E 5,	
15	...	81.5	81	80.7	79	1 10 N	152 3 W	...	...	203	SE 6	
16	...	81.2	81	78.3	78	3 15 N	151 26 W	N, 17° E	22	109	SE 5	
17	To Hilo, 885 miles	81.5	82.3	79.8	78.2	5 28 N	151 16 W	N, 58° E	136	15	In Doldrums	
18	...	83	82	79.7	78	7 54 N	150 36 W	N, 11° W	48	105	NE 5 to 7	
19	...	81	80	77.5	77	10 22 N	152 37 W	N, 22° W	...	160	NE 7	
20	...	79.5	79	77.3	77	13 43 N	152 43 W	N, 18° W	...	212	Lost NE Trades	
21	...	78.2	78	74	73.8	16 28 N	153 28 W	N, 15° W	26	145	in heavy showers.	
22	Arrived at Hilo, Hawaii, at 3.30 p.m.	77.2	...	74.5	...	19 44 N	155 4 W	N, 25° W	202	38	...	
26	Left Hilo at 5.15 p.m.	...	...	...	74.3	...	...	...	...	...	...	
27	Arrived at Honolulu, Oahu, at 5.15 p.m.	78	77.8	76	...	20 42 N	157 20 W	Various	200	...	...	
	Average temperature for the month	80.1°		78.4°								

JANUARY, 1877.

Jan.	Remarks	Temp. of water Noon	Temp. of water 6 p.m.	Temp. of air Noon	Temp. of air 6 p.m.	Latitude	Longitude	Course	Since previous noon Distance Steam	Since previous noon Distance Sail	Wind and weather
		°F	°F	°F	°F	° ′	° ′				
3	Left Honolulu at 5 p.m.	...	...	...	...				...	...	ENE 4
4		78.2	77.8	78.1	76	20 10 N	159 39 W	S. 59° W	65	70	E by S 6 to 8
5		78	77.7	76.8	76.6	20 4 N	164 5 W	W	...	240	SE by S 8
6		79.3	78.1	78.5	77.8	20 3 N	168 53 W	W	...	253	S by E 7 to 9
7		79	77	74.2	74	19 31 N	169 35 W	S. 60° W	...	120	N ½ W 9
8		78.2	77.8	73.2	71.5	17 15 N	173 15 W	S. 59° W	...	244	N by E 9
9		79.8	78	74	71.7	16 44 N	177 15 W	S. 82° W	...	240	E by S 2
10		79.8	79.5	76	74.2	17 15 N	179 6 W	N. 74° W	20	92	Calms
11	180° longitude										
12		80	80	77.8	75.5	16 N	178 28 E	W	102	38	S by E 4
13		80.3	79.8	78.2	75.2	17 19 N	176 29 E	W	...	115	NE 3
14	To Yokohama, 2,700 miles	80	79.3	75.2	75.2	16 1 N	173 25 E	S. 66° W	98	96	NNE 10
15		80.2	80	73.8	73.5	16 2 N	168 15 E	W	...	298	NE 9
16		80.1	79.7	75	74.2	16 38 N	163 47 E	N. 82° W	...	260	ENE 7
17		79	78.2	76	75	17 3 N	159 37 E	N. 84° W	...	240	ENE 6
18		79.8	78	77	75.2	17 30 N	155 40 E	N. 82° W	...	229	ENE 4
19		79	78.4	77	75	18 16 N	153 11 E	N. 74° W	...	148	NNE 2
20		79.2	78	77	75	18 57 N	150 23 E	N. 75° W	151	13	N by W 3
21		78.2	77.2	73.5	72.3	19 36 N	147 19 E	N. 77° W	128	50	N by W to NNW 4 to 5
22		77.5	76.3	67.5	66	20 7 N	144 5 E	N. 81° W	...	185	NNE 8 to 7
23		71	70	62.5	61.5	21 52 N	141 39 E	N. 52° W	...	172	NNE 5 to 3
24		68.5	68	61.5	59.2	23 33 N	139 29 E	N. 50° W	...	158	NE 7 to 6
25		68	67.8	59	59	26 12 N	138 10 E	N. 24° W	...	174	ESE 3
26		65.5	64.5	61	59.5	29 23 N	137 33 E	N. 10° W	100	94	W 9 to 10
27		65.5	64.2	51.5	51	30 59 N	137 49 E	N. 8° E	...	94	NW by 3 to 4
28		64	63.2	48.2	46	32 40 N	138 35 E	N. 21° E	...	108	W by N 7
29	Arrived at Yokohama at 3.30 p.m.	63	52	...	41.2			Various	60	121	Gale
	Average temperature for the month	76.8°			69.7°						

FEBRUARY, 1877.

Feb.	Remarks	Temp. of water		Temp. of air		Latitude	Longitude	Since previous noon			Wind and weather
		Noon	6 p.m.	Noon	6 p.m.			Course	Distance Steam	Distance Sail	
		°F	°F	°F	°F	° ′	° ′				
2	Left Yokohama at 6.30 p.m.	...	...	...	...	...	...	Various: steering along the South Coast of Japan	...	...	NW 3
3	...	53	52	41.2	41	...	...		122	...	NNE 9
4	Arrived at Kobe at 7 p.m.	58	46	40	35.5	...	...		178	...	
12	Left Kobe at 6 a.m. and returned at 2 p.m.	...	...	...	...	...	...		40	...	
15	Left Kobe at 4.30 a.m., and anchored at Ino Ura at 8.30 p.m.	46.1	45	33	32.5	...	...		90	...	W 9
16	Left Ino Ura at 5 a.m.	49.5	50	39	37.5	...	...		110	...	...
17	Anchored off Isaki lighthouse at 4 a.m., Left the anchorage at 8.30 a.m., and arrived at Simono-seki at 11 a.m.	...	...	...	...	...	...		50	...	...
19	Left Simono-seki at 8.30 a.m.	44.2	58	34	41.3	31 16 N	131 54 E		40	...	NW by W 9 to 6
20	...	64	61	51	46.5	29 7 N	129 49 E		64	127	Calm
21	...	69	67	60	59.5	28 13 N	125 53 E	SW	183	208	ESE
22	...	68.2	62	67	62	27 14 N	123 3 E	WSW	13	178	SE
23	...	67.3	65.5	65.2	64.2	25 0 N	119 35 E	S. 65° W	34	183	NE 7 to 10
24	...	55	55	51.8	49	22 35 N	115 38 E		61	288	NE 10 to 6
25	...	61	...	56.5	...	...	...		...	29	...
26	Arrived at Hongkong at 8 a.m.										
	Average temperature for the month	56.5°		48°							

MARCH, 1877.

Mar.	Remarks	Temp. of water Noon	Temp. of water 6 p.m.	Temp. of air Noon	Temp. of air 6 p.m.	Latitude	Longitude	Course	Distance Steam	Distance Sail	Wind and weather
		F°	F°	F°	F°	° '	° '				
7	Left Hongkong at 7 a.m. Arrived at Macao at 1.30 p.m. Left at 6.30 p.m.	...	64.5	...	64.3	...	...	...	45	...	...
8	...	72.5	72.2	72.3	70	20 5 N	113 28 E	...	136	...	E 3
9	...	73.8	72	72	68	18 0 N	113 48 E	S	48	70	NE 3
10	...	78	76.8	73	71.8	15 40 N	112 1 E	SSE	20	128	NE 4
11	...	78	78.2	75.5	74.3	13 45 N	110 32 E	SW by W	...	155	NE 4
12	...	79	78	76.4	76	11 29 N	108 33 E	S, 35° W	...	170	NE 4
13	...	77.7	77.5	78	75.7	9 34 N	107 3 E	S, 46° W	...	171	NE 4
14	...	78	77.7	77.6	76.3	7 34 N	106 16 E	SW by S	...	150	NE 3 to 4
15	...	79.5	79	78	77	4 46 N	104 43 E	S by W, ¼° W	...	176	NE 3 to 4
16	...	80	80	78	76.3	2 51 N	...	SW, ½° S	63	72	NE 3 to 4
17	Arrived at Singapore at 8 a.m.	...	...	...	...	...	...	...	...	...	...
18	Left Singapore at 3 p.m., and arrived at Johore at 8 p.m.	...	...	...	...	...	...	...	...	...	Calms & light airs from NE
19	Left Johore at 4 p.m.	...	83.2	...	79.7	...	...	...	36	...	...
20	Arrived at Malacca at 8 a.m.; left at 11.30 a.m.	...	83.2	80.5	79.5	...	...	...	130	...	...
21	...	88	...	...	...	4 4 N	100 30 E	...	170	...	...
22	Arrived at Penang at 8 a.m.; left at 10 p.m.	...	84.5	88.2	81	5 55 N	98 39 E	...	99	...	...
23	...	85.8	84	82	79	6 10 N	95 5 E	...	109	...	...
24	...	84.2	84	84.2	80	6 26 N	91 41 E	...	212	...	...
25	...	85	84	86	81.5	6 25 N	88 25 E	...	208	...	...
26	...	85.2	84.2	87	79	6 5 N	85 3 E	...	198	...	...
27	...	85.2	...	83	...	5 33 N	82 29 E	...	203	...	...
28	Arrived at Point de Galle at 7 a.m.; left at 9.30 p.m.	...	...	...	...	...	...	...	218	...	...
29	Arrived at Colombo at 11 a.m.	...	...	...	...	...	...	...	85	...	...
30		...	...	...	...	...	...	...	90	...	...
	Average temperature for the month	79.4°		73.3°							

APRIL, 1877.

April	Remarks	Temp. of water Noon	Temp. of water 6 p.m.	Temp. of air Noon	Temp. of air 6 p.m.	Latitude	Longitude	Course	Since previous noon Distance Steam	Since previous noon Distance Sail	Wind and weather
5	Left Colombo, Ceylon, at 1.30 p.m.	°F	°F	°F	°F	° '	° '				
6	...	85.8	85.5	...	80.8	7 26 N	77 10 E	N, 81° W	165	...	W 1
7	...	86	85	83	80.6	7 31 N	74 7 E	N, 88° W	190	...	N 2
8	...	85.8	85	81	78.3	8 16 N	70 31 E	N, ¾° N	216	...	N 4 to 3
9	...	86	84.5	81.3	79	8 59 N	66 59 E	W by N	213	...	Calm
10	...	85	85	79	78	9 38 N	63 32 E	N, 77° W	210	...	NE 1 to 2
11	...	83.6	83.5	81	78.5	10 27 N	60 1 E	...	214	...	ENE 2
12	...	83.8	82.5	83	79	11 14 N	56 30 E	...	213	...	ENE 2 to 4
13	...	83.5	82.6	82.2	79	11 38 N	52 57 E	N, 85° W	210	...	...
14	...	83.2	82.3	82.8	80	12 33 N	49 43 E	...	108	...	E 4
15	Arrived at Aden at 10 p.m.	82.8	82	81	79	12 55 N	46 17 E	N, 84° W	203	...	...
16	Left Aden at 7 p.m.	...	...	...	...	...	...	...	80	...	...
17	Off Island of Perim	...	...	...	...	...	...	...	...	...	...
18	...	82.8	82	83	81.7	16 13 N	41 27 E	...	...	105	S 5
19	...	82	82.2	83.4	81.5	18 13 N	40 7 E	...	...	230	...
20	...	82.5	82	84	83	20 39 N	38 30 E	N, 33° W	29	116	Calms
21	...	83.5	82	84	83.6	23 33 N	36 50 E	N, 30° W	149	22	...
22	...	86.2	82.3	83.5	82.8	26 18 N	34 55 E	...	190	...	...
23	...	78.3	75	82	76	27 13 N	34 1 E	NNW	200	...	...
24	Arrived at Suez at 6 p.m.	75.5	74	71.5	74.5	28 16 N	33 16 E	...	80	27	...
25	Left Suez at 9 a.m. Arrived at Ismailia at 7.15 p.m.	71.3	70.2	71.5	74	...	...	...	89	51	...
26		70	...	71.5	...	...	...	...	22	...	...
27	Left Ismailia at 8 a.m. Arrived at Port Said at 5.30 p.m.; left at 9.30 p.m.	76.5	70	88	83.6	...	...	Working to windward under steam and sail	50	...	...
28	Arrived at Alexandria at 4.30 a.m.	76.7	...	90	...	...	...		50	...	WNW 5
29	...	66.3	64.2	66	64	...	...		174	...	WNW 9 to 7
30	Average temperature for the month	82.3°		78°					117		

MAY, 1877.

May	Remarks	Temp. of water Noon	Temp. of water 6 p.m.	Temp. of air Noon	Temp. of air 6 p.m.	Latitude	Longitude	Course	Since previous noon Distance Steam	Since previous noon Distance Sail	Wind and weather
2	Left Alexandria at 4.30 a.m.	F 68°	F 65.2°	F 70°	F 64.5°	° ′ ...	° ′ ...	WNW	28	2	Calm a.m. Fresh to strong NW winds
3	...	64	64	65.2	64.3	32 30 N	28 39 E	N, 30° W	32	80	
4	...	63.8	63.5	64.2	64	34 35 N	28 48 E	N, 3° E	...	146	NW 7
5	...	65	64	66	64.2	34 48 N	27 13 E	W, ½° S	63	61	NW 7 & calms
6	...	65	62.2	66.2	64	34 54 N	23 11 E	W	125	75	ESE 7 & calms
7	...	63.6	63	64.3	63.6	35 51 N	19 48 E	N, 82° W	46	130	ESE 2
8	Arrived at Malta at 6 p.m.	64	63	64.5	66.2	35 57 N	15 12 E	W	199	16	N 4 to 7
10	Left Malta at 8.15 a.m.	64	64	67	66.5	...	...	Various	20	5	S 2 to 1
11	...	64.5	64	70	66	37 20 N	10 24 E	WNW	186	7	SE & calm
12	...	63	63	69	68.5	37 32 N	6 32 E	S, 82° E	192	...	
13	...	64	63.2	67	66	37 7 N	3 3 E	W, ½° S	173	...	SW by W 5 to 6
14	...	62	62.3	66.3	65	36 50 N	0 20 E	W, ½° N	163	35	SE 5
15	...	...	...	66.2	66	36 31 N	3 43 W	Various	128	26	
16	Arrived at Gibraltar at 6.30 a.m.; left at 7.30 p.m.	67	67	68.2	69	36 27 N	7 58 W	...	48	130	E 8; calm
17	Arrived at Lisbon at 6.30 p.m.	64	...	63.8	...	38 27 N	9 26 W	...	144	6	NNE 5
18	Left Lisbon at 5 p.m., and anchored off Fort St. Julien at 9.15 p.m.	...	...	...	...	...	...	...	...	...	NNE 7
19	Left anchorage at 5 a.m.	...	...	...	...	...	...	...	...	...	N 6
20	...	61.5	64	64	65	39 13 N	9 32 W	...	40	...	
21	...	60.8	59	61	63.5	41 36 N	9 7 W	N, 22° W	60	86	NE 9
22	...	56.5	57	55.5	56.3	43 13 N	10 8 W	N, 16° W	54	120	NE 7 to 5
23	...	58	57	57	50	45 5 N	11 0 W	...	...	9	NE 3 to 5
24	...	56	55	55	54.3	46 40 N	8 41 W	...	149	...	NE 3 to 4
25	Arrived at Cowes at 1 p.m.	55	55	54	...	48 42 N	6 5 W	...	160	...	...
26	Hastings 1.30 a.m.										
27	Average temperature for the month	65°	65°	65.1°					230		

When we finally sailed from Cowes, on July 6th, 1876, the list of persons on board the yacht was as follows :—

THOMAS BRASSEY, Esq., M.P. (Owner)
Mrs. BRASSEY
THOMAS ALLNUTT BRASSEY
MABELLE ANNIE BRASSEY
MURIEL AGNES BRASSEY
MARIE ADELAIDE BRASSEY
Hon. A. Y. BINGHAM
F. HUBERT FREER, Esq.
Commander JAMES BROWN, R.N.
Captain SQUIRE T. S. LECKY, R.N.R.
HENRY PERCY POTTER, Esq. (Surgeon)

ISAIAH POWELL, Sailing Master
HENRY KINDRED, Boatswain
JOHN RIDGE TEMPLEMAN, Carpenter
CHARLES COOK, Signalman and Gunner
JAMES ALLEN, Coxswain of the Gig
JAMES WALFORD, Captain of the Hold
JOHN FALE, Coxswain of the Cutter
HENRY PARKER, Second Coxswain of the Gig
WILLIAM SEBBORN, A.B.
WALTER SEBBORN "
TURNER ENNEW "

WILLIAM MOULTON, A.B.
ALBERT WISEMAN   "
JOHN GREEN   "
THOMAS TAYLOR   "
FREDERICK BUTT   "
HENRY TICHENER   "
THOMAS POWELL, Forecastle Cook
WILLIAM COLE, Boy

ROBERT ROWBOTTOM, Engineer
CHARLES McKECHNIE, 2d ditto
THOMAS KIRKHAM, Leading Fireman
GEORGE BURREDGE, Fireman

GEORGE LESLIE, Steward
WILLIAM AINSWORTH, Bedroom Steward
FREDERICK PARSONS, Saloon Steward
GEORGE BASSETT, 2d ditto

WILLIAM PRYDE, Cook
JOSEPH SOUTHGATE, Cook's Mate

EMMA ADAMS, Nurse
HARRIET HOWE, Lady's Maid
MARY PHILLIPS, Stewardess.

The list of those who were temporarily on board the yacht during the voyage comprised the following persons:—

ARRIVALS.

CREW OF 'MONKSHAVEN' (15) came on board the 'Sunbeam,' Sept. 28.
ARTHUR TURNER, one of the crew, remained on board the 'Sunbeam' as an A.B.
JOHN SEBBORN, from U.S. 'Ashuelot,' Hongkong.
JOHN SHAW (Under-Cook), Hongkong.
ISAAC AYAK, Hongkong.
JOHN AHANG, Hongkong.
MEHEMET, Fireman, Galle.
ABRAHAM, Fireman, Galle.
TOM DOLLAR, Fireman, Galle.
MR. AND MRS. WOODROFFE, Ismailia.

(Total, 24.)

DEPARTURES.

T. ALLNUTT BRASSEY, Rio.
CREW OF 'MONKSHAVEN' (14) placed on board the 'Illimani,' Oct. 5.
CAPTAIN LECKY, Buenos Ayres.
GEO. LESLIE, Ensenada.
CAPTAIN BROWN, Honolulu.
WM. PRYDE, Honolulu.
JOHN FALE, Malacca.
MEHEMET, Fireman, Suez.
ABRAHAM, Fireman, Suez.
TOM DOLLAR, Fireman, Aden.
MR. AND MRS. WOODROFFE, Port Said.

(Total, 25.)

Note.—Many were the preparations to be made before starting on our voyage; the crew had to be selected, we had to decide whether all, any, or none of the children should be taken, what friends we should invite to accompany us, what stores and provisions we should take, and to select from our little fleet of boats those which seemed best suited for the various requirements of the voyage. The whole number comprised

        The 'Gleam,' lifeboat cutter;
        The 'Glance,' large gig;
        The 'Ray,' light gig;
        The 'Trap' (to catch a sunbeam), steam launch;
        The 'Mote,' dingy;
        The 'Flash,' light outrigger.

Of these the 'Trap' and the 'Ray' had to be left behind.

www.ingramcontent.com/pod-product-compliance
Lightning Source LLC
Chambersburg PA
CBHW051844300426
44117CB00006B/268